Studies in Political Economy: Developments in Feminism

Studies in Political Economy: Developments in Feminism

Edited by
Caroline Andrew, Pat Armstrong,
Hugh Armstrong, Wallace Clement
and Leah F. Vosko

Women's Press
Toronto

Studies in Political Economy: Developments in Feminism

Edited by Caroline Andrew, Pat Armstrong, Hugh Armstrong, Wallace Clement and Leah F. Vosko

First published in 2003 by
Women's Press
180 Bloor Street West, Suite 801
Toronto, Ontario
M5S 2V6

www.womenspress.ca

Women's Press gratefully acknowledges financial assistance for our publishing activities from the Ontario Arts Council, the Canada Council for the Arts, and the Government of Canada through the Book Publishing Industry Development Program (BPIDP).

National Library of Canada Cataloguing in Publication Data

Studies in political economy: developments in feminism / edited by Caroline Andrew ... [et al.].

Articles originally published in Studies in political economy.

Includes bibliographical references.
ISBN 0-88961-412-1

1.Feminist economics–Canada. 2. Feminism–Political aspects–Canada. 3. Women–Employment–Canada. 4. Women–Canada–Social conditions. I. Andrew, Caroline, 1942- . II. Title: Studies in political economy (Toronto, Ont.)

HQ1381.S78 2003   305.4'0971   C2002-905274-2

Page design and layout by Brad Horning
Cover design by Susan Thomas/Digital Zone

03   04   05   06   07   08   6   5   4   3   2   1

Printed and bound in Canada by AGMV Marquis Imprimeur Inc.

Table of Contents

General Introduction
Caroline Andrew, Pat Armstrong, and Leah F. Vosko 1

Part One
Production and Reproduction: Feminist Takes
Pat Armstrong and Hugh Armstrong 3

Chapter One
Beyond Sexless Class and Classless Sex: Towards Feminist Marxism
Pat Armstrong and Hugh Armstrong 11

Chapter Two
Spatially Differentiated Conceptions of Gender in the Workplace
Pamela Moss 51

Chapter Three
The Retreat of the State and Long-Term Care Provision:
Implications for Frail Elderly People, Unpaid Family Carers
and Paid Home Care Workers
Jane Aronson and Sheila M. Neysmith 89

Part Two
Flexible Workforces and the Class-Gender Nexus
Wallace Clement 117

Chapter Four
Changing Labour Process and the Nursing Crisis in Canadian Hospitals
Jerry White 125

Chapter Five
The Domestication of Women's Work: A Comparison
of Chinese and Portuguese Immigrant Women Homeworkers
Wenona Giles and Valerie Preston 155

Chapter Six
Flexible Work, Flexible Workers: The Restructuring of
Clerical Work in a Large Telecommunications Company
  Bonnie Fox and Pamela Sugiman 187

Part Three
**Engendering the State in *SPE*: The Interrelations of Theory and
Practice, and of Class, Race and Gender**
  Caroline Andrew 213

Chapter Seven
Classes and States: Welfare State Developments, 1881–1981
  Göran Therborn 219

Chapter Eight
The Conceptual Politics of Struggle: Wife Battering,
the Women's Movement and the State
  Gillian Walker 253

Chapter Nine
Depoliticizing Insurgency: The Politics of the Family in Alberta
  Lois Harder 279

Conclusion
The Pasts (and Futures) of Feminist Political Economy in Canada:
Reviving the Debate
  Leah F. Vosko 305

References 333

About the Contributors 359

Publisher's Acknowledgements 361

General Introduction

Caroline Andrew, Pat Armstrong
and Leah F. Vosko

The title of this book, *Studies in Political Economy: Developments in Feminism*, is intended to evoke two sets of ideas: the ways in which political economy and, more specifically, *Studies in Political Economy* (SPE), have thought about, reflected upon and integrated feminism; and the ways in which feminist thought has been insightful in providing ways for thinking through some of the central issues for a grounded Canadian political economy, the relation of theory and practice, and the relation of actors and structures. Leah Vosko's piece, which ends this collection, completes both these ideas — political economy's efforts to think about feminism develops through a series of stages, and the relation of theory and practice necessarily involves an understanding of context and historical development.

This book has three objectives: to put together a collection of significant articles from *Studies in Political Economy* that illustrate feminist political economy; to reflect on the ways in which political economy, and *SPE* in particular, have incorporated feminism and, finally, to look at the development of Canadian feminist analysis over the past twenty years.

This book was originally conceived as a teaching resource, as something that would be useful in classroom settings. The contents reflect this aim. We felt that students needed to understand how ideas develop over time, so we tried to choose articles from across the period of *SPE*'s existence. We wanted the articles to be available in their original form and we also felt that some contextualization was

1

necessary. For this reason we decided to include brief commentaries on the three sections of the book to provide a guide as to why particular articles were chosen and how they fit into the development of a feminist political economy.

The book is thus organized into three areas: production and reproduction, the workforce and the state. These sections were chosen in order to illustrate, within some of the main areas of scholarship of Canadian political economy, how questions of gender have been raised and discussed. These are not the only areas that have preoccupied Canadian political economists, but they are central ones.

While wanting to indicate the strength and excitement of the feminist political economy scholarship that has been published in *SPE*, we also wanted to indicate clearly that this was an ongoing intellectual effort — not past history — but rather a present and future challenge. For this reason, the conclusion by Leah Vosko, "The Pasts (and Futures) of Feminist Political Economy in Canada: Reviving the Debate," broadens the debate beyond the pages of *SPE* by thinking about how Canadian feminist political economy traditions could contribute to current feminist debates.

"Developments in Feminism" opens up important challenges for understanding the evolving Canadian reality: how to keep gender central to our understanding of social and political processes, and how to use the insights of feminist analysis to renew our approaches to the study of these social and political processes. We hope this collection contributes to meeting these challenges.

Part One

Production and Reproduction: Feminist Takes

Pat Armstrong and Hugh Armstrong

HOW ARE GOODS AND SERVICES CREATED, DISTRIBUTED AND RECREATED? WHAT are the ideas and social relations involved? Who benefits and how do they benefit? How do people individually and collectively participate and respond? What are the pressures, choices and limits? Such questions have been central to the political economy tradition, and critically important not only to understanding how our current societies work but also to how they change and can be changed.

Feminists have little quarrel with these central questions, but they have strenuously objected to where traditional political economy looked for answers. The singular focus on market relations, market goods and market labour, along with the assumption that classes had no gender divisions, have been challenged and rejected. Taking up analytical tools developed in political economy, feminists have struggled to make domestic work visible, valued and transparent in analytical terms.

What came to be known as the domestic labour debate was primarily a theoretical effort to come to grips with these central questions. Postmodernists would later reject such debates on the grounds that they represented grand theory irrelevant for individuals' daily experiences, but these debates did help us understand the interpenetration of households and formal economies, communities and markets. The first article in this section, "Beyond Sexless Class and Classless Sex," summarized and critiqued these debates, using them as a platform to stress the differences between domestic and wage labour as well as the importance of understanding gender divisions at all levels of theoretical abstraction.

3

Our argument that domestic labour creates use value, but is not productive in the sense that it is not labour sold as a commodity and therefore is not subject to the same pressures as wage labour, provoked little response. The argument was complemented in an article by Patricia Connelly and Martha MacDonald that was originally published in the same issue of *SPE* as our article.[1] They used the specific case of a Nova Scotia community to explore both how women can serve as a reserve army of labour because they do domestic work and how women's domestic work is critical to male and female wage employment. The reserve army approach was more a matter of debate than our claim that domestic work was not productive in the Marxist sense, mainly because of what appeared to be the relatively permanent movement of women into the labour market and because of a primary devotion to domestic work. The notion that women form a flexible labour force, in part at least as a result of their domestic labour, fell out of favour as women's labour force participation rates continued to rise. Indeed, current research by Bonnie Fox and Pamela Sugiman suggests that the paid labour of both women and men has become more flexible, in the process reducing sex segregation while increasing tensions related to race, ethnicity and employment status.[2] Women's and men's paid work have undoubtedly become more similar as labour standards and methods for organizing work are harmonized down, feminizing significant portions of the labour force.[3]

Yet Leah Vosko's recent work on temporary service agencies indicates that some women still form a reserve for specific kinds of paid work and that this is related at least to some extent to women's unpaid work at home.[4] This in turn is related to a second argument made in "Beyond Sexless Class and Classless Sex," as well as in many other articles by feminist political economists, namely that analysis must take both domestic and wage labour, as well as the relationship between the two and differences among women, into account.

Many women did move permanently into the labour force as the demand for workers in traditionally female jobs grew enormously, especially with the expansion of the welfare state. The development of state programs also meant that more of the work previously done in the household was now done for pay in the formal economy. This movement contributed, as Meg Luxton's research in Flin Flon makes clear, to shifting work and power relationships within the household.[5] It also contributed to an increase in the number of women working for pay as domestics, a process demonstrated in research by authors such as Sedef Kroc,[6] and Wenona Giles and Valerie Preston.[7] It also led to growing divisions among women based on race and immigration status.

Some domestic work, however, can encourage the development of resistant communities. Pamela Moss's article, included here, draws out these contradictory processes. She pushes us to think through the implications of gendered spaces in paid housekeeping services and to examine the particular gender ideologies created in different workplaces. Although she departs from earlier feminist political economy in terms of her emphasis on place and differences, she relates her analysis to higher levels of abstraction in ways that recall much of the previous work.

In spite of the evidence that a growing number of women are hired to do domestic work in private households, all but the most wealthy of women retain primary responsibility for work in the household. We stressed this continuing responsibility in "Beyond Sexless Class and Classless Sex" when we argued that women's biological capacities played a role in their domestic labour, at least as long as the private home was connected to the free wage labourer and as long as babies were produced in traditional ways. Perhaps due to our ages at the time, however, we were firmly focused on women making and caring for babies and doing the housework, ignoring care for the disabled and elderly. Given the movement of women into the labour force, we were more concerned with explaining how work was being commodified than we were with contradictory tendencies. However, a review we did of research on domestic work helped draw our attention to work that was sent back home as capital sought new means to make profits. The dramatic cutbacks in the welfare state, well underway by the 1980s, had a similar impact on domestic work.

It is this decommodification and relocation of caring work that is the main subject of the article by Jane Aronson and Sheila Neysmith that is included here. This article clearly illustrates the dialogue between theory and evidence, as well as the way theory develops along with changes in service production and delivery. The authors explore more than the increasing transfer of paid work to unpaid female caregivers, however. They also examine the consequences for the paid female caregivers who now enter private households in much greater numbers, and for the women who are the majority of care recipients. Unlike much of the earlier feminist work, this article takes multiple players into account. The stress is on the conflict and inequality among participants, linking these both to the discourse of reforms and to the political economy context. The article thus grounds the grand theory in empirical research and in these times, while stretching the theory to account for current developments.

Equally important, a growing number of women are working for pay in the household not only because they take the major responsibility for domestic work but also because such labour is both cheaper and more flexible than that done in the public sphere. Carla Lipsig-Mummé[8] has analyzed how even women's traditional homework for the garment industry has been transformed by new strategies of deinstitutionalization and deunionization. This is especially the case for women who have recently migrated to Canada. Similar strategies made possible by electronic technologies are rapidly expanding the clerical work that is increasingly done by women at home. Heather Menzies,[9] among others, has taken up the task of exploring what this transfer of paid work to the household means for women's relationships and for the value attached to their work. But much remains to be done in order to make the consequences of, and links among, these new strategies more transparent. The old debates about use value and exchange value, about productive and unproductive labour, may well be helpful once more.

Unlike our argument that domestic labour is more flexible than wage labour precisely because it is not productive of surplus (or what is often called profit), our argument that women's reproductive capacities must be analyzed not only in terms of their contribution to inequality within capitalist societies but also at the highest level of abstraction prompted some strong criticism. It was the link made between free wage labour, women's biological capacities and the logic of capitalism that was particularly contentious within the pages of *SPE*. Patricia Connelly did not see women's subordination as a necessary condition of capitalism, as integral to free wage labour.[10] Instead, she maintained that gender made sense only within the context of particular societies. Likewise, in "Gender and Reproduction, or Babies and the State," Jane Jenson rejected our position on the grounds that it "follows *only* from the a priori assumption that sexual differences are as important as differences in the relationship to the means of production."[11] Our response at the time stressed locating bodies within capitalism at all levels of analysis and in each historically specific case. We were not arguing that capitalism creates, or even needs to create, women as domestic labourers, or that woman's fate is biologically determined. Rather we were arguing that the combination of free wage labour and women's biological capacities (as we knew them then) perpetuates women's subordination, albeit in multiple and complex forms. The debate about how to understand bodies in relationship to capitalism and women's subordination has particular urgency in light of more recent developments in reproductive technologies. As Lorna Weir and Jasmin Habib explain, "[A]ssisted human reproduction is acting to destabilize dominant cultural understandings of how sex and reproduction relate to human bodies".[12] But the issue, as Navsharan Singh reminds us, is not simply about individual women and men, or even exclusively about women as a group and capitalism as a force. Reproduction is racialized, as well as classed and gendered. A terrain of both political and individual struggle, the new technologies reveal "contradictions which underlie notions of women's freedom, self-determination and right to choose."[13] New technologies also expand the possibilities for both profit making and control over the creation of humans by those other than the women who produce the eggs. What does this mean not only for specific groups of women, located in different social and physical spaces, but also for the free wage labour that is at the centre of capitalism? Who is likely to resist these technologies and on what basis, with whose interests in mind?

Such questions take us back to another central issue in political economy, and in our article included here. In traditional political economy, it is classes that make history. It is not surprising then that feminists have been particularly interested in understanding how class analysis could work for women. The focus on market relations meant a focus on classes linked solely to production relations. We argued that all labour, not only that which is productive in direct market terms, must be taken into account when considering how classes are formed and reformed. Patricia Connelly and Martha MacDonald had a much more fully developed analysis that used the specific case of fishing communities in Nova Scotia to show how we can move from a class analysis of women to a gendered class analysis based on the complex relations of market, household and community.[14] Starting from a similar assumption that classes are constructed and reconstructed in concrete social processes, Pamela Moss exposes in the article presented here the contradictory material and subjective forces that simultaneously shape both class and gender relations. More recently, Wallace Clement and John Myles have taken up Dorothy Smith's notion of relations of ruling to explore such questions,[15] as Clement explains in his introduction to the section on production in this volume. These articles clearly demonstrate the need for dynamic conceptualizations of class that encompass all labour whether it is productive of surplus or not, and that take gender, race and region into account.

The debates about production and reproduction have covered all levels of theoretical abstraction and have, at most points over the last three decades, intersected with empirical research on specific cases. The focus over the last decade, however, has been more on the empirical research than on concern with higher levels of abstraction, in part because there is so much interest in differences and specificity. Yet we are now seeing a return to the consideration of debates on production and reproduction, as Leah Vosko's article, which ends this book, makes clear. It is this return that prompts the inclusion of the articles in this section, although many others in *SPE* have also made important contributions to these debates and are well worth searching out.

Notes

1. M. Patricia Connelly and Martha MacDonald, "Women's Work: Domestic and Wage Labour in a Nova Scotia Community," *Studies in Political Economy* 10 (Winter 1983):45–72.
2. Bonnie Fox and Pamela Sugiman, "Flexible Work, Flexible Workers: the Restructuring of Clerical Work in a Large Telecommunications Company," *Studies in Political Economy* 60 (Autumn 1999):59–84.
3. Pat Armstrong, "The Feminization of the Labour Force: Harmonizing Down in a Global Economy," in Isabella Bakker (ed.), *Rethinking Restructuring: Gender and Change in Canada*, edited by Isabella Bakker, 29–54 (Toronto: University of Toronto Press, 1996).
4. Leah Vosko, *Temporary Work: The Gendered Rise of a Precarious Employment Relationship* (Toronto: University of Toronto Press, 2000).
5. Meg Luxton, "Two Hands for the Clock: Changing Patterns in the Gendered Division of Labour," *Studies in Political Economy* 12 (Fall 1983):27–44.
6. Sedef Kroc, "In the Privacy of Their Own Home: Foreign Domestic Workers as Solution to Crisis of the Domestic Sphere," *Studies in Political Economy* 28 (Spring 1989):33–58.
7. Wenona Giles and Valerie Preston, "The Domestication of Women's Work: A Comparison of Chinese and Portuguese Immigrant Women Homeworkers," *Studies in Political Economy* 51 (Fall 1996):147–182.
8. Carla Lipsig-Mummé, "Organizing Women in the Clothing Trades: Homework in the 1983 Garment Strike," *Studies in Political Economy* 22 (Spring 1987):40–72.
9. Heather Menzies, "Telework, Shadow Work: The Privatization of Work in the New Digital Economy," *Studies in Political Economy* 53 (Summer 1997):103–23.
10. M. Patricia Connelly, "On Marxism and Feminism," *Studies in Political Economy* 12 (Fall 1983):153–162.
11. Jane Jenson, "Gender and Reproduction, or Babies and the State," in *Feminism in Action: Studies in Political Economy*, edited by M. Patricia Connolly and Pat Armstrong, 201–236 (Toronto: Canadian Scholars' Press, 1992), 215.
12. Lorna Weir and Jasmin Habib, "A Critical Feminist Analysis of the *Final Report* of the Royal Commission on New Reproductive Technologies" in *Feminism, Political Economy and the State: Contested Terrain*, edited by Pat Armstrong and M. Patricia Connolly, 327–343 (Toronto: Canadian Scholars' Press, 1999), 329.
13. Navsharan Singh, "Of GIFTS, GAMETRICS, Victim Women and Surplus Peoples: Reproductive Technologies and the Representation of 'Third World' Women," in *Feminism, Political Economy and the State: Contested Terrain*, edited by Pat

Armstrong and M. Patricia Connolly, 345–373 (Toronto: Canadian Scholars' Press, 1999), 345.

14. Connelly and MacDonald, "Women's Work."

15. Wallace Clement and John Myles, *Relations of Ruling: Class and Gender in Postindustrial Societies* (Montreal: McGill-Queen's University Press, 1994).

Chapter One

Beyond Sexless Class and Classless Sex: Towards Feminist Marxism

Pat Armstrong and Hugh Armstrong

There can be little doubt that Marxism has been and continues to be, as Heidi Hartmann[1] puts it, sex-blind. True, many journals and anthologies today include at least one article by women on women and much political economy now attaches a paragraph or two acknowledging the existence of women. But this paper is not an attack on discrimination in political economy or an appeal to pay more attention to women's issues. Rather it argues that Marxism must recognize that sex differences are integral to all levels of theory and analysis. The issue is not "women's questions" or "the question of women" but the efficacy of an analytical framework that fails to recognize or explain how and why sex differences pervade every aspect of human activity.

Building on and profiting from a wide range of feminist and Marxist analysis, the paper suggests ways to move beyond the classless sex of much feminist writing, and sexless class of most Marxist work, to a political economy that recognizes sexual divisions as integral to theoretical development. Sex differences were hardly a central concern for the "fathers" of political economy, yet the analytical tools developed by Marx and Engels can help us explore the social construction of the fundamental divisions between men and women. In their initial discussion of the relation between production and reproduction, they laid the basis for such an analysis.

The domestic labour debate, out of fashion in recent years, did attempt to extend Marxist analysis, in order to apply it to the question of women. Not surprisingly, given their pioneering nature, these early efforts were fraught with difficulties. Often mechanical, functionalist and undialectical in trying to relate women to the capitalist production process, these applications sometimes distorted Marxist categories to the point of uselessness. Biological differences were rarely discussed; resistance seldom recognized; ideology frequently ignored. Nevertheless, by focusing on the historical development of the work that takes place outside the market and on the contribution of this labour to the accumulation process, the debate has exposed many of the mechanisms that divide the sexes and subordinate women. It has established the pervasiveness of sex segregation in all kinds of labour and the significance of work in the home for the daily and generational reproduction of free wage labourers. It has shown how market conditions to a large extent shape, and are in turn shaped by, domestic work. Unfortunately, this crucial theoretical work seems to be largely invisible to much of political economy.

Through a critical evaluation of the insights and issues raised in this debate, the paper suggests ways to move towards a political economy that is sex conscious as well as class conscious — towards a feminism that is class conscious as well as sex conscious. Our purpose is to argue that sex divisions should be considered at all levels of analysis and to suggest that theoretical efforts should focus on developing an analysis of class that recognizes the fundamental cleavages based on sex and on an analysis of biology that is historical, materialist and dialectical. The capsule view presented here of the domestic labour debate is intended to illustrate that the development of such theory is itself a collective, dialectical and historical process. As Wally Seccombe[2] points out, "This can never be a merely additive process, like finding the long lost piece in a jig-saw puzzle and happily inserting it in the space left waiting for it." It requires a reworking of theory, not just an "adding on" of women to class analysis, not just an inserting of class differences into feminist approaches. This paper is meant as a contribution to the ambitious reworking project.

Marxist Analytical Tools

Our starting point in this project is — to use C. Wright Mills's term — that of plain Marxists.[3] We seek to work within Marx's own tradition, which requires that we avoid treating his writing as a holy writ through which to search for the correct answers. The danger of creating a vulgar or dogmatic Marxism is nowhere more apparent than in analyzing the position of women. Marx and Engels, most Marxists would agree, did not say much about women, and what they did say is not always useful or illuminating both because they concentrated on explaining capitalist production and because they reflected the particular male bias of their historical period. As Sheila Rowbotham[4] points out, "Despite the depth of their historical analysis, the range of their knowledge and the extent of the commotion their writing has helped to create, Karl Marx and Frederick Engels were still a couple of bourgeois men in the nineteenth century." Or, as Juliet Mitchell[5] puts it, "Raking around in the texts of the master under the heading 'women' is enough to convince the most loyal marxist that the founder was a male chauvinist *par excellence*." But Mitchell goes on to say that it is a ridiculous task to search through Marx for a complete explanation of the situation of women, ridiculous because historical materialism is an approach, a method of analysis.

For us, it is a method that is materialist, dialectical and historical. By materialist, we mean an approach that posits the existence of a real material world, one that conditions the social, political and intellectual processes in general. At the same time, we seek to distance ourselves from the economic determinism that pervades so much of orthodox Marxism and that has so frequently and justifiably been attacked by (among others) feminists of all persuasions. The ways people co-operate to provide for their daily and future needs, combined with the techniques and materials at their disposal, establish the framework within which all human activity takes place. This does not mean that everything can be reduced to or is determined by matter, nor does it imply that ideas are irrelevant, false or the mere products of material conditions. Central to dialectical materialism is the rejection of a false dichotomy between ideas and reality; indeed, of all such separations. Their very relatedness is central to the framework. "Human beings are not active in their productive life and consequently conscious in the remainder of their existence. They are conscious in their productive activity and active in the production of their consciousness."[6]

Marx of course went far beyond the call to begin with an analysis of material conditions. He exposed how capitalism became dominant, and isolated its motivating force, accumulation. In the insatiable drive for capitalist accumulation, more and more goods and services are bought and sold. Labour power, or the capacity to work, is itself increasingly transformed into a commodity as more and more people are separated from alternative means of providing for the basic needs and have to rely increasingly on the purchase of wage goods. Because Marx understood that the commodity production process establishes the broad framework for any capitalist society, he initially focused on how this production process works. He, like the capitalists, left the reproduction of workers largely to themselves. But free wage labour, which is essential to the very definition of capitalism, entails the reproduction of labour power primarily at another location. This separation under capitalism between commodity production and human reproduction (including the reproduction of the commodity labour power) in turn implies a particular division of labour between the sexes, and thus a division within classes. It is a division that pervades all work, whether productive of surplus or not, and one that is fundamental to the understanding of how the capitalist production system operates at all levels of abstraction and of how, and under what conditions, people will rebel.

Two related points following from this line of argumentation need to be underlined. First, by agreeing with Marx to assign pride of place under capitalism to the commodity production process — to the process by which surplus value is produced and appropriated — we distinguish ourselves from those who advocate a dual systems approach, with structures of patriarchy assuming a weight equal to, or at least an independence from, those of capitalism. While acknowledging that the subordination of women predates capitalism, we find that the term "patriarchy" tends to conceal more than it reveals about the many forms of this subordination. More light can be shed on the subordination of women by understanding it as inherent to the capitalist mode.

This leads to the second point, which is that we are able to use Marx's approach in moving beyond his sex-blind position. It is precisely by accepting his argument on the primacy of commodity production that we gain further insight into the subordination of women in capitalist society. We are not being reductionist or more specifically economistic to insist that wage labour is distinct from domestic labour. The logic of the capitalist accumulation process has made them distinct. Furthermore, it is capital, not (faulty) Marxist analysis, that has devalued the domestic labour that is performed normally by women, and which in turn conditions their participation in wage labour.

At the same time, we should of course avoid being carried away by the apparently compelling logic of the system. Marxist analysis is not simply materialist; it is dialectical and historical as well. Just as "materialism" has a double meaning — that there is a real world and that material conditions establish the framework for any society — so too is "dialectical" used in two senses. For Marx, every system produces contradictions at all levels. Not only are capital and labour in constant conflict, but in the process of attempting to cope with this conflict, new contradictions are constantly being created, combatted and partially resolved, generating even more contradictions. At the same time, the term "dialectical" can also mean that social processes and social relations are in themselves contradictory. Seccombe provides an example by arguing that "Although the proletarian condition is formally an open one, the great mass of the class cannot escape its class position even though, as individuals, they are free to try."[7] Similarly, wage labourers are freely compelled under capitalism to sell their ability to work to an employer. So, too, are women freely compelled to marry and to have children, and thus to do domestic work and, under certain conditions and within certain limits, labour force work as well.

With his eyes fixed too firmly on the commodity production process, Marx was unable to incorporate the conflicts between women and men, and between households and capital, into his dialectical analysis. Nor was he able to perceive the contradiction in the free compulsion facing women, who cannot often be full participants in capitalist society unless they are wives and mothers, and cannot often be full participants if they are. His view of contradiction, and thus of struggle, was partial and flawed. While the working class may or may not be differentiated by race, ethnicity, religion, occupation, industry or whatever, it is invariably differentiated by sex. It is perhaps not accidental that for Marx, it is *men* who make their own history, albeit not under conditions of their own choosing. The standard worker was for him at best sexless, at worst always male. As a result, the orthodox Marxist view of class struggle is vitiated by the failure to recognize that the working class has two sexes, a failure that hinders the understanding of men, much less women.

The recognition that the working class has two sexes need not be the grounds for pessimism about the working class as revolutionary agent. After all, the working class household can be an expression of unity as well as of tension between the sexes. More importantly, the seeds of pessimism are sown above all by failure, and an aspect of any successful working-class struggle to create itself is that it must become conscious of itself — a development that entails taking into account its own contradictions. Ignorance is not bliss, at least not for long. So the fact that sex differences cannot be eliminated by an effort of will is of tremendous strategic importance. We can agree with Marxism that the subordination of women is certain to continue as long as capitalism continues. We would add that the demise of the capitalist accumulation process will not necessarily mean an end to the subordination of women, and further that if the revolutionary project is limited to the elimination of this process, it is unlikely to attract many women to its banner. Nor should it. The strategic point then is to stretch dialectical analysis to make it a better tool for understanding and changing reality, for men as well as for women, for women as well as for men.

All these material conditions, contradictions and struggles have a history. In insisting on historical development, Marx was emphasizing the social construction of reality at the same time as he was drawing attention to the wide range of possibilities that exist within any particular mode of production and within any social formation. Where the capitalist mode is dominant, it transforms all aspects of society. Money, class differences, the sexual division of labour — they all predate capitalism, but all acquire a different significance and form under this mode. None, however, remains untouched by the logic of the dominant mode. There are necessary conditions for capitalism, but these can be satisfied in a number of ways. Yet the very workings of capitalism are modified by the struggles both to impose certain capitalist possibilities as against others and to transcend (or maintain) the capitalist mode itself. Indeed, many of the practices and ideas that develop under capitalism are contrary to the interests of capital. So analysis must be historical as well as dialectical and materialist. It must sort out the historical variations between modes of production and within them. More concretely, it must distinguish what is central to the logic of the capitalist mode of production from what is within the range of possible capitalist variations. It is in this spirit that we reject both the historical usage of the concept of patriarchy and assumptions about the unchanging nature of human biology.

With an approach that is materialist, dialectical and historical, it is possible to evaluate critically the domestic labour debate. In our view this debate is most fruitfully seen as starting with the first feminist efforts in the late 1960s to link the subordination of women to the sexual division of labour, and more specifically to relate domestic labour to wage labour. These efforts have involved, but have not been restricted to, considerations of value and domestic labour. Much of the debate has also centred usefully on questions of class and of strategy for women, and thus for men. The debate has helped make more transparent both the subordination of women and the workings of capitalism.[8] It is to an evaluation of the domestic labour debate, broadly conceived, that we turn next. As the debate has shifted to a new terrain, new directions for analysis have emerged. In particular, work needs to be done to make the analysis of human biology more materialist, dialectical and historical. We examine this issue in the concluding sections of the paper.

The Domestic Labour Debate

In 1890, Engels wrote that "Marx and I are ourselves partly to blame for the fact that the younger people sometimes lay more stress on the economic side than is due to it. We had to emphasize the main principle, vis-à-vis our adversaries, who denied it, and we had not always the time, the place or the opportunity to give their due to the other elements involved in the interaction."[9] With the rebirth of feminism in the late 1960s, it is not surprising that, in attempting to provide a material explanation for women's subordination — in trying to counter those who understood women's oppression primarily in terms of the ideas in their heads or the hormones in their bodies — theorists concentrated on women's work and its usefulness to capitalism. Nor is it surprising given the centrality of class to both Marxist analysis in general and to the struggle for change in particular that Marxists asking feminist questions began by trying to fit women into the class concept. These early explorations were thus frequently functionalist and reductionist, dismissing biology and dealing only peripherally with ideology. In the process, they sometimes distorted Marxist categories, reducing their usefulness without making the subordination of women more transparent. The debate quickly became more refined, complex and multidimensional, moving away from an exclusive focus on the movement of matter and away from the equally problematic approach of making women's subordination virtually autonomous from the workings of capitalism, as it tends to be in the dual systems theory. But the analysis continued in many ways to be undialectical. The inherent contradictions in positions taken are only now being explored. Neither resistance[10] nor biology[11] often arose in the debate — at least not on the Marxist side. Women at best appear primarily as victims, at worst as being prepared to collude in their own oppression. It is time to put women back in their own history, to place the sexual division of labour at the centre, not the periphery, of Marxist analysis. It is time to move beyond the domestic labour debate by building on its contribution.

Whether it is Engels claiming that "The first class antagonism which appears in history coincides with the development of the antagonism between man and woman in the monogamous marriage, and the first class oppression with that of the female sex by the male,"[12] or Marx viewing class struggle as the major force for change, an early and continuing issue in Marxist feminist analysis concerns the relationship of women to class.

Engels's statements in *The Origin of the Family, Private Property and the State* were ambiguous enough to form the basis for diametrically opposed approaches to understanding women and class. Shulamith Firestone, in what has stood up as a clear and comprehensive statement of the radical feminist position, commends Engels for observing that "the original division of labor was between men and women for the purposes of childbearing," although she also argues that "Engels has been given too much credit for these scattered recognitions of the oppression of women as a class." Nevertheless, she contends that Marxism provides a method for a "materialist view of history based on sex itself," one that recognizes that women form a class by virtue of their shared biology. For Firestone, sex is class: "The natural reproductive difference between the sexes led directly to the first division of labor at the origins of class."[13] Like the productive technology that will lay the basis for equality in productive relations, scientific developments will free women from the tyranny of reproduction and child-rearing, eliminating the physical differences between men and women and, not incidentally, the basis of all other differences among people as well. Such an approach is clearly ahistorical, denying that women's procreative and child-bearing activities take place within a social context — one that is dominated, although not determined, by decisions and actions taking place in the market. Consequently, it also ignores the class differences among women, differences that have an important influence on the timing, experience and consequences for women of childbirth and child-rearing. It fails to consider the way women have fought for, and gained, some control over their bodies. And the implication that the elimination of the biological differences between men and women will cause all other differences to wither away is difficult to consider seriously. Moreover, technology is not an independent force but one that is developed, introduced and sustained within a social context.

But the importance of women's procreative possibilities and child-bearing responsibilities cannot be so easily dismissed. In searching through the cross-cultural and historical research, among the enormous variety in social formations and practices, only child-bearing and infant care appear as common factors for women, suggesting that these realities play a significant role in women's subordination. While the historical and class variations in the process of child-bearing, birth and caring indicate that the productive factors alter the conditions for the meaning, consequences and experience of the procreative process, and that sex does not therefore make women a class, women's bodies clearly set them apart from men. The implications of these differences too have a history, and also vary with class, but they cannot be ignored in any class analysis.

Nevertheless, sex differences have seldom been acknowledged in Marxist analysis that is not also feminist. Instead of classless sex, or sex as class, we have sexless class. When sex divisions are considered, they often appear as a kind of epiphenomenon, a result of the exclusion of women from capitalist production. Charnie Guettel, an early entrant in the struggle to apply Marxist analysis to feminist questions, argued in *Marxism and Feminism* that "Women are oppressed by men because of the form their lives have had to take in a class society, in which men and women are both oppressed by the ruling class." She too contends that Engel "provides a basis for explaining the origins of women's subjection and, by extension, for discovering the conditions for their emancipation," although she also criticizes him for failing to "develop an analysis of women's oppression under capitalism" and for not mentioning "unequal pay and the responsibilities of maternity." Like Engels, she sees women's labour force participation and the collectivization of domestic labour as the prerequisites of women's liberation because "women's position within the contending classes determines her role in the struggle."[14] Since women's subordination is the result of capitalist organization, women must become wage labourers, become members of the proletarian class, and, as members of that class, struggle for change.

Like Firestone, Guettel finds support for her argument in Engels, but she arrives at the opposite conclusion that women do not form a class. Furthermore, the working class does not, or at least will not, contain fundamental sex divisions once there is "socialization of many of the childcare and domestic functions which are the material basis for women's inequality with men in the labour force."[15] By implication, sex differences will eventually wither away. Indeed, she argues that feminists have underestimated the extent to which they have already disappeared in socialist countries. This approach is also ahistorical in failing to acknowledge the male dominance that predates capitalism. To be sure, under capitalism all relationships are transformed, but in understanding their current nature it is important to examine the factors contributing to their precapitalist existence. Because she fails to examine the persistence of female subordination, blaming it solely on capitalism, she also ignores what women have in common — their bodies and their child-bearing possibilities — and underestimates the significance of domestic labour. Thus the difficulties of overcoming the sex divisions within classes are minimalized and reduced to equal pay for work of equal value, organizing the unorganized, and taxing corporations to pay for universal, democratically controlled daycare. The relationship between men and women within capitalism is developed in a mechanical, undialectical fashion. Only sexless classes resist. Women's control over their bodies and their sexuality is not part of the project, nor is their procreative work integrated into the structure of capitalism. Although women's work in the labour force is the primary, almost exclusive focus of this analysis, thus at best giving a distant second place to sex divisions, at worst denying their fundamental existence, this approach does draw our attention to the importance of women's entry into wage labour — work that cannot be ignored in explaining what divides women from women and from men.

For radical feminists, like Firestone, women's biologically determined shared work experience in child-bearing and child-rearing makes them a class. For Marxists like Guettel, women's capitalist-determined oppression melts into their future work in the labour force, work that will integrate them into an undifferentiated proletarian class. Neither of these approaches pays much attention to the household labour that has become the focus of the domestic labour debate and of other attempts to fit women into the class concept on the basis of this work.

It is difficult now to appreciate the impact of Margaret Benston's "The Political Economy of Women's Liberation" when it appeared in 1969. Although attacked and largely abandoned by later theorists,

Benston's article set many of the terms for the domestic labour debate and was immensely popular at the time because it finally seemed to provide an analysis that grounded women's oppression in their current work. Benston argues that women are already workers and thus a class in the objective Marxist sense of the term under the historically specific conditions of advance capitalism. Using the Marxist distinction between use value and exchange value, she maintains that women can be defined as the group of people who are responsible for the production of simple use values associated with home and family, working in the precapitalist home production unit. Unlike the paid work of men, which produces exchange value as well as use value, the unpaid work of women, which produces only use value, is valueless from the standpoint of capital. Although women might also participate in wage labour, such participation is transient and unrelated to the group definition. They form a reserve army of labour who can be called on when needed for capitalist production, and sent home when no longer required. This women's work is functional for capitalism because it fulfils "the needs for closeness, community, and warm secure relationships," and thus stabilizes the entire economy by maintaining the ideal consumption unit for capitalism — one in which the wages of the man purchase the necessary labour of two people, while allowing for the low-paid labour force work of the woman as required. For Benston, there are two related material conditions for changing woman's position. These are true equality in job opportunities outside the home, and the transfer of work now done in the home to the public economy. "Once women are freed from private production in the home, it will probably be very difficult to maintain for any long period of time a rigid definition of jobs by sex."[16] Nevertheless, she suggests that such changes would be difficult, if not impossible, under capitalism because the socialization of housework would require a massive redistribution of wealth, because women's unpaid labour is profitable and because the women released into the labour force could not be absorbed by it. Furthermore, ideas reinforcing women's inferiority will be difficult to change — indeed cannot change — without dramatic alterations in the structures that support them.

The argument is provocative, confusing and internally contradictory, yet it raises most of the issues that must be dealt with if we are to make the position of women understandable. She does suggest that capitalism has transformed the content and meaning of work, although she does not develop the argument. Cut off from the means of subsistence, money has become increasingly necessary to purchase what is needed for survival, but increasingly can be acquired only by selling the ability to work for a wage. More and more goods and services are commodified, although much of domestic labour is not. The source of power and control is the market and it is this production for the market that relegates unpaid work to a secondary status that creates not only the definition of work but much of domestic work itself. Indeed, domestic work as a separate form of work does not predate capitalism. Yet Benston maintains both that capitalism defines women's work and that this work is precapitalist and preindustrial. She cannot have it both ways. While her distinction between use value and exchange value does expose the dominance of capitalism and does emphasize the fact the women too do work that is both useful and necessary, it does not establish domestic labour as a precapitalist form that will wither away.

The distinction does, however, allow her to introduce the concept of the reserve army of labour, although her definition of women's labour force work as transient, with no structural relation to capital, limits the usefulness of this approach for her. Nevertheless, the concept can be used, as Patricia Connelly has so clearly shown in *Last Hired, First Fired*, in order to "emphasize women's permanent connection to the production process," and to provide "a link between their labour force participation and their work in the home." According to Connelly's expansion of the analysis, "under advanced capitalist forms of production, not only does female domestic labour have no exchange value, but female wage labour receives less than its exchange value."[17] Since women do necessary work in the home, which does not have exchange value, they form a cheap, available labour supply, competing with each other for women's segregated labour force jobs in a way that not only keeps down their wages but those of men as well.

The distinction between use value and exchange value thus indicates how capitalism transforms work primarily into wage labour and domestic labour (making the latter invisible in the process), and allows an exploration of the relationship between the two through the concept of the reverse army of labour; it does not, however, solve the problem of how to fit women into the class concept. While Benston argues that women are now a class on the basis of their production of use values in the home, her conclusions suggest that women are to become part of another class by eliminating their household labour and joining the labour force on equal terms. What, then, is the use of declaring them a class by virtue of their household labour? And how can class differences among women be explained? Like Guettel, she seems to assume that sex distinctions will disappear when women join the working class.

While she does offer a material base for women's oppression, focusing exclusively on women's work and its uses to capitalism, Benston does not understand this work in dialectical terms nor does she see the structure as a result in part of struggles between men and women and between workers of both sexes and owners. Freely compelled to marry, freely compelled to mother and now freely compelled to undertake labour force work, the essence of womanhood can be contradictory. The home is not simply a stabilizing force. The family is not simply created by capitalism. The home is filled with tensions that also result from developments within capitalism. Its existence depends to some extent on the efforts of male workers to obtain a family wage, on their struggles both to prevent women from competing for their jobs and to protect "the weaker sex," on women's attempts to decrease their workload and to maintain what is sometimes a haven, and on the nature of women's work itself, especially their procreative work.

But perhaps the most controversial legacy Benston bequeathed to the domestic labour debate was her statement that domestic labour is valueless from the standpoint of capital. Does domestic labour produce value? Is it subject to the law of value? What does this mean for the women's struggle and for the possibility of eliminating sex divisions within a capitalist society? Concern with these questions gradually shifted the debate away from the class issue towards a focus on the reproduction of labour power and the connection of women's work to capitalist production.

Peggy Morton, in her 1970 article, "Women's Work Is Never Done," was the first to argue that it is necessary to "see the family as a unit whose function is the maintenance of the reproduction of labour power," that "this conception of the family allows us to look at women's public (work in the labour force) and private (work in the family) roles in an integrated way." This position also led her to reject the idea that women form a class on the basis of their work. Although shared domestic labour means that "real contradictions exist for women as women. ... Women are nevertheless objectively, socially, culturally and economically defined and subjectively define themselves through the class position of their husband or their family and/or the class position derived from work outside the home."[18] Not only are there contradictions between both kinds of work; there are also inherent contradictions in the nature of the work in either place. The family does function for capitalism in socializing children, repressing sexuality and instilling appropriate hierarchical relationships through the education of future workers, but this is no smooth process. The very needs of the system create conflicting demands on the family, on women and on children, providing the basis for the development of strategy and militant struggle. Since male supremacy is structural, not just attitudinal, the struggle must be directed towards changing the structure of the system itself.

For Morton then, women do not simply produce use values; they produce something that connects them much more directly to capitalism — labour power. While she did not draw out the implications of this argument, and did not raise the question of value that was to become central to the later debate, she did develop a much more dynamic and dialectical approach to women's work, connecting women's domestic and wage labour, placing them within the contexts of capitalism and ideas about male supremacy, thus illustrating the contradictions that are inherent in this duality of domestic and wage labour. Recognizing the two workplaces of women and the class inequalities among women, she rejects the notion that women form a class. Not addressing directly women's shared procreative capacities, she raises, but does not explore, questions of women's control over their bodies and the class differences in access to birth control and abortion.

Other theorists, like Mariarosa Dalla Costa and Selma James,[19] adopted the argument that women are responsible for the maintenance and reproduction of labour power, but claimed that women constitute a class on the basis of this work in the home. Women are not to demand, as Benston argues, access to the same jobs as men. Instead they are to demand pay for the work they are now performing in the home. For these theorists, women now perform productive labour, that is, work that produces surplus value. The housework of women appears to be a personal service outside of capitalism, but it is in reality the reproduction of labour power, a commodity that is essential to the production of surplus value. The specific form of exploitation that this domestic work represents demands a corresponding specific form of struggle — namely, the women's struggle — within the family. The family is at the core of the capitalist organization of work. It is a social factory. This recognition of the family as a centre of reproduction for labour power — as the other hidden half of capitalist organization and exploitation, and as the other hidden source of surplus labour — entails the recognition of the social power of women. Women must exercise this power by refusing to work, by demanding wages for housework, by throwing responsibility for housework where it belongs — on capital. Thus the significance of defining women as a class on the basis of their domestic labour is that, as a class, they can become central to the class struggle in their own right.

But Dalla Costa and James misuse Marx's distinction between different kinds of labour. They confuse productive and unproductive labour. The purpose of any theory, and therefore its usefulness, rests on its ability to make transparent the opaque — to expose how the thing actually works. By applying to domestic labour categories that make capitalist production transparent frequently requires alteration in definitions and usage. The significance of altered usage does not, however, lie in its being an act of disloyalty to the arcane jargon of a century-old revolutionary. At issue is neither dogmatism nor the claim to be true to Marx. Rather, what is of significance is the capacity of Marx's careful distinctions to expose how capitalism works. Therefore, it is not only "Marxist purists," as Ann Oakley claims, who "need concern themselves with any epistemological uncertainty at this point."[20] It is anyone who wants to find out how and why women remain subordinate.

For Marx, productive labour under capitalism is labour that is exchanged directly (that is, for a wage) with capital in order to provide surplus value. Since housework is not directly exchanged with capital to produce surplus value, it is not in strict Marxist terms productive, and those who do it are not exploited. By collapsing useful and productive labour into one category, Dalla Costa confuses the content of the product with the social relations involved in the labour — the usefulness of the activity in general with its specific social form. It was to avoid this confusion that Marx employed "useful labour" as an ahistorical concept denoting all labour that produces use value, and restricted "productive labour" to capitalism, an historically specific mode of production with, as a result, specific social forms. While all productive labour is also useful labour, not all useful labour is productive. Capitalism was for Marx the social formation in which exploitation normally takes the form of the exchange of commodities and in which labour power is normally bought and sold as a commodity. Thus the social form termed "productive labour," and defined as labour exchanged directly with capital to produce surplus value, is specific to capitalism because it is central to the very definition of capitalism. Without productive labour, there is no capitalism. Without the concept of "productive labour" and without the distinction between it and the concept of "useful labour," the laws of motion of the capitalist mode of production cannot be understood. Since a wide range of behaviour produces use values, to define domestic labour as the production of use values is not very illuminating either since it merely puts it in the ahistorical category of work. Since only labour exchanged directly with capital in order to provide surplus value is productive in Marxist terms, to define domestic labour as productive is simply confusing.

Furthermore, placing domestic labour in the category of productive labour does not, as other adherents to this argument maintain, affect its value. Indeed, defining domestic work as productive leaves no room to explain, as Benston does, why it has become invisible and devalued under capitalism. In addition, it leans towards an idealist explanation, suggesting not only that the cause of the invisibility is the labelling of domestic work as unproductive labour, but also that renaming will increase its value.

There is, perhaps, a more serious problem with this analysis. Paying women a wage would solidify the separation of women from men without altering substantially the nature and conditions of the work and without fundamentally challenging the structure of capitalism. Although some domestic work has already become commodified in the market, capitalism is premised on the very separation of the reproduction of the wage labourer from the productive process, and wages for housework may serve primarily to reinforce this necessary separation. The contradictory needs and processes that develop in capitalism and in women's work form no part of such an analysis — an analysis that leads to a strategy to sustain rather than challenge the subordinate position of women, especially when the analysis does not take explicit account of the nature of women's procreative work.

The argument that women, in providing the care and feeding of men and children, are performing work that produces surplus value shifted the focus of the debate from questions of class to questions of value, sparking a theoretical struggle waged to a large extent on the pages of *New Left Review*. In the initial article of this debate, Wally Seccombe argues that although domestic labour is not productive in the Marxist sense because it is not exchanged directly with capital to produce surplus value, it is nonetheless necessary under capitalism because the commodities bought for domestic consumption, and thus for the reproduction of labour power, have to be converted into their final form before they can be consumed.[21] For Seccombe, the character of domestic labour under capitalism is that it contributes simultaneously to the creation of the commodity labour power while having no direct relation with capital (that is, producing no surplus value). It thus creates value (as does any labour-producing part of a commodity) while not being subject to the law of value. Seccombe develops his argument by means of an analysis of the mystification inherent in the wage, which appears to be exchanged for the labour performed on the job site, but which in fact is exchanged for the labour needed to reproduce labour power. Since domestic labour is part of this labour to reproduce labour power, it creates value that is equivalent to the production costs of its maintenance, despite the fact that it does so under privatized conditions.

Alternative interpretations of the relationship between domestic labour and value arose in the debate. While arguing that domestic labour does not create value, Jean Gardiner maintains that it "does nevertheless contribute to surplus value by keeping down the necessary labour time, or the value of labour power, to a level that is lower than the actual subsistence level of the working class."[22] Housework, although not defined here as productive labour, does result in surplus labour and thus allows the "payment by the capitalist of wages below the value of labour power."[23] Since it lowers the value of labour power, it is necessary to the profits of the capitalist. But this position also became the subject of attack.

Essentially the criticisms of the argument that housework creates value boil down to the fact that domestic labour is not equivalent to wage labour. By claiming that housework creates value, these theorists must be suggesting that housework is itself a commodity that is exchanged for part of the husband's wage. Yet as Margaret Coulson et al. in particular point out, the housewife as housewife does not sell her labour power as a commodity to her husband.[24] Although she does contribute to the maintenance and reproduction of labour power, her participation in the social process is mediated by the marriage contract rather than the labour contract. She is not paid a wage: the exchange between husband and wife is variable and arbitrary, and subject to interpersonal bargaining. This has fundamental consequences in terms of the difference between wage labour and domestic labour. Wage labour is free labour in the sense that the wage labourer sells his labour power to an employer of his choice for a definite period of time in return for a wage. Time not at work is his own and he is free to change employers when he wishes (and conditions permit). The employer constantly attempts to decrease the necessary labour time, which is paid for in the form of a wage, in order to increase surplus value.

Domestic labour, on the other hand, is not free labour. For the housewife, there is little distinction, in terms of either time or space, between her work and her leisure. Since she is not paid a wage and thus does not produce surplus value directly, there is little interest on the part of the capitalist in reducing the necessary labour time by increasing her productivity. Since her work is based on social and emotional as well as economic commitments, it is difficult for her to change "employers" freely. And the relationship between husband and wife is different from that between employer and employee both because it is seldom a strictly economic relationship and because it involves all, rather than part of, the housewife's daily life. Finally, because the relationship is a binding one, there is no tendency towards the equalization of labour that occurs in capitalist commodity production.

Domestic labour and wage labour are not equivalent; they are not interchangeable. Marx revealed the mechanisms that affect a specific form of work — wage labour. These mechanisms do not, however, apply in the same way to domestic labour, precisely because it is not wage labour. As Paul Smith points out, domestic labour is not directly responsive to the price of labour.[25] It is performed even when its product cannot be sold. Because it is not subject to the law of value, there is no social mechanism to define the necessary tasks, no measure of value, and it is not equivalent to other forms of labour. To argue, as Seccombe does, that domestic labour "contributes directly to the creation of the commodity labour power while having no direct relation with capital"[26] does little to expose the nature of the relationship between domestic labour and wage labour. According to Gardiner, "there appears to be no mechanism for the terms of sale of labour power to be determined by the domestic labour performed in its maintenance and reproduction."[27] Better housework is unlikely to result in a better wage.

But to argue, as Gardiner later does, that domestic labour lowers the value of labour power does not make this relationship any more transparent.[28] Because wage labour and domestic labour are not comparable, "there is no basis for the calculation of the transfer of surplus labour-time between the two spheres unless the law of value is redefined."[29] Men married to women who are full-time housewives do not receive lower wages than men married to women who work full-time in the labour force, or men of similar age with no wives at all. In fact, the reverse relationship is more likely; women married to men who receive low wages are more likely to work for pay and thus do less housework. It would make more sense to argue that women entering the labour force who obtain wage work lower the value of labour power by covering at least some of the costs of their own reproduction rather than having all these costs met out of the husband's wage. Even if the cost of domestic labour is hidden, it is still a cost, making it difficult to understand why, in value terms alone, capital would have an interest in maintaining domestic labour — especially when some of its goods and services could be transformed into commodities, thereby producing surplus value.

The early value debate virtually ignored women's wage labour, concentrating as it did on the reproduction of workers, all of whom seemed to be male. In responding to his critics, Seccombe argued that there is an average domestic labour time that can be defined as "that labour time necessary to convert the average wage into the average proletarian household, at the average price of wage goods." From this base, he argues that when real male wages fall, women can compensate for the decrease by either intensifying their housework or by entering the labour force to "supplement the family income."[30] The woman makes a "value trade-off" when she enters the market, compensating for the increased cost of the replacement of her domestic labour with her additional income. But the argument that domestic labour creates value does not, as Seccombe claims, explain movement from one form of labour to the other. If they are equivalent, why would a woman take on the other job? Wage labour and domestic labour are not equivalent. It is precisely because domestic labour is not wage labour that they are not interchangeable. Women cannot decide today that they will quit being pregnant so they can go out to work, but they can decide to stop washing the floor once a week and do it only once a month. There is no "exchangeability of labour time embodied in wage goods for domestic labour time,"[31] as Seccombe argues. While clearly some housework can be replaced by purchasing goods previously processed at home, most women do not replace their domestic chores with McDonald burgers and substitutes hired to clean the toilets and make the beds. They simply leave some work undone, do some work less often and lower the quality of other labour — none of which suggests that there is necessary labour time involved or that this work constitutes average domestic labour time. Indeed, it is precisely because women are not creating value and are not directly subject to the law of value (because they do not produce surplus value) that they can form a reserve army of labour. It is because floors can go unscrubbed and beds unmade, and because they can vacuum less often, that women can in many cases enter the labour force. And it is because they cannot easily transform infant care and child care into purchasable items that many women with small children provide a less flexible supply of labour.

But to argue that domestic labour does not create value or surplus value and is not directly subject to the law of value is not to argue that the law of value does not influence this work. Under capitalism, all labour is transformed, since the law of value impinges on most aspects of human activity. As Seccombe points out in a later article, the household is influenced by both the labour market and the retail market.[32] The household varies in response to wages and the demand for labour, as well as in response to the prices and availability of goods and services, by varying family size and the spacing of children; by varying the wage labour of men, women and children; by adjusting purchases; and by going into debt. Further, women do base their "decision" to take on a second job to a large extent on female wages, male wages and the prices of the commodities their families need.

The debate over the law of value has not shown that women's domestic labour creates value, although it has made clear the fact that women do necessary work at home — work that is useful to capitalism in many ways. While it has not shown that the law of value directly governs the allocation of domestic labour, it has opened the door to an analysis that explores how the operation of the law of value in the market impinges on the household, influencing but not determining domestic labour time and content. In struggling through the implications of applying the law of value to domestic labour, the participants in the debate have revealed the opposite of what was initially intended. They have shown how domestic labour differs from wage labour. They have thus led the way to the argument presented here: that it is the different nature of domestic labour — its existence outside the law of value and the production of surplus value — that creates the flexibility and thus the possibility of domestic workers becoming a reserve army.

It should not be assumed, however, that domestic labour is completely flexible — that there is no minimum necessary labour in specific households. Toilets may go uncleaned, but infants do have to be fed. Nor should it be assumed that women's movement in and out of the labour force is completely flexible and/or simply a matter of choice. Instead of arguing that women were forced out of the labour force in early capitalism and later pulled in and out at the whim of capital, it is necessary to examine, in an historically specific way, which women were entering and leaving, and under what conditions. Patricia Connelly's work indicates that in Canada married men and single women were the first to be forced into wage labour, the first to lose access to the means of directly producing for their needs, the first to have no alternative but to sell their ability to work for a wage.[33] As well, some married women, probably more than official statistics indicate, also worked for a wage from the earliest period, because they too had no alternative way to acquire food and clothes. However, it seems likely that in Canada at least, many married women had access to the means of producing directly for their own survival or of gaining income without entering the labour market. Not only did they have considerable necessary labour in the home, which prevented them from searching for wage work, but they could also directly produce food, sew clothes, do laundry, take on boarders or do other domestic chores without selling their ability to work for a wage. Such alternatives do not mean that most men earned a family wage, nor do they mean that women were completely or even primarily dependent on a male wage. What they do mean is that women were supporting their own reproduction in a way that allowed them to combine this work with the labour they had little chance of escaping — child-bearing and caring responsibilities. More recently, married women have been losing access to the means of production and to alternatives to wage labour. Darning more socks, even if polyester socks could be darned, does not greatly affect family maintenance. The point in this is — a recital that may seem very familiar — that we have been looking at women's work upside down. Instead of seeing women's domestic work as substituting for the wage, we should be seeing the wage as what becomes necessary when, like men, they have no alternative means of providing for their own needs. We should question whether women have ever been dependent on a male wage and, if so, which women — women from which classes. By analyzing domestic labour from this perspective, we will not only expose the class differences among domestic workers — not only trace the transformation and commodification of much domestic work — but also perceive the reduction in women's access to means of support. For larger and larger groups of women, the intensification of domestic labour that is central to Seccombe's argument is not an alternative.

Moreover, women's movement in and out of the labour force should not be understood as being simply functional for capital or as a passive response by women to labour market requirements. By drawing women into the labour force, capital may lower the value of labour power through competition and decrease the costs of reproducing workers by spreading them over more workers, but it also may create a crisis because not all people can be absorbed into paid employment. Capital also encourages tension in the home, for women and men, between women and men. In addition some groups of women, especially those with higher education and training, are fighting to enter the labour force and to abandon their domestic chores; others, especially those with small children, are struggling to escape the compulsion to work at those dull, low-paid, monotonous jobs that create for them the double day. Of course, the alternatives are structured by capitalism itself. Resistance is seldom powerful enough to win, but it does have an influence that cannot be ignored. Women do not passively respond to family or market demands. None of this is to deny that women form a reserve army of labour, especially as part-time and seasonal workers. However, it is to argue that from this perspective, married women are becoming less and less flexible as their alternatives to wage labour are reduced. It is also to argue that some classes of women are more flexible than others and that women are active in directing their labour. And, it must not be forgotten that all of this happens within the context of a society that encourages ideas about male dominance and that values independence and competition, although these values themselves vary from class to class.

This summary and evaluation of the domestic labour debate has been presented here for a number of reasons. First, it is intended to illustrate that while the analysis was frequently mechanical and functionalist, and usually ignored resistance and biology, it did open the door to an approach that is historical, materialist and dialectical.

We seek to expose not only the significance of domestic labour and its relation to wage labour, but also the variable, complex and dialectical development of this work. Through this exposition, it is possible to see the tensions created by the drive for accumulation — for commodification — and the resistance, based on these tensions, that have altered work in the home and in the labour force.

Second, this review is designed to illustrate the centrality of domestic labour and sex divisions to capitalism, to wage labour, and therefore to our theorization of how capitalism operates. Based on sex, separated from production, but conditioned by and in turn conditioning the market, domestic work is both intimately connected to, and a factor in, capitalist processes. Because domestic labour is not wage labour, women form a reserve army for the capitalist productive system. Because wage labour has become dominant and necessary — either directly or indirectly — to the survival of most people, other work and other workers have been devalued. Because domestic work is centred on the reproduction of the next generation of workers, as well as on the daily maintenance of all workers, it is women's work. Finally, this critical summary provides a basis for the next sections of this paper — sections that suggest ways to go forward in developing a political economy that comprehends the fundamental importance of sex divisions at all levels of analysis. The focus is on class, on the separation of domestic and wage labour, and on biological questions as central, but not the only, questions for a sex-conscious theory.

Sex Is a Marxist Issue

Although feminists have focused on domestic labour, or the split between the public and the private, Marxists who are not feminists have concentrated on the production process. If justified at all, this concentration on production is explained either in terms of the dominance of this process or in terms of the level of abstraction. At the highest level of abstraction, it is argued, sex divisions are irrelevant.

But, at the highest level, capitalism is defined as a system that separates capital from labour, with labour power typically bought and sold as a commodity. As Seccombe has so clearly explained, capitalism is premised on the existence of free wage labour.[34] The split between the public and the private is the very essence of capitalism. The sale of labour power as a commodity seems to assume reproduction at home, away from labour force work. It does not, of course, necessitate a particular kind of home or a particular kind of family. The nature and conditions of workers' reproduction are matter for historical investigation at another level of analysis. This does not, however, seem to be the case for the existence of the sexual division of labour itself, which necessarily accompanies the separation of the reproduction of labour power in some kind of home from the production of goods and services in some kind of market. Women, not men, have the babies. If producing the next generation of workers is separated from the commodity production of goods and services, then this split implies a division of labour by sex. The particular duties that are associated with procreation are matters of history, but the division is central to capitalism itself. It is no accident of history that the everyday tasks of maintaining and reproducing the next generation of workers have in fact been disproportionately performed by women.

There is a tendency within capitalism towards commodification; much of domestic labour has already been commodified. But it seems likely that there are real limits to this process if capitalism, and the free wage labourer, are to continue to exist. Some child care work can be, indeed has been, integrated into the market economy. This labour can be equalized and abstracted. But babies can be produced only by fertile women. Such labour, at least given present circumstances, cannot therefore be equalized and abstracted. If all aspects of the reproduction of workers could be commodified, the process would require either the private production of workers with its consequent tendency towards monopoly (a circumstance inimical to the production of a free wage labourer), or an enormous expansion of the state (an eventuality counter to the existence of capitalism). Furthermore, the ideology of the free wage labourer, so important to the capitalist status quo, would be difficult to maintain if people were entirely produced through capitalist production processes or the state. A capitalist society, with its concomitant free wage labourer, seems to imply a separation, in some form, between the reproduction of workers and the production of goods and services. The separation seems also to imply a segregation, and denigration, of women.

Therefore, to insist on distinguishing a highest level of abstraction that entirely excludes consideration of a sexual division of labour is to be sexist — to reinforce the notion of women being hidden from history, or more accurately, from theory. It is also to guarantee an inadequate understanding of capitalism, given that the split between the public and the private, and thus a sexual division of labour, is essential to this mode of production, at the highest level of abstraction. In summary, the existence of a sexual division of labour, although not its form or extent, is crucial to capitalism and therefore to its theorization.

Class Is a Feminist Issue

Few would deny that capitalist societies are class societies or that women as a group are oppressed. But the question of whether or not there is a material basis to that oppression and of whether or not that basis is shared bodies or shared work is still a matter of debate. Are the fundamental divisions those between owners of the means of production and owners of labour power, those between men and women, or those between women and their bodies? Is the main enemy, to use Christine Delphy's terminology, capitalism, men or female anatomy?[35]

While it is essential for a class analysis to locate women in relation to class, the answer cannot be one of these alternatives alone. Women are simultaneously subject to capitalism, male dominance and their bodies. To pose the question in the form of alternatives is like asking whether ideas or material conditions structure women's subordination. They are inseparable. They act together. Patriarchy and capitalism are not autonomous, nor even interconnected systems, but the same system. As integrated forms, they must be examined together.

This is not to argue that women constitute a class. Although it is clear that most of those who own and control the means of production are male, most men own only their ability to work. There are also class differences among women. Lady Astor is not oppressed by her chauffeur and it is questionable whether her cleaning woman is more oppressed by her husband than her employer. Theorists have concentrated on exposing what women have in common, but not all theorists have ignored or dismissed class differences among women. Early in the domestic labour debate, Morton maintained that there were class differences among women — differences based on the class position of their husbands, their families or their own labour force work. Roberta Hamilton explored the different work experiences and life situations of women in peasant, craft, "tradesman" and noble families in the transition to bourgeois and proletarian households.[36] Situating women within the family, and the family in turn within the dominant mode of production, Dorothy Smith argued that capitalism changed all women's work into a personal service, but that there is a crucial difference between working-class and middle-class families. "The household for the working class woman is a means to meeting the needs of its members, and that is her work. Middle class women are oriented by contrast to the values and standards of an externalized order."[37] Bonnie Fox also distinguished between working-class and middle-class women — in this case on the basis of household income and resources.[38] The oppression takes different forms for these women. The consequences, nature and responses to male dominance vary from class to class.

To argue that there are class differences among women and that they do not form a class on the basis of their bodies or their work is not to solve the problem of fitting women into classes. Locating women through their domestic labour either puts most women into the same class or places them automatically in the same class as their husbands. For those women with direct involvement in the labour market, the alternatives are independent class membership with other women because of the domestic labour they also perform. Gardiner's alternative of expanding the definition of the working class to include all those not directly involved in but dependent on the sale of labour power does expose the broad class cleavages, but fails to take into account the fundamental divisions between men and women in the working class.[39] Surely having an indirect, rather than a direct, relationship to production has important consequences for women's class sympathies — sympathies that cannot easily be equated with those of the young and unemployed whose dependency is temporary and transient. Furthermore, such an approach ignores the double work of women, their position as a particular kind of reserve army, their segregation into separate labour force jobs, and the ideology that reinforces and is reinforced by these divisions.

The problem here is more than one of counting, of figuring out how to classify women. Both bourgeois and Marxist categories treat sex differences as irrelevant to stratification and class systems. As Delphy points out, both approaches imply that "wider inequalities have no influence on the (assumed) 'equality' of the couple, and on the other hand that relationships within the couple because they are seen as equal cannot be the cause of wider inequalities."[40] Theories that lump all women together as a class ignore class differences among women. Theories that attach women to their husbands or families ignore women's subordination, their domestic labour and their labour force work. Theories that locate women in terms of their own paid employment forget both the segregation of the labour force and the domestic labour that most women perform. Theories that are blind to sex differences obscure not only divisions fundamental to all classes, but also the structure of capitalism. The working class, as well as the ruling class, has two sexes. Without acknowledging these divisions — without integrating them into a class analysis — neither capitalism nor households can be understood. This is not a plea to add women back in, but a challenge to a theory that has not made the system transparent, has not developed an analysis of class that accounts for a bifurcation of classes — a division that is central to an understanding of how capitalism itself works.

The domestic labour debate does lay the basis for a revision of theory based on an expansion of the class concept. Without denying that the most basic divisions are between those who own and control the means of production and those who own only their labour power — a primacy implied by the dominance of the wage system in capitalist society — it is possible to comprehend the antagonisms between the sexes, and among those of the same sex, by including all labour in our analysis. Those dependent directly or indirectly on the wage are objectively and subjectively divided by their material conditions, by their lived experiences and by the work they do. If work for a wage (or the absence of work for a wage) and work required to transform that wage into consumable form, as well as work necessary to provide the next generation of workers, are included in our approach to class, then divisions between men and women and among women may be better understood. Such an approach would permit the domestic and wage labour of both men and women to be taken into account. Domestic labour would thus form an integral part of the explanation for men's interests just as wage labour would be a basis component in comprehending women's class position and relations. Connecting domestic and wage labour within classes would also extend the analysis to the relationship between domestic and wage labour — to the sex segregation in both areas of work. In this way, it would be possible to develop a theory that exposes the material basis of the subjective and objective antagonisms between sexes. The domestic labour debate suggests a movement in this direction; Marxism provides the tools; political economy should continue the work.

Bodies in History

For Marx, analysis at all levels should begin with the way people provide for their daily and generational needs — with the production and reproduction of goods, services and people. These production and reproduction processes are inseparable aspects of the same whole. They are social processes requiring co-operation, and are subject to historical change. They do, however, have physical components that set limits on possible variations. A minimum of food is necessary, some protection from the elements is essential, and some ejaculation, insemination and gestation must take place for babies to be born. While there are enormous variations in how physiological and socially constructed needs are satisfied, in all societies and throughout history, women have the babies.

That women have babies is not a matter that has relevance only at the level of a particular social formation. How women have babies, and the conditions and consequences of child-bearing, are relative to particular social formations. So is the sexual division of labour related to child-rearing. But the fact that women, not men, have babies is not. To theorize production and reproduction at the highest level of abstraction involves a recognition of the differences in female and male reproductive capacities. Any other approach fails to comprehend the nature of production and reproduction.

Here, we are distinguishing ourselves from much of Marxist analysis. As Hamilton points out, "It is hard not to conclude that the effect of biological differences on the position of women is an embarrassment to marxists, that it is more or less known information which, like the happenings in a Victorian bedroom, is best left unexplored."[41] Those Marxists who fail to discuss the sexual division of labour at all must be assuming, like Guettel, that it is a mere by-product of the capitalist system and thus will wither away with the end of the system — that it is a minor factor in the functioning of capitalism. Those who discuss the sexual division of labour without acknowledging the biological component seem to point in a similar direction. Or perhaps they are assuming that procreative capacities are not amenable to Marxist analysis. But this analysis must be extended to include sexuality, child-bearing and childbirth if the realities of production and reproduction are to be understood and changed in a way that would benefit both women and men.

To recognize that women have the babies is not, however, to resort to a biological explanation of women's subordination, nor to call for the elimination of women's child-bearing responsibilities. Unlike many feminists, we do not see biology as fixed and immutable. We do not see child-bearing as the same for all women in the same society or in different historical periods. We do not see biological factors as primary or even separate factors. Physical capacities do not exist outside — autonomously from — power structures and productive processes. Nor are they beyond human control and manipulation. Procreation is itself to a large extent socially constructed. It has a history. Its process, consequences and meanings also vary from class to class. Capitalism has transformed the productive and reproductive processes. Contradictions are created, resolved and transformed. And women, on the basis of these contradictions, struggle to resist, to gain some control over their biological capacities. What follows is an indication of the direction a Marxist analysis should take if it is to include women's particular reproductive capacities — in other words, their procreative capacities — in the comprehension of production and reproduction in general.

It may be readily agreed that inequality results, not from the different biological capacities but from the social mechanisms that ensure that these capacities become a weakness rather than a resource. To suggest, however, that the very "biology" of the procreation process has varied historically with the economic system may be more a matter of debate. According to Gayle Rubin, "The needs of sexuality and procreation must be satisfied as much as the need to eat, and one of the most obvious deductions which can be made from the data of anthropology is that these needs are hardly ever satisfied in any 'natural form,' any more than are the needs for food."[42] Or, as Richard Wertz and Dorothy Wertz put it in their history of "lying-in" in the United States: "Because people have understood and shaped birth in changing ways, both the means and the meaning of childbirth have a history, an extraordinary one because childbirth is at once a creative act, a biological happening, and a social event."[43] Research on the history of women's role in procreation clearly indicates that the general economic situation, the class structure, the development of technology, women's other work, health care and standards and available food supplies — in short, the economic system — affect the kind of pregnancies women go through, the number of pregnancies they have and their chance of survival.

For example, Louise Tilly and Joan Scott[44] show how low standards of nutrition and health in early modern England inhibited conception, promoted miscarriage, affected the milk supply of mothers and made women infertile by the age of forty or forty-five. Wertz and Wertz report that in the colonies, as in France, "there was a seasonal periodicy to the arrival of children," which "may correlate not only with work demands and consequent exhaustion but also with nutritional variation."[45] In the introduction to her moving collection of English working-class women's testimonials on their experiences with maternity, Margaret Davies argues that the high infant mortality rate and the extensive maternal suffering at the turn of the century were attributable to: (1) inadequate wages; (2) lack of knowledge regarding maternity and of skilled advice and treatment; and (3) the personal relation of husband and wife.[46] Similarly, Neil Sutherland, referring to a 1910 report prepared for the Ontario government, lists the following as agents of high infant mortality rates:

> Poverty, ignorance, poor housing, overcrowded slums, low wages and other social conditions that forced mothers of young children to work outside their homes, impure water and milk, loose controls over the spread of communicable diseases, poor prenatal care, inadequate medical attendance at birth, tardy registration of births, and the lack of clinics and nursing services helping mothers care for their babies properly.[47]

These factors, which also affect the process of pregnancy and child-bearing, result primarily from the existing material conditions. And the very "biology" of menstruation also varies with these conditions over time. According to Janice Delaney, Mary Jane Lupton and Emily Toth, "the fact is, the age at menarche (first menstruation) depends greatly on good food and good health. Those who eat well mature earlier. Today, the average American girl first menstruates when she is twelve and a half years old. Figures from Norway, where the oldest such records are kept, show that in 1850 the average girl had her first period at seventeen; by 1950, at thirteen and a half. For each generation since 1850, then, a girl's period has come about a year earlier than her mother's."[48] Furthermore, as Joyce Leeson and Judith Gray point out, changes in economic and social arrangements have meant that "Thirty-five years or more of virtually uninterrupted menstruation is thus a recent phenomenon."[49] Bodies are not independent of their economic and social surroundings. The conditions are set by the productive system.

Yet changes in the productive system, and more specifically in women's work, do not automatically produce changes in women's experiences with sex and with child-bearing. To quote Stella Browne, a socialist feminist writing in 1922, "No economic changes would give equality or self-determination to any woman unable to choose or refuse motherhood of her own free will." As she so eloquently explained: "Birth control for women is no less essential than workshop control and determination of the conditions of labour for men. ... Birth control is a woman's crucial effort at self-determination and at control of her own person and her own environment."[50] The development of, and the conditions of access to, birth control and abortion technology are clearly of central importance to women.

Some form of birth control has been known since hunting and gathering societies. Yet even the early forms were suppressed if and when this suited the interests of the productive system. As Linda Gordon argues, the coincidence of the suppression of birth control with the development of agriculture is attributable to the need for more labour power and the desire to control inheritance of the accumulating private property.[51] While new technology has been developed in the productive sector, religious and state laws have limited access to, and information on, both old and new methods of birth control and abortion.[52] The research carried out by Wertz and Wertz indicates that the technology and its regulation have had both positive and negative consequences for women.[53] The point is that the interests of women have seldom been taken into account in decisions to develop and to allow access to the technology; consequently, women have had difficulty in asserting control over their bodies through contraception and abortion technology.

Important as this technology and its regulation are to women, there are other ways in which their procreative experiences are conditioned by the productive and state sectors. Procreation is influenced by labour force demands, by state policies and regulations, and by economic requirements and resources. For instance, Tilly and Scott argue that "young populations and job opportunities for young workers kept birth rates from falling" in some French industrial cities during the mid-nineteenth century.[54] According to Angus McLaren, "Factory work often prevented the young mother from being able to nurse her child" in nineteenth-century England, thus reducing even the limited contraceptive protection provided by breast-feeding and consequently encouraging women to seek methods of abortion to prevent birth.[55] The "combination of large-scale immigration from Southern Europe and the causalities of the First World War stimulate[d] widespread alarm over birth and mortality rates,"[56] and resulted in government and private programmes designed to change the conditions of childbirth and child-rearing. In 1937, when depression conditions had dramatically increased unemployment, the Canadian rate of natural increase dropped to a record low of 9.7 (per 1,000 population) in spite of the restrictions in access to birth control techniques and information. During and immediately after World War II, the rate rose steadily from 10.9 in 1939 to a record high of 20.3 in 1954.[57]

In addition, these rates are affected, as many social policy researchers indicate, by existing laws and regulations that "touch on the ability to more effectively plan the number and timing of children by Canadian families (which will bring into consideration abortion and sterilization and contraception), the ability to determine the grounds on which individuals can decide to form or dissolve families (which will involve divorce laws and regulations), and the legal implications of the formation or dissolution of a family unit."[58] Today, in Canada, it is evident that the demand for women as workers in the labour force and the concomitant decline in the economic resources of the family have encouraged women both to participate in the labour force and to reduce the number of children they produce. This reduction itself has been made possible both by the development of birth control technology and by changes in state intervention — especially in the laws that relate to birth control and abortion — but also more generally in the provision of health care services and information.

Like the concept of the virgin mother, procreation has internal contradictions for women. Adrienne Rich has described in eloquent detail the contradictions inherent in mothering within an advanced capitalist society.[59] It is at one and the same time a joyful and painful experience. Women can see the possibility for control over their reproductive capacities, but the control is denied by abortion laws, poor technical development, medical practices and limited information, not to mention the ideology of male superiority. They have "free choice" in marrying and bearing children, but like the wage worker who is freely compelled to sell labour power, women are compelled by conditions of pregnancy, wage work, medical techniques and legal restrictions to marry and have babies in particular ways. Labour force work interferes with pregnancy and birth; pregnancy and birth interfere with labour force jobs.

And while capitalists seek to pursue their interests, the results are frequently contradictory here too. The process is dialectical.

Barbara Ehrenreich and Deirdre English explain that Margaret Sanger's campaign for birth control in the United States was aimed at preventing the problems created by "overbreeding" in the working class.[60] But the consequence of her victory was a greater decline in the birth rate among those Sanger would have described as fit. In Canada, a Crown attorney claimed in 1901, "that employment opportunities permitted women to avoid marriage or to fall back on 'crime' which led to a 'low birth rate'."[61] Women have more recently responded to the growth in demand for women workers and the rising costs of rearing children by reducing the number of children they have and by demanding child care facilities. Now that the demand for female workers is falling off, there are few children to draw women back into the home, although decreasing support for existing child care service increases the pressure on women to go back home.

More generally, the contradiction between the technical possibility for women to control their bodies and the lack of control that results from policies designed for other interests has formed the basis of women's protests for centuries. As Gordon points out in her history of birth control in America, "In no area of life have women ever accepted unchallenged the terms of service offered by men. Sexuality and reproduction were no exception."[62] There are many instances of such rebellion. McLaren argues that in nineteenth-century England, "the workers, and in particular the women workers of the textile areas, should be seen, not as waiting passively for the knowledge to trickle down from their superiors which would permit them to emulate the middle class, but as taking independent action, which might well violate bourgeois morality, in an attempt to achieve their own desired family size."[63] In Canada, "A contributor to the *Canadian Churchman* (1900) went so far as to assert that the pressures of existing society encouraged '... to put it bluntly, in nine cases out of ten, women to murder their unborn children.'"[64]

The entire history of abortion indicates women's resistance to both the law and their procreative capacities. And similar patterns appear in breast-feeding practices. Reporting to the Ontario government in the early part of this century, Dr. Helen MacMurchy argued that women should be convinced to breast-feed their infants in order to prevent high infant mortality rates. "In order to encourage women to breastfeed, a mother's qualms about the cost of such a procedure had to be overcome. A working mother who could not adjust her schedule to a breastfeeding schedule should have a pension, if necessary, to take care of the family."[65] Women have not passively accepted the dictates of the state, the church or men. Indeed, child-bearing itself may be a form of resistance against imposed standards and against powerless conditions. Women may gain power from bearing children — power over children and over men. It should not be seen only as a passive response. Women are not merely vessels. They are active in making their own history.

In various historical periods, women's bodies, and their lack of control over their bodies, have provided the basis for the organized opposition of some women. But, while shared physiology has brought some women together, the variation created by existing material conditions has divided women — has encouraged women in different classes and in different marital situations to experience their bodies in different ways. Women differ in terms of the health care they receive during pregnancy, in terms of their access to information on birth control and on the way their bodies function, and in terms of the ease of gestation as it is related to nutrition, information and exercise. They also differ in the consequences of child-bearing — whether it will cause financial or emotional strain, and whether it will limit free movement and/or labour force participation. Lady Astor and her maid may both give birth, but the treatment they receive and the consequences of childbirth for them vary greatly. This is clearly indicated by the research on women of different class positions. For instance, Ehrenreich and English show that in nineteenth-century America, "It was as if there were two different species of females. Affluent women were seen as inherently sick, too weak and delicate for anything but the mildest pastimes, while working class women were believed to be inherently healthy and robust. The reality was very different. Working class women, who put in long hours of work and received inadequate rest and nutrition, suffered far more than wealthy women from contagious diseases and complications of childbirth."[66] Wertz and Wertz[67] describe how poor women were encouraged to deliver in hospitals so that doctors in training could practise on them. On the other hand, in Canada during the latter half of the nineteenth century, "one of the main reasons for the incidence of puerperal insanity [the 'insanity of childbirth'] in the Victorian era was, ironically, a consequence of medical practitioners delivering babies — a service that the well-to-do were more likely able to afford. ... Today, it is evident that puerperal insanity had less to do with the nature of women than it had to do with the nature of medical treatment."[68] The letters from working-class English women collected by Davies at the turn of the century clearly indicate the "different conditions under which the middle-class and the working-class women becomes a mother."[69] These examples suggest that there is not one procreative process for all women but different procreative processes for women in different classes and in different historical periods.

The alternative analytical approaches are not limited to ignoring sex difference, assuming they are mere social constructs, or concluding that they represent fixed, primary differences that create their own relations — ones that are beyond Marxist analysis. An historical materialist approach not only allows us to situate female sexuality and child-bearing within capitalism but also to show how these processes are conditioned within particular social formations — in different ways for women of different classes. It permits the integration of biological factors as limiting but not determining. Any alternative to capitalist organization must recognize that women, not men, have babies. Like other aspects of the material conditions that human beings face, the goal is to bring procreation under human control, to shape the conditions under which it happens. Theory in political economy should help us understand what these conditions are and how they can be changed; it should direct us towards a strategy to ensure that female bodies, like the ability to do work, are a resource rather than a liability.

That women have babies, albeit under a variety of conditions, does not necessarily mean that they will rear the children or clean the toilets. Nor does it mean that they must live in nuclear families. However, because capitalism is premised on the separation of most aspects of workers' reproduction from the commodity production process, and because women have the babies, women will at times be limited in their access to the production process. Such limitations permit the elaboration of the sexual division of labour (itself not without contradictions) just as they encourage women's dependence on men for financial support and the dependence of higher-paid, wage-earning men on women for domestic services. Access to wage labour is value laden, given the primacy of productive processes and the centrality of the wage. Of course, precisely how this division comes about is a matter of historical investigation, beyond the scope of this paper.[70] But the domestic labour debate and other research suggest that such an approach can expose the mechanisms at work that ensure women's subordination.

Conclusion

The domestic labour debate has honed the analytical tools, has exposed the dual nature of women's work, has shown how this work is useful to capitalism and in the process has laid the basis for an analysis that is more dialectical, more historical, more conscious of active resistance, more conscious of sex divisions. Feminist analysis has shown that bodies and their procreative capacities also condition possibilities, although Marxist analysis helps us to place these bodies in history, in classes, in relationships that are themselves best understood within the context of existing material conditions. In summarizing and evaluating the domestic labour debate, as well as in offering an alternative approach to understanding biological processes, this paper attempts to create a platform on which to build a critique of political economy and a sex-conscious analytical framework.

We have argued that there is a sexual division of labour particular to capitalist society (although many aspects clearly predate capitalism), that this division and the concomitant subordination of women are integral parts of capitalist production and reproduction and that this division has a biological component that cannot be ignored. Moreover, we argue that because capitalism is premised on free wage labour — on the separation of most aspects of workers' reproduction from the production process — women's reproductive capacities separate them out of the production process for child-bearing work. This establishes the basis for an elaboration of sex differences, a sexual division of labour that subordinates women and pervades all levels of human activity under capitalism. Such segregation also fundamentally divides classes.

Any theory of capitalism must be conscious of and provide explanation not only for the separation between home and work but also for that between women and men. It must put women and men back into their history at all levels of analysis. The domestic labour debate suggests that Marxist analytical tools can be applied to the task. That political economy has been sex-blind is a challenge, not an indictment.

Notes

As Roberta Hamilton would say, like all publications this is only a draft gone public. Many people have provided critical comments on earlier drafts, and while few may still recognize the current paper, and while fewer still may want to be linked with it, we would like to thank Jacques Chevalier, Patricia Connelly, Roberta Hamilton, Jared Keil, Angela Miles, George Mitchell, Mary O'Brien, Shirley Pettifer, Wally

Seccombe, Dorothy Smith, Pam Smith, Erica Van Meurs and Bonnie Ward in particular.

1. Heidi Hartmann, "The Unhappy Marriage of Marxism and Feminism: Towards a More Progressive Union," in Lydia Sargent (ed.), *Women and Revolution* (Montreal: Black Rose Books, 1981), 2.

2. Wally Seccombe, "Domestic Labour and the Working-Class Household," in Bonnie Fox (ed.), *Hidden in the Household: Women's Domestic Labour under Capitalism* (Toronto: Women's Press, 1980), 27.

3. C. Wright Mills, *The Marxists* (New York: Dell Publishing, 1962), 98.

4. Sheila Rowbotham, *Women, Resistance and Revolution* (New York: Pantheon Books, 1974), 62.

5. Juliet Mitchell, "Marxism and Women's Revolution," *Social Praxis* 1/1 (1972), 24.

6. Richard Lichtman, "Marx's Theory of Ideology," *Socialist Revolution* 23 (1975), 51.

7. Seccombe, "Domestic Labour," 53.

8. The domestic labour debate itself may seem to have waned in recent years, replaced by a post-Althusserian concern with the autonomy of "patriarchy" and "patriarchal structures." Yet the debate is still powerful enough to have provoked a sustained attack by Christine Delphy and Diana Leonard at a plenary session of the most recent British Sociology Association meetings in Manchester, April 1982.

9. Frederick Engels, "Letter to J. Bloch in Konigsberg," in K. Marx and F. Engels, *Selected Works in Three Volumes*, vol. 3 (Moscow: Progress Publishers, 1970), 488.

10. Of course, the treatment of individual women resisting is common in feminist literature and art. See, for example, Judy Chicago's dazzling sculpture, "The Dinner Party." There has also been some discussion of the suffragette struggles and of women in trade unions, but there has been too little integration of these forms of resistance into a broader framework.

11. Certainly biology has been discussed by some feminists claiming to use a Marxist analysis — notably Shulamith Firestone in *The Dialectic of Sex* (New York: 1970) — but most Marxists ignore the question.

12. Frederick Engels, *The Origin of the Family, Private Property and the State* (Moscow: Progress Pub., 1968), 66.

13. Firestone, *The Dialectic of Sex*, 4, 5, 9.

14. Charnie Guettel, *Marxism and Feminism* (Toronto: Women's Press, 1974), 2, 8, 13, 36.

15. Ibid., 58.

16. Margaret Benston, "The Political Economy of Women's Liberation," reprinted in *Voices from Women's Liberation*, Leslie Tanner (ed.) (New York: New American Library, 1971), 285, 287.

17. M. Patricia Connelly, *Last Hired, First Fired* (Toronto: Women's Educational Press, 1978), 6, 33.

18. Peggy Morton, "Women's Work Is Never Done," reprinted in Canadian Women's Educational Press (ed.), *Women Unite!* (Toronto: Canadian Women's Educational Press, 1972), 53, 51.

19. Mariarosa Dalla Costa and Selma James, *The Power of Women and the Subversion of the Community* (Bristol: Falling Wall Press, 1972).

20. Ann Oakley, *Subject Women* (New York: Pantheon Books, 1981), 168.

21. Wally Seccombe, "The Housewife and Her Labour under Capitalism," *New Left Review* 83 (1974).

22. Jean Gardiner, "Women's Domestic Labour," *New Left Review* 89 (1975), 58.

23. John Harrison, "The Political Economy of Housework," *Bulletin of the Conference of Social Economists* (Winter 1973), 43.

24. Margaret Coulson, Bianka Magas and Hilary Wainwright, "The Housewife and Her Labour under Capitalism — A Critique," *New Left Review* 89 (1975).

25. Paul Smith, "Domestic Labour and Marx's Theory of Value," in Annette Kuhn and Anne Marie Wolpe (eds.), *Feminism and Materialism* (London: Routledge, 1978).

26. Seccombe, "Domestic Labour," 9.

27. Gardiner, "Women's Domestic Labour," 49.

28. Jean Gardiner, "Political Economy of Domestic Labour in Capitalist Society," in Diana Leonard Barker and Sheila Allen (eds.), *Dependence and Exploitation in Work and Marriage* (London: Longman, 1976).

29. Maxine Molyneux, "Beyond the Domestic Labour Debate," *New Left Review* 116 (1979), 9.

30. Wally Seccombe, "Domestic Labour — A Reply to Critics," *New Left Review* 94 (1975), 89.

31. Ibid., 92.

32. Wally Seccombe, "The Expanded Reproduction Cycle of Labour Power in Twentieth-Century Capitalism," in Bonnie Fox (ed.), *Hidden in the Household: Women's Domestic Labour under Capitalism* (Toronto: Women's Press, 1980).

33. Patricia Connelly, "Women's Work and Family Wage in Canada," in Anne Hoiberg (ed.), *Women and the World of Work* (New York: Plenum Press, 1982), 223–238.

34. Seccombe, "The Expanded Reproduction Cycle."

35. Christine Delphy, "L'ennemi principal," reprinted in *Libération des femmes année zero*, Partisans (ed.) (Paris 1972).

36. Roberta Hamilton, *The Liberation of Women* (London: Allen & Unwin, 1978).

37. Dorothy Smith, "Women, the Family and Corporate Capitalism," in Marylee Stephenson (ed.), *Women in Canada* (Toronto: New Press, 1973), 45.

38. Bonnie Fox, "Women's Double Work Day: Twentieth-Century Changes in the Reproduction of Daily Life," in Bonnie Fox (ed.), *Hidden in the Household: Women's Domestic Labour under Capitalism* (Toronto: Women's Press, 1980).

39. Jean Gardiner, "Women in the Labour Process and Class Structure," in Alan Hunt (ed.), *Class and Class Structure* (London: Lawrence and Wishart, 1977), 158.

40. Christine Delphy, "Women in Stratification Studies," in Helen Roberts (ed.), *Doing Feminist Research* (London: Routledge & Kegan Paul, 1981), 115.

41. Hamilton, *Liberation*, 81.

42. Gayle Rubin, "The Traffic in Women: Notes on the Political Economy of Sex," in Rayna R. Reiter (ed.), *Toward an Anthropology of Women* (New York: Monthly Review Press, 1975), 165.

43. Richard W. Wertz and Dorothy C. Wertz, *Lying-In: A History of Childbirth in America* (New York: Free Press, 1979), ix.

44. Louise A. Tilly and Joan W. Scott, *Women, Work and Family* (New York: Holt, Rinehart, and Winston, 1978), 27.

45. Wertz and Wertz, *Lying-In*, 3.

46. Margaret Llewelyn Davies, *Maternity: Letters from Working Women* (Essex: Tiptree, [1915] 1978), 6.

47. Neil Sutherland, *Children in English-Canadian Society* (Toronto: University of Toronto Press, 1976), 62–63.

48. Janice Delaney, Mary Jane Lupton and Emily Toth, *The Curse* (New York: Dutton, 1977), 42–43.

49. Joyce Leeson and Judith Gray, *Women and Medicine* (London: Tavistock Publications, 1978), 93.

50. Quoted in Sheila Rowbotham, *A New World for Women: Stella Browne — Socialist Feminist* (London: Pluto Press, 1977), 62, 63.

51. Linda Gordon, "The Struggle for Reproductive Freedom: Three Stages of Feminism," in Zillah Eisenstein (ed.), *Capitalist Patriarchy and the Case for Feminist Socialism* (New York: Monthly Review Press, 1979), 108.

52. For accounts of the historical development of regulations related to abortion, see Angus McLaren, "Women's Work and the Regulation of Family Size: The Question of Abortion in the Nineteenth Century," *History Workshop* 4 (1977); and Angus McLaren, "Birth Control and Abortion in Canada, 1870–1920," *Canadian Historical Review* 59/3 (September 1978), 319–340.

53. Wertz and Wertz, *Lying-In*.

54. Tilly and Scott, *Women, Work and Family*, 100.

55. McLaren, "Women's Work," 76.

56. Sutherland, *Children*, 56.

57. Canada, Statistics Canada, *Canada Year Book 1975* (Ottawa: 1975), 153.

58. Leroy O. Stone and Claude Marceau, *Canadian Population Trends and Public Policy Through the 1980s* (Montreal: McGill-Queen's University Press, 1977), 37.

59. Adrienne Rich, *Of Woman Born* (London: Norton, 1977).

60. Barbara Ehrenreich and Deirdre English, *Complaints and Disorders* (Old Westbury, NY: Feminist Press, 1973), 72.

61. Quoted by McLaren, "Birth Control," 320.

62. Gordon, "The Struggle for Reproductive Freedom," xiii.

63. McLaren, "Women's Work," 79.

64. McLaren, "Birth Control," 320.

65. Suzann Buckley, "Ladies or Midwives? Efforts to Reduce Infant and Maternal Mortality," in Linda Kealey (ed.), *A Not Unreasonable Claim* (Toronto: Women's Press, 1979), 140.

66. Ehrenreich and English, *Complaints and Disorders*, 16.

67. Wertz and Wertz, *Lying-In*.

68. Rainer Baehre, "Victorian Psychiatry and Canadian Motherhood," *Canadian Women's Studies* 2/1 (1980), 45.

69. Davies, *Maternity*, 3.

70. For an outstanding example of the type of historical investigation we have in mind, see Patricia Connelly and Martha MacDonald, "Women's Work: Domestic and Wage Labour in a Nova Scotia Community," in *Studies in Political Economy* 10 (Winter 1993).

Chapter Two

Spatially Differentiated Conceptions of Gender in the Workplace

Pamela Moss

Introduction

Society and space, their relations and their structures, constitute the social geography research agenda. Although the intricacies of social and spatial relations have been foci of geographic research during the past decade, the articulation of space and ideology is less often addressed in geographic studies of the social urban environment. While ideology as lived experience in the politics of production, reproduction and the state has been part of the analysis, it has not been central to it, with few exceptions.[1] Hence, geographical explanations of the expression of dominant ideologies in specific places do not exist.

Sorting through the spatiality of social relations may be a way to disassemble space in order to understand and explain the constitution of a place at a certain time.[2] Working through the spatiality of ideology may be a way to enhance such a study, incorporating another analytical dimension within place. This can be accomplished in one of two ways: investigating the spatial implications of ideologies, or sorting through the ideological aspects of spatial conceptualizations.[3] Workplace is one such spatial conceptualization. By workplace I mean two things. First, as a general term, workplace$_1$? means the terrain of capitalist labour relations wherein the politics of production and reproduction are played out.[4] "Shop floor politics" refers to the workplace as terrain. Second, the workplace$_2$ is the actual place where the worker performs the tasks she or he is employed to perform. The shop floor per se is workplace as place. In political economy, analysts identify and explain class formation by drawing on dominant ideologies of the workplace$_1$.[5] In work focusing on gender and gender formation processes, links between the workplace$_1$ and the particular gender ideologies dominating that space (workplace$_2$) are being addressed, but these links are not yet fully developed.[6]

In this paper, I draw on my experiences as a "maid" in a housekeeping services franchise to analyze the distinct microspatial shifts in the possession and expression of specific conceptions of gender, both my own and my co-workers. This, then, is an attempt to sort through some of the ideological aspects of gender formation played out in the workplace(s)$_2$ within this specific waged domestic labour process.

Classical Marxism, Ideology and the Divisions of Labour

Marx and Engels provide the foundation for the analysis of the spatiality of ideology in *The German Ideology*. Here they identify the "Real Basis for Ideology" as the successive divisions of labour:

> [t]he greatest division of material and mental labour is the separation of town and country. The antagonism between town and country begins with the transition from barbarism to civilization, from tribe to State, from locality to nation, and runs through the whole history of civilization to the present day. ... In the towns, the division of labour between the individual guilds was as yet [quite naturally derived] and, in the guilds themselves, not at all developed between the individual workers. ... The next division of labour was the separation of production and commerce, the formation of a special class of merchants. ... The immediate consequence of the division of labour between the various towns was the rise of manufactures, branches of production which had outgrown the guild-system. ... Generally speaking, big industry created everywhere the same relations between the classes of society, and thus destroyed the peculiar individuality of the various nationalities. ... The bourgeoisie itself, with its condition, develops only gradually, splits according to the division of labour into various fractions and finally absorbs all propertied classes it finds in existence.[7]

They go on to argue that:

> The transformation, through the division of labour, of personal powers (relationship) into material powers, cannot be dispelled by dismissing the general idea of it from one's mind, but can only be abolished by the individuals again subjecting these material powers to themselves and abolishing the division of labour. Only in community [with others has each] individual the means of cultivating his [sic] gifts in all directions; only in the community, therefore is personal freedom possible.[8]

Later Engels continues the discussion with respect to the origin of the family. He notes that the first division of labour is "that between man and woman" for biological reproduction, or "child breeding," to which he adds: "[t]he first class antagonism which appears in history coincides with the development of the antagonism between man and woman in monogamous marriage, and the first class oppression with that of the female sex by the male."[9] Engels further develops his argument by noting that a society that could no longer reconcile antagonisms had to drive them to a head "in a so-called legal form," the state.[10]

Although steeped in an evolutionary context, Marx and Engels's arguments about the division of labour provide three useful insights with regard to ideologies and the workplace: (1) divisions of labour contribute to the maintenance of class fractions; (2) ideologies can shift with place; and (3) community is a means by which to overcome various divisions of labour. In building upon these insights, I want to extrapolate from them by shifting the focus: (1) from capitalists and labourers in Marx and Engels's work to managers and labourers in the waged domestic labour services sector; (2) from a regional scale of town and country to the microscale of the workplace, with the conceptual distinction between workplace$_1$ and workplace$_2$; and (3) from the community as class alliances to the community of working women employed in the same firm. In this, the works of Harry Braverman, Michael Burawoy and Sheila Cohen are most useful because they address the management/worker relationship, the conceptual distinction between labour and its regulation, and possible strategies for workplace change, respectively.[11]

Extrapolations of Classical Marxist Arguments

Braverman's *Labor and Monopoly Capital* presents a comprehensive analysis of the labour process that challenges some aspects of Marx's *Capital*, Volume I. Braverman bases his analysis on the notion of labour as the inalienable property of an individual. Central to the explanation of the degradation of the worker is a new division of labour: the distinction between the conception and the execution of a task, that is, between managers and workers.

A critique of Braverman's account of the labour process under monopoly capitalism is the departure point for Burawoy,[12] who raises two critical points. First, he argues that capitalist control can be understood only through comparison with non-capitalist modes of production. For Burawoy, monopoly capitalism is but a phase of capitalism; it is a *particular* organization of production relations. Second, Burawoy maintains that the production process is a combination of the economic, political and ideological, wherein the subjective and objective are inseparable. He identifies class interests as simultaneously subjective and objective, permitting both control and resistance to be part of the same relation.

From this argument, Burawoy develops the concept of "factory regime."[13] A factory regime comprises the political apparatuses of production and the labour process. The political apparatuses of production consist of institutions that regulate and shape struggles in the workplace$_1$.[14] The labour process is the coordinated set of activities and relations involved in the transformation of raw materials into useful products in the workplace$_2$.[15] Factory regimes are not monolithic, nor do they take identical forms. The specific character of the regime varies from state to state because of the organization of the labour process, competition among firms and the degree of state intervention.[16]

Burawoy also acknowledges global tendencies, such as the decentralization and democratization of the state, in the transition of one regime to another and emphasizes that workers' struggles shape factory regimes. In discerning connections between separate, yet simultaneous, workers' struggles in different occupations, and extrapolating the interdependent links among coexisting regimes, researchers could build upon Burawoy's contributions to the theoretical interrogation of the relations *of* productions (regulatory apparatuses) and the relations *in* production (labour process). One such contribution would be to draw out the spatial implications of the relations in and of production through identifying the terrain upon which, and the places wherein, the politics of production are played out. Differentiation between workplace$_1$ as a terrain of struggle and workplace$_2$ as the place for the execution of tasks parallels Burawoy's conceptual distinction between the regulatory apparatuses and the labour process.

Cohen introduces an alternative approach that could assist in pulling together fundamental Marxist economic aspects of the labour process with the political aspects outlined in Burawoy's work.[17] In a review of the labour process debate, she calls for a restitution of valorization and exploitation as central components in labour process investigations. She argues that post-Braverman analyses have focused on either "control relations" between workers and management or use value-related issues rather than on relations of production.[18] If refocused, then political and economic struggles of resistance and transformation of the labour process, and power relations within and between classes would once again emerge as central to labour process analysis.

Investigations of "struggles of resistance" and "struggles of transformation" form the basis of Cohen's proposed reorientation. By the former she means struggles against capitalism and its labour processes; by the latter, struggles towards socialism and new labour processes:

> The connection between "struggles of resistance" and "struggles of transformation" cannot be traced without understanding how the structural factors of valorization and exploitation constitute the arena of struggle within capitalism ... [a]nd this lack of class identity, this absence of class politics, is exactly the space in which existing analysis of the labour process has left us.[19]

Class and the processes by which classes are constituted become the community through which the material powers can be overtaken in the struggle for personal freedom. Her work, too, parallels the conceptual and spatial differentiation of production politics and the workplace: "struggles of resistance" refer to relations *in* production and of the workplace$_2$, while "struggles of transformation" refer to relations *of* production and of the workplace$_1$.

A Feminist Critique ...

Conspicuously absent from the class analyses I have drawn upon thus far is gender. Vast literatures exist trying to "determine" the relationships, links, articulations, expressions and dominance of gender and class. Because feminists are chiefly concerned with the imbalance in power relations between women and men, many of the feminist critiques of the labour process literature focus on pointing out the differences between women and men. Since the mid-1980s, socialist feminist studies have moved towards a multifaceted analysis concentrating on the interrelatedness, interconnectedness and entwinement of the processes of the social constructions of gender, class, "race," ethnicity and culture.[20] This movement has been partially in response to the postmodern philosophical challenge to "celebrate difference." Theoretically, then, socialist feminists have moved away from the universal claims that women are connected by virtue of being women and towards a consideration of "woman" as a process comprised of many experiences.[21]

Three theorists provide particularly helpful insights into the ways in which gender and class come together in the workplace. Gayle Rubin, Varda Burstyn and Cynthia Cockburn[22] all attempt to resolve the tension between gender and class by setting them into a wider context of productive and reproductive labour as well as among relations of domination and appropriation.[23] And, all three conceive gender as a process, either implicitly or explicitly, challenging the conventional ways analysts look at gender (and class). Rubin develops an anthropological concept of sex/gender systems to pull together social and biological conceptions of femininity and masculinity to be used in the explanation of differences in the distribution of power between women and men:

> [W]e cannot limit the sex system to "reproduction" in either the social or biological sense of the term. A sex/gender system is not simply the reproductive moment of a "mode of production." The formation of gender identity is an example of production in the realm of the sexual system. And a sex/gender system involves more than the "relations of procreation," reproduction in the biological sense.[24]

This exposition brings the formation of gender and the production of meaning into the sexual realm as *constitutive processes* of gender identity.[25] These gender formation processes involve subjective experiences of gender relations, struggles over sex and gender in all aspects of life and the material conditions of subjectivity. Investigating the constitution of gender in the labour process in this context would thus entail setting subjective experiences of the socially constructed differences between femininity and masculinity and the behaviour associated with them in the context of relations in and of production over time in specific workplaces$_2$.[26] Challenges to the existing set of relations could be formed along the lines of either struggles of resistance (contesting the gender imbued definitions of prescribed behaviour for both women and men as part of the status quo) or struggles of transformation (prefiguring an alternative set of behaviours with an associated ideology as, for example, egalitarian principles for interaction between all workers).

Burstyn, in her analysis of the state, contributes to this understanding of the formation of gender identity as a process through a focus on the politics of masculine domination. In an examination of masculine dominance as the source of the sexual division of labour, Burstyn makes an important distinction between "gender-class" and "economic-class." Gender-class refers to the material and political bases of the control of the relations of appropriation. Economic-class describes the relations of economic exploitation. On the one hand, Burstyn's conceptualization is innovative in that many analyses of masculine dominance would acknowledge only relations of domination at the expense of the relations of exploitation. However, not to attempt to explain these relations of domination in context misses the point of the relational entwinement of gender and class relations (and productive and reproductive labour). On the other hand, Burstyn's distinction lacks integration. Though gender-class and economic-class assist in isolating for analysis relations of domination and of appropriation, what is of equal, if not greater, importance are the concrete processes that shape gender (and class, with regard to this and Burstyn's analysis). Divisions of labour and labour processes are venues within which analysts can investigate these concrete processes. The "trick" conceptually lies in accounting for simultaneously competing and contradictory relations of exploitation, domination and appropriation without necessarily privileging one set of social relations over another, nor holding them in abeyance.[27] If such a conceptualization process is successful, then a socialist feminist argument breaks away from essentialism towards providing a truly dialectical materialist analysis.[28] If held in abeyance, the resulting analysis would be subject to the same criticism as dual system theories.[29]

Cockburn adds an ideological dimension to this conceptualization of gender as a process. She argues that the position technology holds in production relations perpetuates the "gendered" power relations in labour through the labour process.[30] She explains this unequal distribution in terms of "gendering people, gendering jobs."[31] She demonstrates that the labour process not only produces a product (or provides a service), but it also produces culture. In my reading, this culture Cockburn speaks of includes ideology, defined as both the ways in which interests (gender and class) are implicated within and throughout the production process,[32] and as lived experience. For it is within relations in production that gender attributes are ascribed to the people and the job, just as the gender of the job rubs off on the people who hold the positions. Like Cockburn, I want to be careful in distinguishing between men and masculinity. It is not all men who are knowledgeable and in possession of technological and ideological dominance; it is masculinity that has the bond with the machines (power) and therefore technology (ideology).[33] This distinction is useful when investigating concrete processes of gender formation in labour process studies. Personalization of masculine-dominated gendering processes does not crystallize into men per se, and subsequently lead to antagonism in the workplace$_1$. Rather, masculinity is subject to critique, which then shapes and prefigures gender relations within the labour process. Scrutiny and review of situational shifts in the gendering process from labour process to labour process leads to expressions of gender differences in people and in jobs as well as their associated ideologies.

... and a Feminist Analysis

From this critique what emerges is a way to directly address gender in capitalist labour processes while maintaining complex connections between the relations of exploitation, domination and appropriation. Gender is that set of concrete processes through which individuals gain experiences of and attach meaning to the uneven distribution of power between women and men. These concrete processes include daily interactions in the home, workplace$_1$ and sites where individuals do not engage in labour.[34] Also included are individual and social ideas and ideals of femininity and masculinity. Thus, gender forms through situationally specific[35] interaction that embodies not only the relations of exploitation, domination and appropriation, but also each individual's personal experiences to date. Also, gender is simultaneously an ongoing mediation of an individual's experience of these relations, which are often contradictory.[36] Sorting through these contradictions assists the individual in coming to terms with the relations of exploitation, domination and appropriation in specific places. Because of the amount of time spent engaged in waged employment, the workplace$_1$ is a significant venue where individuals forge individual and collective identities, which, in turn, effect change in gender ideologies in other terrains. The forging of these gendered identities actually takes place in the workplace(s)$_2$.

By conceptualizing gender as a set of concrete processes akin to class formation processes,[37] three points emerge as significant in shaping the ways in which analysts should be thinking about gender and class in capitalist labour processes.[38] First, gender and class are not static conceptions. Gender and class are conceived of as concrete social processes constructing and reconstructing gender and class relations, roles and identities within particular organizations of productive and reproductive labour. Second, such conceptualizations embody dialectical change in processes forming gender and class identities within a set of labour relations that implicates both material relations and subjective experiences of those relations. These individual and collective experiences of and (re)actions against uneven distributions of social power reinforce, challenge, contest and even transform gender and class relations. These (re)actions can be demonstrated empirically and can effect change in a specific labour process. Third, conceptualizing gender and class formation takes to heart the concept of process. Rather than describing a set of gender and class relations as a "slice of reality," gender and class as a set of concrete formation processes permit a materially and historically grounded explanation of a specific configuration of social experiences within relations *in* and *of* production. This benefits a theory of capitalist labour processes in that an analyst can more fully account for differences in gender ideologies within a particular labour process and partially explain the emergence of individual as well as collective gender and class identities.

One way to reconnect the scope and range of individual experiences of gender and class is through context:

The word context literally means to weave together, to twine, to connect. This interrelatedness creates the webs of meaning within which humans act. The individual is joined to the world through social groups, structural relations, and identities. However, these are not inflexible categories to which individuals can be reduced. ... While the general constructs of race, class, and gender are essential, they are not rigidly determinant. Context is not a script. Rather, it is a dynamic process through which the individual simultaneously shapes and is shaped by her environment ... [A]n analysis of context, which emphasizes these dynamic processes, is an interpretive strategy which is both diachronic and synchronic.[39]

Recasting *context as process* wherein social relations are seen as threads of a tapestry woven together to produce a richly textured social formation reinforces the notion that specified sets of relations, like gender, class, "race" and ethnicity are not isolated systems of relations operating according to that system's logic. Rather, they are relations that shift in meaning for individuals over time through individual mediation via experience. Thus, unequal power relations based on gender, class, "race" and/or ethnicity can only be understood and, consequently, explained *in context*. In order to avoid relativism as a basis for argument, instead of situating women's experiences in specific contexts, experiences of gender can be incorporated in the formation of one's identity, which in turn shapes the attitudes and actions of the labourer towards her or his labour. By adopting subjectivity in context one must not only acknowledge difference in context, but also recognize sameness in process.

Ideological Aspects of Gender

This sameness in process is the basis for extending the themes identified in the classical Marxist literature outlined above. Both the social division of labour and the relations in production contribute to the maintenance of class fractions among workers employed in the same firm hired to accomplish the same set of tasks. In the case of housekeeping services franchises in southern Ontario in the early 1990s, the spatial fragmentation of the workplace$_1$ provided an opportunity to study the spatial variation in gender ideologies in the workplace(s)$_2$. Ideologies shift with place, not only on a regional scale,[40] but also on a microscale. Economic restructuring processes have not only had an impact on the region in aggregate, but have also affected the detailed division of labour in certain services, wherein spatial fragmentation of the workplace$_1$ fractures experiences of labour and alienates workers even further. So when workers engage in labour relations in various workplaces$_2$, it makes sense that specific gender and class ideologies dominate a specific workplace$_2$ whereas another may dominate someplace else, even another workplace$_2$ within the same labour process. This fragmentation does not alienate the workers into paralysis. Rather, a community emerges that is not based in traditional conceptions of class structure and class conflict. The community is more likely to be based on commonalities among working women as workers and as women.

With this set of extrapolations I argue that gender ideologies, implicated with class ideologies,[41] are constructed through the interaction of individuals in various sets of social relations. Because an imbalance of power is part of all social relations, dominant ideologies emerge and focus on the individual and her or his role in the maintenance of the existing set of power relations. In this way, individual interests are taken to be more important than collective interest, both inside and outside the workplace. Such an emphasis reinforces the fragmenting tendencies of capital by calling on the individual to "look out for your own interests, because no one else is going to." The result is a maintenance and perpetuation of the status quo, which at times is readily accepted and actively supported by the oppressed and disempowered.

As we well know, it is not always the case. At the same time there are competing processes that challenge, contest and transform the existing balances of power between women and men and among classes (struggles of resistance and struggles of transformation). Obviously, ideologies do not simply maintain the existing order. Ideological aspects of social spatial processes can be clarified through meticulous inquiry into daily interactions in specific places. Illustrating gender formation processes in the workplace$_1$ sheds light on the reproduction of ideology as well as on the constitutive processes of individuals. I now turn to an empirical demonstration of the spatially differentiated conceptions of gender in multiple workplaces$_2$ of the same workplace$_1$.

Daily Life as a "Maid"

I gathered information for the case study in this paper over a fifteen-week complete participant observation study as an employee of a franchise.[42] I kept a journal about my experiences. While cleaning I would memorize conversations, the route we took, and the layout of the houses we cleaned. At night I would spend two and a half to three hours recording the day's events on a computer.[43]

My experiences as a franchise housekeeper led me to question the links between the labour I was paid to do and the particular gender ideologies dominating the place I worked. What struck me first and foremost was the fragmentation of the workplace$_2$: the office, the car and the customers' houses. What goes on in these workplaces$_2$? How do the workers see themselves as women in their workplaces$_2$? If the workplaces$_2$ are fragmented, are the women workers fragmented too? Are there specific gender ideologies dominating in these workplaces$_2$? Do they shift from place to place? Is there a dominant gender ideology in the workplace$_1$?

I have culled examples from records of my experiences, either as verbatim journal entries or paraphrases of a set of incidents, that speak to the ideological aspects of gender formation stemming from the workplace$_1$ in the various workplaces$_2$. I present the examples in thematic order, parallel to the three themes identified above: (1) hierarchical social relations, (2) spatiality of the workplaces$_2$ and (3) the community of working women. I do so because the themes build upon one another. Some labour processes, such as the one investigated in this study, fragment the workplace$_1$ spatially into workplaces$_2$. Additionally, some labour processes fragment the workers through this spatial fragmentation. All of this points towards the dissolution and fragmentation of any collective organizing. However, just as fragmentation of space impedes the formation of community, it allows at the same time expressions of a competing ideology to form. Hence, communities form and struggles of resistance and transformation ensue.

Hierarchical Social Relations
From the first day of work, I was quite aware of the social hierarchies. They existed at the office, in the car and in the houses. These power relations were not straightforward or easy to disentangle. They were based on the social division of labour, relations in production and gender relations both within and outside that division and those relations, as, for example, in one's position in the labour process, seniority of employment, womanly defined qualities like nurturing and friendship and various combinations thereof.

Because the most powerful position was held by the manager, all opportunities to invoke this hierarchy were at her discretion. For example, at Easter, Judith,[44] the manager, sent flowers:

It was a pot of pink hyacinth. Of course, I thought first of my mother for she would be the only one who would send me flowers. Wrong. It was from Judith. I presume she sent (sends) everyone flowers. What an interesting management technique. They were sent from the flower shop across the street from the office.[45]

Because of her position as manager, Judith maintains a distance that keeps employer-employee relations intact, yet desires to be a friend and express her care for the women she employs. She said that sometimes she feels like a "mother duck" to the workers more than anything else.[46] She provides them with some opportunities and gives them support. For example, when Candy was two months pregnant, she privately hired Candy to care for her own children in the afternoons after Candy finished work at Clare's. In this way, Candy could earn some extra money for the baby. Judith and her children became very much part of the pregnancy through learning about the development of the fetus.[47] But in the office, another attitude prevailed:

Helen and Candy came in. ... Candy was not well at all. Annie made a comment that Candy didn't look well. She asked when would Candy go see her doctor. Judith was bouncing around for some reason. She had to fix Helen's vacuum. [She finally] came in and looked straight at Candy and said "Remember, these are the best days of your life," Candy glared at Judith and said nothing. Then Judith went on and on about [her kids and] ... the pregnancy book. No one commented. Later, Candy asked how long the [staff] meeting is going to last tomorrow. I inferred that Candy will be sitting with the children tomorrow. ... Candy insisted that she would have to eat a full dinner by 3:00. Judith wouldn't accept this and laughed. Candy didn't say anything. She told her that she wouldn't have time between the end of work and the meeting [to eat]. Candy didn't say anything. Judith relented and told her to make sure she brought something with her.[48]

When the power relations within the labour process were relaxed, less hierarchical and more balanced, the workers responded in kind. Sometimes they "mothered" Judith:

> [They] talked about Nancy's Toppy's party and some of the clothes that they had ordered and liked. Judith had a jumpsuit with her that she had ordered from Toppy's where the zipper had broken. She couldn't mend it. Kelly looked at it and said that she would do it. Judith was going to throw it in the garbage if she didn't get it off to the post office and back to Toppy's. She had forgotten to bring it to the party or to even ask about it. In the car later, Kelly said that there was no way that Judith could have mended it: "she can't do things like that."[49]

Nancy knitted Judith a sweater because Judith can't knit. Kelly is the same age as Judith, thirty-six. Nancy is twenty-four.

Judith's invocation of the employer-employee power hierarchy varied from worker to worker. It was obvious that Judith treated me differently than the other workers. She did not nurture me, nor did she treat me like "just another maid." She treated me more like an equal. Judith rarely looked up when she talked to any of the workers in the office, but "Judith always looks me in the eye when she talks to me."[50] Also, all her employees would get her things while in the office, and even pick up items from local stores for her. One day I offered to get her a coffee: "I went and got coffee. I asked Judith if she wanted me to pour her coffee and give it to her. She said no that she would get it herself."[51]

Further, when I told Judith I was going on vacation, she asked me if I read any of Anne Tyler's books. I had. She passed along *Earthly Possessions* to me. The main character had reminded her of me.[52] At another point, Judith pointed out that "Camille Claudel" was playing at the local independent theatre; she was a Gérard Depardieu fan.[53] My co-workers had never read Tyler, never been to the Broadway Theatre nor heard of Depardieu. Yet Judith knew I had. Though she treated me differently, she still accepted me as a woman; as a "maid," it was just on another set of terms.

In the car, social relations were well defined. When I first worked with Janine and Roberta, Janine drove the car and, as supervising housekeeper, acted as on-site supervisor, money collector and liaison with the customer. Roberta was the housekeeper whose only responsibilities were cleaning. Roberta made it clear to me that I was to sit in the back seat. After all, I was only "in training." But it was even more than that. I was lower in the social hierarchy than she was. This was the case no matter where we were. Though the distribution of power was based initially on our positions within the labour process, the hierarchy was reproduced and maintained through our interpersonal interaction in other places: "Next, we stopped at the variety for Roberta to get some coffee. She got the last cup so I ended up getting chocolate milk. I ate my muffin in the car (... in the back seat) and drank my milk."[54]

And in the office:

> Roberta was going out the door. I handed my cup to her and asked her to get me a cup. She said something like "My name is Roberta, not Mom" and that she "would like a cup with milk" when I got mine. She said it in such a way that I wasn't offended in the least. I got up and away I went.[55]

Even conversation in the car was organized around who was sitting where. Whenever I was in the back seat, I was left out of conversations. Often I was simply forgotten. Lynn as the housekeeper was supposed to review the specifics of the next clean for the team members. Because she and Annie knew the route so well, they never reviewed the cleans in the car. I would peek in the book when they weren't looking so that I had an idea when we would be done for the day. Most of the conversations in the car were not based on the work. Annie, Lynn and I had stopped to grab something to eat before we went to the last house. As was usually the case, I was in the back seat:

> I knew we were on the way to Avondale because I had looked at the book. We stopped at a variety store, one which we had stopped at before. I got out of the car last. Lynn said "She always puts me in the water or a bank." This comment must have been directed at me, because she was referring to where Annie parks the car. I didn't say anything. I slowly climbed out ... [Upon our return, i]n the car, I asked, "Which soap operas do you watch?" After a moment or so, Lynn asks "Who are you asking?" "I saw you buy the magazine." This launched a conversation between

Lynn and Annie. Lynn watches "Days of Our Lives" and
"General Hospital." Annie watches "General Hospital."[56]

No one ever asked me which "soaps" I watched.

I finally got to sit in the front seat when I got a regular cleaning
partner, Nancy. Even then it was a fleeting privilege. Seating
arrangements were not based simply on seniority as employees.
Privilege was tied to the history of the third person with the supervising
housekeeper, or driver. For example, when Lisa, an employee called
back to the franchise to take my place, worked with Nancy and me,
she sat in the back seat. When Kelly, Nancy's previous cleaning
partner, worked with Nancy and me, I sat in the back seat. Lisa had
no history with Nancy; Kelly did.

There was freedom of expression in the car, or at stops in between
houses. Sometimes the stops between "cleans" were the most fun,
and often the most revealing:

> We stopped at a bakery near the high school. I got coffee (I
> was dying for a coffee and dessert), Kelly, a bear claw, and
> Nancy, a danish. We were teasing each other about eating
> and drinking. Both of them had sandwiches and were eating
> sweets. Nancy is in love with Mel Gibson. Nancy and Kelly
> joke about Nancy being "beyond bitch" … Nancy seems like
> things bounce off her fairly easily.[57]

This attitude appears to be a wonderful co-worker coping
mechanism: joking about "bitchiness" in the workplace$_1$. It could also
be a justification for degradation and may actually border on self-
hate.[58]

In the house the supervising housekeeper took on a supervisory
role. Her duties, among other things, included checking on the work
of other housekeepers and allocating tasks among the team members.
Her supervision was limited because she had to acquiesce to the
customer's wishes, especially if that customer was home during the
clean:

> We were supposed to be there for an hour. Mrs. Crown
> wanted us to wash the kitchen floor, clean the spare
> bedroom, and the bathroom downstairs, [all of] which took
> a total of 30 minutes. Janine asked Mrs. Crown what else

she would like done. The upstairs bathroom (disgusting as Roberta so aptly put it), ... you just couldn't get it clean. I tried. Roberta told me not to worry about it.[59]

While we were upstairs, Mrs. Crown asked Janine to move the car as she had parked in the wrong area of the driveway.

Janine had vacuumed all the downstairs by the time we were done. Mrs. Crown called us her "whirlwind girls." How possessive. I learned there to acquiesce to the client.[60]

Janine also had to tell Mrs. Crown (for at least the third time) how to polish furniture properly so as not to get filmy streaks. Acquiescence in this case was less a meek response to oppression and more a strategy for getting through the day without conflict.

Sometimes workers do not yield to customers' more powerful social position and the manager drops the customer from the schedule. One customer had accused Helen of stealing her couch pillows. Judith decided that the customer's complaints were unfounded and suggested that she drop the service. This does not happen each time, and it does not help you feel any better. I told Nancy about a customer who yelled at me and forced me to tears. She responded with a similar incident:

She told me that this one man, Mr. Collins, went off on her because he came home for a photography shoot and his partner/wife forgot to tell him that the "cleaning ladies" were coming that day. He got on the phone with his wife and yelled at her. Then turned and asked Nancy when she would be done. She told him to give her an hour.[61]

Condescension and *ressentiment*[62] are things that the worker gets used to: "Nancy doesn't let these things get to her anymore. 'It isn't worth the ulcers' ... She said that she let this 'roll off her back'."[63] In this case, the feeling of being oppressed and subordinated forced Nancy to develop a more complex way of coping with customers.

Spatiality of the Workplace$_2$
Interaction in the office occurred primarily around administrative details like turning in money, reporting supply use and sorting out weekly

schedules. Interspersed were conversations with a personal tone. Talk was not as free as in the car. Conversations were awkward because of the manager's presence. Sometimes the manager herself made the conversation awkward, perhaps on purpose: "Lynn did make a face though when Judith left the room. Judith had just yelled 'Earth to Lynn. Earth to Lynn.' At the same time, she asked Lynn something in passing that didn't even require an answer."[64]

Workers did not formally register complaints about customers; they would discuss the matter with the manager informally. Judith's attitude towards complaints were first filtered through what she considered important:

> Nancy and Judith were talking about some man who looks
> up "Clare's Cleaning" dresses. Judith was making light of it
> saying that he, Mr. Price, was harmless. Nancy was saying
> that Candy was exaggerating. Judith said that he was that
> bad, but harmless.[65]

The worker could accept the comment as an explanation and actively take on that attitude — "Mr. Price actually is harmless, you know." As with the "Earth to Lynn" incident, no one commented. But "Kelly was looking at her watch while she was cleaning because this man was supposed to get home at 2:00."[66] She finished early.

Judith's opinions were rarely overtly challenged. The employer-employee hierarchy that existed in the office translated into acceptance without confrontation of the opinions Judith expressed in casual conversation. Her attitudes towards gender were particularly revealing. Judith and Nancy were talking about migraines. Judith, unaware of the fact that Nancy did not live with her parents, bluntly told her that if she moved out of her parents' home her headaches would go away.[67] Judith seemed convinced that women suffer illnesses because of their relationships with other people.

Judith's attitudes were subtly apparent in conversation: "Annie told Judith that Judith's [partner] did not look 40. Judith … replied that it was because she took such good care of him."[68] "Judith told me this morning that Annie was pregnant. She said that pregnancies come in three and I had better be careful. Judith said that she had taken herself off the list of possibilities. I told her to take me off, too."[69]

Differences in opinion did exist, but were not direct challenges. Judith told us that her partner's parents bought a house in Florida as an investment, to which they would retire someday. Judith speculated on the money they would "rake in." Whereas when Nancy talked about her parents' retirement to Florida, she had different concerns:

[Florida] is where her mother wants to be. Her father wants to retire to Myrtle Beach, near the golf course. She asked "What would my mother do in Myrtle Beach?" Her mother doesn't play golf.[70]

Expressions of attitudes towards gender differed in the car. The workers talked more freely: "Annie's manner driving home was one of 'bitch', 'for fuck's sake', 'fuck this', 'fuck that', 'damn the other thing'."[71] There was no swearing in the house, nor any flirting. Again with respect to flirting, different rules applied in the car: "One day on the way home with Nancy and Kelly, they let me off on the corner. The men in the truck behind us were 'flirting' and said something like you'd better hurry and get out of that car."[72]

The women flirted, too. Nancy and Kelly commented on how good-looking the construction workers were, especially on hot, sweltering days. Yet Kelly drew a line in her own workplace$_1$. Looking at male construction workers was in direct conflict with the way she would like to be perceived in her job in the workplace:

While I was dusting the master bedroom, Kelly and I were chatting about some of the work. She said that they did one business, Allied Power. All they have to do is the vacuuming, oh yeah, and the bathrooms too. It takes almost three hours. The housekeeper usually stands about because only one person can vacuum with one sweeper. The men usually stand around making stupid, rude comments, calling them girls and whatnot.[73]

She did not like doing this place because of the attitudes of the men and the blatant disrespect.

Specific tasks had to be carried out in the home: wiping down appliances, countertops, splashboards and cupboard fronts; scouring the sink; mopping the floor; and folding the towels. While cleaning, both workers occupied the same space, but were responsible for cleaning specific areas. Each supervising housekeeper had something she was keen about; each worker had a weakness. Kelly emphasized vacuuming under the beds; Lynn always forgot. Everyone liked the chrome to be polished; I could never do it.

On a number of occasions, the supervising housekeeper asked me to rebuff the chrome. After this, I became more diligent. In one bedroom I buffed the chrome so well that I took a step back to look at the shine and knocked the shower door off the rollers. I called in Annie to take a look. We couldn't fix it, so she leaned it up against the wall. Then she reached out and gave the taps a wipe.[74]

It was straightforward and for the most part clean. After I had finished almost everything and actually thought that this was good [all day] I hadn't been reprimanded ... nothing broke, no light bulbs shattered, nothing at all — then Nancy came and said, "Pam, I have to show you something." She told me to BUFF THE CHROME!!!!! ... I can hardly tell the difference. She told me that all that "stuff" comes off ... I spent more time on the superficial buffing than on the actual cleaning.[75]

After a few more instances of this, I finally learned:

I guess I wax floors properly because Nancy stood there and watched me do it. I missed a spot near the beginning; she promptly pointed it out. I also noticed that when she vacuumed the kitchen floor, she stopped and went into the small bathroom and inspected my chrome buffing. I didn't see exactly ... what she checked, but she did go in there and come back out. She didn't say anything.[76]

When customers have complaints, the manager is in contact and can intervene in matters pertaining to the service. The worker must acquiesce in most other interactions with the customers. One retired couple seemed always to be at home when we cleaned. They were nice, but the man would tell derogatory, sexual jokes about women and call us "his girls."[77] Whenever this happened, I felt irritated. On one occasion, the woman insisted that Annie and I stop what we were doing and listen to his joke. We had mixed feelings, because directly afterwards, they gave us gifts: Annie some knick-knacks and me some mugs and a set of pick-up sticks. On our way out, he called us his "kids."[78]

Talking in the house was strictly forbidden, even if the customers were not home. Talk about the labour itself was acceptable and even necessary. Most of the talk centred on instructions for carrying out the tasks:

> Annie said "You do the dusting and vacuuming here. It's easier." Okay ... Annie says, "did you take the vacuum downstairs?" Yes. "You shouldn't have because I need to vaccum here." "I guess I'll go get it." I brought it upstairs ... I finished. Bonnie was vacuuming. I helped her. No problem. Not even a thank you. Just, "It goes there in front of that, that stool." She moved on to the living room. I moved a chair for her. When I moved it back, she said, "Try not to walk where I've vacuumed." Okay. ... "When we're finishing up, you should move chairs and rugs for us." Okay.[79]

Courtesies and pleasantries were not part of our talk, only work. The rest of the talking was "illegal." Although we were not supposed to converse, we did. Lynn once commented on a trip to Paris that the daughter of one of the customers was going to take: "Wouldn't that be nice to have that opportunity?"[80] Nancy told me about the personal history of some of the customers whose houses we cleaned. Sometimes the talk sprang from what we "found" in the workplace.

> Yesterday she commented on my comment that the only way the Miltons' bathtub would get clean, is to rub it for an hour. She said that she could think of other things to rub for an hour. Then, immediately after said, "Aren't I disgusting?"[81]

Or,

> While I was in the first bathroom, Nancy came running up the stairs to give me one of the best chocolate cookies I had ever eaten. She said she always looks to see if Mrs. Scott has this kind; if she does then she has one.[82]

Once conversation specifically about gender evolved in the office when I told Judith and Nancy that I had a date on the weekend. We sat around on a Friday afternoon and talked for nearly two hours.

The consensus about dating and relationships with men was that men are jerks and women are complete people.[83] Of course, this is an oversimplification of our views. Judith insisted that women experience life differently and that men are not women with penises. She went further and said that you cannot get out of a relationship with a man what you need; needs can only be met by other women. I found this interesting, especially in light of Judith's expressions of gender differences in the office. Judith suggested that a woman should try going out (for six months) with a man who is into relationships as much as a woman. After this, Judith thought, she would be so tired that she would want a beer-guzzling, hockey-watching couch potato. Nancy did not think men were the same species. She won't go out just to go out. Regarding relationships, she usually ends up being the daughter the man's mother never had. As for me and my date, he stood me up.

Community for Working Women

Camaradarie among the women in the franchise was not the primary focus of many of the workers. It is not that community does not exist. It is probably more likely that the organization of the relations *in* production obscure the common class interests of working women. Though I wasn't aware of it at the time, there were several occasions on which the interests of the working women came to the fore. For example:

> Roberta said that she gets [about $7.00 an hour]. Bonnie didn't say how much she got. They were also talking about people who would cancel for three or four months and then call Clare's Cleaning back and still get charged a biweekly rate. Sometimes it takes two and a half hours for $55. Roberta was upset. Annie said that Judith couldn't charge an initial cleaning fee because then they would lose the customer. ... Annie takes Judith's side. Roberta doesn't.[84]

The workers receive a percentage of the cleaning fee. Since the service market is tight, the manager tightens the working wages. In this instance, management succeeded in taking out the problems of the market/customer on the worker rather than actually charging the customer for the labour. Annie took up the position of management; Roberta challenged the decision. Yet in another context,

Annie challenged the manager and supported a friend's refusal to go back to work.

> Annie was talking about Judith taking advantage of someone on workers' comp. Her sister used to work for Clare's Cleaning. Her cleaning partner was on workers' compensation for her back. Judith phoned her to come back to work a week early. The woman agreed. Then someone told the [woman] that if she did, workers' compensation would be messed up. So she called Judith back and said no. Judith could not have cared less about that woman's life. Annie said "don't kid yourself," Judith would take advantage of you if she could.[85]

Dental insurance was the only issue that arose as a possible demand around which to organize during my employment. The issue was raised by Nancy. Judith had said that Clare's Cleaning was looking into the possibility of group insurance. Nancy's concern was that everyone else had coverage through their spouses, while she was single.[86] Nancy was going to inquire the following week but never did, and left the company about two months later.

Janine was promoted into a "new" position as quality manager whose duties focused on surprise checks. Resentment of the promotion was rampant. Supervising housekeepers now had to report to Janine about workers' cleaning skills. Another technique the manager used to maintain quality as well as fragment the workers was to assign a team to clean a house that was part of another team's regular route:

> Annie was saying something today that Judith was not treating her (and Lynn) fairly. At the Alexanders', Annie used to be the "maid." Lynn had cleaned the house before with someone else. ... Judith took [the clean] away from her [and gave it to Helen]. Today when we cleaned, it took two hours with three people ... [T]he amount of work we had to do was enormous and it was dirty. It had been a lot dirtier than two weeks of living. This was what I was thinking while I was dusting, mostly, and vacuuming. It really hit home when I did the sills; the mildew was developing for much longer than two weeks. So, when Annie was complaining when we were leaving about the length of time and the dirtiness of the house, it made sense.[87]

Over the incident, Annie said that "she had had enough of Judith, and she was going to tell her everything, whatever that may be."[88] Nothing came of the incident. The Alexander house was put back on Helen's route; Annie was still a supervising housekeeper.

Some of the supervising housekeepers thought that being a supervising housekeeper was not worth the headaches. Janine and Annie were talking:

> ... and I tried to listen to what they had to say. Janine said that she let Roberta get away with a lot when she first started working and she doesn't always do what she is supposed to do. They were both lamenting the duties of a supervising "maid." Neither one liked watching over another worker's work. They don't have the time. Annie said that she didn't like it when Judith would say "Work with her and tell me about her work." They agreed with each other that if the "maid" doesn't do the job, she should be fired. Neither wants to report on the other "maids." Annie doesn't like being given old houses instead of new ones. She thinks that is isn't fair to have to clean up others' jobs. ... Roberta called Janine a stool pigeon because of the position she is in now. Janine goes around and reports back to Judith.[89]

I, too, was subject to the dominant gender ideologies present in the relations in production. It was difficult for me to recognize it when I was embroiled in it.

> I seem to remember lots and lots of times where I was put in a position of "either/or." Either I am hired or I'm not. Either I tell Judith about Lynn or not. Either go crazy or not. Either I report my injury or not. Either I speak up in favour of Candy or not. Either I stand up for myself or not. Each "either" was a situation where if I were to speak, I would always resolve the conflict and would feel much better. However, finding enough gumption or courage was always difficult for me.[90]

It was not until I reread my journal nearly eight months later that I was able to pick out the following incident of community formation. This occurred during my first days of employment, when I was being trained. The women training me spoke freely, as did I.

I told Janine, naively perhaps, about the woman who had a sore shoulder and may be going part-time and then she went on jury duty. Well, it happened to be Janine. She had no plans to go part-time. Janine asked me when I was interviewed, yesterday? No [a month ago]. She [immediately turned and] told Roberta that I had been interviewed six weeks ago. They asked if I were to be full-time. I'm not supposed to; I'm supposed to do leaflet distribution as well. Oh. There is another woman leaving. Maybe she's training you for her job, but she's full-time. The rest of the day neither Janine or Roberta could figure out what Judith was "up to." I wonder, too. Judith did tell me that I seemed like a very systematic person and I should do well.[91]

Judith is supposed to get back to me either tonight or tomorrow morning. Janine and Roberta figured that I was working with another team tomorrow. I wonder. They told me to make sure I read the sheets, because the next time I go out, they might be testing me. Judith also told me that I would have to watch a video soon. Roberta asked about it and commented, "Humph, you're lucky."[92]

An extension of my workplace$_2$ comprised the streets of middle-income neighbourhoods: I delivered flyers. Even on the streets I was subject to a particular gender ideology. Though I felt somewhat restricted, I did talk back:

I went by this one house where two men were sitting, chatting in lawn chairs in the driveway. A woman was mowing the lawn. I handed a flyer to one man and he said that the other man lived here. I turned and handed him the flyer. He told me to give one to the other man. So, I did. Then the first man said [why] does he need one of Clare's Cleaners; he has one over there (he pointed to the woman mowing the lawn). I told him that it should be a gift to her, a belated Mother's Day gift. He wasn't pleased. He said all you women belong in the same union. I said "That's right, we're all women."[93]

Now I would add that we are all working women.

Towards a Hegemonic Gender Ideology?

Although the strength of the hierarchies based on the social division of labour and the relations in production reinforce the spatial fragmentation of the workplace$_1$ into several workplaces$_2$, the evidence I present illustrates the complex ways in which women workers express competing and contradictory gender ideologies. Actions arising from these various conceptions of gender are spatially differentiated and lead to conflict and discord as well as community and concord. In the context of conflict, contradiction and community as part of (re)constructing workers' identities, I think there are two issues that need further elaboration.

First is the issue of the interconnections between class and gender. The explanation I develop of my experiences draws out only two sets of social relations — class and gender.[94] The class-based aspect of this analysis focuses on the hierarchical division of labour between the manager and the employees as well as among the workers. The gender-based aspect of this analysis emphasizes the interactions and expectations the workers have of each other as women and as women workers. These analyses are forwarded in the context of working-class women and are not to be treated as separate analyses. Thus, what I am describing, interpreting and attempting to explain in this context are "gendered class" ideologies.

Conceiving gender and class as processes, not as "slices of reality," allows analysts to get beyond the junctures of gender and class into their simultaneous formation. This conceptualization encourages a less encumbered understanding of how specific ideologies form, reform, conflict and manifest in their complexity in various ways in different places in the workplace$_1$. Through the presentation of my experiences as a "maid" in a housekeeping services franchise, I am able to demonstrate empirically some aspects of this complexity.

I have organized the following discussion around six points. One, the women involved in the labour process express similar ideologies in different places. Two, the women are not necessarily consistent in the expression of any one dominant ideology. Three, when a conflict arises between competing expressions of gender, the social hierarchy of power relations determines whose ideology dominates that particular place at a particular time. Four, places that are for the most part free of regulation lay the foundation for the formation of communities that can engage in struggles of resistance. Five, the spatiality of the workplace$_2$ permits the expression of various ideologies. Six, the workplaces$_2$ encourage a variation in expressions of dominant ideologies.

Specific conceptions of gender held by the women workers were at once the same (Point 1 from above) and in conflict (Point 2). For example, similar notions of mothering were part of the interaction of all the women in the franchise: Judith felt like a "mother duck" and Kelly and Nancy felt they had to "mother" Judith by sewing and knitting for her. Women were sex objects for some of the men we encountered (flirting in the car, Mr. Price looking up Kelly's dress in his house, and the sexual jokes by the retired man in his house) and men were sex objects for some of the women (Nancy talking about rubbing the Miltons' bathtub and Judith in the conversation about men and relationships).[95]

The women workers held contradictory conceptions of gender that, when translated into action, affected the ways in which they made sense of their experiences in the workplaces$_2$. For example, Judith expressed different conceptions of what it was like to be a woman both inside and outside the franchise environment. She was thoughtful about the women she employed (sending flowers), yet sometimes treated them with disrespect ("Earth to Lynn" comment). She treated me quite differently, as if I were in her own social circle. Both Annie and Kelly held competing gender ideologies. Annie supported Judith against co-workers and a co-worker against Judith at the same time on different issues (Annie's discussion with Roberta). Kelly objectified men while they were working, but did not like it when men objectified her while she was working.

The hierarchies in the workplace$_1$, initially organized around the worker's position in the labour process, were sifted through competing ideologies in the various workplaces$_2$ (Point 3). Sometimes the expression of a dominant gender ideology in the workplace$_2$ was linked to relations not regulated by the labour process (my getting coffee for Roberta). Thus, a hierarchy of expressions of specific ideologies emerged with complex rules and interconnections based on both gender and class relations. For example, although I was sitting in the back seat as a housekeeper, Annie and Lynn still left me out of the soap opera conversation; Roberta got the last cup of coffee in the corner store when I was "in training"; I sat in the front seat when I worked with Nancy, and in the back seat when Kelly was around; and Judith silenced Nancy about her headaches. This complexity also allowed Kelly to challenge Judith's ideas about Mr.

Price — being harmless was not enough for Kelly to continue allowing Mr. Price to look up her dress.

Second is the issue of social interaction. The spatiality of the workplace$_2$ assisted in shaping spatially differentiated conceptions of gender in the workplace$_1$. Expressions of gender ideologies are manifested through social interaction among women as women through relations in production, that is, the women as managers, supervising housekeepers, housekeepers and customers. Holding competing gender ideologies led to conflict between workers in some instances as well as contradictions in the women's own conceptions of gender. But this variation in expression also permitted a negotiation of common ground through which women forged alliances, and then led the women to build a working women's community. These ideologies do not exist in a vacuum; they are implicated in the spatiality of our social interaction.

The freedom of the car (workplace$_2$) let us talk freely, often about ourselves, and even to make friends (Annie swearing and Kelly, Nancy and I stopping for coffee) (Point 4). The office, too, was a place where we could be less guarded, at least some of the time. Judith, Nancy and I spent an afternoon in the office talking about men and relationships. Talking in the houses, too, helped break down barriers between us as workers to form a community of working women (talking about going to Paris and about the cleaning at the Alexanders', buffing the chrome, and Janine and Annie talking about supervisory roles within the franchise). My naïve comments to Janine and Roberta set up a working relationship that included their giving me "tips" on how to keep the job in exchange for my information with regard to the manager's "plan."

The building of community was sometimes encouraged and sometimes hampered by the various gender ideologies competing for dominance. For example, because the workplace$_1$ is partitioned into several workplaces$_2$, there is leeway in the behaviour considered to be acceptable and appropriate (Point 5). This permits expression through social interaction (supervised and unsupervised) of a wide variation in gender ideologies. So, when a supervising housekeeper is accused of stealing (in an "unsupervised" workplace$_2$), the manager suggests that the customer drop the service. The customer's assumption about "maids being thieves" is being challenged by the manager. However, in a situation where the assumption is being made that the "maid is a non-person" (in Nancy's case with the photography shoot), the woman must endure the insult and continue "in service" to this customer for the sake of pleasing the customer and the manager.

Also impeding the building of community is the spatiality of the workplaces$_2$ (Point 6). When the workers are to carry out a set of tasks in each of the workplaces$_2$, the interaction involving those specific tasks is imbued with a particular gender ideology. For example, my weak point was buffing chrome. Each supervising housekeeper I worked with was keen on shiny chrome. There were underlying assumptions held by the supervising housekeepers: since I was trained, I should be able to clean a house the Clare's Cleaning way; since I was a woman, I should be able to detect dirt; and since I was working at Clare's Cleaning, I should be able to perfect those tasks. When I went against one of these assumptions, the supervising housekeeper used her supervisory position to point out where I had failed. It was only regarding this particular task (i.e., buffing chrome) that the supervising housekeeper would supervise my work. This example points towards a specific gendered class ideology being invoked when the minimum quality for the clean is not being met. This is a place-specific ideology in that it was expressed only in the customers' houses.

That there exists a community that supports working women within the same set of relations in production brings together these two issues. Through our social interaction, my co-workers and I formed a community wherein we engaged in struggles of resistance. It is not as simple as saying that in some instances or moments class dominates social interaction and in other instances or moments gender dominates. As this empirical demonstration shows, there are indeed links between, more specifically, individual expressions of competing and contradictory gender ideologies and the various workplaces$_2$; between the spatial manifestation of gender ideologies and the relations in the workplace$_1$; and, most generally, between space and ideology.

But the links indicated here are not fully explained. One way to build upon this examination of the expression of competing ideologies in different spaces within the same labour process may be to refine the conceptual tools pulled together in this paper. Detailed accounts of the workplace$_1$ entailing descriptions of the microspatial shifts of dominating gender ideologies in workplaces$_2$ is but one way to investigate gender formation in waged domestic labour processes. This research suggests that there are competing gender ideologies vying for hegemony in the workplace(s)$_2$. There needs to be more detailed investigation of the ways in which women workers' (re)actions build communities in the workplace$_1$ with an emphasis on the spatiality of the workplace$_2$.

I conclude with three additional comments about microspatial studies, conceiving gender as a process and the processes imbricated in capitalist labour processes that shape gender. First, microspatial studies are useful and add to the growing body of literature addressing the processes that "gender" jobs. Geographically, comparative analyses of the spatiality of divisions of labour could address individual responses to global economic restructuring processes. Conceptually, distinctions of social processes between, for example, workplace$_1$ and workplace$_2$, or between class formation and gender formation might be more easily distinguishable in microspatial studies, and therefore refined before being applied at a different spatial scale. Politically, sorting through individual constitutive processes can lead to building co-operative gendered class alliances in struggles of resistance in the workplace, as well as in more widely based transformative struggles. For example, common ground between workers can be negotiated and new relations constructed based on collective gendered class identities.

Second, in order to take seriously gender as a process, analysts must not simply view gender as just a division of labour, nor as an attribute of a social economic or political actor, nor as a "layer" in the state bureaucracy. Rather, gender needs to be conceived as a process in context (spatiality included) whereby workers forge individual and collective identities as women and men and then mediate their experiences as gendered workers in a particular organization of labour. In this way, gender is already implicated in the relations of exploitation, domination and appropriation because workers with individual and collective identities comprise those particular relations. Once the process of "gendering" is incorporated into an analysis, gender then is no longer simply a "slice of reality." Gender as a process, like class as process, is integral to a social formation. Also, because individuals are engaged in multiple sets of social relations at any given time, they continually construct and reconstruct the specific configurations of power by incorporating or "internalizing" their experiences of the unequal distributions of power, experiences that are often contradictory.[96] Their identities, both individual and collective, emerge fragmented and sometimes even place-specific.

Finally, theoretically, explanations of capitalist labour processes lie not so much in gender or work; rather, labour as women's work involves the relational aspects of gender and class, the experiences of these relations and what the individual brings with her to the labour relation. By being engaged in labour, workers are continually constructing and reconstructing their own individual and collective gender and class identities. Since the organization of labour can spatially fragment labour and labourers, workers who try to consolidate their interests can overcome this spatially disjointed labour process as well as their fractured experiences. Workers accomplish this within these labour processes by devising, adopting and adapting individual and collective strategies that resist domination and control as well as transform labour relations so that labourers have more control over the relations in (and possibly of) production and so that the distribution of power within the relations of labour is more equitable.

Notes

An earlier version of this paper was presented at the Annual Meeting of the American Association of Geographers in Miami, Florida, April 1991. I gratefully acknowledge the Ontario Graduate Scholarship program and the partial financial support from the Department of Geography and the Labour Studies Programme, both at McMaster University. I also thank Hugh Armstrong and Gillian Creese as reviewers. Their comments challenged me to clarify the arguments presented in this paper. I also thank the anonymous reviewer for constructive comments, particularly with regard to my methodology.

1. For examples of the ways in which analysts have addressed ideology in geography, see David Henry, *The Urban Experience* (Baltimore: The Johns Hopkins University Press, 1985); David Henry, *Social Justice and the City* (Baltimore: The Johns Hopkins University Press, 1973); Derek Gregory, *Ideology, Science, and Human Geography* (London: Hutchinson, 1978); John Eyles, *Senses of Place* (Warrington; Silverbrook Press, 1985); Richard Walker, "Is There a Service Economy? The Changing Capitalist Division of Labour," *Science and Society* 49/1 (1985), 42–83; Richard Peet (ed.), *International Capitalism and Industrial Restructuring* (London: Allen and Unwin, 1987); Vera Chouinard and Ruth Fincher, "State Formation in Capitalist Societies: A Conjunctural Approach," *Antipode* 19/3 (1987), 329–353; John Eyles, "Housing Advertisements as Signs: Locality Creation and Meaning-Systems," *Geografiska Annaler* 69B/2 (1987), 95–105; James S. Duncan and John A. Agnew (eds.), *The Power of Place* (Boston: Unwin Hyman, 1989); and Jacquelin Burgess, "The Production and Consumption of Environmental Meanings in the Mass Media: A Research Agenda for the 1990s," *Transactions of the Institute of British Geographers* 15/2 (1990), 139–161. See also David Wilson, "Local State Dynamics and Gentrification in Indianapolis, Indiana," *Urban Geography* 10 (1989), 19–40, and Lawrence Knopp and Richard S. Kujawa, "Ideology and Urban Landscapes: Conceptions of the Market in Portland, Maine," *Antipode* 25/3 (1993), 114–139.

2. See Edward W. Soja, *Postmodern Geographies* (London: Verso, 1989), especially Chapter 8, "It All Comes Together in Los Angeles."

3. For example, Kevin Cox and Andrew Mair, "Locality and Community in the Politics of Local Economic Development," *Annals of the Association of American Geographers* 78 (1988), 307–325, and "From Localised Social Structures to Localities as Agents," *Environment and Planning D: Society and Space* 23 (1991), 197–213, have begun sorting through the spatial implications of the ideological aspects of the term "locality."

4. Because I use workplace in two specifically different ways, I want to distinguish them when necessary through the use of subscripts, that is, workplace$_1$ and workplace$_2$. When there are no subscripts, then I mean workplace in both senses.

5. For example, see E.P. Thompson, *The Making of the English Working Class* (New York: Penguin, 1963/1980); Georg Lukàcs, *History and Class Consciousness* (London: Merlin, 1971); Ira Katznelson, *City Trenches* (Chicago: University of Chicago Press, 1981); Charles Sabel, *Work and Politics* (Cambridge: Cambridge University Press, 1982); Michael Burawoy, *The Politics of Production* (London: Verso, 1985); Adam Przeworski, *Capitalism and Social Democracy* (New York: Cambridge University Press, 1985); and David Harvey, *The Condition of Postmodernity* (Oxford: Oxford University Press, 1989). Also of interest is a psychiatric account of workers' alienation by Bernard Doray, *From Taylorism to Fordism: A Rational Madness* (London: Free Association Books, 1988).

6. For example, see Cynthia Cockburn, *Brothers* (London: Pluto, 1983) and *Machinery of Dominance* (Boston: Northwestern University Press, 1985); Ann Ferguson, *Blood at the Root* (London: Pandora, 1989); Phyllis Palmer, *Domesticity and Dirt* (Philadelphia: Temple University Press, 1989); Miriam Glucksmann, *Women Assemble* (New York: Routledge, 1990); and Joy Parr, *The Gender of Breadwinners* (Toronto: University of Toronto Press, 1990).

7. Karl Marx and Friedrich Engels, *The German Ideology* (New York: International Publishers, 1988), 68–69, 71, 72 and 78.

8. Ibid., 83.

9. This division of labour was noted in 1846 when the bulk of *The German Ideology* was written. Quotes are from Friedrich Engels, *The Origin of Family, Private Property, and the State* (Moscow: Progress Pub., 1983), 65 and 66.

10. Ibid., 165.

11. Harry Braverman, *Labor and Monopoly Capital* (New York: Monthly Review Press, 1974), 54; Burawoy, *The Politics of Production*; and Sheila Cohen, "A Labour Process to Nowhere?" *New Left Review* 165 (1987), 34–51.

12. Burawoy, *The Politics of Production*.

13. Ibid., 87.

14. Ibid.

15. Ibid.

16. Ibid., 126.

17. Cohen, "A Labour Process to Nowhere?"

18. Ibid., 37.

19. Ibid., 49, emphasis in original.

20. For example, see Angela Davis, *Women, Race and Class* (New York: Women's Press, 1981); Eva Gamarniko et al., *Class, Gender and Work* (London: Heinemann, 1983); Anne Phillips, *Divided Loyalties* (London: Virago, 1987); Ferguson, *Blood at the Root*; Sherry Gorelick, "The Changer and the Changed: Methodological Reflections on Studying Jewish Feminists," in Alison M. Jagger and Susan R. Bordo (eds.), *Gender/Body/Knowledge* (New Brunswick: Rutgers University Press, 1989), 336–358; Palmer, *Domesticity and Dirt*; and Teresa Amott and Julie Matthaei, *Race, Gender, and Work* (Montreal: Black Rose Books, 1991).

21. See, for example, Linda Nicholson (ed.), *Feminism/Postmodernism* (New York: Routledge, 1987); Andrea Nye, *Feminist Theory and the Philosophies of Man* (New York: Routledge, 1988); Elizabeth V. Spelman, *Inessential Woman* (Boston: Beacon Press, 1988); Personal Narratives Group, *Interpreting Women's Lives* (Bloomington: Indiana University Press, 1989); Tamsin Lorraine, *Gender Identity and the Production of Meaning* (Boulder: Westview, 1990); and Iris Young, *Justice and the Politics of Difference* (Princeton: Princeton University Press, 1990).

22. Gayle Rubin, "The Traffic of Women: Notes on the 'Political Economy' of Sex," in Rayna Rapp Reiter (ed.), *Toward an Anthropology of Women* (New York: Monthly Review Press, 1975), 157–210; Cockburn, *Machinery of Dominance*; and Varda Burstyn, "Masculine Dominance and the State," in Varda Burstyn and Dorothy E. Smith (eds.), *Women, Class, Family and the State* (Toronto: Garamond Press, 1986), 45–89.

23. Compare the analysis of the household by Harriet Fraad, Stephen Resnick and Richard Wolff, "For Every Knight in Shining Armor, There's a Castle Waiting to Be Cleaned: A Marxist-Feminist Analysis of the Household," *Rethinking Marxism* 2/4 (1989), 9–78, which is based on relations of appropriation.

24. Rubin, "The Traffic of Women," 167.

25. See also Lorraine, *Gender, Identity, and the Production of Meaning* for an account of identity formation through interaction and self-strategies.

26. See analyses and case studies by Rosemary Crompton and Kay Sanderson, *Gendered Jobs and Social Change* (London: Unwin Hyman, 1990); Robin Leidner, "Selling Hamburgers, Selling Insurance: Gender, Work and Identity," *Gender and Society* 5 (1991), 154–177; and Glenn Morgan and David Knights, "Gendering Jobs: Corporate Strategy, Managerial Control and the Dynamics of Job Segregation," *Work, Employment and Society* 5 (1991), 181–200.

27. It could be argued that my work here ontologically (and empirically) privileges class. This is not my intention. Rather, I see this specific work as a class-bound analysis of spatially differentiated conceptions of gender in the workplace$_2$, the latter being specific housekeeping service franchise in an urban area of southern Ontario.

28. See Julie Graham, "Theory and Essentialism in Marxist Geography," *Antipode* 22/1 (1990), 53–66.

29. For a review of dual systems theories, see Iris Young, "Beyond the Unhappy Marriage: A Critique of the Dual Systems Theory," in Lydia Sargent (ed.), *Women and Revolution* (Montreal: Black Rose Books, 1981), 43–69; Linda McDowell, "Beyond Patriarchy: A Class Based Explanation of Women's Subordination," *Antipode*

18/3 (1986), 311–321; and Lawrence Knopp and Mickey Lauria, "Gender Relations as a Patriarchal Form of Social Relations," *Antipode* 19/1 (1987), 48–53.

30. Cockburn, *Machinery of Dominance*.

31. Ibid., 167–197.

32. This definition of ideology is from Antonio Gramsci, found in Q. Hoare and G. Nowell-Smith (eds.), *Selections from the Prison Notebooks* (New York: Lawrence and Wishart, 1971).

33. Cockburn, *Machinery of Dominance*, 179.

34. In this instance, by labour I mean all waged and unwaged, productive and reproductive and remunerated and non-remunerated labour.

35. By "situationally specific" I mean the implicit and explicit rules designated for carrying out a specific task. For example, workers employed in housekeeping services franchises are not supposed to talk to the customer while on a clean, yet many forge friendly "mistress and maid" relations and undertake additional labour tasks outside the working relationship (e.g., shopping or banking). Though there are not rules "governing" the interaction between the two in other places, as in the mall (in lieu of the house as part of the workplace$_2$), the interaction is often still based on a set of relations like the "mistress and maid." The "maid" may be ignored and treated like a non-person. This was the case for many of the women who participated in the later phases of the project. Like the social hierarchy in the workplace$_1$, workplace$_2$ relations between the customer and "maid" transcend the specificity of place.

36. That is, behaviour is acceptable in one place and not acceptable elsewhere. For example, a woman can go to a coffee shop by herself and expect not to be bothered, but not to a bar.

37. Class formation has been part of the Marxist theoretical agenda for some time. For example, see Nicos Poulantzas, *Classes in Contemporary Capitalism* (London: New Left Review, 1975); Ralph Milliband, *Marxism and Politics* (Oxford: Oxford University Press, 1977); and Katznelson, *City Trenches*.

38. These arguments can be similarly (but not exactly) applied to other sets of social relations involving relations of domination and appropriation, like race, ethnicity, sexual orientation and culture. This is beyond the scope of this paper. Ferguson, *Blood at the Root*, 77–99, makes a similar argument with her sex-affective production systems.

39. Personal Narratives Group, *Interpreting Women's Lives*, 19, emphasis in original.

40. See Doreen Massey, *Spatial Divisions of Labour* (London: Macmillan, 1984). Linda McDowell, "Life Without Father and Ford: The New Gender Order of Post-Fordism," *Transactions of the Institute of British Geographers* 16/4 (1991), 400–419, makes a similar argument.

41. My investigation of a waged domestic labour process focused on gender and class. I did not focus on race and ethnic relations. In the southern Ontario urban area where I conducted the research, only White, non-immigrant women were employed in housekeeping services franchise.

42. Complete participant observation was only one phase of the project. I talked with women employed as housekeepers in the franchise where I was employed as well

as other area franchises. I spoke with fourteen women three times over a nine-month period. Literature and document surveys were also part of the research project.

43. I went into the employment situation without making my intentions clear to my co-workers or to the manager. It was a difficult decision. While I was aware of the issues of qualitative research possibly being more exploitative of the women who were part of the research process than other types of research, I chose not to reveal my identity. I wanted the experience of a woman cleaning houses by the rules of the franchise and firm, not as a doctoral student wanting that experience. Although I was not totally open about my research, I was not dishonest about my status or circumstances. I was frank about my domestic situation, that I was a student at the university, that I was a teaching assistant, that the money I made from Clare's Cleaning Services (a pseudonym) was an extra income, and about any other topic that came up.

At the end of my employment I wrote a letter to my co-workers and the manager explaining my project, in which I asked each to participate. I subsequently talked with each of the women. Of the nine women employed at Clare's at the time, two women said no, one woman did not return my phone calls, three women said yes but then dropped out because of other commitments (two went on maternity leave and one went back to school), and three women completed the study. (When I was working there were only eight other employees. The ninth employee was hired to take my place. I invited her to participate in the project as well.) The manager participated.

For a more extensive discussion of my decision in the context of ethical considerations of feminist participatory research, see P. Moss, "The 'Gap' as Part of the Politics of Research Design," *Antipode* 27.1 (Jan 1995).

44. All names used here are pseudonyms. I chose names that reflected the names of the women. For example, if the woman's name was Pamela, I chose Samantha. If it was Pammie, then I chose Sammie.

45. Computer field journal (April 1990), 17.

46. Interview with manager (February 27, 1991).

47. Computer field journal (March 1990), 58.

48. Ibid.

49. Ibid. (March 1990), 39. Toppy's is a home-based clothing sales distributor.

50. Ibid. (April 1990), 16.

51. Ibid. (March 1990), 2.

52. Ibid. (May 1990), 28.

53. Ibid., 5.

54. Ibid. (February 1990), 7.

55. Ibid. (August 1990), 57.

56. Written field journal (March 22, 1990).

57. Computer field journal (March 1990), 40.

58. Suzanne Mackenzie helped me work through this aspect of the analysis.

59. Computer field journal (February 1990), 6.

60. Ibid.

61. Ibid. (May 1990), 16.
62. Judith Rollins, in *Between Women* (Philadelphia: Temple University Press, 1985), develops the concept of *ressentiment*, from Nietzsche, in her analysis of the relationship between "maid and mistress." She uses it to describe the emotion that arises from repressed feelings of hatred, envy and revenge in someone who is in a position of subordination or subjugation. Rollins adds to this embodiment feelings of injustice because the person does not feel that she or he deserves to be in a position of subordination.
63. Computer field journal (May 1990), 16.
64. Ibid. (March 1990), 3.
65. Ibid. (April 1990), 17.
66. Ibid.
67. Ibid., 11–13.
68. Ibid. (March 1990), 4.
69. Ibid. (April 1990), 21.
70. Ibid., 11–13.
71. Ibid. (March 1990), 33.
72. Ibid., 63.
73. Ibid. (April 1990), 22.
74. Ibid., 33.
75. Ibid. (April 1990), 9.
76. Ibid., 24.
77. Ibid. (March 1990), 62.
78. Ibid.
79. Ibid., 7.
80. Ibid.
81. Ibid. (May 1990), 52.
82. Ibid., 55.
83. Ibid., 27–32.
84. Ibid. (April 1990), 25.
85. Ibid.
86. Ibid. (May 1990), 58.
87. Ibid. (March 1990), 2.
88. Ibid.
89. Ibid. (May 1990), 72.
90. Ibid. (January 1991), 10. Written with regard to the experiences of February 1990.
91. Ibid. (February 1990), 9.
92. Ibid.
93. Ibid. (May 1990), 43.
94. There are racialized ideologies, especially in the context of women working as waged domestic labourers. See Rollins, *Between Women*, and Mary Romero, *Maid in the U.S.A.* (New York: Routledge, 1992).
95. Sexual objectification by women and by men is different when the social context of the objectification is taken into account.

96. Individuals incorporate or "internalize" these relations of domination and oppression through subjectively mediating material conditions of existence. See Vera Chouinard and Pamela Moss, "Gender and Class Formation in Waged Domestic Labour Processes and the State," paper presented to a special session on "The Politics of the Local State: Production, Consumption and Labour Process in Britain and North America" at the Annual Conference of the Association of American Geographers, San Diego, California, April 1992.

Chapter Three

The Retreat of the State and Long-Term Care Provision: Implications for Frail Elderly People, Unpaid Family Carers and Paid Home Care Workers

Jane Aronson and Sheila M. Neysmith

Over the last twenty years, public policy and debate about health and social services for elderly people (long-term care/LTC) have stressed the importance of moving from institutionally based provision to community-based care. This shift in Canada mirrors developments in most Western industrialized nations and is typically explained in both humanitarian and economic terms: elderly people are thought to prefer being cared for in their own homes, and care in the community is, coincidentally, thought to be less expensive than care in hospitals, nursing homes and chronic care facilities. As governments have been increasingly driven by deficit reduction and cost-cutting objectives, community care has been embraced with mounting urgency. As a matter of public policy, it is presented as an uncontroversial, sensible way of responding to elderly people's needs while also averting demographic and fiscal crisis.

The successful rhetoric of the shift to community/home care in public policy in Canada has not been accompanied by a corresponding shift in public resources. As a result, the shift actually signifies the privatizing of the costs and work associated with frailty in old age. It also signifies a reframing of the relationship between elderly citizens and the state; in effect, the Canadian state is revising previously made promises of social security. In this paper, we examine the implications of this redistribution of costs and reframing of entitlements for those most vulnerable on the LTC stage: frail elderly people themselves;

members of their families who step in to care for them on an unpaid basis; and poorly paid home care workers. We then look beyond the current distribution of costs to these three groups (each of which is, significantly, made up predominantly of women), and the discourse that justifies it to consider alternative ways of framing the LTC debate and of thinking about the place of the state in ensuring adequate and just social provision for the elderly. This examination of political alternatives can usefully expand and unsettle the confining way that issues are posed and solutions countenanced in Canada in the late 1990s.

The Canadian State and Long-Term Care: An Overview

LTC programs for elderly people encompass a wide array of health and social services: from acute, chronic and rehabilitation hospitals for elderly people who are ill, to nursing homes for people requiring fairly constant care and support, to a range of health and social programs (e.g., visiting homemaker services, visiting nursing care, daycare, meals on wheels) that allow people with various degrees of health problems and functional limitations to receive care in their own homes. Partly because of the particular history of health policy development in Canada, with early funding earmarked for the building of hospitals and institutions, the response to the health and social needs of old people has been heavily institution-based and has often resulted in inappropriate care.[1] Through the Canadian Assistance Plan Act (1996) and later the Established Programmes Financing Act (1977), federal and provincial governments structured cost-sharing arrangements that permitted some growth in community-based care and some reduction in unnecessary and relatively expensive institutional care. These statutes did not, however, specify criteria and requirements for health and social services in the community in the way that the Medical Care Act and Canada Health Act specified conditions for provinces' receipt of federal funds for physician and hospital insurance.

During the 1960s and 1970s, provincial governments took up the funding made available by these cost-sharing provisions to offer some community-based services for frail elderly people. In the absence of national standards, however, they took different approaches and various fragmented mixes of public, voluntary and for-profit services resulted. In contrast to the acute care sector, health and social care for frail elderly people in the community remained a service sector held in relatively low social regard and accorded a weak public resource base.[2]

In addition to flagging these dimensions of the weak positioning of community care services in the context of total health care provision, critics of public policy in the 1970s and 1980s also began to articulate the consequences of this weakness for elderly people's families. In Canada and elsewhere, feminist scholars called attention to the reality that women, usually daughters and wives, provided most of the care for frail elderly people; vague allusions to "family care" obscured the extent, social value and costs of this work.[3] This analysis, most developed in the U.K. and Scandinavia, illuminated the ideological construction of family responsibility and family care that is the assumed backdrop to state intervention — a construction that enforces the morality of private, rather than public, responsibility for people in need and effectively limits the citizenship entitlements of elderly people (and other groups deemed dependent).

These early critiques of the underdevelopment of community/ home care and its impact on unpaid family caregivers have been elaborated and voiced with mounting alarm in the face of the diminishing state presence and program cuts of the intervening ten or fifteen years. In response to fiscal constraints, health care is now organized to ensure that fewer people with chronic health problems are cared for in institutions and that people with acute problems are discharged as quickly as possible from expensive hospital care.[4] This "dehospitalizing"[5] and cost-cutting means that increasing numbers of frail older people live in their own homes, often requiring substantial support to do so with security and dignity.

While federal and provincial governments' quests to contain the costs of institutional care accelerated and changed in the last ten years, the basic planks of policy and funding arrangements for community care did not; rather, the permissively framed, non-mandatory arrangements for cost-sharing, introduced thirty years ago, stayed in place.[6] Now, with the prospect of cuts in federal transfer payments and the shift to block funding, it seems improbable that the small fraction of total health care spending presently allocated to home care — still less than 1 per cent — will increase significantly.[7]

Policy Discourse Pressing Long-Term Care into the Private Domain

This brief description of the development of government activity in LTC in Canada brings us to the 1990s, to a picture of hastening retreat in public provision. This retreat is occurring with relatively little controversy or debate. Rather, it unfolds through a discourse about imminent fiscal crisis and debt reduction that generates a logic justifying sacrifices and cutbacks.[8] Cutting back on social programs is presented as an inevitability as Canadian society is buffeted by the winds of the global economy. It is presented as self-evident that survival in the global economy requires the appeasement of international capital and money markets, and thus the reduction of any costs that constrain capital accumulation.

With respect to state responses to the elderly in particular, this presentation of cost-cutting inevitabilities is bolstered by knowledge that population aging will mean higher numbers of old people and, most significantly, of very old people who typically experience greater physical and cognitive impairments. This demographic reality is interpreted to confirm the view that elderly citizens' entitlements can legitimately be revisited. Such revisiting has already resulted in the scaling back of elderly people's pension entitlements. Universal entitlements to Old Age Security, once a seemingly unassailable right of citizenship, have been eroded and, at the time of writing, entitlements under the Canada Pension Plan are being reviewed.

Alongside this renegotiation of previous assurances of economic security, we also see assaults on earlier promises of health security. With funding cuts to the provinces and the introduction of the Canadian Health and Social Transfer, the federal government is retreating from its role in framing a national commitment to universal health care. At the provincial level, promises of health care security are being questioned as balancing budgets becomes entrenched as the paramount public policy goal. At the local level, the security of community services is threatened as agencies lose assured base funding and depend precariously on short-term project funds, income from charity drives and private sector donations.

In the LTC arena, specific forms of instability result from this general climate of insecurity. For example, the cost of hospital and chronic care beds is pictured as so unaffordable that cost-savings achieved by early discharges and home-based care are readily embraced. Ironically, the closing of beds has acquired the political capital once reserved for announcements of new hospitals. Policy making and planning aimed at effecting such cuts and rearrangements in LTC are couched in the language of industry and the marketplace, stressing efficiency and rational management. Ontario's LTC Reform Act, for example, focused on the streamlined coordination of community care for elderly and disabled people.[9] Even as the Act proclaimed the centrality of the "consumers" of community-based services, it also reaffirmed the importance of cost-containment and of the role of their families in assuring their well-being. Thus, like most legislation of its kind, it communicated very oblique commitments to public service provision and to entitlements previously promised to elderly citizens.

This kind of obliqueness, along with the logic of cost-containment that has become numbingly ordinary in public debate, shrouds the reality that the costs of LTC are being redistributed to the private sphere. Watching a similar process of privatization of care of the elderly in the U.S., Bergthold et al. caution: "Social costs and disadvantages do not simply disappear; they must be borne by the individuals and families concerned."[10] The suggestion in the efficiency-driven policy discourse that costs have been or can be better managed and cut out is, in large part, a deception. Many are not eliminated but, rather, shifted to the "community" — a euphemistic and insubstantial concept. In reality, Western industrialized societies are characterized by privatized households and dispersed social connections rather than by local ties and readily available support networks.[11] Regardless, the rhetoric of community is invoked and put to use in deinstitutionalization and community care policies of all kinds. In LTC, this empty invocation means that the costs of frailty and care are simply hidden from public view in the private lives and homes of old people and their families and in the isolated work worlds of paid home care providers.

Tracing the Implications of Privatizing Long-Term Care

In tracing the way that the economic and social costs associated with frailty and disability in old age are being privatized, we consider the experiences of three groups crucially implicated in the policy shift to community-based care. First, we consider elderly people themselves, the supposed beneficiaries of the policy emphasis on care at home. By providing inadequate or meagre responses to their needs, the costs of frailty are effectively transferred to their shoulders to be endured or dealt with privately or alone. Some of the costs also shift to family members — our second group of concern — who typically step in to provide needed care. And, thirdly, costs are shifted to paid home care providers who are, for the most part, cheaper, less well organized and more isolated than their institutional counterparts and thus more open to exploitation.

Our knowledge of the costs borne by these three groups is uneven. As with patterns in all societal stocks of knowledge, this unevenness reflects power differences and legitimated patterns of attention and inattention. In examining the experiences and interests of each group below, we both review our current state of knowledge and consider the significance of the emphases and omissions within it.

Frail Elderly People and the Privatization of Long-Term Care: Shrinking Entitlements and Mounting Insecurity

To examine the implications for elderly people of the emphasis on community-based care in the LTC policy discourse, we draw on a review of relevant literature and insights generated in our own and others' earlier research. These sources are few in number, but we can distill from them two themes of particular concern: first, the deceptiveness of policy rhetoric that depicts elderly people as either central, self-determining actors or as informed consumers exercising choice in the LTC marketplace; and, secondly, the discrepancy between these rhetorical images of elderly people's positioning and what we know of their actual experiences of needing care and support to cope with frailty and ill health.

In the public policy discourse, the shift to community-based care is often explained as a response to elderly people's preference to remain in their own homes. As the language of private economic enterprise has enveloped discussion of social programs, such allusions to preference and choice have become commonplace. We hear less now of the older population's entitlements of citizenship than we do about elderly consumers' rights to exercise choice in the LTC marketplace. Closely examined, these images of choice and involvement — evoked in other comparable welfare regimes as well — prove hollow and misleading.[12] Preferences or choices can be exercised only if real alternatives exist or can be demanded and if knowledge about them is accessible. These conditions are not satisfied when, in reality, elderly people face: a shrinking institutional sector, already unattractive by virtue of its forbidding history; fragmented and often meagrely funded home care services; and, as a result, enforced dependence on the care of relatives, if they have any. Further, they do not "shop" for services as free agents but, rather, are assessed and accorded priority by professional gatekeepers of various kinds, whose decisions are contingent on the shifting availability of resources and funds, rather than on more stable and assured assessments of need.

Just as consumer sovereignty proves an ill-fitting image for capturing old people's individual experiences of need and service receipt, it also proves hollow in the rhetoric of consumer participation and community consultation in policy development. While rather ostentatiously invited to participate in narrowed, consultative policy making processes, elderly people's voices are seldom included in decision making about the actual design and operation of resources that are provided to respond to their needs.[13] The Ontario experience in developing a LTC policy in a supposedly consultative and inclusive fashion revealed the conceptual poverty of both "participation" and "community."[14]

Elderly people negotiate this complex terrain at a time when their relationship with the state is in flux, when, as noted above, assurances of economic and social security are being reviewed and compromised. Unsurprisingly, this climate translates into a sense of disentitlement and instability for many older people. Participants in studies exploring older people's wishes for themselves in the face of frailty reflect this instability, for example: "The economy can't keep all these old people — we're a drag on the younger generation"[15]; "Old people come to expect so little. ... we've made a contribution and should be entitled to help now. We shouldn't be swept aside."[16] Regardless of the particular degree of submission or protest voiced, such observations are not remotely in accord with the images of consumerism asserted in the policy discourse.

Elderly people's own accounts of what it is like to need support or care reflect the insecurity of their dependent positioning. Research suggests that, given alternatives, elderly people do not want to rely on the care of family.[17] The help of relatives was, however, recognized among a sample of elderly women as an inevitability and a buffer against less desirable options: "I don't know what I'd do without my daughter — she'll keep me going here. I couldn't bear the thought of a home." "I'm very lucky to have my niece. She comes in regularly and helps out with the things I can't do."[18] Relying on family members' help in this way often evoked feelings of indebtedness and flew in the face of closely held ideals about independence and self-reliance. "I don't want to be a burden" was a frequently voiced concern and subjects spoke of difficult and contradictory efforts to balance their increasingly obvious needs with their pride in not being dependent.[19]

These observations and anxieties about depending upon relatives of a younger generation capture the realities of only one segment of the frail elderly population. We know rather less about elderly people's experiences of relying on elderly spouses for care and support. Significantly, too, relatively little research attention has been given to people who do not have children, who do not live in heterosexual partnerships or who do not live in Western, nuclear family forms — in short, who do not fit in with the homogeneous picture of "family care" painted in the LTC policy discourse.[20] Research on the diversity of social ties can both expand the narrowed framing of "family care" that underpins the public policy discourse and highlight groups who face frailty in old age in especially unsupported circumstances.

Our knowledge of elderly people's perspectives on receiving paid care at home is also limited, but, again, the powerlessness of their positioning is striking. For example, an older woman imagined how she would feel receiving care at home:

> When you're an old lady, frail, maybe a little helpless, you haven't the gumption to stand up against a person who's coming to do a service and say: "That wasn't good enough." You just let it happen.[21]

The submission implicit in this statement was also identified in a study of elderly recipients of home care services in the new British mixed economy of social care. Claiming to streamline people's access to needed community services, a care manager is charged with coordinating individual consumers' packages of resources from the public and for-profit care markets. Recipients of this model of care reported considerable insecurity at what seemed unpredictable services arranged on their behalf and delivered by a bewildering array of providers. Their confusion and passivity points, the authors suggest, to the discordance between the design and provision of needed care and a market approach to supplying uniform services:

> The problem is not just that care cannot be a standardized commodity, it is not clear that it can be a commodity in the market sense at all. It is qualitatively different from a commercial product in that it must carry within it a non-standardized affective component: caring.[22]

This reference to the individual and particular quality of care relationships is echoed throughout the small literature on home care recipients' perspectives. Service users report appreciating care providers who have time to listen and talk, who get to know their particular needs and with whom they have stable relationships.[23] It is sobering to realize, therefore, that it is exactly these personalizing aspects of care provision that are being squeezed out of home care services as cost-cutting leads to the speed-up and intensification of home care workers' jobs.[24]

In sum, it seems that the rhetoric of community-based care and consumer choice corresponds very little with what we know of frail elderly people's realities. Rather than choice and security, we see pressure to depend on relatives (if available) and a lack of confidence in increasingly meagre, standardized services.[25] In the public discourse on LTC and in the kinds of research it legitimates, these realities and their consequences receive relatively little attention. Seniors' groups certainly express protest at the impact of cost-cutting, for example: "Care and compassion have given way to closing beds, inappropriate discharges, indignities to persons, unnecessary suffering and in some cases premature death."[26] However, their voices are fairly faint in the face of the dominant public discourse and, until recently, they have not been joined by the voices of seemingly related advocacy movements (e.g., feminist groups, the labour movement, the disability rights movement). This lack of political mobilization can be understood partly as a reflection of the fragility of old age as a basis for collective identity or action, and partly as a reflection of the ageism that permeates our wider culture. These forces serve to stifle resistance to policy changes and diminishing citizenship entitlements in the LTC arena.

Unpaid Family Carers and the Privatization of Long-Term Care: Ultimate Responsibility for Increasing Work

Compared with our knowledge of frail elderly people's positioning, we know considerably more about women's activities in caring for elderly relatives. It is now commonly acknowledged that family members, predominantly women, provide the great proportion of LTC for frail elderly people. It is a proportion hard to specify since it is not counted as work of social value, though the Ontario government recently estimated it to be as high as 90 per cent.[27] While acknowledged in the public policy discourse and the health policy literature, this division of care between the private sphere of families and the public sphere of state activity is still depicted as a self-evident, uncontentious phenomenon. Family members are seen to choose to fulfill natural commitments to relatives in need. As a result, women's unpaid caring work comes into public view only when it breaks down or threatens to do so. Community-based services are provided to buttress and sustain family carers, not to substitute for them.

Critical observers of these processes call attention to the politically constructed character of the line dividing family and public responsibility for the care of old people.[28] Rather than a natural unfolding of family care and unintrusive state interventions, the line is revealed as a shifting division determined by political and economic interests. Just as the broad rhetoric of "family care" proves a blunt analytic category for understanding diversity in old people's private experience of entitlement and support, it also obscures important differences among family carers. The basis of commitment, for example, between spouses or between children and parents is substantially different, and the capacity to care for an elderly spouse or parent are very differently shaped. Adult daughters' capacities may be limited by the necessity of paid work, child care or geographical distance, while spouses' capacities are likely to be influenced by the limitations that come with their own aging; both may be constrained by their lack of training for the work of caring. The simplifying invocation of "family care" that underpins the LTC policy discourse also leaves no room for appreciating the jeopardies and risks of abuse and neglect hidden within families.[29]

Regardless of such differences in family carers' material or emotional resources, cost-cutting in LTC presses caring work out of the pubic domain and onto their shoulders. Cuts in public provision (for example, early hospital discharges, reduced nursing home beds, cuts in home care) shift the work of caring to families, "demonstrating how capitalism reorganizes the labour process to make use of free service labour."[30] Claimed as cost reductions in public accounting, such cuts represent cost increases for family carers. In this section, we review what we know of how these cost are actually shifted and of the consequences for those who pick them up.

Analyses of everyday encounters of elderly people and their families with formal service providers reveal how the line between public and private responsibility for care is actually drawn. Women in a study of caregiving daughters described, for example, how physicians, social workers and other key gatekeepers communicated the assumption that patients and families should fend for themselves; they felt that professionals expected them to appreciate the limits of public resources but to overlook the limits of their own. For example, a woman working full-time and with two children at home described how a doctor urged her to take her very frail mother home from an acute care hospital while she waited for a bed in a nursing home: "I always felt the doctor and social worker were suspicious. I always felt they thought we were going to *dump* her or ... we didn't *care* about her."[31] From the hospital's vantage point, this woman's mother would be deemed a frustrating and expensive "bed blocker."[32] Her daughter's unpaid services could free the bed and enable the hospital to meet its commitments to cost-efficiency.

Besides illuminating the way that costs are redistributed from the public to the private sphere, subjects in this study pointed, too, to the ways in which responsibility for caring is distributed within families. Research reveals that responsibility for caring typically falls to women (wives, daughters, daughters-in-law) rather than men.[33] Analysis of this pattern highlights its origins in gender socialization and in women's and men's differential participation and rewards in the labour market, and explains general differences in how caring is experienced subjectively — as an obligation for women and as an active choice for men.[34] Research suggests, too, that men and women carers meet with different responses from the formal service system as male carers tend to receive more formal support and relief than do women.[35]

Recognizing women's unpaid caring as an obligation rather than a choice parallels a theme emphasized in our consideration of frail elderly people's positioning in the LTC discourse. There we saw that the rhetoric of consumer choice obscured the oppressive realities of having to rely on family members or to accept meagre public services. Here we see women in families pressed into caring by virtue of the absence of alternatives for elderly relatives. In her articulation of women's ultimate responsibility for family labour, Saraceno captures this positioning vividly: "It is the woman who, above all, knows and experiences the dimension of inescapable necessity which structures family relations, especially as far as intergenerational relations ... are concerned."[36]

Depending on the extent and duration of women's care for elderly relatives, the inescapable necessity of responding to their needs can come at considerable cost. For reasonably well older people, care might mean practical help with shopping or heavy housework, emotional support and the continuation of an otherwise fairly reciprocal relationship. For elderly relatives with more serious physical or mental impairments, it can involve twenty-four-hour care. With cuts to hospital services and institutional resources for the aged and chronically ill, more and more frail and sick elderly people require increasingly complex and demanding support in their own homes. The costs to women of providing such support are varied and complex.[37] Costs in time and energy can result in serious strains and tensions. Caring for an elderly relative can also be a source of emotional stress and lead to social isolation. Such strains can result in physical or mental exhaustion or illness for the carer. Materially, too, caring for an elderly relative may impose immediate financial costs. It can also prompt younger women to withdraw from the labour force or to decide not to seek advancement in their paid work and, ultimately, can lead to diminished income and diminished pension entitlements in old age.[38]

Theoretically, family carers could be a source of potential resistance to the privatization of LTC: they have inside knowledge of its implications and costs for themselves and for the elderly relatives for whom they care. A subject in the study of caregiving daughters cited earlier alluded rather tentatively to the possibility of resistance:

> In my case, for example, with full time jobs and a family and children and a home to run, *we're* under pressure too. I mean, not as badly, we could provide support, but there were *limits* — there really were limits. ... It sounds awful, but my mother's been a Canadian citizen for umpteen years and I pay a hell of a lot in income tax every year, my husband pays a hell of a lot ... and now and then, when we need some short-term help, I don't think it should be difficult to find.[39]

That such a claim, from a relatively privileged White, middle-class woman, feels "awful" suggests that resistance will be readily stifled by guilt at appearing undaughterly. In addition, there are few contexts where women like this one can gather to recognize themselves as a collective with common interests. In Ontario, Concerned Friends of Seniors in Care Facilities (an organization of people with relatives in nursing homes) and At Home/Chez Nous (an organization of family care providers) assert a small voice in the LTC arena. Mostly, however, family carers' resistance tends to be expressed as advocacy focused more narrowly on the interests of their individual relatives. An interesting though, as yet, small body of literature focuses on family carers' efforts to advocate for and secure the best possible treatment for relatives who receive home care or live in institutions.[40] This work highlights the possible political value of their knowledge of the shortcomings of public LTC. However, it also points to the potential for conflict between family carers and key paid providers (like nursing assistants and home care workers) who are likely to be the targets of family criticism and frustration with inadequate care.

In sum, the implications for family carers of public cost-cutting, and the deceptive rhetoric of community-based care take the shape of unpaid work that, even if lovingly and willingly given, is exacted by the lack of publicly provided alternatives and can be costly. Clearly the potential costs of this unpaid caring unfold differently for women in different social locations. Those with more resources, by virtue of class, race or age, will be better able to offset the costs of caring, whether by purchasing private help or by being able to negotiate public resources from a more privileged position. To date, we understand these differences poorly — a result of the feminist caring literature's relatively narrow focus on middle-class, White women providing unpaid care for relatives.[41] This focus, reflective of the social positioning of those who generated the literature, has resulted in relative inattention to the experiences of paid care providers in the community who are typically working class and, increasingly, immigrant women. In the next section, we turn to consider the consequences of the ongoing shifts in LTC for this vulnerably positioned labour force.

Home Care Workers and the Privatization of Long-Term Care: Publicly Unrewarded Skills and Labour

The shift towards community-based care for frail elderly people accomplishes cuts in public spending by moving the work of caring from hospitals and institutions to cheaper care providers, specifically to unpaid family carers (as discussed above) and to paid workers in home care services. Home care services encompass a wide array of health and social services and employ a variety of care providers (e.g., nurses, physiotherapists, social workers, nutritionists and visiting homemakers). We focus our discussion here on visiting homemakers (now commonly referred to as "home care workers," a term we use throughout the paper), who represent a significant proportion of the home care labour force and are seen as "the backbone" of home health care.[42] As a labour force of low-paid paraprofessionals (drawn increasingly from immigrant populations in metropolitan areas) who do what is understood in our culture as the ordinary activities of women in the privacy of old people's homes, the jeopardy of their positioning merits particular attention.

Home care workers seldom appear as subjects in the dominant policy discourse. Instead, attention is directed to the management and organization of their work and to questions of quality assurance and costing.[43] The critical literature on institutional nursing work offers some valuable insights into paid care work in the current political and economic climate, revealing, for example: the complexity and invisibility of the emotional work involved in caring for people's personal needs; the poor employment conditions and devalued status of nursing assistants and aides who are key care providers for chronically ill and frail elderly people; and the negative effects of managerial practices that seek to cut government costs by intensifying and pressing the caring labour process into the standardized form of industrial production.[44] While these patterns are likely to unfold in comparable work carried out in the community, there are likely to be some differences too. In particular, home care workers' ambiguous positioning as public workers in the private, isolated work sites of old people's homes structures particular tensions and forms of exploitation.

Our observations of the ways that home care workers shoulder some of the burdens of government cost-containment in LTC are derived from a study undertaken in two home care agencies in southern Ontario.[45] The employment conditions of these paraprofessional workers suggest that government costs are indeed reduced by shifting care out of institutions. The hourly rate of pay for workers whom we interviewed ranged from $9 to $12 and they had limited benefits — conditions inferior to those of their counterparts in hospitals and nursing homes.[46] This visible and proclaimed reduction of government costs is not, however, our main focus here. Rather, we address some less visible ways in which home care workers shoulder some of the redistributed cost of LTC.

First, we found that some aspects of home care workers' labour and skill go unremarked and unrewarded as a result of the significant discrepancy between their official job descriptions and their own accounts of what they do in the course of helping old people. Official accounts of home care work underscore its practical character, specifying such tasks as cooking, cleaning, bathing, dressing and laundry. Couched as a list of tasks, the job can be broken down into standard, measurable units of work and is thus amenable to the kinds of industrial management practices not commonplace in hospital care. In contrast, workers' own descriptions of their day-to-day work revealed how unstandardized it was, and how they constantly adapted their practical activities to clients' individual needs and situations; "every case is different" and "it depends" were frequent qualifiers to descriptions of particular tasks. For example, a worker reflected on the complexity of helping clients with bathing: "When you work in personal care you have to develop a handling of the client. They have to get used to you handling them. You have to get used to how they like to be handled."

Home care workers prided themselves on their ability to personalize their work in this way, on building relationships and on caring well for their clients. They found the attachment they developed with clients an inevitable and often rewarding aspect of their work:

> The supervisor might say well you're going in there to do the laundry, do the shopping, do the cleaning, … but eventually you find yourself that you're more involved, you know. And they might say, well try not to get involved. Well, you cannot not … get involved. If you're going in there regularly and you're seeing the situation, you become part of that person.

Such processes of becoming familiar with individual clients, getting to know their histories and responding to their preferences, also noted in other research, require considerable time and skill.[47]

Just as homemakers perceived these aspects of their work to be important and valuable, family carers and elderly people do so as well. As noted earlier, elderly care recipients value continuity in their relationships with paid care workers, and family carers report a protective concern that care workers treat their relatives in ways that are affirming and individualizing. These skilled and crucial aspects of caring work are, however, accorded little visibility in home care workers' job descriptions and in the public discourse on home care. As a result, workers' performance of them goes (publicly) unvalued and uncompensated. This invisibility and the resulting exploitation are made possible by dominant typifications of work that eclipse women's interpersonal caring activities, rendering them the natural outcome of disposition rather than skilled work of social value.[48] Socialized in these constructions of work themselves, home care workers lack a vocabulary in which to claim caring activities as skills or even as real work, and resist the low valuation of their work in the public discourse.[49]

A second and related aspect of home care workers' exploitable positioning in LTC emerged in their engagement in unpaid "extra" activities on behalf of their clients. Workers described various ways in which their work seeped out of its formal boundaries. For example, they put in time beyond their official allocations of hours. They also carried out tasks that lay outside their officially defined repertoire (e.g., gardening, cutting toenails, keeping clients company), which they judged would benefit their elderly clients. They sometimes breached the formal, non-reciprocal relationship with clients specified by their employers by, for example, giving and accepting gifts or keeping in phone contact with clients in between paid visits or after their assignments were over. Home care workers' assumption of this kind of extra, personalizing work has been identified in others' analyses of home care providers.[50]

Workers' motivations for undertaking such extra, unpaid work warrant particular attention as we try to identify and anticipate the consequences of inadequate public LTC provision. Home care workers alluded to a sense of moral responsibility for elderly clients that parallels the ultimate responsibility felt by family care providers: "[W]hen you know that the client doesn't have any other person going in, it makes a big difference too. You know that you're the only one they see from basically one week to the next a lot of times."

The pressure of knowing they were the clients' last resort is likely to be higher for community- than institutionally based care workers. In institutional settings, workers share their knowledge of and sense of responsibility for clients with co-workers and supervisors. Isolated in old people's homes, with no co-workers, with little support from supervisors (the result of budget cuts) and often with exclusive knowledge of clients' situations, home care workers are more likely to feel pressed into being responsive. In effect, the context and conditions of their work are ideally suited to extracting labour that exceeds their officially defined jobs.

While extra labour was often provided out of moral obligation, it was also extracted by virtue of home care workers' vulnerable social status. This vulnerability originated, for them all, in their status as workers deemed relatively unskilled and easily replaceable. Conscious of this, they needed to sustain workable relationships with clients, even if that meant responding to unfair demands: "[I]f I don't have them (my clients) I don't work. I don't have pay. And I need my pay to eat." In addition to this class-based vulnerability, home care workers who were women of colour or who had accents that marked them as not Canadian-born reported a heightened sense of jeopardy. They felt, for example, unable to refuse clients' or families' unreasonable demands or to challenge racist and demeaning treatment. If they risked complaining to their supervisors, they were usually supported to some degree. Typically, supervisors transferred them to other cases. They did not deal more directly with clients' and families' racist behaviour as an issue of occupational safety and basic human rights.[51] In the private home care market, we could expect workers to be even less protected.[52]

All these oppressive conditions in home care work are intensifying with managerial practices designed to cut government costs. In our study, cost-cutting was felt in various ways: as reductions in time allotments to clients; in the introduction of split shifts and of unpaid "on call" duties; in reduced support and supervision; and in caseloads of more needy clients being discharged earlier from hospitals or unable to find a place in the shrinking supply of institutional beds. In other jurisdictions, observers describe organizational arrangements designed to intensify home care workers' labour in even more systematic ways. In schemes tried, for example, in the U.S.,[53] the U.K.[54] and Sweden,[55] home care workers are assigned to clients on random or rotating bases so that time-consuming relationships cannot develop and tasks can be accomplished with assembly-line efficiency.

In other jurisdictions, too, the privatization of home care services is seen to contribute further to the systematic degradation of home care workers' employment conditions.[56] In New Zealand, for example, where privatization has been a matter of government policy for ten years, home care workers are cast as independent contractors and home care services are managed as profit-motivated businesses. No longer entitled to even the most minimal occupational rights and protections, home care workers' jobs are extraordinarily unregulated and devalued and are, at the time of writing, the focus of legal challenge and union activity.[57] In anticipation of such developments here in Canada, home care workers in Manitoba went on strike in the spring of 1996 to protest the provincial government's plan to shift a large portion of home health care to the private sector. Such a shift is, of course, facilitated by the North American Free Trade Agreement, which paved the way for private providers from the U.S. to enter the Canadian health care arena in pursuit, implicitly, of profit and their shareholders' interests, rather than of the collective health or occupational welfare of Canadians.[58]

We have documented the implications of governments' cost-cutting and the policy shift to community-based LTC for three crucially affected groups: frail elderly people, unpaid family carers and paid home care workers. Before moving on to set their perspectives in broader analyses of state responses to elderly people's needs and to women's caring work, it is important to acknowledge that the three groups have permeable boundaries and that their respective jeopardies intersect. Their blurred boundaries emerge when we recognize, for example, that many spouses caring for frail partners are themselves elderly and in uncertain health; that many home care workers also look after elderly people in their own families; and, of course, that women providing care on paid and unpaid bases (and those who conceptualize what they do) will themselves probably live to be old. It is also the case that the three groups shape each other's realities. For example, the availability of a responsible and generous home care worker who overextends herself can relieve the stresses of a caring daughter and the jeopardy of her elderly parent; a demanding elderly person can exploit a home care worker desperate for work as a new immigrant to Canada; a confused elderly person deemed difficult or unmanageable by frustrated family members and paid care workers may live alone at some risk. Effectively, these three participants on the LTC stage are thrown into interdependent relationships crosscut by inequalities and potential conflicts based on race, class and age differences. It is important to understand the origins of such conflicts not as interpersonal problems but as the direct result of shrinking public care provision that entraps and oppresses them all.[59]

Future Directions in Long-Term Care: The Possibilities of a More Active State

In responding to fiscal pressures over the last decade, the Canadian state has resorted almost exclusively to cost-cutting measures, pleading an absence of other options. However, recognition that other liberal welfare states, faced with similar fiscal pressures, have pursued alternative policies in LTC exposes the actions of the Canadian state as accumulated political choices rather then neutral inevitabilities. In this final section, we consider first how pursuit of alternatives requires an active rather than a retreating state presence in the development of social policy. Secondly, we discuss how, with such a presence, the discourse on LTC could be reframed to guarantee access to minimum levels of specified services for all elderly citizens and to redistribute the costs of those services more equitably.

An Active State Presence in Social Policy Development?

In order to develop public policies that assure elderly citizens access to specified LTC services and that distribute their costs equitably, the active intervention of federal and provincial governments is needed. We see instead a federal government in retreat, transferring resources to the provinces through block grants that specify neither minimum criteria for entitlement nor national standards of service. We also see both federal and provincial governments simply watching the expansion of the market and informal sectors.

The challenge of considering the possibilities of a more active state presence is significant because an interventionist liberal state has been subject to attacks from the left as well as from the right. It has been criticized, with justification, for its frequent support of market forces and organized interests and its failure to promote the interests of oppressed groups. However, assuming an anti-state position in response to these concerns does not challenge the vulnerability of the kinds of groups discussed here and, arguably, it may actually jeopardize them further. Despite the mixed and contradictory effects of state intervention, analysis of its history can remind us of its capacity to disrupt capitalist and patriarchal power.[60] We know, for example, that in countries like Sweden and Denmark, where an active state exists, women have registered real gains from policies that recognize the social benefits accruing from child care and elder care programs.[61] We can identify examples of similar gains in Canada; for instance, despite resistance from the market sector, federal and provincial governments initiated pay and employment equity policies, as well as property-splitting at divorce, anti-violence programs and welfare schemes that have benefited different groups of women. The Canada Pension Plan disrupts gender-specific employment assumptions found in most private pension schemes. Similarly, and perhaps most significantly for our consideration of LTC, the Canada Health Act clearly disrupts class privilege.

These observations are not presented to idealize past achievements of welfare states or to gloss over their contradictions but to give some social context to the current debate so that it is less ahistorical and so that we can recognize the possibilities of more active state intervention. Feminist analyses of the liberal state have alerted us to both its positive and negative potential for women's welfare and security. In order to visualize its positive potential in LTC, two particular themes in this now extensive body of work warrant our attention.

First, feminist critiques have highlighted how the liberal state focuses narrowly on the individual and "his" freedom of action. Such a state does not recognize that individuals' relationships or group memberships influence their power or positioning and determine their freedom of action and ability to negotiate. Translated to the arena of LTC, this construction of individuals as free and equal actors means, for example, that family carers are seen to do their caring work by choice and that elderly people are seen to choose to rely on them. In a minority of situations, choice may indeed be exercised. The possibility of choice is greatest where: financial resources are sufficient to purchase services on the market; family structures are such that a spouse is present and in reasonably good health; and the care needs of the elderly person are minimal. These conditions are, of course, exceptional; many of the elderly are widows with limited resources, they do not have readily available kin on whom they want to depend, and most elderly people needing care require more than the occasional bit of help.[62]

A second significant flaw in assumptions underlying the liberal state concerns the separation of public and private spheres. Social policies and the activities of the state are, it is assumed, confined to the public arena and are not seen as affecting the organization of private life. The fallacy of this separation of spheres emerged throughout our discussion of the three groups involved in LTC; home care policy has a profound effect on their private lives. We saw, for example, how hospitals balance their budgets by releasing patients earlier, and how the necessity of providing care to an elderly family member affects the daily rhythm of a carer's life, her career pattern and future pension entitlements, yet the patriarchal model of the liberal state defines such issues as private matters to be negotiated among family members who freely enter the caring contract as equals. Our earlier discussion of the coercion and lack of choice that characterized the experiences of frail elderly people and their unpaid and paid carers reveals the inaccuracy of this liberal imagery.

Long-Term Care: Part of the Broader Renegotiation of Social Security in Canada

If, as a result of political mobilization, advocacy, public debate and research, Canadians endorsed the kind of active state presence in LTC that we see reflected in the framing of medicare, what would be some of its key features and how would it be discussed? We identify two related elements in a more interventionist LTC policy: first, it would guarantee citizens access to minimum levels of specified services; and secondly, it would require the reframing of a pluralist model of state intervention to ensure equitable outcomes for the unequally positioned actors on the LTC stage.

Policy attention to assuring access and entitlement to defined LTC services would bring LTC policy into line with the original framing of the Canadian Health Act. In that Act, access and service are guaranteed but, except for patients' entitlements to choose physicians, "choice" does not loom large in the principles framing legislation — a stark contrast to the imagery of choice that pervades the LTC discourse. A LTC policy framed in a similar tradition would stress meeting the specified needs of old people. It would not assume that need will be met if elderly people and their caring daughters or spouses just "choose" from a LTC marketplace in which there are not clear guarantees of service availability or stability. This framing of LTC policy would transform elderly consumers into elderly citizens with rights and responsibilities. It would also make visible the political nature of need interpretation and of responses to defined need.[63] Acknowledged as politically determined phenomena, need definition, services and programs would be revealed as open to contestation, not depicted as the inevitable and undebatable results of market forces.

The transformation of elderly consumers into politically positioned citizens requires a reframing of the nature of welfare pluralism in Canada. The four sectors that comprise what is explicitly referred to and debated in Europe as the "mixed economy of welfare" are: (1) the public/state sector, (2) the private/market sector, (3) the voluntary sector and (4) the informal sector.[64] The particular mix and balance of these four sectors has not been the subject of clear public debate in Canada. Rather, growth in the market and informal sectors has happened by virtue of cost-cutting in the public sector. Determining the mix more openly and equitably requires the presence of the state as a key player in the LTC arena — an arena in which the interests of those whose well-being is critically affected by LTC would occupy significant space.

This model of state intervention assumes conflict and inequality between the participants in LTC. The realization that an active state would always be formulating policy among unequal participants with conflicting interests eliminates the deceptive concept of an overriding national interest that must take primacy, whether it be deficit reduction or health care.[65] This acknowledgement of conflict provides a frame for attending to the inequities embedded in current models of community-based care. With more active state involvement, the oppressive and exploitative potential structured into home care work and the various conflicts, discussed above, that are now contained in the private world of home-based care but rooted in broader class, race and age inequalities would all be matters for explicit public policy attention.

Bringing a more active state into LTC policy making in Canada clearly represents a huge challenge. Historically, the Canadian state has not been as active a presence in social policy development as have some of its European counterparts. Presently, too, state *in*activity is fostered and confirmed in the dominant policy discourse in Canada. However, even if an active state — with all its contradictions — seems a distant possibility at this moment, it is still important that it be articulated as an alternative way forward that promises greater security and equity in policies affecting old people and those who care for them. Without the articulation of this alternative, unchallenged marketplace imperatives will move us towards greater insecurity and inequity in LTC and in other social policy domains. At stake are not just the pragmatics of funding and organizational arrangements, as the dominant discourse implies, but the very basis of our future social security in Canada.

Notes

Part of the work reported here was supported by the Social Sciences and Humanities Research Council of Canada (Women and Social Change) through a project grant (882-92-0015) and a network grant (816-94-0003).

1. N.L. Chappell, L.A. Strain and A.A. Blandford, *Aging and Health Care: A Social Perspective* (Toronto: Holt, Rinehart and Winston, 1986); P. Manga, "Health Economics and the Current Health Care Cost Crisis," *Health and Canadian Society* 1 (1993).

2. Chappell et al., *Aging and Health Care.*

3. J. Finch and D. Groves, *A Labour of Love: Women, Work and Caring* (London: Routledge and Kegan Paul, 1983); H. Holter (ed.), *Patriarchy in a Welfare Society* (Oslo: Universitisforlaget, 1984); S.M. Neysmith, "Parental Care: Another Female Family Function?" *Canadian Journal of Social Work Education* 7 (1981).

4. H. Brown and H. Smith, "Women Caring for People: The Mismatch Between Rhetoric and Women's Reality?" *Policy and Politics* 21 (1993); L.A. Bergthold, C.L. Estes and A. Villanueva, "Public Light and Private Dark: The Privatization of Home Health Services for the Elderly in the United States," *Home Health Care Services Quarterly* 11 (1990); Economic Council of Canada, *Aging With Limited Resources* (Ottawa: Ministry of Supply and Services, 1986).

5. N.Y. Glaszer, *Women's Paid and Unpaid Labour: The Work Transfer in Health Care and Retailing* (Philadelphia: Temple University Press, 1993), 112.

6. National Advisory Council on Aging, *The NACA Position on Community Services in Health Care for Seniors: Progress and Challenges* (Ottawa: Ministry of Supply and Services, 1995).

7. Ontario Ministry of Health, Ministry of Community and Social Services and Ministry of Citizenship, *Partnerships in Long-Term Care: A New Way to Plan, Manage and Deliver Services and Community Support* (Toronto: Queen's Printer for Ontario, 1993), 7, 15; Manga, "Health Economics," 198.

8. D.J. Cooper and D. Neu, "The Politics of Debt and Deficit in Alberta," in G. Laxer and T. Harrison (eds.), *The Trojan Horse: Alberta and the Future of Canada* (Montreal: Black Rose, 1995); L. McQuaig, *Shooting the Hippo* (Toronto: Viking, 1995).

9. Government of Ontario, *An Act Respecting Long-Term Care* (1994).

10. Bergthold et al., "Public Light," 27.

11. M. Bulmer, *The Social Basis of Community Care* (London: Allen and Unwin, 1987).

12. J. Baldock and C. Ungerson, "Consumer Perceptions of an Emerging Mixed Economy of Care," in A. Evers and I. Svetlik (eds.), *Balancing Pluralism: New Welfare Mixes in Care for the Elderly* (Aldershot: Avebury, 1993); A. Walker, "The Future of Long-Term Care in Canada: A British Perspective," *Canadian Journal on Aging* 14 (1995).

13. J. Aronson, "Giving Consumers a Say in Policy Development: Influencing Policy or Just Being Heard?" *Canadian Public Policy* XIX (1993).

14. R.B. Deber and A.P. Williams, "Policy, Payment and Participation: Long Term Care Reform in Ontario," *Canadian Journal on Aging* 14 (1995).

15. J. Aronson, "Are We Really Listening? Beyond the Official Discourse on Needs of Old People," *Canadian Social Work Review* 9 (1992), 81.

16. Aronson, "Giving Consumers a Say," 371.

17. S. Daatland, "What Are Families For? On Family Solidarity and Preference for Help," *Ageing and Society* 10 (1990).
18. Aronson, "Are We Really Listening?" 77.
19. J. Aronson, "Old Women's Experiences of Needing Care: Choice or Compulsion?" *Canadian Journal on Aging* 9 (1990).
20. H. Graham, "Social Divisions of Caring," *Women's Studies International Forum* 16 (1993); L. Strain and B. Payne, "Social Networks and Patterns of Social Interaction Among Ever-Single and Separated/Divorced Elderly Canadians," *Canadian Journal on Aging* 11 (1992).
21. Aronson, "Are We Really Listening?" 79.
22. Baldock and Ungerson, "Consumer Perceptions," 311.
23. H. Qureshi, "Boundaries Between Formal and Informal Caregiving Work," in C. Ungerson (ed.), *Gender and Caring Work: Work and Welfare in Britain and Scandinavia* (London: Harvester Wheatsheaf, 1990); M.Y. Stricklin, "Home Care Consumers Speak Out on Quality," *Home Healthcare Nurse* 11 (1993).
24. J. Aronson and S. Neysmith, "'You're Not Just in There to Do the Work': Depersonalizing Policies and the Exploitation of Home Care Workers' Labour," *Gender & Society* 10 (1996).
25. R. Phillips, *A Second Look at the Clients in the Community Programs for People with Cognitive Impairments in Metro Toronto (January 1–March 31, 1994).* (Toronto: Toronto Long Term Care Office, Ontario Ministry of Health, 1995).
26. Mae Harman of Canadian Pensioners Concerned, quoted in K. Toughill, "Health Care Cuts Killing Seniors, Group Says," *Toronto Star* (April 20, 1995), A1.
27. Ontario Ministry of Community and Social Services, *Redirection of Long-Term Care and Support Services in Ontario* (Toronto: Queen's Printer for Ontario, 1991), 10.
28. E.K. Abel, *Who Cares for the Elderly? Pubic Policy and the Experiences of Adult Daughters* (Philadelphia: Temple University Press, 1991); C.T. Baines, P.M. Evans and S.M. Neysmith, *Women's Caring: Feminist Perspectives on Social Welfare* (Toronto: McClelland and Stewart, 1991).
29. S.M. Neysmith, "Power in Relationships of Trust: A Feminist Analysis of Elder Abuse," in M. McLean (ed.), *Abuse and Neglect of Older Canadians: Strategies for Change* (Toronto: Thompson Educational Publishing, 1995).
30. N.Y. Glaser, "The Home as Workshop: Women as Amateur Nurses and Medical Care Providers," *Gender & Society* 4 (1990), 479.
31. J. Aronson, "Women's Sense of Responsibility for the Care of Old People: 'But Who Else Is Going to Do It?'" *Gender & Society* 6 (1992), 13.
32. D. Grant, "Bed-Blockers Blamed for Emergency Ward Crunch," *The Globe and Mail* (February 18, 1985), 16.
33. H. Qureshi and A. Walker, *The Caring Relationship: Elderly People and Their Families* (London: MacMillan, 1989); C. Saraceno, "Division of Family Labour and Gender Identity," in A. Showstack Sassoon (ed.), *Women and the State* (London: Unwin Hyman, 1987).
34. C. Ungerson, *Policy Is Personal: Sex, Gender and Informal Care* (London: Tavistock, 1987).

35. D. Gibson and J. Allen, "Parasitism and Phallocentrism in Social Problems of the Aged," *Policy Sciences* 26 (1993).

36. Saraceno, "Division of Family Labour," 199.

37. P. Armstrong, "Closer to Home: More Work for Women," in P. Armstrong, J. Choiniere, G. Feldberg and J. White, *Take Care: Warning Signals for Canada's Health Care System* (Toronto: Garamond, 1994).

38. M. Townson, *Women's Financial Futures: Mid-Life Prospects for a Secure Retirement* (Ottawa: Canadian Advisory Council on the Status of Women, 1995).

39. Aronson, "Women's Sense of Responsibility," 13.

40. B. Bowers, "Family Perceptions of Care in a Nursing Home," in E. Abel and M. Nelson (eds.), *Circles of Care: Work and Identity in Women's Lives* (New York: SUNY Press, 1990); M.T. Duncan and D.L. Morgan, "Sharing the Caring: Family Caregivers' Views of Their Relationships with Nursing Home Staff," *Gerontologist* 34 (1994).

41. Graham, "Social Divisions."

42. N.N. Eustis, R.A. Kane and L.R. Fischer, "Home Care Quality and the Home Care Worker: Beyond Quality Assurance as Usual," *Gerontologist* 33 (1993), 64.

43. R. Kane and A. Caplan, *Ethical Conflicts in the Management of Home Care: The Case Manager's Dilemma* (New York: Springer Publishing, 1993); H. Schmid and Y. Hasenfeld, "Organizational Dilemmas in the Provision of Home Care Services," *Social Service Review* 67 (1993).

44. M. Campbell, "Management as 'Ruling': A Class Phenomenon in Nursing," *Studies in Political Economy* 27 (1988); T. Diamond, *Making Gray Gold: Narratives of Nursing Home Care* (Chicago: University of Chicago Press, 1992); N. James, "Care = Organization + Physical Labour + Emotional Labour," *Sociology of Health and Illness* 14 (1992); L.S. Weintraub, *No Place Like Home: A Discussion Paper About Living and Working in Ontario's Long Term Care Facilities* (Don Mills: Ontario Federation of Labour, 1995); J. White, "Changing Labour Processes and the Nursing Crisis in Canadian Hospitals," *Studies in Political Economy* 40 (1993).

45. Aronson and Neysmith, "'You're Not Just in There'"; S.M. Neysmith and J. Aronson, "Home Care Workers Discuss Their Work: The Skills Required to Use Your 'Common Sense,'" *Journal of Aging Studies* 10 (1996).

46. W. Crown, M. McAdam and E. Sadowsky, *Caring* (April 1992), 34–38; R. Donovan, "'We Care for the Most Important People in Your Life': Home Care Workers in New York City," *Women's Studies Quarterly* 1 (1989); A. Martin Matthews, *Homemakers' Services to the Elderly: Provider Characteristics and Client Benefit, 1989–1992* (Guelph: Gerontology Research Centre, 1992).

47. L.W. Kaye, "Worker Views of the Intensity of Affective Expression During the Delivery of Home Care Services for the Elderly," *Home Health Care Services* 7 (1986); L. Warren, "'We're Home Helps Because We Care': The Experiences of Home Helps Caring for Elderly People," in P. Abbott and G. Payne (eds.), *New Directions in the Sociology of Health* (London: Falmer Press, 1990).

48. M.L. Devault, *Feeding the Family: The Social Organization of Caring as Gendered Work* (Chicago: University of Chicago Press, 1991); A. Kaplan Daniels, "Invisible Work," *Social Problems* 34 (1987).

49. Aronson and Neysmith, "'You're Not Just in There.'"
50. S. Cunnison, "Gender, Consent and Exploitation Among Sheltered Housing Wardens," in K. Purcell, S. Wood, A. Waton and S. Allen (eds.), *The Changing Experience of Employment: Restructuring and Recession* (London: MacMillan, 1986); C. de la Cuesta, "Fringe Work: Peripheral Work in Health Visiting," *Sociology of Health and Illness* 15 (1993).
51. S.M. Neysmith and J. Aronson, "Negotiating Issues of Culture and Race Within the Home," paper presented at the conference of the Canadian Association on Gerontology, Vancouver, 1995.
52. Donovan, "'We Care for the Most Important'"; R. Donovan, P.A. Kurzman and C. Rotman, "Improving the Lives of Home Care Workers," *Social Work* 38 (1993); E. Jones, "The Privatization of Home Care in Manitoba," *Canadian Review of Social Policy* 37 (1996).
53. E.R. Chichin and M.H. Kantor, "The Home Care Industry: Strategies for Survival in an Era of Dwindling Resources," *Journal of Aging and Social Policy* 4 (1992).
54. Qureshi and Walker, *The Caring Relationship*.
55. M. Szebehely, *Vardagens Organisering: Om vardbitraden och gamla i hemtjansten* [The Organization of Everyday Life: On Home Helpers and Elderly People in Sweden] (Lund: Arkiv Forlag, 1995).
56. Bergthold et al., "Public Light"; J. Kelsey, *The New Zealand Experiment: A World Model for Structural Adjustment?* (Auckland: Auckland University Press, 1995); R.J. Owens, "The Peripheral Worker: Women and the Legal Regulation of Outwork," in M. Thornton (ed.), *Public and Private: Feminist Legal Debates* (Melbourne: OUP, 1995).
57. *Cashman and Others v. Central Regional Health Authority*, Employment Court Wellington Registry, WEC3/96, W119/95; Interview, Luci Highfield, Service Workers Union, Wellington, N.Z., March 1996.
58. M. Cohen, *Free Trade and the Future of Women's Work: Manufacturing and Service Industries* (Toronto: Garamond Press, 1987).
59. For discussion of the possibilities of care that enhances the rights of both recipients and workers, see: M. Carpenter, *Normality Is Hard Work: Trade Unions and the Politics of Community Care* (London: Lawrence and Wishart, 1994); L. Sky, *Lean and Mean Health Care: The Creation of the Generic Worker and the Deregulation of Health Care* (Don Mills: Ontario Federation of Labour, 1995).
60. M. Harrington, "What Exactly Is Wrong with the Liberal State as an Agent of Change?" in V. Spike Peterson (ed.), *Gendered States: Feminist (Re)visions of International Relations Theory* (Boulder and London: Lynne Reinner Publishers, 1992).
61. S. Daatland, "Recent Trends and Future Prospects for the Elderly in Scandinavia," *Journal of Aging and Social Policy* 6 (1994); B. Siim, "Toward a Feminist Rethinking of the Welfare State," in K. Jones and A. Jonasdottor (eds.), *The Political Interests of Gender: Developing Theory and Research with a Feminist Face* (London: Sage, 1988).
62. S.M. Neysmith, "Toward a Woman Friendly Long-Term Care Policy," in P. Evans and G. Wekerle (eds.), *Women and the Canadian Welfare State: Challenges and Change* (Toronto: University of Toronto Press, 1997).

63. N. Fraser, *Unruly Practices: Power, Discourse and Gender in Contemporary Social Theory* (Minneapolis: University of Minnesota Press, 1989).

64. A. Evers, "The Welfare Mix Approach: Understanding the Pluralism of Welfare Systems," in A. Evers and I. Svetlik (eds.), *Balancing Pluralism: New Welfare Mixes in Care for the Elderly* (Aldershot: Avebury, 1993).

65. Harrington, "What Exactly Is Wrong," 77.

Part Two

Flexible Workforces and the Class-Gender Nexus

Wallace Clement

MUCH OF THE FEMINIST CRITIQUE OF THE 1970S AND THE EARLY 1980S focused on "gender blindness" and "missing the domestic." An important breakthrough, however, came in the mid-1980s. As expressed by Suzanne Mackenzie, "socialist-feminist analysis focuses not primarily on production, not primarily on reproduction, but on the relations between the two. The nature of this intersection is seen to define gender relations."[1]

In *Relations of Ruling: Class and Gender in Postindustrial Societies*, John Myles and I argued that "there is more to production relations than class relations, that relations of ruling in the market not only develop to organize relations between capital and labour but also between men and women."[2] We took a macrocomparative approach to the class-gender nexus. This was located in the rise of a working class characterized as "the postindustrial, female service worker." Postindustrial work had become a crucial site for struggles about gender relations.[3] Much of our analysis focused on the complex, bidirectional relationship between domestic and paid labour. Our study could not address the links between structures and practices with anything like the specificity possible in case studies. In this section we have three Canadian case studies of the class-gender nexus that were published in *SPE* between 1993 and 1999, focusing on the practice of flexible workers.

In an uneven way, earlier issues of *SPE* had included some key works marking phases of feminism, as Leah Vosko's rich conclusion to this collection documents. Meg Luxton's justifiably renowned ethnography,

117

More Than a Labour of Love: Three Generations of Women's Work in the Home,[4] set in the mining community of Flin Flon, Manitoba in 1976–1977, was updated to 1981 for *SPE* 12 (Fall 1983). The piece, "Two Hands for the Clock: Changing Patterns in the Gendered Division of Labour," was much more than an update. Through it Luxton introduced a key nuance into the primarily theoretical and methodological discussion that had been published at the same time by the same press as her case study, under the editorship of Bonnie Fox, *Hidden in the Household: Women's Domestic Labour Under Capitalism*.[5] Returning to "her" community a few years later, Luxton found many more women in the paid work they had been excluded from earlier. She observed, however, that "when married women get paying jobs they continue to do most of the domestic labour." Many of the women now worked outside the home, yet they still performed most of the housework. Men retained "breadwinner power" because they earned more than their wives. Moreover, the men who started doing domestic labour upset the control women had over domestic labour. Luxton captured the complexity and emotional disruption cause domestically by these changing material conditions.

Luxton's piece went beyond "gender-blindness" and "missing the domestic" and into the complexities and paradoxes of women's paid and unpaid work. Getting women into the labour force did not destroy the unequal division of domestic labour, but it did disrupt it. The extent that men were drawn into aspects of domestic labour was itself problematic because this had been staked as "women's domain" of control. Luxton understood this as an economic, political and personal matter, upsetting the culture women had created to delimit their sphere. Moreover, the economic authority gained by having their own jobs did not measure up to the economic power of the male "breadwinner." Instead they acquired double burdens and no empowerment. Substantial changes were still required in both the paid and unpaid spheres. The transitions were to be at times painful in terms of relationships and identities for these working-class women.

Parenthetically, it is of interest to read Sedef Arat-Koc's "In the Privacy of Our Own Home: Foreign Domestic Workers as Solution to the Crisis in the Domestic Sphere in Canada" in *SPE* 28. Middle- and upper-class women have addressed some of their domestic demands regarding child care and housework by hiring offshore help. Arat-Koc's article addresses the articulation of gender, class and citizenship. This reinforces the theme that middle- and upper-class women have generally benefited by increased female labour force participation and postindustrial work, but working-class women have become more disadvantaged. Also see Pamela Moss's "Spatially Differentiated Concepts of Gender in the Workplace" in *SPE* 43 (and in this volume) for an account of housekeeping by firms.

Luxton's article in *SPE* did not stand entirely alone on the topic of women and work. Notable was Alicja Muszynski on fishery shore workers in British Columbia where women, especially Native women, are demonstrated to be important for class consciousness in B.C. unions (*SPE* 20). Carla Lipsig-Mummé explored garment workers through homework and unions in Montreal (*SPE* 22). Rosemary Warskett published a case study of bank workers and unionization, emphasizing legal impediments and the contradictions of liberal laws (*SPE* 25). She also had an article on unequal pay that shifted discussion beyond gender discrimination to include the place of skill hierarchies in class analysis (*SPE* 32).

What distinguishes the three articles selected for this section and links them to Luxton's early observation is the connection between home and work producing relations of ruling for class and gender. Each is a case study in how "women's work" is produced and what characteristics it has, including its class content. Also remarkable is how they are about resistance in various forms — how nurses refuse to work longer hours and full careers under the conditions of work intensification; how changes in women's employment in the form of homework occurs; and how dissatisfaction results with the restructuring of clerical work.

Jerry White examines changes in Canadian nursing, a traditional female job. With the dramatic restructuring of state services, especially health care delivery, this means an intensification of the labour process for nurses and flexible work for managers. It has also produced new forms of working class militancy as strategic responses to these changes. White identifies the paradox of a shortage of nursing labour, not a shortage of nurses. The question is why do nurses refuse to work? He contends it is the intensification of the labour process that poses a barrier to the quality of their work experience and patient care. The barrier is nurses' subordination to the decision making of doctors as a profession and, more recently, hospital management under conditions of restructuring.

Central to the account is the place of gender and class in nurses' struggles. It includes nurses' "place" in hospital decision-making authority about the type and delivery of care linked to their identity as care providers and hospitals as places of care provision. This is part of the explanation for shortages. Trained nurses are leaving. Many cut back to part-time hours and for many others this is a prelude to resignation from the profession. Strikes have also become much more prevalent across the country. These strikes have in common a concern about the quality of health care and, embedded in that, the quality of nurses' labour process and the care they can deliver. Also embedded in the nursing experience are what White calls the "home/work interfaces." Women do not have the same domestic supports and priorities as men. This is especially prevalent in nursing where issues of scheduling for shift work, child care, elder care and husband care are compounded by the increased stress from job-derived work intensification.

The synergy of class and gender in the context of workplace restructuring goes a long way to offering a rich explanation of so-called nursing shortages and the rise of nursing militancy. To address the "causes" will require revamping hospital administrations and management practices, addressing relationships between doctors and nurses and changing how nursing work is valued. Flexible work must prioritize the lives of workers themselves and value their commitment to patient care. Nurses will gain "breadwinner power" only when their incomes match those of men and their careers can be given equal priority to their husbands'. Moreover, a more equitable allocation of child, elder and family obligations is a prerequisite for workplace empowerment. This may involve changes in men's behaviour at home or a socialization of these responsibilities through adequate child care facilities, eldercare services and/or greater commodification of domestic responsibilities.

It is ironic that in the midst of Canada's postindustrial heartland that substantial numbers of women are working outside formal employment and located in their homes in ways reminiscent of preindustrial work. Suzanne Mackenzie's study of homework illustrates its prevalence and diversity in Canada, especially the number of "craft workers" who service members of their local community.[6] Women who work from home sewing for each other offer a contrast with those who sew from home for multinational corporations.

Wenona Giles and Valerie Preston contend that two processes characterize a major segment of women's flexible work today: informalization and domestication. These twin processes are the paradox of postindustrialism. In contrast to the new managerial and professional frontiers for women is the downside of the polarization of women's workforce in the form of contingent workers. They are the fallout of the decline of factory work and the rise of homework as a "survival strategy." The domestication of paid work is the greatest for marginal members of the labour force, namely immigrant working-class women with weak English skills. Using Toronto as a case study, they demonstrate that immigrant women are far from homogeneous in their experiences. Informalization and domestication doubles the invisibility of women workers, especially in the garment industry where most are Chinese without knowledge of English and who work from home. These homeworkers are nominally self-employed, but seek recognition as de facto employees in order to organize themselves.

The social isolation of homeworkers, more than their domestic obligations, keeps them working in the home. It is the absence of alternatives rather than the demands of households that keep them working up to fifteen hours a day. Chinese husbands often control the decision to do homework, while Portuguese women seem more autonomous in household matters. Portuguese husbands are also reported to be more involved in domestic work like meal preparation and child-rearing, while Chinese men are not supportive. The type of activities matters for the experience of homeworkers. Service work in the form of child care, housekeeping, cleaning and typing, which is more frequently done by Portuguese women, is a more satisfying experience than industrial work, mainly garments, done by Chinese women who express a preference for factory work.

Types of cultural practices, especially the relationships between men and women, strongly influence the experience of women engaged in paid work in the home. Once again, however, the nature of domestic sharing is a critical factor in the labour process of women who work from their homes. Portuguese women, who seem to have somewhat greater language skills and may have been in Canada longer, have been more effective in utilizing the benefits of flexibility. For the Chinese women, however, their work at home is because of the absence of alternatives and a part of their patriarchal household structure. The formalization of factory work would give them greater access to alternatives and, potentially, representation. It would certainly make their condition more visible and subject to elementary forms of regulation. Unfortunately, we learn very little about the work of these women's husbands and their class experiences. Nor do we really know much about the extended families of these women and whether they are available to cover domestic responsibilities in the event they had factory work available. Do they live in single or extended family houses? Clearly households are the appropriate unit of class and gender analysis, not individuals.

Bonnie Fox and Pamela Sugiman report on another form of flexibility and restructuring, this time in a core postindustrial sector — telecommunications. They investigate the introduction of a highly computerized billing system and the application of the most "advanced" human resource management system in a Toronto office. They identify several contradictory outcomes for the "new office." The new system introduces "teamwork" and the rise of contingent workers in the form of part-time and temporary workers.

One of the contradictions is the recruitment of more men into clerical work traditionally performed by women. The characteristics of the work as a whole, however, are more typical of women's work. There has been a "levelling down" of the work. In addition to the older staff of established women, there have been younger recruits who are more diverse ethnically, especially people of colour, and more men. Contradictions are rampant: the new equipment, designed to improve routine work, also increases surveillance and allows the introduction of quotas. At the same time, the health of workers is deteriorating. Tensions include promoting teamwork and individual responsibility; homogeneous job classifications yet varied skill and responsibility requirements; a mixing of temporary and permanent workers. Using national-level data, Marjorie Griffin Cohen has some similar findings about recent-entrant women that are not optimistic about the equality effects of restructuring. She concludes that "The restructuring that is occurring will inhibit the possibilities for equality between men and women, and is likely to increase disparities between classes of women."[7]

Postindustrial work, as exhibited in this advanced telecommunications company, has had gender effects. It has begun to break through traditional occupational segregation, but has done so in the least progressive way. High technology and modern management systems do not necessarily lead to effective work patterns or to productive work relations. The strongest rift currently introduced within this newly created labour force is across generations: young people of both sexes and people of colour are congregated into dead-end, low-paying contingent jobs in the name of flexibility and service. We learn very little about the home lives of these workers. Clearly the contingent workers do not earn a "living wage" and must work several jobs, continue to live with their parents or live in poverty. They have little prospect of a career or gaining meaningful experience through this most modern postindustrial workplace.

Flexible for whom is a question that needs to be asked of all these cases. For a state system striving to reduce health services, for clothing manufacturers seeking to compete with Third World labour and for core postindustrial firms cutting their wage bill, "productive" does not mean productive for healthy, well-rounded individual workers and households. It does not even mean productive in terms of the work produced.

"Productive" has become equated with cheaper, not with quality and value. The key socialist-feminist analysis insight into the multifaceted nexus between class and gender as expressed by the link between the formal and informal economies, paid and unpaid work and the labour force and household remains germane under postindustrial capitalism.

Notes

1. Suzanne Mackenzie, "Women's Responses to Economic Restructuring: Changing Gender, Changing Space," in Roberta Hamilton and Michèle Barrett (eds.), *The Politics of Diversity: Feminism, Marxism and Nationalism* (Montreal: The Book Center, 1986), 84. For an important intervention building towards a feminist political economy in Canada, see Heather Jon Maroney and Meg Luxton, "From Feminism and Political Economy to Feminist Political Economy," in their edited collection *Feminism and Political Economy: Women's Work, Women's Struggles* (Toronto: Methuen, 1987). Their views were extended in "Gender at Work: Canadian Feminist Political Economy since 1988" in Wallace Clement (ed.), *Understanding Canada: Building on the New Canadian Political Economy* (Montreal: McGill-Queen's University Press, 1997).
2. Wallace Clement and John Myles, *Relations of Ruling: Class and Gender in Postindustrial Societies* (Montreal: McGill-Queen's University Press, 1994), ix.
3. Ibid., 243, 249.
4. Meg Luxton, *More Than a Labour of Love: Three Generations of Women's Work in the Home* (Toronto: Women's Press, 1980).
5. Bonnie Fox (ed.), *Hidden in the Household: Women's Domestic Labour Under Capitalism* (Toronto: Women's Press, 1980).
6. Mackenzie, "Women's Responses to Economic Restructuring," 89ff.
7. Marjorie Griffin Cohen, "The Implications of Economic Restructuring for Women: The Canadian Situation," in Isabella Bakker (ed.), *The Strategic Silence: Gender and Economic Policy* (London: Zed Books, 1994), 103.

Chapter Four

Changing Labour Process and the Nursing Crisis in Canadian Hospitals

Jerry White

Introduction

Few issues have sparked such multidisciplinary interest as the crisis in nursing. Health care is seen as a social good in Canada, and we have come to expect a high-quality, low consumer cost service. Today, such a service is threatened and a number of fingers point to a shortage of nurses as the cause.

Nurses in our hospitals are leaving the profession, opting for part-time arrangements, and/or going on strike. We have beds closing down, delays in operations, and reports of increasing work-related stress in hospitals. The variety of explanations for this situation have added to our understanding of women (the nursing profession is 98.6 per cent female) and the organization of work. However, the principal shortcoming of the leading sociological and political economy explanations lies in the fact that they tend to downplay the role of gender and worker resistance in the context of labour process change.

This paper attempts to address this problem by drawing on these multidisciplinary debates and using an interview and survey-based study[1] to uncover the relationship between gender, class, labour process and militancy. I argue that nurses are no longer playing a passive and subservient role. Nurses individually and collectively have been awakened to resistance by a fundamental change in their labour process. There is a serious and growing divergence between how nurses want to do the job — how they feel the care should be delivered

— and how the hospital, management and government see nursing delivered under the present conditions. In order to understand the crisis, we have to grasp the roots of this divergence and contradiction. Nurses want to provide a different kind of care in the hospital, but cannot. Denied more say in how the work is organized, they are instead encouraged to adapt to the new environment.

How gender plays itself out through the understandings, desires and expectations that women bring to the job is one focus of this paper. As a result of their own understandings and expectations, nurses want to keep the level and quality of care high. Their job satisfaction is dependent upon it. This has created and fanned resistance among them. The current crisis is the result and manifestation of the resistance of nurses to the changing labour process, changes brought on by a fiscal crisis of the state.

The argument begins with a brief discussion of the mainstream explanation given for the crisis in nursing — that there is a shortage of nurses. The concepts used in constructing a less reductionist model for interpreting the current crisis in hospital nursing are then discussed. This included a model for understanding labour process across its multiple dimensions of space, time and form, incorporating the role of gender as well as an analytical discussion of resistance. In light of the data gathered in the study, I then argue that the crisis is best understood in terms of resistance to managerial initiatives aimed at cost-cutting. The three forms of resistance identified are: the strike; an outright resignation from activity in the profession; and the move to part-time work. Given that non-labour process and non-class/ gender models place the onus for the current situation on supply-and-demand relationships (which can be corrected with financial incentives), a follow-up survey that indicates monetary issues are not in fact driving the current staffing problems is very briefly discussed. The final section of the paper draws together conclusions based upon the theoretical discussions regarding gender, labour process, class and control.

A Shortage of Nurses?

We know there is a problem recruiting and retaining nurses. This has led some analysts to claim we have a simple supply-and-demand problem,[2] yet the evidence indicates that there is no absolute shortage of nurses. While there are no increases in people entering the profession, there is a very large pool of trained nurses who have left full-time nursing. In a very real sense we can say that, while at the micro level of the hospital there is unfilled demand based on management-defined needs, there are nurses in the wider labour market capable of filling the demand. They have simply chosen not to work.

TABLE 4.1
Nurses in Ontario 1983–1987

Year	Total	Employed	New	Other*
1983	100,091	68,284	2,801	29,006
1984	100,171	70,411	2,962	26,798
1985	101,704	73,677	3,985	24,042
1986	103,517	75,935	3,005	24,577
1987	105,356	78,735	3,039	23,582

* This includes those who were voluntarily unemployed and a small number who have left the jurisdiction.

Source: *College of Nurses of Ontario, Registration Data.*

The province with the greatest reported "shortages" — Ontario — has a residual group of voluntarily unemployed nurses approaching 30 per cent of the total nursing population. Reports vary on the extent of the actual shortfall in the hospitals; however, Ministry of Health officials report in an interview that as of mid-1988, Ontario was experiencing a shortage of 1,143 nurses.[3] Table 4.1 indicates that it is not a supply side problem in the traditional sense. Nurses are choosing not to work.[4] The number of nurses who have withdrawn from the profession far outweighs demand.

Before we leave the general area of labour market explanations, it is important to at least raise the issue of flexibility.[5] The move towards the use of more flexible labour is helpful in explaining several hospital management actions over the past years, such as the substitution of registered nurses (RNs) for RNAs (registered nursing assistants).[6] While this move does affect the demand side, and does exacerbate the apparent shortage of nurses, it could not cause the shortage, nor could it cause the crisis. The move to flexible labour in the hospital is a fragment of the mosaic of management strategies aimed at cost reduction. This certainly is a contributor in the current crisis, but it is not the primary cause.

To summarize, there is no shortage of nurses, but for a variety of reasons, which are explored later, many refuse to work. In order to explain this we must develop some new tools or at least reshape some of the ones we have at our disposal. The labour market paradigm does explain certain aspects of unsupplied demand, which can account in part for the difficulties that hospitals have retaining full-time nurses. However, the question is not how to deal with the "shortage" of nurses in the sense that the neoclassical economist would see it. To uncover the reasons why so many trained nurses choose not to work requires an examination of the changing work process in the hospitals, and the introduction of the concepts of resistance and gender in the context of a revamped labour process analysis.

Labour Process Theory and Practice

When we speak of labour process we refer to a dynamic mechanism that has many facets. The labour process consists of purposive human activity, or labour itself, that, with the help of the instruments of labour including both tools and methods of work, brings about changes in the object of the work. Central to the understanding of labour process is the recognition that in the course of work we realize part of our own purpose. We not only change the object of the work but ourselves as well. If work is unpleasant, unchallenging or however different from the wishes and expectations we have, then there will be reduced achievement, growth, satisfaction and fulfillment based on our understood abilities.[7] As Corrigan comments, "production is both a material and social process, an activity whereby people transform both their circumstances and themselves. Each of its facets, in Marx's view, conditions and constrains the other."[8]

The work that people carry out in a labour process is purposive, conscious and conceptual. This allows several things: workers form relationships at the social level that include values, intimacy and a workplace culture; people who associate share values, norms and knowledge; and people develop a portion of their self-identity through the process of work. These aspects are conditioned by several factors. Firstly, there are the expectations, ideas and understandings that people bring with them into the job. Secondly, the process itself conditions attitudes and self-identity. Thirdly, forces outside of the workplace — structural influences such as the business cycle or state policy — condition the entire process.

Changes in the labour process will alter the organization, social interactions and the actors themselves. It is in the labour process where we find the nexus of structure and human agency, where resistance conditioned by gender and class is promulgated. This implies that if there are labour process changes in the hospital, then there will be a change in the nurses themselves in both their attitudes and their relationship to work.

A Model for Evaluating Labour Process Change

Working with labour process change as an explanatory concept requires that we be more specific regarding its constituent dimensions. First, there is the "time" within which work is done. That is, as we use our physical and mental skills, along with tools, to carry out tasks within the context of certain power relations (control relations/social relations of production), there is an explicit expectation regarding what is often called "work intensity." This is the amount and the pace of work to be done in a certain period. This is one plane along the "time" dimension.

The second dimension is the scope and content of the tasks associated with the particular labour process. This has two planes. One is the "completeness of the task," or the integrity of the task, and includes the technical division of labour and Braverman's idea of the processes of deskilling. The second plane constitutes the definition and boundaries of the total job and involves the conception of the occupation. The two planes affect each other where the realization of the concept of productive job (what the worker imagines or conceives the job to be) and the integrity of the job vis-à-vis division of labour, meet. We can imagine a job being broken down so finely by the technical division of labour that the worker no longer views it as the job he or she trained for.

The third dimension relates to the interaction of tools and people through "space" (which can be understood also as place). This is the configuration of the worker and the tools at his or her disposal. Integral to this configuration is where the work is done.

The implication of this model of labour process is that if there are labour process changes in the hospital, then there will be a change in the nurses' attitudes and their relationship to work. Based on some preliminary qualitative data, it appears that nurses have increasingly found the changes in the labour process intolerable.

Changes in the Hospital Labour Process

This explanation of the crisis in nursing depends on interpreting the responses of nurses to changes in their work in the hospital. The key areas in which changes occurred included: the tasks themselves; how the nurses approached the tasks; the condition of the patients (greater acuity); the satisfaction gained in caring for people who were recuperating; the speed of the work; the charting; the work scheduling; the "changing tools" (i.e., technology); the changing mix of skills in the work team, etc. If we look at these features of changing labour process in the context of our model of time, place and content, an interesting view of the complex of factors motivating the resistance of the nurses emerges.

Changes in the Time of Work

Changes in "intensification" have taken many forms. The shorter stay of patients, referred to as "turnaround time," has meant that each of the patients is at greater "acuity," and the range and number of interventions is increased. The changes in acuity have been extreme. Fifteen years ago one-third of the patients might have been severely ill; today that number is closer to 90 per cent.[9] Patients are sent home to recuperate, with the result that the satisfaction nurses experienced in the process of caring for recuperating patients has been diminished. At the same time there are fewer nurses employed for the patient load, which puts a greater burden on those working, forces a quicker movement through the tasks that can be done, and leaves more tasks undone. The mix of RNs and RNAs has been altered, with fewer RNAs to take up aspects of the work. The final change in intensification has been in the monitoring of "productivity," with computers used to keep track of the procedures done and the time it takes to execute them. This creates a "for productivity" rather than a "for care" orientation, a step the nurses have found totally unsatisfactory.

Changes in the Scope and Content of Jobs

The second dimension discussed in the labour process is the "scope and content" of the tasks performed, or what we might refer to as "job" characteristics. These have changed a great deal. The work of Marie Campbell indicates that nurses are caught in a system where organizational changes in nursing management have pushed them to become part of a government restraint program.[10] Through technologies and practices involving workload measurement and control, nurses monitor their own work and thus implement "textually mediated nursing management practices."[11] This mediated management practice is a documentary process that classifies patient needs into levels and assigns standard care required by level, thereby eliminating professional judgment and establishing cost-efficiency as the criteria for decisions about patient care. Efficiencies can be monitored through computerized charting of tasks performed, and controlled through pre-set budgets. Accordingly, nurses must give what looks like good care on paper and find ways to cope with cuts in funds.[12]

The introduction of patient classification systems threatens the nurses' labour process in a number of ways. There are several "kinds" of systems, yet they are all basically categorical systems that allot labour based on some projection of the amount of care that the patient will need. One system has each patient assessed for the amount of care, meds, baths, counselling, feeding, etc., that he or she might need. Each patient is then assigned a value, which, when added to other values, gives the head nurse the total number of nurses necessary for that shift. Another system classified patients according to sickness and known complications. This classification allows certain treatments (actually laying out procedures and times) and a set number of hours/minutes for bedside care. These systems displace the nurse's working skill, understanding and knowledge of the patient. The systems also force nurses to avoid certain procedures that they feel are important because they have not been designated. For instance, consoling and other family interactions are not recognized in the categorical systems.

Growe writes: "The standardized formula may not be providing a scientific basis for what is *actually* needed as much as a hospital's expected level of production."[13] The best way to describe nursing and the quest for efficiency today is the art of "giving fewer and fewer services to more and more patients faster and faster."[14] With the demand for nurses to prioritize time, combined with the push for charting, we see a real shift in the work. As we will see below, this work change is not well received.

The intensification of work also has direct effects on work content. Nurses in Goldfarb's study indicate that intensification and new monitoring practices mean "no time for patients."[15] The new technologies, which are part of the patient classification, and machine-generated "care" plans contribute to a change in what the nurse does. Particularly important is the reduction in the skilled judgments that nurses were trained to carry out. This is exacerbated by a changing division of labour, in which nurses may be given a part of a total nursing care job to do on a repetitive basis. For example, a nurse might be given the task of giving everyone a bath, and not get to participate in or learn about the total care of any single patient. This is reminiscent of Taylorism's deskilling and technical division of labour.

Other fiscally driven labour process changes not already mentioned include such things as reductions in the number of housekeepers available for dealing with emergency spills, so that nurses must add this job to their work schedules. As well, the cuts in chronic care funding and building over the last few years mean that often one-third, and sometimes as many as one-half, of the patients in a work area are waiting for chronic care beds to open up. Nurses have generally been trained for acute work and the necessity of nursing chronic patients represents an aberration in the labour process for many.

Changes in the Location of Work: Working Space
The third dimension, which we called "space or place," has also changed. Nurses often find themselves rotated between several work settings. This contributes to stress because they do not know the patients. They are not aware of the peculiarities of the ward they are on — for example, where machines and supplies are stored, or what supplies exist.

All these changes contribute to a contradiction that develops at the level of the individual and the collective, and changes the content of work, moving it away from what nurses find acceptable within their framework of understanding. There were strong indications of this in the initial investigation and the results of the more thorough study reported below corroborate the hypothesis that this contradiction has led to resistance.

While this discussion does not exhaust the changes in labour process, it does give a clearer view of the basic changes that have caused a high level of resistance. We must remember that nurses experience changes in their labour process as a profound alteration in their professed identities and their personal and collective notions of the meaning of nursing. Adam, who puts forward a notion of system conception of nursing that is congruent with nurses' own conception, argues that nurses are worried that new systems, which move towards treating diagnoses and away from treating the patient in a holistic way, will move nursing away from its former system conception to a new one. She also places the personal conception within the same bounds as this study, i.e., "seeking to put the patient in the best position for recovery."[16]

Warburton and Carroll also examine the changing nature of work in hospitals as a source of stress and frustration, attempting to explain how class and gender relations provide the broad framework in which contemporary problems can be understood.[17] They situate nurses' work in the context of class relations, in which nurses are dominated by the medical profession and, more recently, by management. The major implication of the nurses' status as female, employed workers has been their incorporation into hospital settings in subordinate and passive roles under male supervisors.[18] While important, the problem here is that the effects of gender are reduced to the subordination of women to men, and the continued domestic labour responsibilities that must be shouldered by female nurses. In this framework, nurses are seen mainly in a class perspective as producers or reproducers of labour power because of their "repair" function. This is not the primary manifestation of gender. We turn now to a more complete examination of gender as a factor in the nursing crisis.

Gender and the Nursing Crisis

Gender is crucial to an understanding of the current crisis in nursing, not only because nursing is overwhelmingly female, but because it is linked back to the very essence of human interaction at work. It weaves its influence through the entire problem in a myriad of ways. Just as "class" in E.P. Thompson's work is the sound and feeling — the experience, not just the category — so it is that gender is a structural prism through which the specificities of the problem at hand should be understood. There are three ways in which the role of gender is understood in this study. The first two are the observable and interactive dimensions, and the third is best understood as a more internalized dimension.

The gender effects that emerge from the qualitative data operate on both the observable and internalized dimensions. The *observable* are often power relationships between women and men such as the following. First, there is women's subjugation to men. Doctors and administrators are often male. When nurses seek access to the loci of power in their work world, they necessarily confront gendered relations. The subjugation thus influences the demand for increasing professional standards. The Canadian Nurses Association sees improved credentials as increasing their bargaining power in the highly "human capital"-conscious hospital setting.

Second, there is the home/work interface. The vast majority of nurses are women, approximately 98 per cent in most jurisdictions.[19] In seeking to gain control over their lives, they must try to facilitate socially imposed family roles. However, women lack the social supports that men have (i.e., wives), and therefore have difficulty doing this.[20] This process creates a contradiction over time and scheduling. Goldfarb corroborates this when he reports that "shift work, family responsibilities and lack of accommodation for mothers" are three problems reported by nurses.[21]

An examination of the *internalized* dimension involves trying to understand the connection between the worker and pride in work. Women's attachment to nursing (which we would argue is a gender-mediated attachment) is broken as they are forced to carry out their work in ways that are not commensurate with their understanding of what is necessary. In a previous study, female hospital workers reported that they were very tied to patient contact and caregiving functions. When the process of work changes and, as in this case, the bond with caregiving is broken, the intrinsic rewards are diminished. This causes a reaction because the women have come to the workplace with a notion of what they feel they should be doing there. This breeds resistance to the change.[22]

In order to adequately begin to move the analysis forward, it is necessary that all three of the dimensions related to gender be understood and that the third — the conceptions of work or the connection between women and the nursing care they provide — be seen as primary. This is the interaction that is closest to, and indeed intertwined with, the labour process. We want to look at the effects of a changing labour process, while accepting that the whole process is mediated by gender.

When we speak of problems related to a change in the labour process, we are referring to problems involving how work is done, its speed, content, form, intensity, etc. As noted above, when people engage in a process of labour, they form social relations and develop an identity. This is conditioned by the expectations they bring to the job, as well as their ideas and understandings. One of the key activities through which these understandings and expectations are developed is work.[23] Our identity is partially forged as we develop our social relations at work and engage in an established labour process.[24] These relations are mediated by, and associated with, the expectations and understandings we bring to work. Gender affects expectations and understandings, influences the relationships, and conditions the interaction between the work and the worker — the act and the actor.

Gender influences (conditions) what we want from our work and our perception of how to do it. Warburton and Carroll contribute to our understanding of this process when they focus on the external interactions that shape the relationship of workplace change and gender.[25] In this paper, the focus is on the more complex form of interaction between nurse as female and worker and the strategies of change that are transforming work. Warburton and Carroll make one other contribution. They argue that as nurses resist proletarianization and link their working conditions in the hospitals with a fight for improved health care, they *will* contribute to a wider labour agenda. Further, Warburton and Carroll indicate that nurses, as members of a feminized semiprofession, *could* play a role "challenging ... notions of women's place ... [and] attacking the sexual division of labour on both the industrial and home fronts."[26] There are two problems with this view. First, it looks at present-day nurses in the context of *future* resistance. Second, it creates some ambiguity in the class analysis by linking the fight in "defense of professionalism in opposition to proletarianization" with the defence of health care and problems in working conditions. These are both seen to make *potential* contributions on the class front. The difficulty here is that the professionalization issue and proposals to make the baccalaureate the minimum qualification for all nurses should not be seen as part of the more active class response.

Warburton and Carroll introduce the idea of resistance in a limited way, characterizing it as motivated largely by economic self-interest and never concretizing it. This inadvertently leaves us with nurses accepting a role in their own subordination, and then demanding compensation for the responsibility. Their resistance is, however, a more complex phenomenon that has much more to do with the current crisis than the analysis of Warburton and Carroll would suggest.

Resistance and the Nursing Crisis

What is resistance? In the simplest sense, the term describes an action (or actions) aimed at either passively or actively slowing, reversing, avoiding or protesting management directions or control strategies in the workplace. Opposing actions may arise from structurally induced change in the organization and a wider process of work, and may arise in part from the individual or agency level. This paper attempts to look at both the structural elements and the agency involved in these forms of behaviours.

Resistance can best be understood in the context of control and in opposition to consent. The coordination of work, or what Edwards refers to as the control of others' labour through the exercise of authority, evokes a response from workers that may be represented along a continuum such as the one pictured below.[27]

Response to control system

more
consent
(compliance)

⟵————————————————————⟶

more
resistance

The linear perspective, however, obscures the fact that the two states (consent and resistance) overlap much in the way Venn diagrams do. There is both consent/compliance and resistance in every situation (with the possible exception of strikes and lockouts where consent is formally abrogated). The nature, form, elements or outcomes of these responses depend on the control systems in place, and the understandings and attitudes (not to mention the strength of the class forces) in the workplace.

The resistance recorded in this investigation is simply a response to the managerial exercise of control of the labour process, a control that negates the more creative side of nursing work. The consent, which Badgely, Brown and Ehrenreich all argue is so astounding among women service workers in general, and nurses in particular, is replaced by resistance,[28] a resistance that is both passive and active.

Resistance need not be the stuff of Gurr's rebellions or Moore's injustice.[29] Actions can arise on any scale, from workplaces to entire nations. Theoretically, any workplace relation is temporary, and represents a combination of resistance and consent. Therefore it can and does change. When faced with change in managerial strategy, the workers sometimes adjust (i.e., re-establish) their consensual relations, sometimes are coerced into consent, and sometimes dramatically resist.

Resistance and consent are often seen as opposites, but they share some common points, particularly their origin (or source). Consent, which Thompson calls compliance,[30] and resistance are constructed historically and socially by the material interaction and assessment of the actors in the workplace labour process. Their interactions take place over time and are conditioned by both an individual and collective perception of possible gains or losses. Resistance and consent are then both linked to the same historical process that develops a worker's identity. Willmott reaffirms the notion that a link exists between a worker's general identity and resistance.[31]

Some approaches to the problem of understanding resistance focus on workers' "imagination" of their work: workers "conceptualize the labour as an object" based on concrete experiences prior to the labour. The activity of the work itself forces the worker to confront the difference between the ideal or the imagined, and reality. Changes are then made in the "imagined" so that it corresponds with the reality, and a new set of guiding intentions is created.[32] What happens if workers cannot adjust their perception of the work to the reality of a new set of conditions? It is here, I would argue, that the relationship between consent and resistance alters, and resistance increases. This is the process in which nurses are currently embroiled.

This analysis is informed by a wide set of contributions to the field. Braverman's initial contribution has generated an incredible amount of thought and comment.[33] Important criticisms have been levelled at Braverman's work because he underrated the resistance of the worker in the workplace, both as an individual actor as well as a member of a class.[34] He saw scientific management as the key and central control mechanism in advanced capitalism. A number of theorists, such as Friedman, Edwards and Burawoy, maintain that the scientific management revolution did not, in fact, have an enormous long-term impact.[35] It was too rigid and ran in contradiction to the aspirations of workers to participate creatively in their work.[36] Friedman argued that capital had to develop ways of dealing with this contradiction in the labour process. He proposed that management should attempt to create a "responsible autonomy" in which workers would be encouraged to identify with the aims of management, particularly the necessity of competitiveness, and would thereafter act responsibly with a minimum of supervision.[37] Thus, the accommodation struck in the workplace would vary according to the level of pressure the workers could exert through their resistance to management tactics.

Edwards developed a typology of evolving forms of control from simple to technical through to bureaucratic.[38] The transition of these forms is precipitated by resistance to the control system that is in place. For example, the simple control structure depended on the direct influence of the owner — a form of personal pressure. As the workplaces grew, this became untenable and resistance forced experimentation and development of alternatives. Are we in a period in which the managements of hospitals are seeking new forms of control aimed at finding a new point of accommodation with the workers? This does not seem to be the case.

Burawoy also sees the movement towards gaining consent as central to control, although his "game playing" and "making out" theory does take a different direction.[39] Workers are somewhat atomized and seek to relieve boredom, pass time, reduce fatigue, etc., by setting up systems and games in the workplace. This, Burawoy argues, is a form of integration that reduces resistance. In this study, we find that nurses enjoy their work and are stimulated by it. Perhaps if they were able to forgo such attachment, we would see little if any resistance, but this is not the case.

While these past studies of resistance do inform the present study, there are real differences. For example, the hospital is a service setting, a caregiving setting, with a female-dominated workforce. Most previous studies were conducted in commodity-producing, male-dominated settings. Resistance in this setting is not diminishing, but rather increasing. Moreover, nurses have been described as very committed, "what the private sector manager would hope for" in terms of their integration of purpose. The following sections illustrate that the new labour processes in the hospitals are being subjected to collective, albeit fractured, responses — forms of resistance that can be derived from the particularity of the labour process as it intersects with gender and class. Women bring their gender-specific expectations to the workplace and have a conception of what they want over and above the wages from work. When a change in the labour process challenges these expectations, there is reaction and resistance. The interview and archival data discussed here indicate that the resistance, which I argue is at the centre of the crisis, is manifested along three dimensions: strikes; moving to part-time work; and quitting the job outright.

Strikes as Resistance

A form of direct or active resistance is the job action, which includes the strike. Strikes and job actions are not normally thought of as endemic among hospital nurses. Many things mitigate against strike action: the illegality of the strike (in many jurisdictions); the "Florence Nightingalism" and professionalism of nurses; and, finally, the preconception that women are less likely to strike.[40] Nevertheless, there have been a growing number of job actions in the hospitals, including strikes, over the past few years.

In 1988 Alberta and Saskatchewan nurses went on strike; in 1989, it was B.C. and Quebec nurses.[41] The purpose here is not to describe these strikes in full, but to draw on the consultations and archival data to look at the nurses' key demands. In the Alberta and Saskatchewan strikes, concerns about health care quality surfaced in demands related to: (1) hours of work; (2) cuts in types of service offered or possible; (3) staff shortages; (4) working in unfamiliar venues or being moved from ward to ward; and (5) working conditions in general.

Hours of Work

There were many comments concerning the increasing hours of work. An acute care nurse of nine years says, "I can't tell you how many times I had to stay on just to catch things up for the nurses coming on, or how many doubles (extra shifts) I've had to do. I love nursing, but I cannot take the extra hours when things are like they are now."[42]

According to Judith Firth, an Alberta RN: "Often we had to forfeit breaks and stay after shifts just to complete paperwork."[43] Nurses were consistent in reporting problems with long shifts.

Care Issues

One demand, won in 1982, was for the establishment of a Professional Responsibility Committee to allow nurses to discuss their concerns about nursing care in committee with management. Management wanted this right removed in the 1988 negotiations.[44] In 1986 the Saskatchewan nurses won the right to talk to management about patient safety, understaffing and related conditions affecting health care delivery. The hospitals wanted to remove this clause. They feared that the clause could be used to publicize problems in hospital care.

Nurses complained publicly that they were told to cut back on the care given if the workload was too heavy. Heather Smith of the

United Nurses of Alberta negotiating committee reported: "We were told in negotiations that nurses should stop providing frills — *frills*. Do you consider a backrub a frill?"[45]

A Calgary nurse noted:

We have felt powerless to make changes in our hospitals. When you want to deliver a first-rate service and feel good that you have really helped make people well or more comfortable, but you cannot because someone or something is stopping you, then ... then you have to take some sort of action.[46]

A nurse in Regina, Saskatchewan:

You can't feel good about the job you do if you take from one pocket to put in the other. All day I let care for one slide so I can take care of someone else. ... You can't be serious when you ask me why we choose to strike. What is that expression? "We ain't going to take it any more."

Cathy Cameron, a Saskatchewan nurse:

If an elderly patient rings for assistance to get to the washroom at night and you are busy with someone, ... the person gets up on their own, falls, and breaks a hip. You feel terrible, but it's the shortages of staff. There is a problem in the quality of health care delivered. We want to keep the right to talk about these problems.[47]

A nurse of twelve years explains:

We are not really like they made us out to be. The increases in salary were important, but not *the* most important. We wanted to be able to do our job. It is hard to explain to you how it feels to go home after work knowing there were people who did not get adequate care. I was on strike to change that.

Staff Shortages

Shortages figured heavily in many assessments of the reasons why nurses were unhappy on the job. One said: "If it takes three people to even partially cover the patient needs, try it with two. That's what we are faced with on too many shifts."[48] In Alberta the story was the same: "I've been forced to categorize my nursing duties into priorities. Duties such as turning a bedridden patient every two hours to prevent skin breakdown, blood clots ... have to be put low on the list of priorities because of staff shortages."[49]

There is little doubt there was a shortfall in nurses, but the shortfall created conditions for both strikes and a further exodus from nursing.

Work Space/Place Questions

Nurses also noted that the policy of frequently moving nurses from ward to ward had ill effects. Judith Firth of Alberta notes: "We've been faced with selected ward closures and staff layoffs. Remaining staff are floated to other units in unfamiliar settings with little or no orientation, making patient care unsafe and increasing staff frustration."[50]

In a 1988 interview, a Saskatchewan nurse said: "We are expected to cope in unfamiliar areas with minimal or no orientation. It's not unusual to be asked to work on two or three different units a day."

Working Conditions

Public statements and letters to newspapers tended to emphasize the importance of working conditions in strike demands: "The main issue in the strike is working conditions. Monetary benefits are very secondary."[51] "The major disappointment of the settlement is the lack of improvements in hospital working conditions."[52] "Working under the severe staff shortages leaves no time for the types of care people require."[53]

There was a consistency to the commentaries on working conditions. Nurses had expectations of what the work should be — what it had to be like in order for the delivery of service to achieve a standard that was adequate. We can see from the above that "working conditions" include much of what we might consider to be the labour process in nursing.

Interview and archival material indicated that monetary issues played a secondary role. On the surface, the strike in B.C. appeared to contradict this, as wage increases amounting to 33 per cent were placed at the forefront of demands, along with a negotiable timetable and more say in health care delivery. However, when the negotiating committee put forward a package for ratification, which included essentially little more than a healthy wage increase, the members rejected it saying that the "wage increase, schedule and various shift premiums didn't make the job stresses worthwhile."[54]

The changing nature of work (labour process), resulting in actual or perceived workload increase and the deterioration of job satisfaction, prompted strikes in which nurses hoped they could slow down and/or reverse the worsening situation, or at least raise public awareness of the problems. The desire to gain control of the work, its performance and quality, is at the "eye of the storm." A nurse in Saskatoon sums it up:

> I'll tell you what the issues are. We cannot do the job we are trained to do. There are too few of us, patients in hospital are older and more ill than they used to be, managements are cutting every corner because the province does not give them the funds. I speak for a lot of others when I say the stress is burning me out.

The increasing crisis in funding and utilization has intensified the work of the RNs. This, in microcosm, is the contradiction. Financial questions push workforce composition changes and labour process changes, which in turn cause critical labour participation declines.

It is important to note that there are differences among nurses' organizations with regard to how they should respond to the current situation. The professional associations, such as The Canadian Nurses' Association (CNA), have opted for increased professionalization. If we think of Wright's notion of "contradictory class location," the professional associations and many managerial nurses are trying to reaffirm the autonomy of nurses, separating them from the occupations "beneath them" in the medical hierarchy, and placing them closer to the petite bourgeoisie rather than the working class in the overall class structure.[55] Through the CNA, professional associations have taken up the demand for an all-baccalaureate nursing staff. The hope is that this will bring more respect and greater rewards to the profession.

The unions and, to a large extent, nurses on the floor are opting for a different approach based on a different class perspective. It is a mistake to see the union response as *only* an attempt to evade proletarianization. The nurses feel that delivering care and doing a day's work that is productive and useful is at stake. Where deskilling and proletarianization coincide with the challenge to the nurses' conception of the proper labour process, we find a crisis linking class and gender issues.

Part-Time Work: A Second Form of Resistance

The second form of resistance adopted by some nurses involves the move from full-time to part-time work.[56] It is a passive form of resistance in the sense that nurses are leaving full-time work in order to avoid a changing workplace and to escape the kind of problems that were mentioned in the strike section.

Before we look at the comments of the interviewees on why they went part-time, we should examine how serious a phenomenon the opting for part-time status is. Data indicate that it is very widespread:

TABLE 4.2[57]
Number of Registered Nurses in Canada
Employed in Nursing Full-time and Part-time
1970–1986

Year	Total Number	Full-time (%)	Part-time (%)
1974	128,675	74	26
1976	137,858	69	31
1978	161,125	67	33
1980	155,309	64.7	35.3
1982	164,231	62.6	37.3
1984	188,074	55.8	44.2
1986	184,067	63.2	36.8

The Canadian data show that there was a shift from 74 per cent full-time nurses in 1974 to a low of 55.8 per cent in 1984. The seeming reversal in the 1984 to 1986 period is accompanied by an actual drop in the number of nurses employed. One explanation for this is that nurses were leaving the profession rather than moving to part-time status.

Why are nurses moving to part-time work in such numbers? The study indicates that nurses perceived many dramatic measures being taken to reduce hospital expenditures, such as support staff reductions (orderlies and RNAs), technological changes and more casual staff in the team mix. Two other structural changes were also taking place — an increasing acuity on the ward and a quicker "turnaround" time.[58] In the past, a patient might stay five days in the hospital after an operation. Today that same patient may be in and out in three days. Recuperation occurs at home, so people on the ward are, on average, more ill. There is a movement towards putting the very ill, those who previously might have been in an intensive care setting, on the ward. This situation has serious effects. One effect is summed up by an Ontario nurse of nineteen years: "What we mean by increasing acuity is a sicker patient and that means the nurse makes more frequent interventions." The increasing acuity also means that "people in the wards today would have been in ICU [intensive care unit] 10 years ago."[59]

Increasing acuity lowers the nurses' job satisfaction. They no longer get to see the results of their work. Whereas the nurses in times past could look forward to having the patients improve "before their eyes," patients must now convalesce at home. Gone are the smiling chats with people pulled back from the brink of serious illness. There are more interventions and fewer chances to see the result of those hard hours of patient care.

A nurse of eleven years said: "As a person recovers from surgery, they are interested in yakking and it's part of the job to do it, an enjoyable part. It seems we get a lot less of that now. Patients are gone before you get to know them. ... Some of the best parts of my work are gone."

These changes left nurses with two choices: "Should I walk out? I could not stand what was happening to *my* job, *my* responsibilities. Leaving seemed like the only choice, but I could not afford it. Maybe with fewer hours it would be easier to take."

Nurses reported that they hoped to reduce the pressure with shorter hours. They felt that they could have more control over which shifts they would have to work. However, they found that they did not gain control of their work lives. The type of work, the hours they were asked to work and the pace of work on the job remained significantly out of their control. Interview data indicate that the frustration resulting from their inability to carry out "traditional bedside duties" was not diminished.

A part-time nurse in London, Ontario, commented: "I find that my life is often more complicated. With the strange shifts I get [as a part-time nurse] I feel I have less control than before." Another nurse found her power to bargain curtailed: "Perhaps I was foolish, but I did believe I would get more say about when I would work; but now I have to work [in order to make enough to live]. I can't do without the shifts, so I cannot be as picky [about when to work] as I hoped."

Our interviews and other research indicate that part-time work fails to reduce the intensification of the labour process: "At first I felt a level of relief, almost freedom, as I did not have to get ready for the shifts I was so used to. Very soon I found myself feeling just ... no ... even more uptight after the shifts I did work. ... I found changing wards and having few patterns affected me."[60]

In the Goldfarb study, part-time and full-time nurses had very similar responses in terms of their dissatisfactions and complaints, despite the fact that most full-time nurses opted for part-time work in order to alleviate the frustration they felt in the full-time positions.[61] Mathera finds that the part-time nurse in an acute setting works more hours and receives fewer benefits.[62] This was echoed in our research: "I may work less hours, but at work it seems even more pressure. I use to think it was me ... not being used to being in harness, but I think our assignments are heavier."[63]

While many nursing unions have declared the part-time option a right, and have called it a way for women to deal with pressures of home and work, it is often a method adopted by nurses to escape the problems at work. The common assumption is that nurses want part-time work to permit them to raise families. From a more patriarchal perspective, they need less money because they are supplementing a spouse's wage. Yet another assumption is that there is no choice, that managements create part-time employment in order to cut the costs associated with full-time workers' benefits. In this case, quite a different scenario is playing itself out. Nurses are choosing part-time work as an alternative to full-time work because they do not want to work under the new conditions.

According to the data, the attempt to gain control over one's work life is a major impetus to the selection of part-time work, but it generally fails to improve the part-timers' lot.[64]

All I have ever wanted to do is have the chance to practise my nursing up to my ability. I do not mean adequate given the time or given the load. I thought part-time would give me that chance. I do not know the patients. ... When you do not come in regularly, things change, people change. I think it is harder to be the kind of nurse you want to be.[65]

The full-time nurses find that the workplace deteriorates as more people opt for part-time status. This finding was almost universal in my interviews: "More part-timers, more problems." "You just cannot run a ward with all the part-time nurses. You need more full-time people." "Part-timers change. They get moved from place to place. When you do not know the person who is coming in and they don't know the routines, the equipment locations, the patients or whatever, then I get to do too much."

The part-timers themselves report to their nurses' unions that they are used to having to fill in on a variety of units without being given any orientation.

So while this form of resistance contributes to the crisis by creating a further "shortage" of nurses, it does not benefit the nurses directly. It should be noted that while the unions have defended their members' rights to be able to move to part-time status, they have explained that there are pitfalls and that job sharing may be preferable.

Part-time work has often been used as a management strategy both in and outside of the hospital. In the late 1970s and early 1980s, hospital administrators increased the number of part-time workers and this included nurses. The aim was to save labour costs and create a more flexible workplace (see discussion on numerical flexibility in note 5). However, the strategy was

> ... abandoned by many administrations as: nurses became very hard to get and the agencies supplying temporary nurses began to charge considerably inflated hourly rates. You cannot blame them. It was a supply-and-demand problem, but we certainly didn't encourage part-time nursing from that point.[66]

I have argued that nurses experienced the changing labour process and related time problems on the job, and reacted. Their reaction was to release the pressure by reducing hours and, most importantly, to give themselves what they perceived as a lever to exert some control. The interview material supports this interpretation, but indicates that nurses feel this passive strategy has failed.

Quitting as Resistance

As noted at the outset of this paper in discussing the mainstream explanation for the current shortage of nurses, there are adequate numbers of nurses available in the system. However, many nurses are simply unwilling to work under the present organization and conditions of work. Nurses are challenging the changes in the hospital nursing labour process by resisting with their feet — by walking out.

If we were to generalize the concerns of the nurses with the changes in labour process, we could say that they are focused on both the increasing workload and *a change in the composition of that workload*. There have been changes in how the work is done, its speed, content, form, intensity, who it is delivered to, how it is reported and classified, as well as how it is evaluated. The changes that have taken place have made it difficult for nurses to deliver the care they feel is their responsibility. Nurses repeatedly commented on this:

> There are times when dressings cannot be changed. We have no support staff, so we have to do everything and we cannot. You certainly cannot be proud of the work you do anymore ... not that I don't care. Heavens, if that were the case I would be happier, but I do care — that is the problem.

As Campbell noted, the whole process of assessment and delivery has changed,[67] yet nurses have not acquiesced, they have resisted. Is this resistance aimed at increasing the extrinsic rewards? It is true that nurses on strike have said, in effect, "*If* you will not change the work conditions, then you must pay," but the qualitive data indicates that monetary issues are secondary.

We conducted an exploratory survey in order to see if there was support for the contention that monetary issues are secondary to labour process issues in generating conflict.[68] The survey indicated that content of the work and issues related to labour process outweighed monetary issues by more than two to one. Asked what factors might influence them to leave nursing, only 25 per cent pointed to pay issues, while labour process issues were cited by over 70 per cent. On the whole, the exploratory survey was consistent with and lends support to the qualitative findings.

Concluding Remarks

In a 1988 article for *Healthsharing*, Pat Armstrong asked, "Where have all the nurses gone?"[69] This paper has attempted to explain why they are absenting themselves from the hospitals. The mainstream scientific explanations, which rely on a labour market and a supply-and-demand framework, simply do not account for the complexities of the current situation. Many policy analysts argue that the way to deal with the nursing crisis is with dollars. There are a number of problems with this approach, not the least of which is the fact that the foundational or structural cause of the situation is a fiscal crisis: finding *more* money when there is already a shortfall will prove very difficult. But even if additional funds *could* be found, this would not necessarily resolve the crisis. As this investigation has sought to demonstrate, the current crisis has much more to do with the role of the nurse — the time, place and content of her nursing work. The expectations of the nurse, or her conceptions of what a nurse is and does, have been challenged. They have been challenged by managerial strategies, provoked by a fiscal crisis of the state, that have created a new regime of work — a new labour process. As interviews reveal, there is widespread feeling that this labour process runs counter to ideas, feelings, understandings and conceptions of nurses, both collective and individual. Nurses told us that they were not able to "to do the job they were trained to do," not able to use the skills they had acquired. They were confronted with a decision: Should they come to a new consensual relation with the managerial regimes or should their response shift to resistance?

Studies of strikes and the exploratory survey demonstrate that the issues involved are work-related, not monetary. The desire to challenge managerial control over the labour process is evident, whether in demands relating to the professional responsibility committees, shape of the work day, realigning the paper/real care divide, the content and form of work, the time of work or even where the work was to be done. Dissatisfaction with all facets of the new labour process was overwhelming. This is consistent with our propositions concerning the roots of the current problems. These problems led to the strikes — that seems very clear.

But what of the more controversial forms of resistance identified here? Nurses, confronted with the changing nature of work, had to make hard decisions. The commitment to patients was very high and the organizational commitment — marvelled at in the 1960s and

1970s — was still there, but the problems that nurses confronted made it impossible to maintain such commitment. Some nurses believed initially that perhaps "fewer hours would make it easier to take." In the simple model of response to control presented here, nurses were shifting the mix of consent/compliance to resistance in response to managerial strategies. Moving to part-time protected the attachment to care. Nurses hoped for relief from stress and some increase in control over time and place of work, if not over the core content. This strategy has not worked.

While the move to part-time was initially one managerial strategy aimed at cost reduction, administrators found shortages of full-time workers and *abandoned* the goal of increasing the part-time complement. As well, the Ontario Nurses' Association began successfully pushing a job-share approach, making it an alternative for those who wanted part-time hours. This did not save the management any wages.

Is part-time a preferred option because nurses as women were still responsible for the home in addition to employment? This is a whole question in itself. The issue came up only peripherally in the study, but the interviews, documentary evidence and other commentators indicate that there are no more "appliance nurses" — those who wish to work only a few shifts a week in order to supplement a male income. Nurses want more work and seek stability of employment, more defined hours and greater input into the content of health care.[70] Nurses, like other women, work because they want to make a productive contribution, and because they must in order to support themselves and their families. The supplementary survey, although hardly conclusive, indicates that part-time work is not chosen primarily to deal with the work/home interface problems, but rather to cope with a changing workplace. The problems of balancing responsibilities at work and home are there as they are for most working women, but they are exacerbated by the problems of a changing workplace.

The labour process framework developed here allows us to examine the causes of the problem, while at the same time it allows us to integrate an understanding of the role of gender. All people bring to their work a set of understandings and expectations that are developed through life experience. One's gender has a powerful effect on what these experiences and understandings are going to be, because gender influences the life we lead and how we are treated at a profound level. So it is that women bring their gender specific expectations to the workplace and have a conception of what they want over and above wages from work. When a change in the labour process challenges these expectations, there is reaction and resistance.

Notes

1. Confidential interviews were conducted with thirty-four nurses from four acute care hospitals in Ontario cities and union officials in two other centres. A small number of nurses were consulted in Calgary, Regina and Saskatoon concerning their respective strikes.

2. The most influential study focusing on the labour market supply and demand for nurses is N. Meltz, *The Nursing Shortage* (Toronto: Registered Nurses' Association of Ontario, 1988). He concludes that supply is the key causal factor in the nursing shortage, as it has not increased at the same pace as demand. The supply shortfall is due to reductions in college spaces for nursing, and that this "will be solved by the market" (Meltz 1988, 65). He proposes a series of extrinsic rewards including but not restricted to: wage premiums in certain areas, cash in lieu of benefits as an option and increased job ladders. All of these are good suggestions for improving the material lot of nurses and cushioning a deteriorating work situation, but it is our contention that it misses the cause of the problem.

3. J. McArthur, "Pay Is Not the Problem," *Toronto Star* (February 16, 1988), A2.

4. This is verified by J. McArthur in ibid.

5. Flexibility is a vast subject. In the simplest terms, flexibility is management's attempt to seek adaptability to product market fluctuation. There are two distinct types of flexibility. One relates to technological manipulations in the workplace such as small-batching and cluster organization development (the Benetton model) and has generally been seen to apply more to the private sector in the production of commodities. However, this need not be so. The second type relates to labour market flexibility. The "flexible firm" seeks to segment the labour force into a small core of permanent full-time employees and a large periphery of part-time, casual, on call, temporary and subcontracted workers. See M. MacDonald, "The Flex Spec Debates," *Studies in Political Economy* 36 (Autumn 1991); I. Dey, "Flexible Parts and Ridged Fulls: The Limited Revolution in Work-time Patterns," *Work, Employment and Society* 3/4 (December 1989); A. Pollert, "Dismantling Flexibility," *Capital and Class* 34 (May 1988); C. Hakim, "Trends in the Flexible Workforce," *Employment Gazette* (November 1987); P. Jones, "Labour Market Flexibility," *Labour and Society* 12/1 (January 1987). The flexible firm is dependent on the core workers having certain characteristics that include functional flexibility in the labour process through multiskilling (crossing occupational boundaries) and time flexibility, which allows overtime or work intensification. It is possible to see the roots of this flexible firm in the new "just-in-time" (JIT) inventory strategies (applied in this case to labour) and the Japanese employment system adapted by the British, German, French and Italians to their national situations. See J.P. White, "Women, Labour Process and Public Sector Militancy," Address to the 8th Annual Conference on Labour Process, University of Manchester Institute of Science and Technology,

Manchester, 1988. In the public sector the flexibility model is used to vary labour with demand for service and lower ongoing variable capital costs by shrinking the fixed labour force.

6. In a study done in 1986–1987 for CUPE, I investigated the substitution of registered nurses (RNs) for registered nursing assistants (RNAs). The RNs are more expensive and are therefore not a cost-efficient substitute for the assistants. RNs can, however, do the range of tasks that nursing assistants do, as well as perform duties that RNAs cannot. Pat Armstrong, "Where Have All the Nurses Gone?" *Healthsharing* (Summer 1988), points out that the technology exists to put RNs on part-time rotating shifts. This allows for more management flexibility. This creation of labour flexibility in hospital nursing provides the only possible rationale for the shift to RNs on management's part.

7. K. Marx, *Capital*, Vol. 1 (New York: International Publishers, 1967), 170.

8. P. Corrigan, H. Ramsey and D. Saver, *Socialist Construction and Marxist Theory* (London: Macmillan, 1978), 2; P. Thompson, *The Nature of Work* (London: Macmillan, 1983), 40.

9. Interview data; J.P. White, *Hospital Strike: Women, Unions and Conflict in the Public Sector* (Toronto: Thompson Educational Pub., 1990); S. Growe, *Who Cares?* (Toronto: McClelland and Stewart, 1991).

10. M. Campbell, "The Structure of Stress in Nurses' Work," in D. Coburn (ed.), *Health and Canadian Society: Sociological Perspectives* (Markham: Fitzhenry and Whiteside, 1987); M. Campbell, "Management as 'Ruling': A Class Phenomenon in Nursing," *Studies in Political Economy* 27 (Autumn 1988).

11. Campbell, "Management as Ruling."

12. Ibid., 36–39.

13. Growe, *Who Cares?*; Interview data.

14. Ibid.

15. Goldfarb Corporation, *The Nursing Crisis* (Toronto: Ontario Nurses' Association, 1988).

16. E. Adam, *To Be a Nurse*, 2nd ed. (New York: W.B. Saunders, 1991), 28.

17. R. Warburton and W. Carroll, "Class and Gender in Nursing," in D. Coburn (ed.), *Health and Canadian Society: Sociological Perspectives* (Markham: Fitzhenry and Whiteside, 1987), 371.

18. Ibid., 369–701.

19. J. Jenny, *Issues Affecting Nurses' Hospital Employment in the 80s* (Toronto: Canadian Hospital Association, 1982).

20. White, *Hospital Strike*, Chapter 3.

21. Goldfarb Corp., *The Nursing Crisis*.

22. There are many interrelations between paid and unpaid work that could be considered. Earlier studies of non-nursing staff in the hospitals indicated that women seek things in the labour market that they do not get from domestic work. See White, *Hospital Strike*, 38–41. Women reported that the productive involvement outside of the home increases their identity, independence and power in the family. Women work because they must work, but they seek intrinsic rewards as well. In the previous study, it led to an illegal strike. In the present case, resistance manifests itself along the lines described.

23. Marx, *Capital*; J. Rinehart, *The Tyranny of Work*, 2nd ed. (Toronto: HBJ, 1987).

24. G. Salaman, *Working* (London: Tavistock Pub., 1986).

25. Warburton and Carroll, "Class and Gender," 372.

26. Ibid., 372.

27. R. Edwards, *Contested Terrain: The Transformation of the Workplace in the Twentieth Century* (London: Heinemann, 1979).

28. R. Badgely, "Health Workers Strike," *International Journal of Health Services* 5/1. (1975); C.A. Brown, "Women Workers in the Health Service Industry," *International Journal of Health Services* 5/1 (1975); B. Ehrenreich and J. Ehrenreich, "Hospital Workers: A Case Study of the New Working Class," *Monthly Review* 24/8 (1973).

29. T.R. Gurr, *Why Men Rebel* (Princeton: Princeton University Press, 1970); B. Moore, *Injustice: The Social Basis of Obedience and Revolt* (London: Macmillan, 1978).

30. Thompson, *The Nature of Work*.

31. H. Willmott, "Subjectivity and the Dialectic of Praxis: Opening Up the Core of Labour Process Analysis," in D. Knights and H. Willmott (eds.), *Labour Process Theory* (London: Macmillan, 1990).

32. G. Lukas, *Labour* (London: Merlin Press, 1980); P. Wardell, "Labour and Labour Process," in D. Knights and H. Willmott (eds.), *Labour Process Theory* (London: Macmillan, 1990).

33. H. Braverman, *Labour and Monopoly Capital* (New York: Monthly Review Press, 1974).

34. White, *Hospital Strike*; S. Wood (ed.), *The Degradation of Work* (London: Hutchinson Press, 1982), 15.

35. A. Friedman, *Industry and Labour* (London: Macmillan, 1977); M. Burawoy, *Manufacturing Consent* (Chicago: University of Chicago Press, 1979); M. Burawoy, *The Politics of Production* (London: Verso, 1985); Edwards, *Contested Terrain*.

36. Thompson, *The Nature of Work*, 133.

37. Ibid.; Friedman, *Industry and Labour*, 48.

38. Edwards, *Contested Terrain*.

39. Burawoy, *Manufacturing Consent*.

40. This preoccupation is increasingly shown to be false. In a study of women and strikes, I argue that propositions portraying women as more passive and less likely to strike are incorrect and grounded in patriarchal stereotypes. See White, *Hospital Strike*; White, "Women Labour Process." For a discussion of the reasons why women have been gender-typed as more passive, less militant and more stable with regard to strikes and job actions, see R. Milkman, *Women, Work and Protest* (New York: Routledge and Kegan Paul, 1985); K. Purcell, "Militancy and Acquiescence Amongst Women Workers," in S. Burman (ed.), *Fit Work for Women* (London: Croom Helm, 1979); White, *Hospital Strike*; L. Tentler, *Wage-Earning Women: Industrial Work and Family Life in the United States, 1900–1914* (New York: Oxford Press, 1979).

41. In Quebec, close to 40,000 nurses engaged in ongoing illegal strikes, defying the Bourassa government's repeated attempts to intimidate them. Nurses received unprecedented public support and the support of the wider labour movement.

Their demands were similar to those across the country. See M. Gagnon, "Reflections on the Public Sector Contract Negotiations," *Studies in Political Economy* 31 (Spring 1990), 173–175.

42. Interview, Alberta, 1988.
43. Letters, "Frustration Caused Strike" *Edmonton Journal* (February 11, 1988), A7.
44. Heather Smith, interview, "Morningside," CBC Radio, October 11, 1988.
45. Ibid.
46. Interview, acute care nurse, Calgary, 1988.
47. Heather Smith, interview.
48. Interview, Saskatchewan nurse, 1988.
49. Letters, "Frustration."
50. Ibid.
51. Ibid.
52. J. Boehm, Letter, *Edmonton Journal* (February 13, 1988), B1.
53. Interview, Alberta nurse, 1988.
54. *Ottawa Citizen* (July 13, 1989), A3.
55. For Wright's discussion of the semiautonomous contradictory category, see E.O. Wright, "Class Boundaries in Advanced Capitalist Societies," *New Left Review* 98 (1976), 26; E.O. Wright, *Class Crisis and the State* (London: New Left Books, 1978); E.O. Wright, *Classes* (London: Verso, 1985); as well as his rejection of the category in E.O. Wright, *The Debate on Classes* (London: Verso, 1989).
56. For the purpose of this study, part-time nurses are those who are permanent employees available for twenty-four hours of work per week. This corresponds to two twelve-hour shifts, or three eight-hour shifts.
57. There are a variety of sources used to compile this table: Canadian Nurses' Association, *Countdown 1975–85*, Table 2, Section A; Health and Welfare Canada, *Health Personnel* (1986, 1987), Table 13.4; and Statistics Canada, *Nursing in Canada 83-226*, Table 2.

    The data includes a sizable "not stated" category: 7,363 in 1984 and 20,512 in 1986. These are largely in the province of Quebec. The percentage was calculated by subtracting the "not stated" category from the total and recalculating the percentage. This biases the data towards full-time employment because a *larger* proportion of nurses in Quebec are part-time. P. Armstrong reports that fully 60 per cent of Quebec nurses are part-time.
58. White, "Women, Labour Process"; Jenny, *Issues Affecting*, 15.
59. B. Lee, "ICU a Real Pressure Cooker," *Hamilton Spectator* (April 25, 1988), B1.
60. Interview, part-time acute care nurse, Hamilton, 1988.
61. Ontario Nurses' Association, *An Industry in Crisis* (Toronto, April 1988).
62. D. Mathera, "Nurses Pay: How Part-timers Are Doing," *R.N.* (December 1985), 33.
63. Interview, part-time nurse, London, Ontario, 1988.
64. Jenny, *Issues Affecting*, 25.
65. Interview, part-time nurse, Burlington, Ontario.
66. Interview, administrator, acute care hospital.
67. Campbell, "The Structure of Stress."

68. The survey was conducted in May 1989 at an acute care hospital in a medium-size Canadian city. On a day chosen at random, questionnaires were distributed to all nurses on duty on two consecutive shifts. Sixty-four of sixty-five registered nurses completed the questionnaire. The sample, all female, was 62.5 per cent full-time and 37.5 per cent part-time. In addition to the survey, three unit managers were interviewed to explore a management perspective and unidentified, numbered exit interviews were provided by the personnel department for review. The survey was conducted to give another indication whether the Meltz propositions about pay adjustments as a remedy for the crisis, or the labour process propositions that arise from the interview and archival research had support.
69. Armstrong, "Where Have All the Nurses Gone?"
70. Interview data; Growe, *Who Cares?*

Chapter Five

The Domestication of Women's Work: A Comparison of Chinese and Portuguese Immigrant Women Homeworkers

Wenona Giles and Valerie Preston

Changes in the Canadian political economy, including trade liberalization, economic recession, the shift to post-Fordist forms of production and monetarist economic policies, have intensified two processes that define the nature of women's work in the 1990s: informalization and domestication. According to Castells and Portes,[1] informalization refers to processes that lead to "work activities or economic transactions, paid or unpaid, that occur outside the conventional market economy and are not regulated, mentioned, audited or counted by any official agency in the society,"[2] making them insecure and sometimes "illegal." The recent closure of manufacturing and industrial firms and concomitant job loss have accelerated the informalization of work.[3]

Increased informalization has been accompanied by the domestication of work, a shift in the locations and sites of paid work from formal workplaces to domestic premises.[4] Domestic household space is the "interface of productive and reproductive resources and spaces."[5] At this "interface," paid work blurs the distinctions between productive and reproductive relations. The individual worker's identity as a member of the paid labour force is obscured as work is reduced to a series of items or "pieces of work" and as family members become involved in production. Household relations change to accommodate and resist the accompanying relations of production. Homework is an old phenomenon,[6] but the emergence of new types of production in the home, new forms of worker-employer relations and changes in household relations occurring in response to domestication are altering ethnic, gender and class inequalities.

The speed and nature of informalization and domestication reflect local conditions. Labour markets are constituted locally, so that the effects of international, national and regional trends depend upon local circumstances, which may be more important for women than for men.[7] Women often rely on local social networks and services to learn about job openings and to accommodate the demands of home and workplace, and many women's activities are more limited spatially than men's.[8]

In Canada, the transition from a goods-producing to an information-based urban economy is well underway in the largest city, Toronto.[9] Manufacturing employment has declined in absolute and relative terms, employment in business and consumer services has increased as Toronto has become the pre-eminent financial centre of Canada and manufacturing and routine service employment have decentralized. The effects of restructuring have been heightened since 1990 by a severe recession that has accelerated job loss. Between 1990 and 1992, total employment declined annually by 4.4 per cent, for an average loss of 78,000 jobs per year in the Census Metropolitan Area. Employment has declined most precipitously in manufacturing, retail and wholesale trade and construction, the industrial sectors in which immigrant workers of both sexes have been concentrated. Rising unemployment and an increase in part-time employment have accompanied these industrial shifts.[10]

Economic restructuring has led to significant changes in women's employment. While initially women's employment increased as men left manufacturing jobs in the early 1980s, some female-dominated jobs, particularly clerical and semiskilled production jobs, have declined in the last recession.[11] The female workforce is increasingly polarized between well-paid, well-qualified women in professional and management jobs and the majority of women in poorly paid, insecure and often part-time service and sales jobs. In the United States and Britain, polarization is associated with increasing division on the basis of race and ethnicity.[12] Minority women, mainly African American and Hispanic in the United States and mainly Asian in Great Britain, are clustered in less desirable jobs while White women are overrepresented in full-time, well-paid jobs. Polarization is one result of employers' efforts to create a contingent workforce whose numbers can be expanded or reduced according to demand. Workers are segmented into a primary labour market offering opportunities for career advancement, training, job security and good wages, or into a secondary labour market of contingent workers hired on a part-time, temporary and seasonal basis.[13]

For employers, homeworkers are one of the most attractive types of contingent worker. Homework reduces labour costs and other operating costs while providing a workforce that is on call as demand requires.[14] Several studies have documented the adverse working conditions of many homeworkers who labour long hours for low wages that are often less than the statutory minimum wage.[15] The unpredictable flow of work and the lack of benefits compound the financial disadvantages of homework that is often unsafe and unhealthy.[16] Even when homeworkers enjoy the same salary and benefits as their counterparts in the formal workplace, costs of heating, shelter, and other utilities are borne by the employee working at home.

Recently, homework has been promoted as a desirable working arrangement for employees who may be able to accommodate better the demands of domestic and paid labour by working at home while enjoying relative autonomy.[17] Homework is also supposed to be advantageous for entrepreneurs who can reduce capital and operating costs by locating in domestic premises.[18] However, many of the advantages of homework are outweighed by its disadvantages. With unpredictable and demanding deadlines, much homework does not provide the flexibility often described as an advantage of working from home.[19] Even self-employed proprietors and professionals who enjoy more control of their work schedules are concerned about potential barriers to career advancement, social isolation and responsibility for health and safety while working at home.[20]

The trend towards the domestication of paid work is most pronounced for those who occupy marginal positions in the labour market, particularly immigrant women who are non-English-speaking, working class and women of colour.[21] Concentrated in declining economic sectors where employers are seeking the greatest flexibility from workers, many immigrant women have few alternatives to homework. The loss of unskilled and semiskilled production jobs in manufacturing during the current period of restructuring has placed immigrant women at a serious disadvantage in contemporary labour markets.

This paper reports the findings from a pilot study exploring working-class, immigrant women's evaluations of homework in Toronto. The pilot study was designed to document the histories of immigrant women who work at home and their assessments of current working conditions. From interviews with first-generation Portuguese women and first-generation Chinese women, we examine how immigrant women evaluate paid work at home in terms of its impact on their work lives and on their home lives. The work histories, domestic relations and assessments of Portuguese and Chinese women are compared to identify some of the commonalities and differences among female homeworkers from different ethnic groups. In this comparison, we seek to establish how ethnicity contributes to differences in the experiences of a group of women who often are deemed marginal and lacking in resources.

An empirical study of immigrant women's homework faces several challenges. The very nature of homework, which occurs in private homes, means it is difficult to identify and locate homeworkers, and workers may be hesitant to reveal information that could jeopardize them legally or with jobbers and agencies that supply work.[22] These difficulties may be compounded by the immigrant status of women. Language difficulties, limited knowledge of the policies and institutions of the Canadian state, and fear of state authorities discourage many immigrant women from speaking with strangers. Finally, gender relations in the household may also prevent immigrant women from expressing their opinions.[23]

To overcome these challenges, a pilot study modelled on previous studies of immigrant women's work[24] was conducted in Toronto. Using a snowball sampling procedure, six Portuguese and six Chinese immigrant women who were working at home were identified and interviewed.[25] They were located through contacts with voluntary agencies in each community and suggestions from Portuguese and Chinese immigrants known to the researchers. Identifying participants was an arduous process and the interviews were completed slowly between March 1991 and September 1992. The sample is not representative in a statistical sense, reducing the extent to which the empirical findings can be generalized. However, the nature of homework precludes large random samples. Furthermore, the sampling strategy is consistent with the study's aim to explore in depth the work and immigration histories of homeworkers and the evaluations of homework.[26]

Immigrant Women

Certain groups of women are especially vulnerable to recent changes in the nature and location of paid employment: recent immigrants, poorly educated women, women of colour and women with little knowledge of the dominant languages of work in Canada.[27] Such women fall into two broad categories. Lipsig-Mummé identifies one group as rural or urban women who are born in the country in which they work, and have limited education.[28] Her research implies that the women she describes are of the dominant ethnicity. Their participation in work at home is linked to such factors as competition for limited jobs, poverty and the traditional gender division of labour. The second group comprises immigrant women who lack skills in the dominant language and child care resources, and are also constrained from participating in the formal economy by racism and traditional gender divisions of labour.[29]

Immigrant women in Canada are not a homogeneous group, but experience differences in class, ethnicity/"race," sexuality, English/French fluency, education, etc. As well, the label "immigrant woman" is used differently by researchers. In some cases, immigrant women are defined by their generational status in Canada, i.e., the first generation only, referred to as "immigrant women."[30] This is a diverse group that ranges from wealthy English-speaking and French-speaking women who have professional qualifications and work experience widely recognized by Canadian employers to refugees who arrive in Canada with few resources and limited ability to speak English or French and who struggle to have their educational qualifications and experiences recognized. Other researchers use this label in a critical way to describe women who are socially constructed as immigrant women of colour, etc.[31] In this study we focus on women who, on the one hand, are first-generation immigrants (i.e., they have been born elsewhere); on the other hand, we recognize that the social construction of these women as "immigrant women" often affects their access to jobs and services.

The women we describe in this paper are part of a growing segment of the labour market. With labour force participation rates that exceed those of Canadian-born women, immigrant women in general are more likely to participate in paid labour than Canadian-born women and their experiences in the labour market are diverse. Women immigrating from the United Kingdom, the United States, and other Northern European countries who are also fluent in English or French are likely to be employed in the primary labour market where their earnings match those of Canadian-born women.[32] For women from other countries of origin that today are the main sources of immigrants, language skills, education and "visible minority" status critically influence their earnings and occupations. According to Boyd, recent arrivals who lack English- or French-speaking ability and "visible minority" women suffer lower earnings. They are far more likely than their Canadian-born counterparts to hold semiskilled and non-skilled positions in the manufacturing sector.[33]

The potentially adverse effects of economic restructuring for some immigrant women are apparent in a recent Australian study.[34] Lacking local experience, possessing few skills suitable for the jobs being created in financial and producer services, with limited fluency in English, and with low levels of education, recent immigrants to Australia from Central European and South Asian countries are particularly vulnerable to the domestication and informalization of work. After losing factory jobs, many immigrants have fallen back on self-employment, employment in family businesses and homework as the only means of earning an income.[35]

The same is likely to be true in Toronto. Between1981 and 1986, the concentration of immigrant women from Central and Southern Europe, Asia and Africa in skilled and semiskilled manual manufacturing jobs increased,[36] so these immigrant women were among the groups most vulnerable to the loss of manufacturing employment. The residential concentration of many immigrant groups in central districts of the Toronto Census Metropolitan Area will also have diminished their access to manufacturing jobs that have relocated to the outer regions of the urban area.[37] The factory jobs that remain are simply beyond the travel range of many immigrant women. Firms that rely on an immigrant workforce are also likely to have shifted to various forms of homework so as to reduce production costs.[38]

Diversity of Experience

Immigrant communities differ in terms of several factors that may influence women's participation in the labour market. These include labour force experience prior to arriving in Canada; education and identified skills; language ability; and gender roles inside and outside of the household. Boyd notes that when examining differences among immigrant women, ethnicity is also a factor and ethnic minorities persist in low-wage job sectors, even when education, previous experience, language ability, etc., are taken into account.[39]

Today in Canada, in an era of global restructuring, ethnicity plays a critical role in the labour market and is also shaped in the struggles regarding capitalist production. The informalization and domestication of wage work are important aspects of these struggles and affect both production and reproduction by bringing the wage workplace into the home. Women in working-class immigrant family households are pulled into this dynamic in a particular way depending upon their personal histories (pre- and postmigration) as well as the historical struggles regarding their ethnicity.

Our understanding of how ethnicity alters immigrant women's decisions about paid work depends upon how we think ethnicity is constructed. Ng argues that ethnicity is part of the organization of production in Canada and the triad of gender, ethnic and class relations are "inextricably linked to the Canadian state, if we see the state as the culmination and crystallization of struggles over the dominant (in the case of Canada, capitalist) mode of production."[40] She regards ethnicity as being historically constructed "in and through productive and reproductive relations."[41] Another view has emphasized the ways that social relations in the household shape ethnicity and vice versa. This perspective argues that women's ethnicity must be distinguished from men's, just as women's experiences and struggles in the household and outside of it are different from men's. Within a collectivity, women will experience ethnicity differently depending on their class, age, marital status, sexuality, education, etc.[42] Bottomley has emphasized the interrelationship of ethnicity with other factors such as work, family responsibilities and language. She points to the importance of relating discussions of migrant/immigrant women to wider issues "about women in society, ideological forms, cultural transformations and resistance" and the dangers of essentializing the experiences of women, for example, to solely their work history or their ethnicity.[43]

We suggest that in the Canadian context, immigrant women's ethnicity is influenced concomitantly by conditions within the group as well as those outside the group. For example, public policies, economic conditions and social relations prevailing at the time of arrival in Canada, combined with experiences in their countries of origin, have led to multiple Chinese-Canadian ethnicities.[44]

The link between ethnicity and the informalization and domestication of work is well recognized in recent investigations of the garment industry.[45] The relative invisibility of homework in the garment industry is attributed as much to the marginal positions of the women who do the sewing as to its location in the home. For example, the vast majority of homeworkers in the Toronto garment industry are Chinese immigrants who lack fluency in English. These women, who often have limited education and even less knowledge of relevant employment legislation, can find little alternative employment that accommodates their domestic responsibilities.[46] They are easily exploited by jobbers and subcontractors. In the cases of Chinese women in Toronto, Chinese ethnicity contributes to the invisibility of their work and domestic lives in the Canadian context.

Recent British research[47] has underscored ethnic divisions in women's experiences of homework. Several groups of homeworkers with very different working conditions were identified. They included industrial and clerical homeworkers[48] who were hired on demand by subcontractors. Nominally self-employed, these women had little control over the number and scheduling of their working hours, low wages and non-existent employee benefits. At the other end of the spectrum, technical and professional employees enjoyed renumeration and employment conditions similar to those of their counterparts in formal workplaces. While all of the homeworkers were concerned with the welfare of their children, their reasons for taking up homework and their evaluations of their working conditions varied significantly. Industrial and clerical homeworkers felt most constrained by external factors that limited their job opportunities and as expected, they were least satisfied with their wages, benefits, work schedules and working conditions. Even professional and technical workers who wanted to work from home expressed concern about the difficulties of combining child care with paid work and possible barriers to career advancement.

Several ethnic and racial divisions were apparent. Black and Asian women, particularly immigrants, were concentrated overwhelmingly in the least attractive clerical and industrial homework. Within each group of homeworkers, minority women had lower wages and worse working conditions than their White native-born counterparts. The employment opportunities of minority women were constrained mostly by external factors. In addition to discriminatory hiring practices, minority women who were immigrants had to contend with state regulations that limited their access to social assistance, child care and training, and thereby forced them into homework in a desperate attempt to find any source of income. With few social contacts outside their immigrant communities, the job searches of these immigrant women were more restricted and less successful than those of their native-born counterparts.

To take account of the diversity of women's experiences, this study explores the link between ethnicity and domestication in several economic sectors and within two ethnic groups. Ethnicity is interrelated with many of the other social characteristics that influence women's experiences and evaluations of homework, for example, class and gender relations. We focus on the differences and similarities between Portuguese and Chinese working-class women and their experience of the informalization and domestication of their wage work in Toronto.[49] We turn briefly now to their differing migration experiences that are part of the context within which ethnicity is forged.

Portuguese immigration to Canada peaked in the 1970s, declining from 1977 onwards with fewer Portuguese landing each year.[50] The majority (approximately 75 per cent) of Portuguese immigrants were relatively unskilled, rural migrants from the Azores Islands for whom the move to Canada meant a transition from a rural to urban industrialized society.[51] In contrast, the numbers of Chinese immigrants have tended to increase annually and their backgrounds are very diverse. The largest numbers of Chinese immigrants arrive directly from Hong Kong, a highly urbanized and commercial economy where English is frequently a language of instruction.[52] Immigrants of Chinese origin continue to arrive from the People's Republic of China as sponsored family immigrants and refugees. Some are from rural backgrounds and lack the education and language fluency to integrate easily into Canadian society, while many are well-educated former students, some of whom sought refuge after the massacre in Tiananmen Square.[53] As well, ethnic Chinese arrive from Taiwan and other countries.

The Move to Working at Home

Information about immigrant women's paid work at home was elicited in lengthy semistructured interviews in each woman's first language: Mandarin, Cantonese and Portuguese, and participants were paid a small honorarium. The interviews were conducted at each woman's home by interviewers of Chinese and Portuguese backgrounds. Interviews were guided by a schedule that concentrated on immigration experience, work history and current working conditions, family and household relations, and personal history. Semistructured interviews allowed us to explore in detail the reasons for women's immigration and employment decisions and their evaluations of homework. The interview schedule was flexible, giving participants control over the sequence and depth of questions about each topic. The completed interviews were lengthy, between one and a half and three hours long.[54]

The participants in this study have diverse immigration experiences, as well as personal and work histories that interrelate with ethnicity. The majority of the women are currently married with children. (See Table 5.1.) Half the women have preschool and school-aged children at home, while five have adult children who are working or attending postsecondary education. In most cases, the adult children lived away from home, even before they married. Ethnic differences are apparent in the women's educational achievements and abilities to speak English. The educational backgrounds and linguistic abilities of Portuguese women were fairly consistent. Only two had completed some high school, while the others had finished elementary education. All of the Portuguese women judged that they could speak some English, but none was satisfied with her proficiency, for example, "It's enough for my work and to do things, ... I can't carry on a fluent conversation" (Lucy, cleaner).[55]

> I know how to speak English, but it's not the kind of English that people who went to school speak — they know more. And some things I can't read and I ask my daughter or my son. ... (Augusta, garment worker)

In comparison, Chinese women have more diverse educational backgrounds and linguistic abilities. One Chinese woman had never attended school and at the other extreme, one woman had completed medical school. Their ability to speak English also varies from three women who cannot speak any English to two who claimed some proficiency. The more varied backgrounds of Chinese women are reflected in their immigration histories. In general, the Chinese are more recent immigrants of whom the majority arrived after 1979. Although five of the six Chinese participants were born in the People's Republic of China, three of them came to Canada from a second country. In contrast, most of the Portuguese women immigrated directly to Canada between 1955 and 1979. Only one of the six Portuguese women had lived in a second country before coming to Canada.

TABLE 5.1
Social Characteristics and Immigration History

Name[a]	Country of Birth	Year of Immigration to Canada	Marital Status	Children[b]	Education Completed	English Proficiency[c]
Lucy	Madeira, Portugal	1971	Separated	3 adult	Elementary	Not fluent
Marie Jose	Azores, Portugal	1955	Married	2 adult	Elementary	Not fluent
Belmira	Azores, Portugal	1975	Married	2 sons (14, 9)	Some high school, commercial courses	Not fluent
Ricanda	Mainland, Portugal	1988	Married	Daughter (13), 2 sons (8, 9)	Elementary	Not fluent
Augusta	Azores, Portugal	1965	Married	Daughter (16), 2 sons (12, 7)	Elementary	Not fluent
Fernanda	Mainland, Portugal	1969	Married	2 adult	Some high school	Not fluent
Ming Lai	China	1975	Married	Daughter (14), son (15)	High school graduate	None
Fu Jun	Bangkok, Thailand	1980	Single	None	Some high school	Some fluency
May Ying	China	1971	Married	5 adult	None	None
Qin	China	1984	Married	Daughter (1), son (6)	Some high school/ commercial courses	Some fluency
Ying Chan	China	1991	Widow	2 adult	Medical school graduate	None
Madelaine	China	1989	Divorced	Daughter (NA)	Some law school	Not fluent

[a] Pseudonyms are used to protect the identities of all informants.
[b] Except in the case of adult children, ages of children are listed in parentheses. Adult children have all finished or left high school. They are employed or attending college, technical schools and university, although some still live at home.
[c] Each woman's English proficiency is based on her own self-assessment. "None" indicates the woman does not speak English, "Not fluent" indicates she speaks English but not well, and "Some fluency" indicates the ability to speak English well, but not perfectly.
NA = Not available

Women from both ethnic groups were involved in various types of homework that were weakly related to their educational backgrounds. (See Table 5.2.) One well-educated Chinese woman worked as a typist, while three less-educated Chinese women did industrial homework as garment workers. The experiences of two other Chinese women illustrate the weak effects of education. The two Chinese women engaged in child care and housekeeping are poles apart in terms of education. One has never attended school, while the other is a former physician who retired in China before immigrating to Canada. (See Table 5.1.) Among Portuguese women who generally had less education than Chinese women, the relationship between education and type of homework is also complex. Portuguese women were working as cleaners, operating small family

TABLE 5.2
Working Conditions: Past and Present

Name[a]	Current Occupation	Working Hours (per week)	Previous Occupation	Location of Previous Job
Portuguese:				
Lucy	cleaner	50–55	cleaner	offices
Marie Jose	child care worker	55–65	garment worker	factory
Belmira	garment worker	52–56	cleaner	offices
Ricanda	child care worker	NA	cleaner	offices
Augusta	child care worker	55–65	auto parts producer	factory
Fernanda	electrolysis	15–20	cleaner	factory
Chinese:				
Ming Lai	garment worker	50–60	garment worker	factory
Fu Jun	garment worker	50–55	garment worker	factory
May Ying	child care worker	50–55	cleaner	offices
Qin	typist	NA	typist	office
Ying Chan	child care/ housekeeper	65–98	pediatrician	office
Madelaine	garment worker	72–90	garment worker	factory

[a] Pseudonyms are used to protect the identities of all informants.
NA = Not available

daycares and providing aesthetic services. (See Table 5.2.) Only one Portuguese woman was employed as a garment worker.

Regardless of women's ethnic backgrounds, the interviews highlighted the link between the decline in factory work and the rise of paid work at home that has been observed elsewhere.[56] Prior to taking up homework, women from both ethnic groups had worked in a variety of jobs. In their home countries, they had worked in factories, as waitresses and as a photographer's assistant; they had done agricultural labour and practised medicine. Only two Portuguese women and two Chinese women had worked at home as seamstresses, embroiderers and toy makers before immigrating to Canada. All of the women found jobs outside the home after arriving in Toronto. (See Table 5.2.) They were engaged in a wide range of activities, including production work in factories, cleaning offices, secretarial work and personal services. There was some ethnic segmentation: four of the six Portuguese women cleaned offices and factories, while half the Chinese women worked in garment factories. Chinese and Portuguese women pointed to the loss of factory jobs and declining wages, injuries on the job and conflicts with supervisors as major reasons for leaving formal work settings. Three Chinese women and four Portuguese women left factory and cleaning jobs because they were laid off and the amount of work had declined. For all but two of the remaining women, medical problems associated with working conditions and conflicts with supervisors were the main reasons for leaving paid jobs outside the home.

In this group of immigrant women, concerns about child care costs rarely motivated women to abandon paid employment in a factory or office setting for homework. Only one Chinese woman said that she started doing homework because she was worried about the costs of child care. Sometimes the departure from a formal job coincided with a pregnancy, but none of the women described pregnancy as the precipitating reason for leaving factory and cleaning jobs. The relative insignificance of child care costs is the same for Portuguese and Chinese women despite the differences in their immigration and work histories. This is in contrast with findings from previous surveys of Chinese garment workers that mentioned child care costs as a major reason for working at home.[57] Family considerations, particularly the need to care for young children, were not among the reasons given by Chinese or Portuguese women for becoming homeworkers; rather the possibility of caring for children while earning a wage was sometimes given as a reason for remaining in homework, or described as one of the benefits of homework.

The interviews also confirmed that the invisibility of homework is as much a consequence of the immigrant status of the women who resort to it as it is of its location in the home. Portuguese and Chinese women did not feel that they had any alternatives to working at home. Their limited education and language fluency prevented them from seeking formal employment other than factory and cleaning jobs. Portuguese and Chinese garment workers had looked for factory jobs, but they had accepted homework because it was available and, ironically, because they described it as more secure and steady work. Cleaners and child care workers who had lost factory and office jobs pointed to suggestions from friends and relatives as the major reason for beginning to work at home. In all cases, homework was viewed initially as a short-term economic survival strategy that would tide the women over until factory and office jobs were available.

The work histories confirm that these immigrant women resorted to working at home when there were no feasible alternative forms of paid employment. During this period of rapid restructuring, many of the production and service jobs held previously by these immigrant women disappeared or relocated, while employers recruited a contingent workforce that would increase their flexibility and reduce labour and operating costs. When compared to unemployment, homework was considered the lesser of two evils, at least for these Chinese and Portuguese immigrants who are marginalized in the labour market by virtue of their skills, language fluency, ethnicity and domestic relations. While Allen and Wolkowitz do not examine the complexities of ethnicity and the enormous variety of types of homework in their early research, little seems to have changed since the 1970s when they noted that "the unemployed lack the resources to participate either in the formal or informal sections of the economy as self-employed, but homeworking in the manufacturing sector may be an available form of paid work for them. This cannot be interpreted as a viable "lifestyle" or a freely chosen option. ..."[58]

Among these immigrant women, working at home is mainly a response to macroeconomic changes. It does not represent a brave new future where work and home life are accommodated successfully by domesticating the workplace.[59]

Working conditions of women from both ethnic groups are similar to those reported elsewhere for industrial homeworkers.[60] In general,

Portuguese and Chinese women worked between fifty and sixty hours per week, more than permitted by legislation. (See Table 5.2.) Daily work hours often exceeded the number permitted under the *Employment Standards Act*, which regulates the paid work of employees. Many women worked up to fifteen hours per day, a trend that has also been observed among service workers based at home.[61] The length of the work day was extremely variable, often depending upon the demands of the employers. Chinese and Portuguese garment workers laboured long hours to meet short deadlines, while child care workers were occupied as required by parents. Cleaners worked equally long hours except where they had been able to negotiate a flat rate for cleaning by the house rather than cleaning by the hour. Cleaners and garment workers were frequently asked to work on the weekends, while child care workers reported more ability to refuse requests to babysit outside regular hours unless they "lived in" at their employer's home.

Poor working conditions were associated with inadequate compensation, which is also typical of homework.[62] Weekly variations in working hours caused pay to vary. Most of the homeworkers do a form of piecework, being paid by the number of children they cared for, the amount and "quality" of sewing they completed and the number of houses they cleaned. None of these Chinese and Portuguese women received benefits, overtime premiums or vacation pay. Despite the fact that homework is regulated by the *Employment Standards Act* and homeworkers are "employees" under the Act, employers consistently ignored the legislation and illegally treated their homeworking employees as "self-employed" workers, solely responsible for making all contributions to any benefit plans for which they qualified. As self-employed workers, none is eligible for unemployment insurance or workers' compensation.

Despite the similarities in their working conditions, the interviews revealed important differences in their evaluations of homework. To illustrate and elucidate the nature of these ethnic differences, we outline briefly the major advantages and shortcomings of homework identified by the immigrant women themselves. Beginning with Chinese women, we discuss their views of homework and its impact on their household and family relations. A similar description from Portuguese women follows. The discussions centre on four factors that underlay commonalities and differences between the two groups. Gender relations in the household form part of the context within which Chinese and Portuguese women accommodate the competing demands of paid homework and unpaid domestic labour. Cultural notions about the value of education also seems to influence Chinese and Portuguese women's evaluations of homework. Finally, the women's prior experience of paid work at home in Canada and elsewhere and their work histories as immigrants in Canada in a period of restructuring contribute to different views of homework in the two ethnic groups.

Chinese Women

We detected a certain resignation in the interviews with Chinese women. They regarded work as an investment in the education and the future of immediate and extended family relatives ("family" being defined as those living in the same household in Toronto and possibly those living elsewhere). Homework was a means to an end that might benefit the women indirectly via the future kindness of their educated children. Although, as one Chinese babysitter expressed, in Canada respect for the elders was not important:

> The children, even though I feed them and provide food and housing, when they're grown up they don't want you to live with them. That's the life here, that's the life in the West, they don't want to live with you. They want to have their freedom, they want to have their nuclear family, they want to have their own family and you're an old woman or an old man. They don't want to be with you. (May Ying, babysitter)

The Chinese women described themselves as subordinate to their spouses who were openly criticized by the Chinese women and described as either being too strict with the children, gambling away the money or wanting too much control over household income and over their wives' activities. The women from mainland China described a greater independence from men in their home country than in Canada:

> For instance, in China, when I was angry, I just showed my anger. And when I wanted to complain, I just complained. Now, with my husband, I say one sentence and he will retort ten sentences back to me. So I have decided — never mind, forget it. It's better to be quiet to avoid the fights. (Qin, typist)

I think traditionally Chinese men have more power, more control, but in China it has been changed after the liberation. Now in China wives don't have to obey husbands because they have jobs and they are independent financially. (Ying Chan, live-in babysitter)

Chinese men in Toronto were described as wielding control over women's decisions to do homework, their working conditions and their earnings:

My husband said to me that it's impossible for me to find my old job, the type of job that I worked in China [she was an accountant]. He told me that I could never do what I did before and I would have difficulty doing the same profession, so I believed in him. (Qin, typist)

All my money is in my husband's hand. Even my mother is quite angry about it. My mother said, what's wrong with me? She said, "How could you let this happen? How would you not even have a penny to yourself?" She couldn't believe that I don't even have my own private savings. (Qin, typist)

I don't really interfere with my husband's private life. But on the other hand, he does want to control me, to have power over me. For example, when I have to work late because of my work, he didn't want me to do it, and he would complain. But on the other hand, he doesn't help me. (Ming Lai, seamstress)

The Chinese women referred to themselves as central to the economic survival of the family — of children, siblings and parents — and to the dream of education for family members, and these were the reasons that they worked so hard. Unlike the Portuguese women, Chinese women tended to describe the purpose of their work as benefiting others rather than themselves:

I support my children with my money, so I cannot afford not to work. ... I'm very stingy on myself. But in terms of the children, I try and get them as much as they need. My husband, once in a while, he gives them a little bit of money. ... Ninety-eight per cent of the time I pay for everything. I feel that with my two children, I have to try my best to support them until they become mature, until they become independent. I would also like them to go to university. (Ming Lai, seamstress)

All my brothers and sisters are either attending university or have university degrees, except me, of course. ... I give everything I make to my parents, and my parents pay for everything. (Fu Jun, seamstress)

My parents were traditional, very conservative and I was the oldest daughter and my mother wanted me to be her servant. ... My brother and sister, though, they have gone to university, they have university education. It's only me that I have not gone to school at all, not even for one day. That's why I really put all my energy on my children, so that, you know, it's a good thing that my children proved to be rewarding for me. Even though my life is bitter, it's also sweet. (May Ying, babysitter)

The Chinese women complained of various ailments that they attributed to their work — digestive problems due to bad nerves for May Ying (babysitter), indigestion and ulcers, hay fever and rheumatism for Ming Lai (seamstress), and eyesight and pains in the hands for Qin, the typist. For the most part, they saw few solutions to these problems. The Chinese homeworkers often felt unable to escape the conflicts that arose when productive and reproductive activities occurred in the same space.

Chinese women varied in their ability to speak English. Some women spoke little English, although their husbands' language needs had been addressed more adequately and at some cost to the women:

I have studied for a few months English for immigrants. I used to study from seven to nine. But my husband had to take care of the kids, so then after a while it didn't work out. ... My husband, he studied English too. But he studied when he first came. But, yes, he's better than me. He studied longer. He can speak better than I do. (Ming Lai, seamstress)

Others who had been professionals or semiprofessionals in China had learned English among other languages in school. The perceptions of these women regarding the link between their lack of language skills and job choices are accurate and poignant.[63] The women saw few possibilities for improvement in their own job status in Canada. Only two Chinese women aspired to professional careers, although both felt constrained by their limited knowledge of English. One woman spoke for several others when she referred to her retirement as a time when she would finally be "free":

> I'm just looking forward to when I retire in five years. In five years I feel that I will be free and I'll be on my own and I can go anywhere — north, south, east and west — who knows. When I get to sixty-five, I'm not going to bother with the family. (May Ying, babysitter)

Chinese women were resigned to the rigours of homework. Many women were frustrated juggling the competing demands of paid and unpaid work in households where men were described as dominant. Nor did education ensure success in the labour market, where lack of English proficiency hampered all Chinese homeworkers. Lack of fluency also restricted the types of homework in which Chinese women were involved, possibly reducing their satisfaction with this type of work. All of the Chinese homeworkers complained about their hours of work, which were inflexible and largely outside their control. The garment workers often worked long into the night to have one day free each week, while the child care worker and housekeeper were at the mercy of their employers, who often arrived late to care for their children.

·There were some differences in the assessments of various homeworkers. The three garment workers were isolated, forced to work alone for long and unpredictable hours. They also resented their dependency on jobbers who scheduled work unpredictably and with little consultation. The child care worker and housekeeper were more satisfied with their jobs, largely because enjoyment of the children compensated somewhat for lower wages and long working hours. Social interaction, even if it was mainly with the children in their care, was an important source of job satisfaction for the child care worker and housekeeper. Both workers felt that they did essential work for their employers, whose job status was a source of pride for both women. They enjoyed the autonomy of domestic work, where each was her own boss for much of the day.

Portuguese Women

The majority of Portuguese women also like working at home. They enjoy the work, particularly the child care workers and cleaners.

> ... I started working in the private homes because I liked it and that's what I'm still doing today. It's work that I love. (Lucy, cleaner)

> ... this kind of work, I've always like it, always. ... Let me tell you, I wouldn't exchange my work life for anything! (Marie Jose, child care worker)

The Portuguese women mentioned several advantages of homework including having no boss, being able to schedule their own hours and not having to travel and be away from home. Two women also referred to the health benefits of homework, which allowed them to avoid catching colds when commuting or working with others in a factory. The women prize the characteristics of homework that contrast most with the characteristics of their previous factory and office jobs. It is not surprising that they value autonomy since several had quit work after disputes with bosses and supervisors. Flexible work hours may be more of an illusion than a reality, but the idea of setting one's own hours is an important aspect of autonomy. Finally, before leaving formal workplaces, some women had commuted long distances by public transit from central Toronto to suburban Scarborough as factories relocated to the suburbs. Working at home offers welcome relief from these lengthy, time-consuming trips.

Unlike the Chinese women, the Portuguese women participate in the household's financial management. They see themselves as having some authority within the household unit. Financial decisions, everyday purchases and earnings are pooled and disbursed after the women and their spouses reach an agreement.

> We agree on things together. We plan together to see if we agree. ... He gets his cheque, he gives it over to me. He doesn't even verify the bank book, he trusts me. And, of course, he works and we are on this together. (Ricarda, food preparation)

Indeed, in some households, the homeworkers largely control everyday expenditures:

> Either one of us goes to the bank. We've always had a good understanding on that, and I've always had my money. I know people, where the wife works, and she never sees a cent. Even if I didn't have money and didn't work, I'd *still* have money. If it's me who goes to the bank, I keep the money in my purse and then I'll give it to him … so when he needs it, he goes and takes it from my purse. But he has to warn me because then I don't count on that money anymore. I don't want to be surprised. He does it in front of me, and we don't have any kind of secrets between us. (Belmira, garment worker)

Despite the emphasis on pooling earnings and collective decision making, Portuguese men and women do not always agree completely about financial matters. Several women commented about their husbands needing money for beer and other amusements, while they needed less money because of working at home.

> I don't drink beer, but I don't need much money because I stay home. So when he needs it, he goes and takes it from my purse. (Belmira, garment worker)

For many of the Portuguese women, working at home seems compatible with their rural backgrounds and limited educational attainments.

> I have this job that I like. I don't mean as it relates to the quality of the work, but because I can stay at home. I already came from Portugal like this, not liking to get out of the house. I only went out when I really needed to. And here it was difficult too because I wasn't used to working outside of the home. I learned to do all the work at home, but with my mother, I didn't have foreladies [female bosses] or the like. When I came here I was obliged to go and work outside, and it was extremely difficult, and added to other hardships I went through. (Belmira, garment worker)

These women are not naïve. Other studies have shown that Portuguese women who work in formal settings are highly politicized.[64]

The Portuguese homeworkers recognize some of the serious disadvantages of homework. They are concerned by the lack of benefits. As one woman who works for a private daycare agency said:

> Now I don't have any kids, but I can't go on unemployment. But I'm private daycare so I don't get those benefits. So I don't get anything, no benefits whatsoever ... So she [agency person] told me I'd have to pay out of my own pocket to get some benefits. ... It would be much better for me, of course. I don't think I should pay out of my pocket because the mothers pay them [the agency] more than what they pay us per child. (Augusta, child care worker)

Several women were exploring how to pay for pension, unemployment and workers' compensation plans at the time of the interviews. They were also concerned about low wages and the failure of employers to offer pay increases.

Many women regret their lack of English and education. Remarking that they "had to work," they say that they would have liked to have been professionals in the same (or related) field. The child care workers want to be teachers or operate licensed daycares, and a garment worker wants to be a hairdresser. Limited fluency in English and restricted educational opportunities have reduced their future job possibilities.

The Portuguese women convey an attitude of acceptance when discussing their work at home. Working at home was not their first job choice in most cases. Many Portuguese women emphasize that they work at home because there were no other jobs available at the time that they were looking. Out of work, they learned about homeworking opportunities from friends and relatives. Having begun homework, some have come to enjoy it and their working conditions.

Differences and Commonalities

It is clear that Portuguese women found working at home more acceptable than Chinese women. The various evaluations are striking, particularly in light of the women's common reasons for taking up homework. Paid work at home was a survival strategy adopted as jobs in factories and offices disappeared. Despite their common employment histories, Portuguese and Chinese women expressed very different opinions about doing paid work at home. The varied opinions are rooted in ethnic differences in gender relations in the household, cultural notions about the value of education, prior experience of working at home and type of homework.

Gender relations within the household seem to be important factors influencing women's views of homework. In the Portuguese households, women felt that their husbands were supportive of their work. They commented that their husbands did a variety of domestic work ranging from preparing meals to caring for young children as needed to accommodate the demands of the women's homework. In the case of a garment worker, the husband helped her complete work by picking up materials and delivering the finished garments, particularly when she was pressed for time. Whether or not the men actually did many domestic tasks was not discerned; however, the women's beliefs that their husbands were willing to help them certainly contributed to their satisfaction with this form of work. In part, the support of their spouses may have compensated for the loss of social contacts at factories and other formal work settings.

In contrast, the married Chinese women reported that their husbands were of little support or assistance. Indeed, as their comments about financial management indicate, gender relations in the Chinese households appear on the surface to be very unequal. Isolated by work at home and without the support of spouses and other family members, Chinese women are more dissatisfied with homework than their Portuguese counterparts. Only one of the Portuguese women stated that she would return to factory work if a job became available while all of the Chinese garment workers expressed this preference. For Portuguese women, the opportunity to be at home while working was attractive. For Chinese women, who were more dissatisfied with gender relations within their households, being at home was a disadvantage of homework.

Cultural notions about the importance of education influence evaluations of homework. There was a positive and clear commitment regarding the importance of education among the Chinese women. In all cases they worked to support the education of children, siblings, nieces and nephews who were in Canada or still in the home country. This was less likely to be the case among Portuguese women who often regarded hard work as a means of more immediate accumulation of material goods for the benefit of the whole family unit. Portuguese children were more likely to be encouraged to find jobs, even if it meant leaving high school before graduating.

The type of homework and women's past experiences with homework also seem to influence women's evaluations. Some of the Portuguese women had worked as embroiderers in their country of origin. The skill involved in embroidery is not easily transferable to the Canadian job market. With limited education and little transferable work experience and skills, Portuguese women end up doing cleaning and child care. Compared with industrial homework in the garment industry, child care and cleaning were considered less isolating and more personally satisfying. The four Portuguese women and both Chinese women who worked as cleaners and child care workers commented about how much they liked the children in their care and the people for whom they worked. They emphasized the importance of these social relations in their descriptions of their work. In contrast, the Chinese workers sewing at home who had previous experience as seamstresses or as factory workers described themselves as very isolated. They all expressed interest in returning to factory work whenever possible, a measure of their dissatisfaction with industrial homework. Type of homework plays an important role in immigrant women's evaluations, which are also influenced by ethnicity.

Ethnic differences in the views of homework arise from several sources. Faced with the need to earn a living as Toronto's economy is restructured, the Chinese and Portuguese women in this study all took up homework. However, their evaluations of homework are influenced by gender roles that have evolved as the women moved from their countries of origin and established households in Canada, cultural notions about the importance of education, their experiences as immigrants in the Canadian labour market and work experiences elsewhere. In general, Portuguese women are more satisfied with homework than their Chinese counterparts; however, ethnic differences diminish once type of homework is considered. The question that we have begun to address is how ethnicity interrelates with work experience, education and immigration experience[65] so that women from each ethnic group have ended up in different types of homework. Ethnicity is only one of several factors that influence immigrant women's experiences and evaluations of homework, but its relative importance can only be established in a larger study.

Conclusion

The case studies have confirmed that homework is a survival strategy adopted in the face of the economic restructuring that has led to job losses in offices and factories. To reduce labour and operating costs, employers have domesticated paid workers, creating a contingent workforce that is available on demand as production needs require. Our findings in Toronto are similar to those reported in a much larger British study[66] in so far as working-class immigrant women who do paid work at home tend to be in the least remunerative and most precarious forms of homework. All of the women in our study complained about low wages, lack of benefits and the unpredictability of work. For these working-class immigrant women whose employment opportunities are limited by lack of Canadian experience, limited fluency in English and lack of training, homework does not provide stable, secure and satisfying employment. Sometimes unsafe and unhealthy, working conditions were always demanding because of long, unpredictable hours.

The case studies suggest that homeworkers are not passive victims of macroeconomic changes outside their control. Having taken up homework, some women came to prefer working at home. All of the women found working at home were available to their children. However, the women in service occupations, employed as child care workers, housekeepers and cleaners, reported greater satisfaction with homework than industrial homeworkers. In service occupations homeworkers found more autonomy and control than they had in previous jobs in factories and offices. When these advantages were combined with freedom from commuting and social interaction with employers and children, domestic service jobs were preferred over employment in factories and offices. This contrasts with industrial homeworkers who found few advantages in working at home and, without exception, preferred to work in a factory if work were available.

The literature on immigrant women has tended to treat them as a homogeneous group. By extension, diversity among immigrant women homeworkers has been inadequately explored.[67] This pilot study has suggested that there is a good deal of variation in the way immigrant women evaluate their paid work at home. Although our findings are only suggestive, the diversity of women's experiences of homework revealed in the interviews underscores how involvement in paid work is defined by and through their ethnicity. While Portuguese and Chinese women share a desire and need to work, their success as homeworkers reflects in part their abilities to overcome constraints imposed by patriarchal relations within the family, limited access to state services, class position, the racism that ethnic minorities experience in Canada and the working conditions characteristic of homework.

By concentrating on the household rather than a single industry, the pilot study has suggested the potential range of women's experiences at homework. Among Chinese and Portuguese immigrant women, homework encompasses a wide variety of jobs from typing and hairdressing to industrial sewing and domestic work in the form of child care, food preparation and cleaning. Studies of only one industrial sector (e.g., the garment industry) are complemented by investigations of the variety of work done at home. Comparisons reveal differences in job satisfaction across industrial sectors, although working conditions are described as poor in all sectors included in this study.

The need for comparative studies is underlined by the homeworkers' stories, which illustrate how changes in the way that capitalism organizes production are altering home and household relations. Mediating institutions,[68] such as the state and employers, set the terrain on which each homeworker negotiates conditions of work. In turn, these working conditions influence and are influenced by household relations. Thus, in a study of ethnicity, it is important to understand not only the role of mediating institutions and the way they formally regulate employment, but also their relationship with the domestic enterprise.

Additional research on a larger scale is needed to confirm the findings from the pilot study. In particular, more attention should be given to exploring the politics of homeworkers' struggles. Homeworkers are striving to be viewed as employees rather than independent self-employed workers, so they may obtain benefits that are rightly theirs under current employment legislation. Responding to the concerns of homeworkers, the International Ladies Garment Workers' Union is lobbying for enforcement of the Employment Standards Act vis-à-vis homework[69] and homeworkers themselves have begun to organize in the Homeworkers' Association in Toronto. Both the private and public struggles of homeworkers regarding the conditions of domesticated paid work can be advanced through a fuller comprehension of the diversity of immigrant women's experiences in homework.

Notes

This research was completed with funding from SSHRC grant 816-93-0131 awarded to W. Giles, S. Arat-Koc, W. Lem and V. Preston. We are grateful for the assistance of our co-investigators. Research assistance was ably provided by Ilda Januario, Guida Man and Meilian Lam. We thank the reviewers for their helpful comments. An earlier draft of this paper was presented at the Canadian Sociology and Anthropology Meetings in Calgary, June 1994.

1. Manuel Castells and A. Portes, "World Underneath: The Origins, Dynamics and Effects of the Informal Economy," in A. Portes, M. Castells and L.A. Benton (eds.), *The Informal Economy: Studies in Advanced and Less Developed Countries* (Baltimore and London: Johns Hopkins University Press, 1989).
2. Michele Hoyman, "Female Participation in the Informal Economy: A Neglected Issue," *The Annals of the American Academy of Political and Social Science* 493 (1987).
3. Marjorie Cohen, "The MacDonald Report and Its Implications for Women" (Toronto: National Action Committee on the Status of Women, 1985); Marjorie Cohen, *Free Trade and the Future of Women's Work: Manufacturing and Service Industries* (Toronto: Garamond, 1987); Daniel Drache and Duncan Cameron, *The Other Macdonald Report* (1985); Ontario Advisory Council on the Status of Women, *Recommendations for Changes to the Employment Standards Act* (Toronto, 1989); Alice de Wolff, *Review of the Situation of Women in Canada* (Toronto: National Action Committee on the Status of Women, 1992); Martha MacDonald, "Post-Fordism and the Flexibility Debate," *Studies in Political Economy* 36 (1991).
4. International Ladies Garment Workers' Union (ILGWU), *Homeworkers: Fair Wages and Working Conditions for Homeworkers: A Brief to the Government of Ontario* (1991); Virginia Galt, "Oh Give Me a Home ...," *The Globe and Mail* (Sept 19, 1992).
5. Suzanne MacKenzie, "Building Women, Building Cities: Toward Gender Sensitive Theory in the Environmental Disciplines," in C. Andrew and B.M. Milroy (eds.), *Life Spaces: Gender, Household, Employment* (Vancouver: U.B.C. Press, 1988).
6. Belinda Leach, "'Flexible' Work, Precarious Future: Some Lessons from the Canadian Clothing Industry," *Canadian Review of Sociology and Anthropology* 30/1 (1993), 64–82.
7. Susan Hanson and Geraldine Pratt, "Dynamic Dependencies: A Geographic Investigation of Local Labor Markets," *Economic Geography* 68 (1992), 373–405.
8. Isabel Dyck, "Integrating Home and Wage Workplace: Women's Daily Lives in a Canadian Suburb," *The Canadian Geographer* 33 (1989), 329–341; Susan Hanson and Geraldine Pratt, "Geographic Perspectives on the Occupational Segregation of Women," *National Geographic Research* 6 (1990), 376–399; Jaqueline Tivers, *Women Attached: The Daily Lives of Women with Young Children* (London: Croom Helm, 1985).
9. Robert Murdie, "Economic Restructuring and Social Polarization in Toronto: Impacts on an Immigrant Population," mimeo (North York, ON: Department of Geography, York University, 1994); Glen Norcliffe, Michael Goldrick and Leon Muszynski, "Cyclical Factors, Technological Change, Capital Mobility, and Deindustrialization in Metropolitan Toronto," *Urban Geography* 7 (1986), 413–436.
10. Murdie, "Economic Restructuring and Social Polarization."
11. Alice de Wolff, *Job Loss and Entry Level Information Workers: Training and Adjustment Strategies for Clerical Workers in Metro Toronto*, Report of the Metro Toronto Clerical Workers' Labour Adjustment Committee (July 1995).

12. Teresa Amott, *Caught in the Crisis: Women and the U.S. Economy Today* (New York: Basic Books, 1993); Anne Phizacklea and Mary Wolkowitz, *Homeworking Women: Gender, Racism and Class at Work* (London: Sage Publications, 1995).

13. Bennett Harrison, *Lean and Mean, The Changing Landscape of Corporate Power in the Age of Flexibility* (New York: Basic Books, 1994); Harvie Ramsay, Anna Pollert and Helen Rainbird, "A Decade of Transformation? Labour Market Flexibility and Work Organization in the United Kingdom," *New Directions in Work Organization: The Industrial Relations Response* (1992), 169–189.

14. Phizacklea and Wolkowitz, *Homeworking Women*; Leach, "'Flexible' Work,"; Kathleen Christensen, presentation at "A Conference on Homeworking: From the Double Day to the Endless Day," Regis College, Toronto, November 13–15, 1992; Sheila Allen and Carol Wolkowitz, "Homeworking and the Control of Women's Work: in Feminist Review (ed.), *Waged Work: A Reader* (London: Virago Press, 1986), 238–264.

15. Jan Borowy, "Super Fitness, Super Scam," *Our Times* 15/2 (1996), 19–23; Jan Borowy and Fanny Yuen, *The International Ladies Garment Workers' Union 1993 Homeworkers' Study: An Investigation into Wages and Working Conditions of Chinese-Speaking Homeworkers in Metropolitan Toronto* (Toronto: ILGWU, 1993); Barbara Cameron and Teresa Mak, "Chinese Speaking Homeworkers in Toronto: Summary of Results of a Survey Conducted by the ILGWU" (Toronto: ILGWU, 1991); Women and Work Research and Education Society (WWRES) & the International Ladies Garment Workers' Union (ILGWU), "Industrial Homework and Employment Standards: A Community Approach to 'Visibility' and Understanding," brief prepared for Improved Employment Legislation for the Ministry of Women's Equality, Vancouver, British Columbia, 1993.

16. Conference Handbook Committee (CHC), *From the Double Day to the Endless Day*, Proceedings from the Conference on Homeworking (Ottawa: Canadian Centre for Policy Alternatives, 1992).

17. Kathleen Christensen, *The New Era of Home-based Work* (Boulder: Westview Press, 1988).

18. Barbara Orser and Mary Foster, *Home Enterprise, Canadians and Home-based Work* (Ottawa: The National Home-based Business Project Committee, 1992).

19. Phizacklea and Wolkowitz, *Homeworking Women*; Leach, "'Flexible' Work,"; CHC, *From the Double Day to the Endless Day.*

20. Christensen, *The New Era of Home-based Work*; Claire Letourneau, "Telecommuting and Electronic Homework in Canada" (Ottawa: Womens Bureau, Labour Canada, 1990).

21. Leach, "'Flexible' Work"; Urban Dimensions Group, *Growth of the Contingent Workforce in Ontario: Structural Trends, Statistical Dimensions and Policy Implications* (Ontario Women's Directorate, 1989); Susan Christopherson, "Flexibility in the U.S. Service Economy and the Emerging Spatial Division of Labour," *Transactions Institute of British Geographers* 14 (1989), 131–143; S. Seward and K. McDade, *Immigrant Women in Canada: A Policy Perspective* (Ottawa: Canadian Advisory Council on the Status of Women, 1988); Alma Estable, *Immigrant Women in Canada: Current Issues* (Ottawa: Canadian Advisory Council on the Status of Women, 1986); S. Mitter, "Industrial Restructuring and Manufacturing Homework: Immigrant Women in the Clothing Industry," *Capital*

and *Class* 27 (1986), 37–80; Saskia Sassen, "The Informal Economy," in J.H. Mollenkopf and M. Castells (eds.), *Dual City, Restructuring New York* (New York: Russell Sage Foundation, 1991), 79–102; K. Ward, *Women Workers and Global Restructuring* (Ithaca: L.R. Press, 1990); Roxana Ng, "Sexism, Racism and Canadian Nationalism," in Snega Gunew and Anna Yeatman (eds.), *Feminism and the Politics of Difference* (Halifax: Fernwood, 1993), 197–211; Monica Boyd, "Gender, Visible Minority and Immigrant Earnings Inequality: Reassessing an Employment Equity Premise," in V. Satzewich (ed.), *Deconstructing a Nation: Immigration, Multiculturalism and Racism in 90s in Canada* (Toronto: Fernwood Press, 1992), 279–321; Borowy and Yuen, *The ILGWU 1993 Homeworkers Study*; WWRES and ILGWU, "Industrial Homework and Employment Standards."

22. Jobbers are typical of the garment industry where a clothing manufacturer may subcontract production of a garment by arranging for fabric to be ordered and cut according to the pattern. The jobber will subcontract garment assembly to individual seamstresses who are hired to complete piecework as self-employed workers. Jobbers act as middlemen between the manufacturer and individual workers. There may be a hierarchy of jobbers, according to Leach, "'Flexible' Work." See also Louis A. Ferman, Stuart Henry and Michele M. Hoyman, "Issues and Prospects for the Study of Informal Economies: Concepts, Research Strategies, and Policy," *Annals of the American Academy of Political and Social Science* 493 (1987), 154–172.

23. Wenona Giles, "Clean Jobs, Dirty Jobs: Ethnicity, Social Reproduction and Gendered Identity,"*Culture* 13/2 (1993), 37–44.

24. M. Labelle, G. Turcotte, M. Kempeneers and D. Meintel, *Histoires d'Immigrées, Itinéraires d'Ouvrières Columbiennes, Greques, Haïtennes et Portugaises de Montréal* (Montréal: Boréal, 1987); ILGWU, *Homeworkers: Fair Wages and Working Conditions.*

25. Snowball sampling involves asking initial informants to identify subsequent informants. Each informant is known to at least one other informant. The sample is not random, raising questions about its ability to represent the population. Earl Babbie, *The Practice of Social Research* (Belmont: Wadsworth, 1983).

26. Andrew Sayer, *Method in Social Science: A Realist Approach* (London: Hutchinson, 1984).

27. Labelle et al., *Histoires d'Immigrées*; Giles, "Clean Jobs, Dirty Jobs"; Ruth Fincher, Ian Campbell and Michael Webber, "Multiculturalism, Settlement and Migrants' Income and Employment Strategies," in G. Clark, D. Forbes and R. Francis (eds.), *Multiculturalism, Difference and Postmodernism* (Melbourne: Longman Cheshire, 1993); A. de Wolff, *Review of the Situation of Women in Canada*; Roxana Ng, "Managing Female Immigration: A Case of Institutional Sexism and Racism," *Canadian Women's Studies Journal* 12/3 (1992), 20–23; Sedef Arat-Koc, "Importing Housewives: Non-Citizen Domestic Workers and the Crisis of the Domestic Sphere in Canada," in M. Luxton, H. Rosenberg and S. Arat-Koc (eds.), *Through the Kitchen Window: The Politics of Home and Family* (Toronto: Garamond Press, 1990); Monica Boyd, "Immigrant Women: Language, Socioeconomic Inequalities and Policy Issues," in S.S. Halli, F. Trovato and L. Dreidger (eds.), *Ethnic Demography, Canadian Immigrant, Racial and Cultural*

Variations (Ottawa: Carleton University Press, 1990), 275–293; Donna Gabbacia (ed.), *Seeking Common Ground: Multidisciplinary Studies of Immigrant Women in the United States* (Westport: Praeger, 1992), Introduction, xi–xxvi.

28. Carla Lipsig-Mummé, "The Renaissance of Homeworking in Developed Economies," *Industrial Relations* 38 (1983), 545–567. See also Margaret Oldfield, "The Electronic Cottage — Boon or Bane for Mothers," in A.M. Letito and I. Ericsson (eds.), *Proceedings of the Conference on Women, Work and Computerization* (Helsinki, 1991); Theresa Johnson, "Work at Home: New Draft Policy: But What Does It All Mean?" *Alliance* (Public Service Alliance of Canada) (Spring 1992), 4–6; U. Huws, *The New Homeworkers, New Technology and the Changing Location of White Collar Work* (London: Low Pay Unit, 1984); Canada, Treasury Board, *Telework Policy* (1992); Testimony of Dr. Kathleen Christensen before the Employment and Housing Subcommittee, Committee on Government Operations, U.S. House of Representatives, Washington, D.C. 1988; Christensen, *The New Era of Home-based Work*; Christensen, presentation, "Conference on Homeworking."

29. ILGWU, *Homeworkers: Fair Wages and Working*; Belinda Leach, "Ideas About Work and Family: Outwork in Contemporary Ontario," Ph.D. dissertation, Department of Anthropology, University of Toronto, 1992.

30. Giles, "Clean Jobs, Dirty Jobs"; Boyd, "Gender, Visible Minority"; Fincher et al., "Multiculturalism, Settlement."

31. On diversity among first-generation immigrant women, see Boyd, "Gender, Visible Minority"; For critical use of the term "immigrant women," see Ng, "Sexism, Racism and Canadian Nationalism."

32. Boyd, "Immigrant Women."

33. Valerie Preston and Wenona Giles, "Ethnicity, Gender and Labour Markets in Canada: A Case Study of Immigrant Women in Toronto," paper presented at the Canadian Sociology and Anthropology Association Meetings, Kingston, Ontario, 1991.

34. Michael Webber, Ian Campbell and Ruth Fincher, "Ethnicity, Gender, and Industrial Restructuring in Australia, 1971–1986," *Journal of Intercultural Studies* 11 (1990), 1–48; Fincher et al., "Multiculturalism, Settlement."

35. Fincher et al., "Multiculturalism, Settlement."

36. Preston and Giles, "Ethnicity, Gender and Labour Markets."

37. Murdie, "Economic Restructuring and Social Polarization."

38. Leach, "Ideas About Work and Family"; Saskia Sassen, *The Global City* (Princeton: Princeton University Press, 1990).

39. Boyd, "Gender, Visible Minority"; Boyd, "Immigrant Women"; Roxana Ng and Alma Estable, "Immigrant Women in the Labour Force: An Overview of Present Knowledge and Research Gaps," *Resources for Feminist Research* 16/1 (1987), 29–33.

40. Roxana Ng, "Sexism, Racism and Canadian Nationalism," in Himani Bannerji (ed.), *Returning the Gaze: Essays on Racism, Feminism and Politics* (Toronto: Sister Vision Press, 1993), 193.

41. Ibid., 195.

42. Nira Yuval-Davis, "Identity Politics and Women's Ethnicity," in Valentine Moghadam (ed.), *Identity, Politics and Women: Cultural Reassertions and Feminisms in International Perspective* (Boulder: Westview Press, 1994), 410.

43. Gill Bottomley, "Living Across Difference: Connecting Gender, Ethnicity, Class and Ageingin Australia," paper presented for the Workshops on the Political Economy of Marriage and the Family, York University, November, 1995, 5–6. See also, Gill Bottomley, "Representing the 'Second Generation': Subjects, Objects and Ways of Knowing," in G. Bottomley, M. de Lepervanche and J. Martin (eds.), *Intersexions: Gender, Class, Culture and Ethnicity* (Sydney: Allen and Unwin, 1991); Gill Bottomley and Marie de Lepervanche (eds.), *Ethnicity, Class and Gender in Australia* (Sydney: Allen and Unwin, 1984).

44. Women's Book Committee, Chinese Canadian National Council, *Jin Guo: Voices of Chinese Canadian Women* (Toronto: Women's Press, 1992); Peter S. Li, *The Chinese in Canada* (Toronto: Oxford University Press, 1988).

45. CHC, *From the Double Day to the Endless Day*; WWRES and ILGWU, "Industrial Homework and Employment Standards."

46. Borowy and Yuen, *ILGWU 1993 Homeworkers' Study*; Cameron and Mak, "Chinese Speaking Homeworkers in Toronto."

47. Phizacklea and Wolkowitz, *Homeworking Women*.

48. While the move to clerical homework is only beginning in Canada, a recent study of clerical workers predicts that once supervisory mechanisms are in place, there will be a massive restructuring of clerical work to homework in the Metropolitan Toronto region. See de Wolff, *Job Loss and Entry Level*.

49. Both Chinese and Portuguese immigrant women in Toronto are racialized, but their racial experiences differ. In her research in the U.S., Ruth Frankenburg argues for "historically specific, politically engaged and provisional" definitions of "race difference" or racialization; Ruth Frankenburg, *White Women, Race Matters: The Social Construction of Whiteness* (London: Routledge, 1993), 12. Frankenburg defines Native Americans, Latinos, African American and Asian/Pacific Americans alike as current targets of racism in the United States. Wenona Giles, *The Gender Relations of a Labour Migration: Two Generations of Portuguese Women in Toronto* (working title; forthcoming) provides a more detailed discussion of the racism experienced by the Portuguese in Toronto.

50. Lucia Grosner, "A Canadian Profile: Toronto's Portuguese and Brazilian Communities" (Toronto: Portuguese Interagency Network, 1995).

51. Jose Carlos Teixeira and Gilles Lavigne, *The Portuguese in Canada: A Bibliography* (Toronto: Institute for Social Research, York University, 1992); Ilda Januario, "Some Statistical Data on the Portuguese-Canadian Population," mimeo (Toronto: Portuguese-Canadian Educators' Association, 1993).

52. According to immigration statistics that are available by country of birth, in 1990, 23,134 immigrants from Hong Kong gained permanent residence in Canada and another 14,193 immigrants from the People's Republic of China became permanent residents. Together, these two countries accounted for 17.4 per cent of all "legal" immigrants in 1990. The number of people emigrating from the People's Republic of China has declined slightly, but it remains an important source of immigrants. C. Inglis, A. Birch and G. Sherington, "An Overview of Australian and Canadian Migration Patterns and Policies," in H. Adelman, A. Borowski, M. Burstein and L. Foster (eds.), *Immigration and Refugee Policy: Australia and Canada Compared*, Vol. 1 (Carlton: Melbourne University Press, 1994), 3–30; Xiaofeng Liu, "New

Mainland Chinese Immigrants: A Case Study in Metro Toronto," Ph.D. dissertation, Department of Geography, York University, 1995.

53. Liu, "New Mainland Chinese Immigrants."

54. The taped interviews were translated by the interviewers. Translations were checked by two of the principal investigators who speak Portuguese and Cantonese. English transcripts were typed by professional transcribers.

55. All names used in this document are pseudonyms.

56. WWRES and ILGWU, "Industrial Homework and Employment Standards"; Fincher et al., "Multiculturalism, Settlement"; CHC, *From the Double Day to the Endless Day.*

57. Borowy and Yuen, *ILGWU 1993 Homeworkers Study*; Cameron and Mak, "Chinese Speaking Homeworkers in Toronto."

58. Allen and Wolkowitz, "Homeworking and the Control of Women's Work," 263.

59. Orser and Foster, *Home Enterprise.*

60. Phizacklea and Wolkowitz, *Homeworking Women*; CHC, *From the Double Day to the Endless Day*; Christensen, presentation, "Conference on Homeworking."

61. Letourneau, "Telecommuting and Electronic Homework", Wenona Giles and Sedef Arat-Koc, *Maid in the Market: Women's Paid Domestic Labour* (Halifax: Fernwood Publishing, 1994).

62. Borowy and Yuen, *ILGWU 1993 Homeworkers' Study*; CHC, *From the Double Day to the Endless Day.*

63. Boyd, "Immigrant Women."

64. Giles, "Clean Jobs, Dirty Jobs"; Louis Lamphere, *From Working Daughters to Working Mothers: Immigrant Women in a New England Industrial Community* (Ithaca: Cornell University Press, 1987); Rusty Neal and Virginia Neale, "'As Long as You Know How to Do Housework': Portuguese Canadian Women and the Office Cleaning Industry in Toronto," *Canadian Women's Studies Journal* 16/1 (1987), 39–41.

65. Bottomley, "Living Across Difference"; Bottomley, "Representing the 'Second Generation.'"

66. Phizacklea and Wolkowitz, *Homeworking Women.*

67. Gabbacia, *Seeking Common Ground*, Introduction, xi–xxvi.

68. Louise Lamphere, *Structuring Diversity: Ethnographic Perspectives on the New Immigration* (Chicago and London: University of Chicago Press, 1992), Introduction, 1–34.

69. Borowy and Yuen, *ILGWU 1993 Homeworkers' Study*; WWRES and ILGWU, "Industrial Homework and Employment Standards"; CHC, *From the Double Day to the Endless Day.*

Chapter Six

Flexible Work, Flexible Workers: The Restructuring of Clerical Work in a Large Telecommunications Company

Bonnie Fox and Pamela Sugiman

Today, in the context of strong global competition, deregulation of labour and a proliferation of micro technologies, work is being restructured at a quickening pace.[1] In the words of David Harvey, we are in the midst of an era of "flexible accumulation," which "rests on flexibility with respect to 'labour processes,' 'labour markets,' products and patterns of consumption. It is characterized by the emergence of ... above all, greatly intensified rates of 'commercial, technological and organizational innovation' (emphases added)."[2]

Rapidly changing technologies and "flexible" human resource management (HRM) strategies are arguably the most important elements of the restructuring of paid work. New technologies, after all, bear the potential to revolutionize work. Yet sociologists and organization theorists have long recognized that technology alone does not determine the nature of jobs. The reshaping of work through technological change is often determined by the "authority of capital," not the "authority of technical know-how."[3] The content of jobs is a product of the way management organizes the labour process and deploys its workforce, rather than an objective (technical) necessity.[4] The dominant goal of human resource management is "flexibility." Most popular among flexibility strategies are the flexible organization of work (known as " flexible specialization" ["flex-spec"] or "functional flexibility") and employing labour in non-standard jobs ("numerical flexibility").

187

Research and debate about the nature and consequences of restructuring have burgeoned over the last couple of decades. Yet the literature is lacking in some important respects. First, much of the discussion has revolved exclusively around ideal-typical constructs such as Atkinson's model of the "flexible firm," which equates functional flexibility with "core" labour forces and numerical flexibility with "peripheral" labour forces.[5] Second, many writers contributing to the debate about the effects of flexible specialization have assumed that flex-spec operates alone. In short, much of the scholarly writing is problematic in failing to carefully examine how various flexibility approaches have been implemented and played out in real work settings. Empirical accounts of restructuring, though relatively few, have highlighted the complexities of such workplaces. These studies suggest that real workplaces host a web of management strategies, are in constant state of flux and bear evidence of old organizational forms alongside the new.[6] Such studies prompt questions about what strategies different firms are actually using and when; for what kinds of work and workers; how functional and numerical flexibility interact (when they do); and their joint and separate effects on the workforce.

At a more general level, few contributors to the current restructuring debate have systematically examined management's own belief that workplace reorganization is based on rational, uniform, well-planned strategies.[7] An implicit assumption in much of the literature is that restructuring follows a clear, linear course and where it has unanticipated consequences, these are solely the outcome of resistance by labour.[8] Researchers thus need to further interrogate the rationality of management plans, highlight their ambiguity and explore the effects of those plans with an eye to inconsistent and conflicting results.

Inquiries about management intentions have, to some extent, been eclipsed by questions about the outcomes of restructuring. The effects of flexible specialization, in particular, have generated considerable debate. Many researchers have asked whether the multiskilling (or cross-training), job rotation and team organization that are often a part of flexible specialization reverse the job fragmentation, job simplification and erosion of workers' control, which Taylorist management strategies entailed.[9] Much of this discussion too still needs to be grounded in empirical research.

Moreover, though questions about social relations among workers, and between labour and management, pervade the restructuring literature, the existing research is motivated primarily by inquiries about class, and largely overlooks gender and race relations. Given that class is unquestionably entangled with gender and race, a failure to understand the nexus of these sets of social relations will likely distort any analysis.

In this paper, we examine the process of restructuring as experienced by clerical workers in a Customer Payments Centre (CPC), the billing department of a major telecommunications company in Toronto, Canada. This department represents an interesting microcosm of larger trends in the economy. Directly following the introduction of advanced computer technology, management began to pursue both of the major types of "flexible" HRM strategies in the CPC: they organized workers into teams and flexibly specialized the labour process, and they hired increasing numbers of workers on a part-time or temporary basis.

This case study allows us to examine the restructuring process in its specifics. It reveals the nature of reorganization in a particular firm, workers' experiences of it and its implications for worker-management relations and relations among employees themselves. It forces us to drop the assumption that flexible specialization and numerical flexibility are applied to different parts of the labour force, and prompts us to ask what happens when the two HRM strategies are used together for the same workers.[10] More generally, it highlights the complexity and indeterminacy of management strategies — and the contradictory outcomes that sometimes follow from them. As well, our examination contributes to ongoing discussions about the feminization of clerical work. Although employees in the CPC perform work that may be described as typically "women's," significant numbers of men now fill the unit and work alongside women. We suggest that as jobs for both sexes increasingly take on the characteristics of "women's work" (that is, as they become bad jobs), gender divisions in the workplace may lessen somewhat, while class, racial, ethnic and other lines of demarcation may deepen.

The Literature

Several parallel bodies of literature examine restructuring, its impact on work and workers' experiences of it. Studies of clerical work have been primarily concerned with the effects of computer technology. A much smaller body of research discusses the application of flexible human resource management (both numerical and functional) to women in clerical employment. Most discussions of flex-spec, however, have been based on studies of manufacturing jobs that are typically performed by men. We briefly review the major arguments and findings.

Studies of the introduction of microchip technology to clerical work indicate that the effects are neither simple nor obvious. While mainly concerned about predicting the job loss that can be expected from automation, research on the transformation of clerical work accompanying technological change has also had much to say about how clerks experience the new office.[11] Some researchers argue that clerical work has been deskilled as a result of office automation; others argue that the effects are mixed: routine jobs undergoing greater fragmentation and simplification but other jobs necessitating greater skill.[12] Many writers claim that the new technology has intensified clerical work; some find increased monitoring of workers by management as a result of the new technology.[13] The effects of the new information technology vary by industry, size of office or firm and management policies.[14] The only uniform finding is that health problems increase for clerical workers as a result of automation.[15]

The general conclusion of the most comprehensive reviews of this research is that technology itself has no necessary consequences for the contents of clerical work, its organization and thus workers' experiences. Researchers agree that technology cannot singlehandedly change the organization of work, and that management policies intervene to determine the way work is organized, and thus the effects of new technology.[16]

For manufacturing jobs, the focus of research on restructuring is on the effects of flexible work organization, or functional flexibility. A flex-spec labour process involves a cross-trained workforce, working in teams and rotating among jobs in a flattened job structure. Typically, it is accompanied by a goal of co-operation and flexible arrangements between labour and management, rather than adversarial relations based on strict contractual agreements.[17]

Where Taylorist management strategies have rationalized production by eliminating the need for workers to make decisions, a flex-spec organization attempts to eliminate "waste" by employing workers' knowledge of their jobs in the rationalization process.[18] Working in teams, employees are given responsibility for scheduling, planning the work, rotating workers among jobs and meeting quotas. Increasing workers' responsibility, team organization diminishes the need for supervision, although it provides employees with no added authority.

Teamwork in manufacturing often occurs in the context of a "lean production" model whereby stock is acquired "just in time," barely sufficient numbers of workers are hired and thus buffers and cushions in the labour process are eliminated. The absence of "excess" labour under the "lean and mean" model means that employees must absorb the costs of production problems by extending their workday into mandatory overtime — becoming "accordion workers."[19] Additionally, management squeezes "wasted" time out of the production process by moving workers from job to job whenever there is "slack time." The cross-training of employees is aimed at reducing turnover time and eliminating downtime rather than upgrading workers' skills.[20] Most writers argue that workers are simply acquiring a number of job-specific and company-specific skills for highly simplified jobs.

Meanwhile, weakened worker unity often accompanies a flex-spec labour process. Writers speculate that the organization of the workforce into teams may encourage competition among groups of workers insofar as they monitor each other's performance to ensure that no one "slacks off." As well, in many cases, management has eroded "internal labour markets," or job ladders, as it has flattened the occupational structure and even attacked entrenched seniority systems and other protections won by organized labour.

While the literature assumes that flexibility for women workers means part-time work, some studies show that women are also subject to flex-spec HRM.[21] Research on the insurance industry — a large employer of women — suggests that the white-collar work done by many women is being significantly reorganized. In tandem with computer technology, the reorganization of insurance work has meant not only degraded jobs for clerks doing data entry but also multitask positions involving teamwork for women with good educational credentials.[22] The questions raised about flex-spec with respect to manufacturing jobs — requiring a close examination of the labour process and workers' experiences — have yet, however, to be pursued even with respect to the insurance industry.

Restructuring in the Customer Payments Centre

The Customer Payments Centre is located on an upper floor of a large, grey, nondescript building situated in a bleak industrial area just outside of Metropolitan Toronto. The Centre is staffed by approximately 200 clerical workers who process bill payments. Although these workers belong in a union, their collective power is extremely limited. Many members have long relinquished the belief that this union acts as the collective voice of workers, and some union stewards openly claim that one of their primary objectives is to ensure that workers do not file grievances against the company. The union, commonly referred to as "the Association," is affiliated with neither the provincially based Ontario Federation of Labour, nor the country's central labour body, the Canadian Labour Congress.

We interviewed ten groups of workers employed at this site. Each group consisted of four to five randomly selected individuals. In addition, we spoke with three supervisors and two representatives of mid/upper management. These interviews were supplemented by a review of selected union and company documents and observations of employees performing their work.

The clerical workforce in the CPC is divided into eight units, each of which is headed by a supervisor. Each supervisor, in turn, is accountable to a single manager who oversees the entire department. Staff in the various units of the CPC perform distinct but interrelated functions. These include processing "regular" residential customer payments made either by mail, preauthorized cheque withdrawal or through a bank; processing "irregular" mailed payments, including those by business clients; investigating and dealing with "problem" payments; and balancing the daily total payments. Altogether, CPC employees process between 100,000 and 120,000 transactions daily, in order to make a bank deposit by early afternoon. Work shifts begin as early as 6:00 a.m. and end at approximately 3:00 p.m.

In recent years, the Centre has undergone tremendous technological and organizational change. Change is now constant in this firm and it is occurring at an accelerated rate. For employees, its pace and intensity are alarming. The most notable recent transformation began in 1991 with the technological redesign of the workplace. In an effort to heighten efficiency and avoid impending mechanical problems, the company replaced highly outdated machinery with sophisticated new computerized equipment. Often referred to as "recognition technology," the newly introduced machines have the capacity to encode cheques and bills, read codes, match codes between cheques and bills, create microfilm and leave an audit trail for proof of deposit.[23] As well, personal computers were installed throughout the department, allowing workers access to central files containing customer information. The introduction of this new machinery was independent of a human resource management strategy; although some of the new technology facilitated the team organization that followed it, most did not.

Prior to these departmental changes, management began to seek greater flexibility in its clerical workforce on a company-wide basis. In 1990, upper-level management made a decision to hire workers on a temporary basis only. They also made a strong commitment to part-time employment. In the CPC, this meant that management was relying increasingly on temporary and part-time workers while introducing new technology and pressuring employees to work extra hours in order to adapt to the new machines and still meet pre-established work quotas.

In addition to numerical flexibility, approximately one year after the introduction of the new computer equipment the company adopted a philosophy known as Total Quality Management (TQM), with its goal of functional flexibility.[24] As a first step, management flattened the department's occupational structure and compressed related pay scales. Higher-wage workers were transferred out of the CPC, leaving employees in only two (lower) wage bands. The majority of these workers occupy the lower of the two bands. Following this, supervisors introduced various employee initiative schemes, organized the workforce into teams, and began job rotation among team members. As well, in an effort to move away from its negative connotations, the firm abandoned the designation "clerical worker," replacing it with the now fashionable title of "associate." Furthermore, in teams, workers themselves took over many functions that were previously in the exclusive domain of management. For instance, team leaders became responsible for settling disputes among team members and scheduling teamwork.

Meanwhile over this period, there was a gradual transformation of the social composition of the workforce. Years ago, the CPC was informally known as the "blue-rinse floor" and the "hen house," as it was staffed largely by middle-aged women. The majority of these women were of British or European descent and they entered full-time employment after their children were grown. Coincident with the technological and organizational changes that transformed the CPC, many of these women "retired." Those who remain are in the units handling "irregular" mail and "problem" payments and checking the daily balance. Most of the current staff are young in comparison, ranging in age from their early twenties to early thirties. These newer employees are especially apparent in entry-level, temporary and part-time jobs in the "regular" mail units.

Recently hired employers are also of diverse ethnic and racial origins. East Indians, West Indians, East Asians, South Asians, Italian Canadians, African Canadians and a number of other ethnic and racial groups are now represented in the CPC. Some of these workers are first-time immigrants to Canada. While such racial and ethnic diversity reflects the growing heterogeneity of the wider Toronto area, it is striking in this particular work site as such diversity is not characteristic of the workforce in the company's other locations.

As well, the sex composition of the Centre has shifted over the last several years. Clerical jobs in the CPC have traditionally been held by women, but increasing numbers of men have recently joined them. Young men are now scattered throughout the CPC and, in many cases, they work alongside women. In the regular residential mail units (where the least skilled jobs exist), 26 to 31 per cent of employees are men. In the department where workers run the computer system and make daily balances, 44 per cent of the workforce is male. While fewer men are located in other departments, their numerical representation is still not insignificant. Only one department in the CPC is filled exclusively by women. Here, workers are long-term employees of the company, and occupy the preferred permanent, full-time, better-paid jobs.

Costly New Technology

Beginning with the publication of Harry Braverman's *Labour and Monopoly Capital*, writers contributing to the labour-process literature (usually discussing scientific management) have tended to assume that management takes a carefully reasoned approach to the deployment of labour.[25] After all, given the high cost of capital investment, it is commonsensical to assume that employers attempt to utilize technological potential fully. In the CPC, however, use of the costly new technology, as well as the decision making and implementation processes surrounding it, were haphazard and ill-conceived. Indeed because of misguided decision making and poor planning on the part of management, the implementation period was one of chaos. Though a committee made up of supervisors from the various units in the department was officially responsible for the resystemization, this committee was headed by a business graduate who was recruited from outside the firm. This outside consultant ignored many of the suggestions made by in-house supervisors. In turn, management introduced an insufficient number of machines, and employees were inadequately trained to operate the new equipment. Staff ended up doing their work largely by trial and error.

Furthermore, for almost a year after the new machines were introduced, everyone in the Centre, workers and supervisors alike, was putting in eleven- to thirteen-hour days, and also working on Saturdays, in an effort to process payments in accordance with the usual production goals. Even part-time employees became "accordion workers." In fact, because part-time workers had put in excessively long hours, company policy eventually required management to convert many of them to full-time status. Management thereby lost the flexibility that these workers were meant to provide. The transition was so chaotic that for some time the department faced the prospect of having its work grind to a halt. It paid dearly to avoid that: it pressured employees to work overtime, at time-and-a-half or double their standard rate of pay.

In the end, payments were processed daily largely because of employees' own initiatives. With little guidance, workers taught themselves how to operate the new machines. Some workers viewed the firm's increased use of machinery as contradictory precisely because of the importance of worker ingenuity for doing the job well. Critical of the subordination of workers and the labour process to the authority of the machine, one woman stated that when one's work is totally dependent on a machine, "everything has to grind to a halt" when the machine breaks. She said, "Before, so many hands would pick up the work and get it going, and now we're waiting for one machine to do it all." This worker continued, "Hundreds of thousands of dollars [are spent] for just maintenance of these machines. That money would pay for a lot of bodies who have eyes and can see and they don't break down completely." Paradoxically, a process aimed at removing some of the need for thinking on the part of workers relied, in the short term, on precisely this capacity. The job-specific knowledge possessed by long-term employees was especially important to the continuation of the labour process at a time when the firm was moving to temporary labour.

Not only was the company haphazard about introducing the technological change, ultimately it also failed to take the steps necessary to realize the productive potential of the new machines.

According to a supervisor who was well versed in the technical details of the redesign, because employees were not properly trained, they did not utilize the equipment to its full potential. Yet management made no effort to rectify this. Indeed, it had not even collected the statistics necessary for an analysis of productivity before and after the conversion to new equipment.

Its chaotic introduction notwithstanding, the new machinery did enhance managerial control and intensify the labour process. With "state of the art" computer equipment, the company could more effectively enforce productivity quotas and monitor workers, especially those who performed highly routine tasks such as opening (regular) mail. On the mail-opening machines (on which workers check and sort documents), employees' names are automatically recorded, along with the number of documents they process and the speed at which the work is done. This method of surveillance had serious repercussions for employees because management adopted a harsh rate system at the same time that it introduced the new machines. When asked what happens if a worker does not meet the set rate, one (temporary) employee stated, "I was told if I didn't get to 600 [800 is the rate] by the third or fourth month [after starting], I wouldn't have a job." In the face of such threats, most workers attempted to work harder and faster in a race with the machine. Not surprisingly, many women and men described the CPC as "a very high-stress environment."

Though most employees recognized that the microchip technology facilitated greater managerial control and an intensification of the labour process, the extent to which it contributed to a further routinization and degradation of work depended largely on the specific nature of the job (including the degree of mechanization), and thus the unit in which people worked.[26] Jobs that had already been made routine with the old machinery were further degraded with the introduction of more advanced computer technology. Most regular mail processors, for example, likened their jobs after the resystemization to those typically performed by the manual working class. In describing this work, a number of women and men used the terms "mindless," "no challenge" and "brain-dead boring." "You're a robot. [You] take [the bill] out, put it in," remarked one worker. A woman who had been with the firm for ten years commented, "I have never worked like in a factory before."

Alongside workers who processed regular payments, however, were those who handled the non-standard payments. While the same machinery was introduced in each unit, the mix of tasks that workers performed in a non-standard mail necessitated that they continue to handle payments on a case-by-case basis, and decide themselves how best to proceed with each. Workers in these more challenging jobs believed that the new technology improved some aspects of their work. The computer created in many of these employees a feeling of greater control over the labour process as it permitted easier access to information about customer accounts. Notably, it enabled them to solve problems for the customers directly, and this generated in some workers a feeling of personal effectiveness. "We can do it all ourselves instead of sending problem payments to other units," explained one long-term employee. In short, the new technology reintegrated some jobs that previously had been fragmented. The technology in itself was not a predetermined, universalizing force.

Whatever their feelings about the impact of the new machinery on the exercise of skill and autonomy, employees uniformly believed that in combination with the rate system and the goal of same-day processing, the technology was highly detrimental to their health and well-being. While workers believed that the ergonomics of the new machines and recently purchased office furniture constituted some improvement over the old, most of them complained vociferously about experiencing more frequent and aggravating health problems than in the past. In part, this may have been because the department regularly violated official company policy that an employee should work on any one machine no longer than two consecutive hours.

Many workers suffered from repetitive-strain injuries such as tendonitis and carpal-tunnel syndrome and/or back and neck problems, eye strain, vision problems, chronic headaches, fatigue, nausea and dizziness. Even those individuals who investigated problems with payments (generally a more varied task than routine mail processing) felt that their jobs had worsened with the resystemization: scanning microfilm for errors is apparently harder on people's eyes than scanning paper. One woman described her experience: "We are processing different [kinds of] payments. ... I have bifocal glasses. ... I feel sick. I feel I cannot sit more than half an hour. I feel really dizzy and sick. ... We have to look always a little down and it's too much pressure on your neck."

In spite of the number and severity of complaints, however, company officials claimed that health and safety were not matters of grave concern. One senior manager dismissively stated that such problems resulted from workers' own lack of knowledge about how best to use the chairs and machinery, for example. For the most part, management promoted a definition of "health and safety" that placed individual blame on workers and exonerated the company itself from taking any responsibility for the workers' problems. Not surprisingly, management's definition had little to do with the organization of work (the political economy of the workplace), and this view was not challenged by representatives of the employees' "Association." In summarizing the company's position on workers' health, a group of employees sarcastically reported that the corporation employs forty-one physicians on staff, and recently held a flu-shot campaign. One employee said, "I took the St. John's Ambulance course. They [the firm] paid for it."

Working in Teams

Soon after the department acquired its new equipment and, in the process, increased its reliance on part-time and temporary workers, the company began to openly promote the managerial strategy known as Total Quality Management. In the CPC, TQM centred on the organization of workers into teams of varying sizes.[27] Team leaders established weekly work schedules and organized job rotation. Leaders were appointed by the supervisor of the unit. In theory, team leadership was to rotate among all members of the teams, but in practice some workers did not want to assume the positions and others were never selected for it.

Central to the teams was a functionally flexible work organization. Workers were trained to do all of the jobs in their unit, as well as some jobs in other units within the department. They were then to rotate among the jobs in their unit on a daily basis, according to the work schedule. Less frequently, they would perform jobs in other units as needed. Because workers typically moved laterally within a unit between jobs of equivalent skill level, their tasks became more diversified (that is, they performed multiple tasks). Few employees upgraded their firm-specific skills, nor did they have an opportunity to acquire new skills that would be transferable outside the firm.

Management encouraged competition among the teams in the regular mail units by measuring and publicizing team productivity every week. In addition, the company had established various employee award programs to recognize contributions (by teams or individuals within teams) to objectives such as the team concept itself, heightened productivity and "service excellence." Yet alongside such company practices stood management's rhetoric that all employees, regardless of team membership, should work co-operatively to meet the challenges of the highly competitive climate in which the company operated. This contradiction was one of many. TQM, as applied in this unit, made little sense to workers.

Another contradiction centred on job classifications, work content and pay scales. Flex-spec was predicated on a flattened occupational structure and, consistent with this, the labour force had become fairly homogeneous with respect to pay. Nevertheless, jobs in the CPC varied considerably in content, and thus skill requirements and levels of responsibility. Some of the work (most of it in the regular mails) was automated and monotonous, requiring virtually no thought; but in some of the other units (such as that in which the daily balance was made) the jobs demanded knowledge, skill and problem solving.

Variation in job requirements bore a rough correspondence to differences in the employee's term of employment. The three standard mail units were composed of a mixture of permanent and temporary employees; many of the employees were part-time. The other units employed mostly permanent staff working on a full-time basis; four of the five had only full-time employees. Despite the above-mentioned differences in employment status, skill and level of responsibility, however, workers were all paid approximately the same wages, and all faced extremely limited prospects of upward mobility. Cognizant of this, workers from every category felt that they were being unjustly treated. The dearth of opportunities for mobility, and the absence of clear distinctions in pay and benefits from newer staff, especially angered senior employees working at jobs involving significant responsibility. In turn, more recently hired staff had higher levels of formal education than the more senior workers and resumés at odds with their unchallenging jobs. Workers were frustrated on both counts.

Overall, workers' views of the team structure varied with their relationship to the company as well as the nature of their work. Long-term employees, many of whom strongly identified with the company and were performing jobs that both required extensive knowledge and allowed autonomy and decision making, generally held a positive view of teamwork (as they did of the new machinery). These workers, did, however, resent being handed greater responsibility under the team organization. To the extent that supervisors had withdrawn from the actual work, the weight of the decisions employees made daily was greater than previously. According to a worker in non-standard mail, "It looks like you're just pushing paper, but you're making decisions all the time, and informed decisions at that." In non-standard mail, the responsibility and limited discretionary power that workers held, in fact, was a source of stress. One employee explained that she worried excessively about decisions she had made during the day long after she left the workplace. She would think to herself, "'Oh, but this [payment] is a lot of money! What am I gonna do?'... You can't sleep at night 'cause you're afraid to come in the morning [for fear you handled the payment incorrectly]."

The majority of workers, many of whom were employed in the routine mail processing units, were highly critical of working in teams. The main complaint was about tensions arising among team members. One employee stated, "I don't think anybody's got a problem with the work. People have a problem with the people." A co-worker likewise remarked, "Before, you did your job and that was it; now you have to keep people happy." Yet another woman explained, "That's the biggest conflict up here — between people. It never was before."

What was most at issue was how quickly and competently co-workers performed their work. For many employees, who was and who was not "pulling their weight" on the team became an overriding concern. "Instead of one pair of eyes watching you, you've got more," said one woman. Another commented, "It's not management you have to worry about. ... It's the people you work with." Thus, even workers who did not closely identify with company goals of heightened productivity and efficiency effectively patrolled one another.[28]

It is notable, though, that tensions among workers were not random. Some of the strongest conflicts and most bitter resentments in the Centre were between permanent (full-time and part-time) employees, on the one hand, and the temporary (part-time) workers on the other. While permanent employees were willing to co-operate and sometimes even make concessions in order to help the company prosper in a competitive market, they argued that temporary workers had no such identification with the company.[29] They believed that because of their relative indifference about the future of the company, temporary workers were neither responsible nor hard-working. According to one permanent worker, "We are aware that our company is going through a transition now. And this is another thing: we resent that they bring in all these temporary people who have no stake in the company."

The company did, however, drive temporary workers to sell themselves aggressively in order to remain in their jobs. And one way of doing this was to work at an extremely high rate, which meant avoiding handling any problematic payments, thus leaving them for more experienced workers. Temporary workers, therefore, had little inducement to work co-operatively in teams and indeed were motivated to outperform their co-workers. Accordingly, many of the workers felt that the team concept posed a fundamental contradiction: while employees were expected to work collectively, they were at the same time forced to promote themselves within the firm on an individual basis. "How [then] do they expect the team spirit to carry?" asked one worker.

Tensions between temporary and permanent workers peaked several months prior to our interviews. The workers' own proposals for resolving such tensions underlines the seriousness of the division among these two categories of workers. Following the adoption of the new machinery in the regular mail unit, and prior to the introduction of teams, management removed the rates that set the standard for productivity. Shortly after the teams were established, several permanent employees made an astonishing move. They requested that management reinstall the old rate system. They took this extraordinary action because they believed that without the rates, the more recently hired temporary workers were avoiding the harder jobs and thus shifting the burden onto the shoulders of the (decreased number of) experienced permanent workers. Permanent employees felt that the new workers were simply not "pulling their weight." In their view, (former) close and careful supervision — notwithstanding its problems — meant that no one could avoid the harder work and everyone got credit for what they did.

What is clear here, then, is that functional flexibility and numerical flexibility (non-standard jobs) can, in practice, be incompatible with organizational strategies. Introducing flex-spec, or any other kind of team organization, into a workplace in which temporary employees are working alongside permanent employees is problematic. The different structural positions of the two categories of workers made for conflict between them. Of course, the resulting division within the workforce is favourable to management to the extent that is deflects anger based on class exploitation and directs it horizontally.

In this case, however, workers also displayed growing resentment towards supervisors for abdicating their "traditional" managerial role under the team organization. The withdrawal of supervisors from direct supervision was made possible by the mutual patrolling among workers. Employees noted, though, that under this arrangement conflict among workers in teams had at times escalated to such heights that they themselves had appealed to supervisors to intervene and mediate. In response to such requests, supervisors suggested that employees handle the problems on their own. One woman explained, "If there's a problem and you go to [your] manager, she'll turn around and say, 'You should deal with this on your team!'" A co-worker in the same unit added, "So, we've [workers] already killed each other. We can't agree on anything, and we come to you [the manager] and you still won't help us." Another worker complained, "Now everything's on us."

Furthermore, because supervisors no longer managed in direct view, workers wondered what they did, and the resulting resentment towards management was palpable. One woman exclaimed, "I can't figure out why they're called management!" Another worker expressed her belief that "Management never does anything." According to even the general manager of the CPC, managers do not know the "work" of the department "at all." Yet in his view, management's withdrawal from direct supervision is a positive product of team organization — a more efficient use of managerial time and talent in that this redistribution of responsibilities permitted supervisors and managers to attend meetings and courses about market trends, company goals, policies and methods of managing.

Most workers disagreed with this view. Especially problematic in their eyes is that an absent management cannot adequately assess the performance of individual workers. In evaluating employees' performance, managers often relied on rates. But the rates used to measure productivity in the deskilled mail processing jobs, for instance, fail to indicate quality, complexity, level of difficulty and the like. Some employees thus compared current practices unfavourably with the previous system whereby supervision was much tighter. In their view, under the old system resting on much closer supervision, at least good work was noticed.

Workers were highly critical of their annual evaluations by management. The consensus was that only people who "blew their own horns" did well. Many employees also noted that supervisors' "favourites" were treated differently and evaluated more positively than others. Indeed, workers perceived favouritism to be the biggest problem in the department. Other employees claimed that management preferred to keep good workers in place because they were too valuable to lose; troublemakers were less useful and therefore were often promoted out of the unit. Management's distance from the labour process clearly generated distrust among the workers.

More directly contrary to management goals is that the tensions among workers on teams sometimes hampered productivity. After learning that productivity levels were down in her (regular) mail unit, one supervisor, with a nod from upper management, arbitrarily suspended job rotation and the team allocation of work for a week-long period. Employees in her unit were consequently forced to work in the same job, day after day. The result was a dramatic increase in productivity in this unit. Workers themselves had no say in determining this sudden shift in policy. Management's commitment to job rotation and teamwork was conditional upon workers' ability to meet established productivity/efficiency targets. When these work arrangements conflicted with the firm's bottom line goals, job rotation and teamwork were readily abandoned.

Team organization exacerbated other tensions among the workforce as well. Because teamwork enhanced the interdependence of workers, and replaced the formal rules and orders of supervisors with negotiations among co-workers, the stage was set for ethnic, racial and gender-based tensions. In fact, racial and ethnic strains were rife in the units processing the standard mail. That is, in the units featuring degraded work, teamwork promoted racial and ethnic tensions in addition to those between permanent and temporary workers, and the former tensions crosscut the latter. In separate interviews, several women of colour reported that ethnic stereotyping and racial discrimination greatly affected their work lives, both structurally and experientially.[30] Many employees claimed that the workforce was divided hierarchically into ethnic cliques. Those at the bottom of the ladder felt marginalized and subordinated by both supervisors and co-workers on the basis of ethnic and racial origin. A long-term employee commented, "I am the only Indian in my department. They are all Italian. They treat me like dirt. They are together. They cover each other and I am the only one in trouble all the time. ... I don't understand what is going on."

In contrast to these racial and ethnic tensions, gender differences did not produce divisions. Some researchers have argued that restructuring in general, and flex-spec in particular, should reinforce and strengthen unequal gender relations, and even increase hostility between women and men — assuming that women and men are in different positions in a company.[31] Only a few writers have focused on how the current restructuring is creating more "women's jobs" for both women and men, and thus potentially eroding one source of conflict between the sexes.[32]

In the CPC, women and men reported that they got along very well, and liked working together. Our observations supported that assessment: women and men in the CPC seemed to interact easily and genially. Both women and men commented to us that the workday was made more pleasant by the presence of the other sex. Indeed, the undercurrent of sexuality sometimes present when women and men work together seemed to lighten the monotony of working in the units processing the regular mail. Ironically, then, the erosion of sexual segregation that may accompany restructuring can, in some cases, produce a reduction in gender tensions in the labour force.

Of course, there are overriding negative consequences. As we saw, in spite of variation in job content across the CPC, management views all jobs in the department in the same light — namely, as "women's work" — and produced a flattened structure that reflected that view. This means that the men in these jobs are treated as women (that is, badly). A long-term, permanent male employee who had helped install the present computer system, and was responsible (along with one other employee and a technician from outside) for its operation, was classified in a lower band than that of most workers in the department. In order to move up, he was forced to file a union grievance. In spite of his sex, he had been treated like a female clerk.

Servicing the Customer

Exacerbating these new and deepening divisions within the workforce was a strong managerial emphasis on the individual merit and competitive drive of employees. While managers expressed an ideological commitment to the team concept, they clearly conveyed the message that the success of a worker depends on her or his independent ability to exceed the official job description. One recently upgraded woman said, "If you want to achieve, you have to push yourself. You have to initiate a lot of stuff." Another commented, "Just doing the work alone doesn't get you a promotion." The additional effort expected of workers, however, was only vaguely defined.

It was apparent, though, that the company was expanding all jobs to include a sales/personal service component. Management expected each and every worker directly to promote sales and increase the company's business, not only by providing efficient and informed telephone customer service but also by drawing on their personal talents and interpersonal skills in an attempt to make the customer feel valued and respected. According to one of many leaflets distributed by the company, employee "success" was measured in part by "[g]oing above and beyond the call of duty" in an effort to "delight the customer. ... "

On the job daily, employees experienced this sales/service emphasis as an additional pressure. In the unit that was responsible for handling problem payments, workers attributed much of their daily stress to the company's unrelenting push to compete for new customers and "enhance company loyalty." Functioning within a "service economy," most business clients themselves expected special treatment by the people who processed their payments. "You have more customers [now] who want kid glove treatment," observed one worker.

To some extent, the relationship between customer and employee seemed to eclipse that which had formerly existed between supervisor and employee. Service workers have long been aware of the need to please a public clientele. In this new workplace scenario, however, the customer is a more direct participant in the monitoring and evaluation of workers.[33] For example, customer complaints were a key source of poor ratings in workers' annual reviews. Conversely, workers who could win new clients or keep important existing clientele by going "out of their way," "above and beyond" (for example, by meeting clients in the CPC lobby to review account statements or spending several hours on the telephone with one customer) — often on their own time and of their own initiative — were noticed and rewarded by management.

Some workers themselves expressed pride in their ability to display strong social skills on the job. Indeed, a number of women in the unit stated that their role in "helping the customer" allowed them to derive some meaning from otherwise alienating work. They did so by defining their job as a service to people rather than as routine paper processing. For offering this "service," furthermore, some women said they felt "appreciated" by customers. One employee remarked, "[S]ometimes a customer is really nice and makes you feel happy for the whole day. ... [T]hey'll ask your name, how's the weather. ... I feel so good."

Without denying the importance of workers' own attempts to humanize their work and thereby dignify themselves, it is important to note that this emphasis on customer satisfaction also emerged as part of a refashioned, decentralized, managerial strategy of control — one that rests on shifting authority from the supervisor and employer to "the shoulders of non-managerial individuals."[34] Indeed, customers can be more effective disciplining agents and managers, in part because the relationship between employees and their many anonymous clients does not, on the face of it, appear to be hierarchical and adversarial. Although servicing the customer was a source of strain, many workers felt obliged to process payments efficiently precisely because "the customer" was depending on them.

Along with enlisting the customer, management attributed the least popular and most brutal corporate decisions to the seemingly objective laws of the market.[35] Indeed, these two forces, the customer and the market, were often used in tandem. For example, top management periodically relied on television monitors in the cafeteria to broadcast to workers the message that the company's survival depended on their being fiercely competitive. And they claimed that one way to maintain a competitive advantage was to offer outstanding customer service (especially to corporate clients). During these assemblies, managers delivered a punitive message, warning that jobs would be lost if workers did not make special efforts (and even concessions) in the interest of the firm's survival. One woman expressed the sentiments of many employees: "I'm doing my best for that customer. I'm conscious of it because that customer means my job." Another worker explained that company broadcasts often sound like "the axe is falling. ... People are afraid to lose their jobs. They'll do what they need to do to keep their jobs." A co-worker added:

> I wouldn't call it threats. They just tell you what the facts are. ... If you want to help out by taking a reduced work week or whatever, then it's gonna make it easier. ... Look in the papers, how many companies are just laying off. ... You're lucky that, at least, they give you a choice to help them.

In this refashioned workplace, even workers themselves were held accountable for the viability of their jobs.

This management approach, then, is one in which supervisors and managers are seemingly absent, yet retain strong (indirect) political control over the workforce. Management did not abdicate power; its power merely became diffused. Along with ensuring that workers regulate one another in team arrangements, management handed over some supervisory control to the customer and accountability to the market. Management's retreat from the workplace, of course, was illusory. Workers never stopped feeling the "presence" of management. Paradoxically, it seems that as managers physically receded from the shop floor, they spent more time developing strategies of managing.

But because the power and logic of capital is unyielding, regardless of how well workers service the customer or concede to aid the health of the company, they will lose their jobs. Not satisfied with the organizational changes to date, as our interviews ended, company executives entered a new phase of restructuring — pursuing a philosophy they term "business transformation." According to the firm's spokespersons, the new business transformation means "looking at every single thing you do, backwards and forwards and upside down, and coming up with a way to do it faster, smarter." According to this philosophy, each unit in the firm must be accountable for its profitability. "If it's not successful, get rid of it," says one manager. As part of this plan, the company will "outsource" functions such as customer payments and close down the CPC.

Discussion and Conclusions

The case of the Customer Payments Centre throws into question the assumption that managerial strategies are always rationally planned, consistent and effective — a view that managers themselves often reinforce in their promotion of TQM as a seamless method of managing. We observed irrationality, inconsistency and contradictions in this unit of clerical workers. The employer was managing largely by trial and error. While company officials undoubtedly intended that the new computerized equipment would reduce their reliance on labour, the process of technological change in the CPC not only resulted in an unnecessarily high increase in labour costs (albeit temporarily), but it also served to underline the ultimate dependence of management on workers' job-specific skills and initiative (again, at least in the initial period of adjustment). Meanwhile, the company introduced a management strategy that purported to humanize the workplace, championed a philosophy of worker involvement and aimed to promote worker loyalty to the firm (TQM). Yet these organizational and ideological goals were advanced in the context of technological innovations that had already served, in part, to degrade and dehumanize the work. According to one worker, the philosophy of TQM makes little sense in the CPC because "it's [the unit] totally not people oriented; it's machine-oriented."

Adding to the contradictions, management heightened numerical flexibility, relying increasingly on part-time and temporary employees from whom loyalty could not be expected. The structural conditions of their employment made such a commitment unlikely. In turn, the insecurity that underlay part-timers' minimal commitment propelled them to protect their own interests. In so doing, they were poor candidates for working in teams. Clearly, in the case of the CPC, numerical flexibility and functional flexibility are at odds.

The indeterminacy of managerial methods, however, has not diminished the power of capital. In spite of these contradictory outcomes, the company continues to dominate the telecommunications market and boasts an exorbitantly high rate of profit. Furthermore, notwithstanding haphazard shifts in organizational policies, management has intensified its control of the workforce and the labour process. What has happened is that in the face of contradictory outcomes and unforeseen developments both within the organization and external to it, driven in its relentless pursuit of efficiency and profitability, employers have resorted to a "multiplicity of control strategies."[36] As sociologist Vicki Smith states, enlisting customers to regulate service workers and relying on workers in teams to monitor one another (as well as promoting the idea of the objective necessity of the market) are "decentralized and subjective strategies that mesh with an occupational structure increasingly characterized by service and flexible manufacturing work."[37] They reflect the growing diffusion and open-endedness of managerial evaluation and control. These new strategies coexist with the old (for example, a harsh rate system, the routinization of many jobs, flattening the occupational structure).

The implications of this example of restructuring for worker-management relations generally, and worker resistance in particular, are not clear. New lines of division are being drawn in the CPC. While the feminization of women's and men's work has seemed to lessen both sex segregation and workplace conflicts between sexes, there are growing tensions and rivalries among workers based on race and ethnicity and employment status (temporary, part-time or permanent, full-time) in intersection with seniority and skill level.

These new lines of demarcation, however, have not served to displace workers' anger towards management. Workers' consciousness of their exploitation by management has been heightened by a number of contradictions in their situation. Broad-banded jobs, with similar rates of pay and similarly poor promotion opportunities, host a labour force that is highly variable in terms of educational credentials, skills and knowledge of the department's labour process. Consequently, workers feel unjustly treated. Team organization, which removes management from direct supervision and precludes responsible evaluation of workers' performance, also induces clear resentment of management by employees. Given that the anger workers feel towards management is mediated by divisions among themselves, however, the form that worker resistance will assume is uncertain. Collective resistance will depend on the entry of another actor — a strong labour organization that must unify workers along fundamental bases. But insofar as workplace democratization has been illusory, workplace conflict is certain to persist, even if this particular work unit disappears.

Notes

We wish to thank the Metro Toronto Clerical Workers Labour Adjustment Committee, and especially Alice De Wolff, for allowing us the opportunity to do this case study for them. For helpful comments on an earlier draft of the paper, we thank Leah Vosko, Kate Bezanson, Tania DasGupta, Alice Dewolff, Marnina Gonick, Meg Luxton, David Rapaport, Ester Reiter and Robert Storey.

1. J. Stanford, "Discipline, Insecurity and Productivity: The Economics Behind Labour Market 'Flexibility,'" in J. Pulkingham and G. Ternowetsky (eds.), *Remaking Canadian Social Policy* (Halifax: Fernwood Press, 1996), 130–147.
2. D. Harvey, *The Condition of Postmodernity* (Oxford: Basil Blackwell, 1989), 147.
3. D. Pignon and J. Querzola, "Dictatorship and Democracy in Production," in Andre Gorz (ed.), *The Division of Labour* (Sussex, England: Harvester Press, 1978), 63–99.
4. H. Harman, R. Kraut and L. Tilly (eds.), *Computer Chips and Paper Clips*, Vol. 1 (Washington, DC: Panel on Technology and Women's Employment, Commission on Behavioral and Social Sciences and Education. National Research Council, National Academy Press, 1987).
5. J. Atkinson, "Recent Changes in the International Labour Market Structure in the UK," in W. Buitelaar (ed.), *Technology and Work* (Aldershot: Avebury, 1988),

133–149; see also G. Betcherman, K. McMullen, N. Leckie and C. Caron, *The Canadian Workplace in Transition* (Kingston: Queen's University, Industrial Relations Centre, 1994). In Canada, Betcherman et al. pose two "paths" for the new HRM models: (1) a "low-cost" path characterized by non-standard jobs, and (2) a "high-performance" path that features a skilled labour force, flexible work organization, commitment to training, employee involvement in decision making, etc.

6. B. Russell, "The Subtle Labour Process and the Great Skill Debate: Evidence from a Potash Mine-Mill Operation," *Canadian Journal of Sociology* 20/3 (1995), 359–386; Pignon and Querzola, "Dictatorship and Democracy."

7. But see B. Garson, *The Electronic Sweatshop* (New York: Simon & Schuster, 1988); S. Proctor, M. Rowlinson, L. McArdle, J. Hassard and P. Forrester, "Flexibility, Politics and Strategy: In Defense of the Model of the Flexible Firm," *Work, Employment and Society* 8/2 (1994), 221–242.

8. See Russell, "The Subtle Labour Process."

9. D. Dohse, J. Ulrich and T. Malsch, "From 'Fordism' to 'Toyotism'? The Social Organization of the Labor Process in the Japanese Automobile Industry," *Politics and Society* 14/2 (1985), 115–143; K. Hadley, "Working Lean and Mean: A Gendered Experience of Restructuring in an Electronics Manufacturing Plant," unpublished Ph.D. thesis, Ontario Institute for Studies in Education, 1994; M.J. Piore, "Perspectives on Labour Market Flexibility," *Industrial Relations* 25/2 (1986), 183–201; D. Robertson, J. Rinehart, C. Huxley and the CAW Research Group on CAMMI, "Team Concept and Kaizen: Japanese Production Management in a Unionized Canadian Auto Plant," *Studies in Political Economy* 39 (1992), 77–107; J. Reinhart, C. Huxley and D. Robertson, *Just Another Car Factory? Lean Production and Its Discontents* (Ithaca, NY: ILR Press, 1997); Russell, "The Subtle Law Process"; H. Shaiken, S. Herzenberg and S. Kuhn, "The Work Process Under More Flexible Production," *Industrial Relations* 25/2 (1986), 167–182; M. Parker and J. Slaughter, *Choosing Sides: Unions and the Team Concept* (Boston: South End Press, 1989); J. Toomaney, "The Reality of Workplace Flexibility," *Capital and Class* 40 (1990), 29–55.

10. Atkinson, "Recent Changes."

11. See H. Menzies, *Women and the Chip* (Montreal: the Institute for Research on Public Policy, 1982); H. Menzies, *Whose Brave New World?* (Toronto: Between the Lines Press, 1996).

12. E. Applebaum, "Technology and the Redesign of Work in the Insurance Industry," in B.D. Wright, M.F. Ferree, G. Mellow, L. Lewis, M.D. Samper R. Asher and K. Claspell (eds.), *Women, Work and Technology* (Ann Arbor: University of Michigan Press, 1987), 182–201; B. Baran and S. Teegarden, "Women's Labor in the Office of the Future: A Case Study of the Insurance Industry," in L. Beneria and C. Stimpson (eds.), *Women, Households and the Economy* (New Brunswick, NJ: Rutgers University Press, 1987), 201–224; R. Crompton and G. Jones, *White-Collar Proletariat* (London: MacMillan Press, 1984); A. Machung, "Word Processing: Forward for Business, Backward for Women," in K. Sacks and D. Remy (eds.), *My Troubles Are Going to Have Trouble with Me* (New Brunswick, NJ: Rutgers University Press, 1984), 124–139.

13. R. Feldberg and E.N. Glenn, "Technology and the Transformation of Clerical Work," in R. Kraut (ed.), *Technology and the Transformation of White-Collar Work* (Hillsdate, NJ: Lawrence Erlbaum Associates, 1987), 77–98; C. Lane, "New Technology and Clerical Work," in D. Gallie (ed.), *Employment in Britain* (Oxford: Basil Blackwell, 1989); Machung, "Word Processing."

14. V. Carter, "Office Technology and Relations of Control in Clerical Work Organizations," in B.D. Wright et al. (eds.), *Women, Work and Technology* (Ann Arbor: University of Michigan Press, 1987), 202–220; Hartmann, Kraut and Tilly (eds.), *Computer Chips and Paper Clips*.

15. Hartmann, Kraut and Tilly (eds.), *Computer Chips and Paper Clips*.

16. Ibid;.Lane, "New Technology."

17. D. Wells, "Are Strong Unions Compatible with the new Model of Human Resource Management," *Relations Industrielles* 48/1 (1993), 56–83.

18. Dohse, Ulrich and Malsch, "From Fordism to Toyotism"; Hadley, "Working Lean and Mean"; Parker and Slaughter, *Choosing Sides*; Robertson, Rinehart, Huxley and the CAW Research Group on CAMMI, "Team Concept and Kaizen"; Shaiken, Herzenberg and Kuhn, "The Work Process"; Tomaney, "The Reality of Workplace Flexibility."

19. Hadley, "Working Lean and Mean."

20. Ibid.; Tomaney, "The Reality of Workplace Flexibility."

21. For a discussion of flexibility and part-time work, see V. Beechey, "Conceptualizing Part-Time Work," in V. Beechey (ed.), *Unequal Work* (London: Verso, 1987), 149–169; J. Jenson, "The Talents of Women, the Skills of Men: Flexible Specialization and Women," in S. Wood (ed.), *The Transformation of Work?* (London: Hutchinson, 1989); S. Walby, "Flexibility and the Changing Sexual Division of Labour," in S. Wood (ed.), *The Transformation of Work?* (London: Hutchinson, 1989). Actually, numerical flexibility (non-standard work) is probably a more common management strategy than flexible specialization. See Atkinson, "Recent Changes." Certainly non-standard work is on the rise in Canada. See A. Duffy and N. Pupo, *Part-Time Paradox: Connecting Gender, Work and Family* (Toronto: McClelland & Stewart, 1992); P. Armstrong, "The Feminization of the Labour Force: Harmonizing Down in a Global Economy," in I. Bakker (ed.), *Rethinking Restructuring: Gender and Change in Canada* (Toronto: University of Toronto Press, 1996), 29–54. In 1992, 30 per cent of the Canadian labour force worked in non-standard jobs. See Betcherman, McMullen, Leckie and Caron, *The Canadian Workplace in Transition*.

22. Applebaum, "Technology and the Redesign of Work"; Baran and Teegarden, "Women Labour."

23. A. De Wolff, "Job Loss and Entry-Level Information Workers: Training and Adjustment Strategies for Clerical Workers in Metro Toronto" (Toronto: Report of the Metro Toronto Clerical Workers Labour Adjustment Committee, 1995).

24. We asked several middle-level managers and two more senior managers about the decision-making process, especially the relationships between technological changes and organizational changes. None of the middle managers were able to offer an adequate explanation of the sequence or logic of decision making in the company. The two upper-level managers suggested that decisions were made by one or two

individuals only who seemed to have the power to implement whichever managerial philosophy was currently popular.

25. H. Braverman, *Labour and Monopoly Capital* (New York: Monthly Review Press, 1974).

26. See also R. Milkman and C. Pullman, "Technological Change in an Auto Assembly Plant: The Impact on Workers, Tasks, and Skills," *Work and Occupations* 18/2 (1991), 123–147; S. Zuboff, *In the Age of the Smart Machine: The Future of Work and Power* (New York: Basic Books, 1988).

27. In the regular mail processing units, each team consisted of twelve workers; in the irregular mail unit, seven people made up a team; and in the other units a team contained three or four workers.

28. See also H. Gottfried and L. Graham, "Constructing Difference: The Making of Gendered Subcultures in a Japanese Automobile Plant," *Sociology* 27/4 (1993), 611–628; Robertson, Rinehart, Huxley and the CAW Research Group on CAMMI, "Team Concept and Kaizen"; A. Sinclair, "The Tyranny of a Team Ideology," *Organization Studies* 13/4 (1992), 611–626.

29. Some of the workers we interviewed reported that they were banking their overtime hours rather than receiving financial compensation for overtime worked in an effort to "help out the health of the company." In addition, for the same reason, a number of employees said that they had "voluntarily" agreed to take reduced work weeks at a loss of pay.

30. This outcome was predicted by Hadley, "Working Lean and Mean."

31. See S. Hacker, "Sex Stratification, Technology and Organizational Change: A Longitudinal Case Study of AT&T," *Social Problems* 26 (1979), 539–557; Jenson, "The Talents of Women"; Walby, "Flexibility and the Changing Sexual Division."

32. See Armstrong, "The Feminization of the Labour Force", L. McDowell, "Life Without Father and Ford: The New Gender Order of Post-Fordism," *Transactions of the Institute of British Geographers* 16 (1991), 400–419.

33. See also L. Fuller and V. Smith, "Consumers' Reports: Management by Customers in a Changing Economy," *Work Employment, and Society* 5/1 (1991), 1–16; R. Leidner, *Fast Food, Fast Talk, Service Work and the Routinization of Everyday Life* (Berkeley: University of California Press, 1993).

34. V. Smith, "Braverman's Legacy: The Labour Process Tradition at 20," *Work and Occupations* 21/4 (1994), 415.

35. See Pignon and Querzola, "Dictatorship and Democracy," 75.

36. Smith, "Braverman's Legacy," 414.

37. Ibid., 415.

Part Three

Engendering the State in *SPE*: The Interrelations of Theory and Practice, and of Class, Race and Gender

Caroline Andrew

SPE DOES NOT BEGIN WITH A GENDERED ANALYSIS OF THE STATE, BUT IT CERTAINLY does begin with a state analysis. This was central to the intellectual project of those who founded *SPE* — the same group of scholars who produced *The Canadian State: Political Economy and Political Power* under the editorship of Leo Panitch in 1977. The project was to present an analysis of the state capable of understanding the links between class and state. Historical specificity was important and, influenced by the work of Ralph Miliband, so too was the understanding of the different institutions of the state. It brought together the theoretical contributions of Marx and particularly the neo-Marxists — Miliband, Poulantzas, O'Connor and Gramsci — with the historical development of Canada. The analysis of specific state institutions, programs and activities were to be understood in terms of class.

This was certainly the frame of the early issues of *SPE*. One of the few articles with a gender perspective, and one that comes indirectly to an analysis of the state through a study of civil society, is Joey Noble's description of charitable organizing in Toronto in *SPE* 2 ("'Class-ifying' the Poor: Toronto Charities, 1850–1880"). It was the wives of the bourgeois leaders who visited the poor to judge their worthiness to receive assistance. It is an analysis of the state only indirectly in that state policy was to give the responsibility for social services to private charities, but it does have a clear sensitivity to gender relations as they intermesh with processes of social control.

The first text included here is that of Göran Therborn, from *SPE* 14 (Summer 1984). It focuses on understanding welfare state developments by the interplay of class and state. To this extent it continues the tradition of state/class analysis, but in its sensitivity to the specific historical analysis of civil society-state relations and to specific cultural traditions as linked to state forms, it opens up ways of understanding gender/state relations. Indeed, Therborn explicitly recognizes the gendered nature of the state/class interactions he describes:

> The labour movement has always been male-dominated and, in spite of the explicit demands for the legal equality of women, this workers protection orientation often includes a patriarchal, special protectionist attitude towards women (often assimilated with children) and women's work. Class also has a gender aspect. (Chapter Seven, this volume)

Therborn situates welfare state developments as political responses to the organized strength of the union movement and to the links between the union movement and a political party supporting its demands. But the way each specific state responds depends on the forms of state action already available to that state in terms of its own cultural traditions. He therefore focuses his analysis on the organizations of civil society and on the ways in which state action takes account of civil society/state relations in a broad context. This includes legal traditions, levels of the state, dominant ideas, church-state interactions — all factors that will facilitate the inclusion of gender. Therborn's analysis of the welfare state does not include gender, but it explicitly provides a framework for analysis that opens the way for the inclusion of gender.

The inclusion of gender through the contextualized detailing of civil society-state relations has found its place in *SPE*. Heather Jon Maroney's article (*SPE* 39) on nationalism, pronatalism and the construction of "a demographic crisis" in Quebec 1960–1988 is one such example — with a focus on thinking through the strategic choices for the women's movement. Maroney (1992, 13) analyzes the organizational work of the Quebec women's movement before 1980 when it formulated demands for "reproductive self-determination and reformed maternity and childcare." Confronted by a new pronatalism in the mid- to late 1980s articulated and "objectified" by the scientific discourse of demography, the feminists were largely marginalized. Maroney's analysis of state policy takes account of the organizational strengths of different parts of the women's movement, from the incorporation of liberal feminism to the marginalization of the more progressive elements.

Sue Findlay (*SPE* 42) also situates her analysis of the state in its relations with civil society, looking explicitly at the way community is represented in the development of state policies. By examining the representation of "women" in the Equal Opportunity Program at the City of Toronto and in the Citizenship Branch of the Federal Secretary of State, Findlay argues that these processes actually limit the autonomy of the groups and therefore neither act to democratize the state nor to democratize the community organizations. Supporting the efforts of the women's movement to truly reflect diversity and celebrate difference is central to democratic reform, and part of these efforts is to understand the ways in which their representation in the state reinforces their problems of leadership that does not represent the diversity of women. Once again, understanding civil society puts a gendered focus to the analysis of the state.

The second text, by Gillian Walker, is from *SPE* 33 (Autumn 1990). It deals with how to understand the relations between the state and the women's movement, particularly that part of the women's movement active in issues involving wife battering. It is an analysis stemming from the interplay of practice ("The result of this process is that, although we have achieved much and are still working, struggling and angry, the sites of our struggles are dispersed, disconnected and depoliticized," Chapter Eight, this volume) and of theory ("The analysis developed in my study reveals a layered web of negotiated discursive relations in which ideological constructs play a coordinating role," Chapter Eight, this volume). This has been an important area of feminist activism, state policy and feminist analysis in Canada, and Gillian Walker's article and her book made an early and important contribution to understanding the interplay of the state and the women's movement. In its concern to understand processes of control and the ways in which concepts organize issues and link them to institutional processes of ruling, her work reflects the intellectual influence of Dorothy Smith. Understanding the ways in which language socially constructs issues and therefore organizes the interrelations of the women's movement and the state is crucial for activists and analysts alike. Walker argues: "'Family violence' deflects the focus from the legal system towards health, welfare and social services institutions, but 'male violence,' reformulated in professional discourses in terms such as 'spouse assault,' paves the way for the entry of legal discourse" (Chapter Eight, this volume).

The state categorizes and institutionalizes. It seeks to organize the problem of violence and sees it as a question of management, certainly not as a question of women's oppression. Different institutions of the state — the legal system and the social services — articulate the issue differently and therefore propose different programs and different treatments. Walker looks at government programs, but her analysis is centred in understanding how the ways in which women's groups, service deliverers and researchers articulate issues help to explain how wife battering is lodged "within particular institutional sites of the state's 'social problem apparatus'" (Chapter Eight, this volume). She does this, among other ways, by analyzing presentations made to parliamentary and legislative committee hearings. A concern for discourse has methodological consequences, and learning to understand the social consequences of language is of practical as well as theoretical importance to the women's movement. Walker ends her article by coming back to the issues of practice: "How to organize to change the oppressive conditions of women's lives, without being appropriated through our interactions with the ruling apparatus and participation in the relations of ruling, is the dilemma which confronts the women's movement as it moves into the nineties" (Chapter Eight, this volume).

The ways in which the interactions between the women's movement and the state shape state policies remain an important theme within *SPE*. Margaret Little's "The Blurring of Boundaries: Private and Public Welfare for Single Mothers in Ontario" (*SPE* 47) returns to some of the themes discussed by Joey Noble — the influence of maternalism and the role played by women's organizations and charitable organizations in lobbying for, and in administering, Mothers' Allowances in Ontario. As Little (1995, 90–91) states, "By exploring the 'maternal origins' of the Canadian welfare state we can examine the important role women played as lobbyists for such policies, and the manner in which women were defined and incorporated into the state as citizens and as clients." The article by Katherine Scott (*SPE* 50) on women and social assistance reform in the 1990s carries this same story forward in time. As she states, "social assistance is the classic example of how women were identified with the social functioning of mothering, rather than in their capacity as individual citizens or as workers" (Scott 1996, 18). The introduction of a gender-neutral worker-citizen model within the context of neo-liberal state restructuring presents the women's movement with a dilemma: "the extension of liberal rights through social assistance reforms may result in a roll back of social citizenship rights in the name of equality" (Scott 1996, 29). In this case state policy incorporates gender equality but within a context of the reduction of entitlement.

Our third text picks up these themes of struggles regarding the construction of women within state policies, of struggles within civil society and those between civil society and the state. Lois Harder (*SPE* 50) writes about the politics of the family in Alberta as an attempt "to contain Alberta feminists' demands for equality" (Chapter Nine, this volume). She looks particularly at the initiatives taken by the Getty government in the early 1990s to emphasize families and traditional family values, particularly through the creation of the Premier's Council in Support of Alberta Families. Harder uses the work of Iris Marion Young and Nancy Fraser to construct a framework for interpreting Alberta politics. Young's idea is of claims-making as a struggle between insurgency and containment, as groups attempt to press new claims and the state attempts to contain claims within a traditional framework. Fraser's analysis of the politics of needs interpretation adds to this the idea of groups struggling not only with the state but with other groups within civil society. In the Alberta case, this is central; the Alberta Status of Women Action Committee (ASWAC) had to counter the discourse of the Alberta Federation of Women United for Families (AFWUF) in order to press the claims of Alberta women on the government. In addition, Fraser's categorization of oppositional, reprivatization and expert discourses permits an understanding of civil society-state interactions as struggles about defining the questions to which government should answer. The family as a reprivatization discourse had two significant advantages for the government according to Harder. Firstly, in a period of uncertainty and rapidly changing values and ways of life, an appeal to the past is reassuring. Secondly, the appeal to the family placed feminists in a dilemma because it related directly to the contradictions of making claims based on women's difference. But this was the position that feminists had taken in order to deal with the diversity of the women's movement. Equality-based claims created the vision of a generic "woman" without race, class, disability and so on. However, making claims on the grounds of difference raises inevitably the question of mothering and, therefore, of families. As Harder acknowledges, "it is this vulnerability to the reprivatization discourse of family values and the manifestations of this discourse in public policy that has posed the most significant challenge to feminist claims for justice" (Chapter Nine, this volume). Containment and depoliticization on the part of the state; struggles for equality and justice from the Alberta women's movement.

The main argument of this section is that the gendering of state analysis in *SPE* has come primarily through authors who took civil society seriously and who centred their analysis of state-civil society relations in an examination of the organized women's movement in interrelation with the state. It is in analyzing specific examples of these interrelations — the relations of different parts of the women's movement to each other and to other parts of civil society, the intersections of race, class and gender, the forms and conditions of the interactions with different parts of the state — that one begins to build up an understanding of the state that incorporates not only sex but class and race as well. In this way Therborn, Walker and Harder illustrate a line of analysis.

Understanding the state has always been a practical as well as a theoretical concern. Understanding how the state constructs women in public policy allows important theoretical insights about state behaviour in general, which in turn allows a better strategic understanding of how the women's movement should act. *SPE*'s understanding of the state has evolved considerably over the first sixty issues — feminist analysis centred on the organized women's movement in its interactions with the state has been one of the factors in this evolution, and a rich collection of studies of feminist political economy of the state has also been one of the beneficial results of this evolution.

References

Findlay, Sue. 1993. "Reinventing the 'Community': A First Step in the Process of Democratization." *SPE* 42 (Autumn).

Little, Margaret. 1995. "The Blurring of Boundaries: Private and Public Welfare for Single Mothers in Ontario." *SPE* 47 (Summer).

Maroney, Heather Jon. 1992. "'Who Has the Baby?' Nationalism, Pronatalism, and the Construction of a 'Demographic Crisis' in Quebec 1960–1988." *SPE* 39 (Autumn).

Noble, Joey. 1979. "'Class-ifying' the Poor: Toronto Charities, 1850–1880." *SPE* 2 (Autumn).

Panitch, Leo. 1977. *The Canadian State: Political Economy and Political Power*. Toronto: University of Toronto Press.

Scott, Katherine. 1996. "The Dilemma of Liberal Citizenship: Women and Social Assistance Reform in the 1990s." *SPE* 50 (Summer).

Chapter Seven

Classes and States: Welfare State Developments, 1881-1981

Göran Therborn

The Working Class and the Perspective of 1881

1881-1981: At Two Ends of a Tunnel

History, in her intricate running through time, seems almost always to elude the hopes and the extrapolations of the ideologist and the correlations and the hypotheses of the sociologist. Her enigmatic smile, therefore, brings forth historians, even outside the guild of Clio, like amateurs to the Louvre. The welfare state is one of the major institutions of advanced capitalism, but, like capitalist democracy, the welfare state is one of capital's children out of wedlock — unexpected by protagonists and antagonists alike. In an earlier piece, I have tried to lay bare the complex processes of the conception and birth of capitalist democracy, also arguing against current and prevailing misreadings of the past.[1] There are some similar problems with current research on the welfare state. That is, current conceptions do not seem to reach or link up with the past.

A fairly non-controversial starting point for the contemporary welfare state is the German social insurance legislation of the 1880s, beginning with the Health Insurance Act of 1883. At least in Germany, where the centenary was celebrated in 1981, the *ouverture* of this legislation is held to be the Imperial Enunciation (*Kaiserliche Botschaft*) of November 17, 1881 (edited by *the* political entrepreneur of Wilhelmine social insurance policy, Bismarck).

219

Let us revive the perspective of the 1880s, listening to the message of the Kaiser and his chancellor:

> We already, in February of this year, expressed our conviction that social depredations cannot be redressed by the repression of Social-Democratic excesses, but that this must be accompanied by the positive advancement of the workers. ... To this end a revision of the Bill on workers' insurance introduced by the federated governments in the previous session will be submitted. ... A more intimate connexion with the real forces of the life of the people and their concentration in the form of corporate associations under State protection and with State encouragement will, we hope, also render possible a solution to the tasks which the State administration alone would be unable to handle to the same degree.[2]

Two things come out with utmost clarity from this message as being of central concern to the new departure: *class relations* or, more specifically, the integration of the working class into the existing society and state through support-cum-repression; and the *role and structure of the state*, or a reorganization of state-society relations (concretely by effacing the strict liberal demarcation of civil society versus Parliament-cum-bureaucracy by means of corporatist arrangements). These issues — class and state — were decisive both to Bismarck and to his opponents.[3] The *Reich* government withdrew its first proposal of 1881, after the Diet had accepted the insurance, but not what the government regarded as the proper role of the state in it. One of Bismarck's administrative collaborators, Theodore Lohman, wrote about Bismarck in a private letter in 1883:

> The accident insurance in itself is a secondary point for him; the main point is to use this opportunity to bring corporative associations into existence, which little by little would have to be extended to all the productive classes of the people, so that the foundation for the establishment of a representative instance of the people may be brought into being, which would constitute an essentially participatory legislature, replacing or alongside the Reichstag. ...[4]

Now let us listen to the cumulative wisdom a century later, through the words of, in my humble opinion, two of the very best and most historically informed contemporary social-scientific experts on the welfare state, Peter Flora and Arnold Heidenheimer:

> What is the essence of the welfare state? The concept of
> the welfare state cannot be defined by relating its meaning
> too closely to the specific reform-minded spirit of Britain in
> the 1940s, which was characterized by an unusual situation
> of war and austerity creating a high degree of solidarity among
> its citizens. Nor should the concept be defined, without regard
> to historical context, by a mere designation of policy
> boundaries and their underlying principles. Rather, the
> concept is defined by interpreting the welfare state as an
> answer to basic and long-term development processes and
> the problems created by them. From the perspective of a
> theory of political development, it is interpreted as an answer
> to increasing demands for socio-economic equality in the
> context of the evolution of mass democracies. The theory
> of modernization or structural differentiations on the other
> hand, leads us to understand the welfare state as an answer
> to the growing needs and demands for socio-economic
> security in the context of an increasing division of labour,
> the expansion of markets, and the loss of "security functions"
> by families and other communities. In this sense, the basic
> goals and legitimizing principles of socio-economic security
> and equality are interpreted as the core of the welfare state.[5]

There is little connection between, on the one hand, the "blood and iron" concerns of the *Reich* government of the 1880s to repress (through banning of the extraparliamentary activities of Social Democracy) and integrate the working class by reorganizing the state in a corporatist direction and, on the other, the latter-day Whig interpretation along the lines of "an answer to the increasing demands for socio-economic equality in the context of the *evolution* of mass democracies" (emphasis added).

The working class is held to be significant only as the main beneficiary of welfare state development, particularly in the latter's democratic responsiveness to demands for socio-economic equality and security, and the state's acquisition of a new legitimacy through social services and transfer payments. With a discrete understatement, it is noted in passing, though, that "the creation of the modern welfare state did not precede the aggravation of business cycle effects and the intensification of class conflict in the last decades of the nineteenth century."[6]

However, it would be unfair to judge two independently distinguished scholars on the basis of their lowest common denominator, even though that tells us something about the state of well-informed scholarly opinion. To the volume cited above, Heidenheimer has contributed a paper that opens up a new vista on the trajectory of welfare states. He introduces public secondary and tertiary education as one of the welfare state's possible features and analyzes mass higher education as a possible alternative to social security legislation. Flora, in his personal contribution, shows the fragility of industrialization and urbanization explanations for the beginnings of the welfare state, and brings out the importance of state structure in the form of constitutional monarchies (more progressive) versus parliamentary democracies. In an even more thought-provoking essay, Flora puts the welfare state in a historical context comprising six major features: industrial society, capitalism, international system, nation state, mass democracy and family/population.[7]

These are major contributions to our knowledge of the welfare state and its background. But both authors evade the questions of 1881 — those of the status and the effects of the working class, and of the reorganization of the state. Heidenheimer does this by sticking to the problematic of individual educational opportunities and social security entitlements; Flora by subsuming the problems of class relations and state structure under the notions of monarchy-parliamentarism and mass democracy.

That the present weighs very heavily on the common understanding of the past is also underlined by another great and very impressive project on the development of the welfare state: the West German-based legal historians' project, "A Century of Social Insurance — Bismarck's Social Legislation in European Comparison." In the editors' introduction to a volume of national reports, the development of the welfare state is collapsed into "state answers" to a set of "social risks" of income loss for individuals.[8]

In more conventional welfare state sociology, of which Wilensky is probably the best representative,[9] the welfare state is reduced to social expenditure as a proportion of gross national product. And the debate rages between those who hold that it is basically determined by economic growth and demography, and those who argue that parliamentary and cabinet seats of political parties make a difference. Wilensky belongs to the former, and among the latter the most thorough and interesting are Francis Castles and his collaborators, who argue that it is not the positive influence of left-wing parties, but the negative influence of right-wing parties that is important.[10]

There are several attempts at reviewing class and state contexts of the welfare state in a comparative manner. But so far the major one, by the Swedish sociologist Staffan Marklund, concentrates on correlating class structures and social insurance patterns, while refraining from historiographic and organizational analyses.[11] Ian Gough has made an outstanding contribution from the perspective of Marxist political economy, involving a complex, history-conscious framework, but with an empirical focus on Britain in the 1970s.[12] Others, such as those by Korpi and Esping-Andersen, are still being developed from the vantage point of Swedish social democracy.[13]

This paper claims no more than an exploratory status. But what it claims to explore is the apparently dark tunnel between the 1880s and the 1980s. In particular, the paper attempts to bring out the class context of the beginning of the welfare state; differential forms of welfare commitments and their determinants; and the location of the welfare state in the history of states, including an answer to the previously unasked and unanswered question of when the state became a welfare state.

Two Centenaries: Marxism and Social Insurance

Implied by the Imperial Enunciation quoted above is a break with liberalism, not only in the usual sense of a break with laissez-faire and its socio-economic legacy,[14] but also as a conception of what the state is, or has to be, in relation to classes and not just to individuals. There seems to be a not irrelevant coincidence between the emergence of modern social-security legislation and of the *modern labour movement*.

Labour historians and social law historians do not seem to mix very well, but it is, of course, a striking fact that the first modern welfare state legislation developed in the country of the first — and for a long period the dominant — modern labour movement. A "modern labour movement" involves (1) a political party appealing to and trying to organize the workers as a class, different from other classes, with a view to gaining political power; and (2) a trade union movement organizing the workers as a class for economic struggle with capital. The crucial constitutive movement in both respects is the establishment of permanent, unified party and trade union organizations having the same territorial range as state authority (i.e., a "national" party and a "national" trade union confederation).

The Paris Commune of 1871 was a watershed in labour history as well as a crucial trigger of modern welfare state developments. With regard to labour history, the Paris Commune was the last major manifestation, in Western Europe, of the insurrectionary crowd, and the international repression it unleashed brought to an end the heterogeneous proto-labour movement, the First International. In its place came the working-class mass party and the unified trade union movement.

The new class-specific labour movement, like the welfare state, meant a break with the traditions of the bourgeois revolution — both its radical-plebian and bourgeois-liberal variants. Being a country of vigorous industrial capitalism and of an aborted bourgeois revolution, Germany led the way. Lassalle's successor, Schweitzer, brought together a German trade union confederation as early as 1868, the same year as the Trades Union Congress (TUC) was founded in Britain, a country that had started to industrialize almost a century earlier. In 1875, at the Gotha Congress, which brought together the Lassalleans (who founded their organization in 1863) and the Eisenachers (who founded their party in 1869), the first modern labour party of the world was founded.

The Paris Commune had an enormous impact upon Bismarck and some of his closest social policy associates as well. After visits and a brief Prussian ambassadorship to France, Bismarck became a fervent admirer of Napoleon III and of the latter's attempts at a social appeal. The Commune also occurred during the Franco-Prussian War and involved the killing of two German generals. Bismarck's social policy adviser, Hermann Wagener, was an eyewitness to the event in Paris.[15] The prevention of a similar occurrence in Germany became one of Bismarck's and his associates' major preoccupations.

The Paris Commune had immediate effects on the three countries pioneering modern welfare state developments — Germany, Austria and Denmark — although not in a direct institutional way. At Bismarck's initiative there occurred, in 1872, a Prusso-Austrian conference about measures to meet the challenge of the international labour movement. In thirteen sessions, questions such as workers' education, producers' co-operatives, housing, women's and children's work, insurance and mutual aid societies were discussed.[16] In 1875, the Danish government set up its Workers' Commission against the background of the formation of a Danish section of the First International, dealing with questions of health insurance, industrial accidents and unemployment.[17]

At this stage, a couple of specifications might be in order. It is *not* being argued that ruling class fear was *the* decisive precipitant of the beginning of the welfare state, nor that the labour movement had any direct influence upon it. What *is* being argued is (1) that a threat from the working-class movement perceived by the political rulers was a necessary (but not sufficient) condition for welfare state initiatives; (2) that there is a structural affinity between the first major welfare state initiatives and the modern labour movement; and (3) that there is a chronological relationship between the emergence of the modern labour movement and the beginning of the welfare state, which makes it probable that there is a causal link between the two, the nature of which remains to be demonstrated.

The only thing that will be added here to the evidence of the impact of the Paris Commune is a reference to the general political character of the three major political leaders of the pioneer efforts (Bismarck in Germany; Taaffe in Austria; Estrup in Denmark). All were strong political leaders, as well as clear and outspoken conservatives. None of them were connected with any humanitarian movement, but all were very forceful, power-conscious politicians. From the repressive efforts against the organized labour movement of all three, as well as from their general ideological orientation, the conclusion seems to be warranted that a perceived threat from below was a necessary condition for the welfare legislation of 1883–1891. The break with poor-law repression and humiliation meant a recognition of a *collective* category of *persons*, in contrast to living objects or fortunate individuals to be kept alive.

In German and Austrian social insurance, this was expressed in the explicit recognition of industrial workers as a class of insurees; and the Danish pensions and health insurance acts of 1891–1892 recognized a broader category of non-propertied proletarians and semiproletarians as deserving public support of a kind different from that given to paupers.

The parallel to the modern labour movement — and popular movement — is striking. Members of the labour movement are expected to pay their dues with the same regularity as social insurees are expected — and obliged — to pay their insurance. In other words, social insurance, as well as the modern labour movement, presupposes what the German writer Conze once called a transformation "from a mob to the proletariat."

This perspective fits with the otherwise anomalous lateness of Britain and Belgium — the first industrializers of Europe — and also with the lateness of the Netherlands, which was urbanized at an early date. (See Table 7.1.)

A reference to the constitution of a modern labour movement may contribute to an explanation of the lag between industrialization and public social security in the two pioneer countries of industrialzation, Britain and Belgium. Britain had, in Chartism, the first mass labour movement of the world, but it was crushed in the 1840s. Only much later and gradually did the British working class free itself from bourgeois tutelage by developing its own institutions of economic and political struggle. The first major British social insurance — in the form of the Old Age Pensions Act of 1908 — had a complex background. But two aspects of it were very important: the new independent politics of labour expressed in the National Committee of Organized Labour for Old Age Pensions (part of the new labour politics after 1900); and the example of Germany, where Lloyd George and British trade unionists had gone for first-hand study.[18]

Except for intermittent rebellions, the workers of Wallonia, the industrialized part of Belgium, remained subdued for a long time. The founding of the Belgian Workers' Party in 1885 was basically a Flemish and Brussels affair. Modern Belgian social history begins with the riots of the Wallonian miners in 1886, a development more similar in form to an old peasant *jacquerie* than to a modern labour movement.[19]

Thus, Britain and Belgium pioneered in industrialization, and Germany pioneered in working-class organization and social policy. The latter correlation hardly seems to be spurious. Bismarck, for his part, was never silent on the significance of Social Democracy, both during the Imperial Speech from the Throne under his chancellorship and in more private comments such as: "If Social-Democracy did not exist, and if there were not masses of people intimidated by it, then the moderate advances which we have managed to push through in the area of social reform would not yet exist. ..."[20]

Marxism rapidly became the language and the social perspective of the new modern labour movement. From Karl Kautsky's journal,

TABLE 7.1

Timing of Working-Class Party Unification, Trade Union Unification, and First Major or Moderate Social Insurance Law

	Party	Trade Union	Social Insurance
Germany	1875	1868	1883
Austria	1888–1889	1893	1888
Denmark	1878	1898	1891
Norway	1887	1889	1894
France	1905	1895	1898
Belgium	1889	1910	1900
Netherlands	1894	1905	1901
Britain	1900 (1918)	1868	1908
Switzerland	1888	1880	1911
Sweden	1889	1898	1913
Italy	1892	1906	after 1914

Notes: Dates are taken from national labour history monographs and refer to the constitution of nationally unified working-class parties and trade union confederations. The selection of countries is that used by Peter Flora in his "Solution or Source of Crisis? The Welfare State in Historical Perspective," in W.J. Mommsen (ed.), *The Emergence of the Welfare State in Britain and Germany* (London: 1981).

Statistically, the relation between party foundation and social insurance legislation is not very compelling. The rank correlation is 0.46. However, compared with the relationship between the rate of industrialization during the 1880s and 1890s, the figure is quite respectable. The rank correlation between first significant social insurance legislation and rate of industrialization is –0.07. See Jens Albers, *Von Armenhaus zum Wohlfahrtsstat* (Frankfurt and New York: 1982), 120.

If the complex Swiss constitution is taken into account, the correlation becomes considerably higher. Already in 1889, the Swiss Federal Assembly commissioned the federal government to enact social insurance legislation. But this meant a constitutional change, which first had to be submitted to a referendum, which in turn carried the proposal in 1890. But then the referendum institute thwarted government and parliamentary initiatives until 1911. If 1889 or 1890 is taken as the year of Swiss legislation, rank correlation with labour party foundation would be 0.65, as compared with a correlation with the rate of industrialization of 0.11. See A. Maurer, "Landesbericht Schweiz," in P. Köhler and H. Zacher (eds.), *Ein Jahrhundert Sozialversicherung* (Berlin: 1981), 780ff.

Such statistics speak to statisticians. To social and political historians, another figure is perhaps more telling. In 1877, when a modern labour party had not yet been founded anywhere else, the SAPD (German Socialist Democratic Party) polled 39.2 per cent of the votes in Berlin, the capital of social insurance. See H. Wachenheim, *Die deutsche Arbeiterbewegung 1844–1914* (Cologne: 1967), 188.

Neue Zeit, backed by the undisputed party leadership of Bebel, Marxism spread in the 1880s as *the* idiom and vision of the organized working-class movement, carried across political and cultural boundaries by the inspiring authority of the unrivalled German example.[21]

From the perspective of the conventional wisdom of the 1980s, it might seem symbolic that Marx died the same year as the first social insurance bill was passed. However, the Marx centenary and that of social insurance are related rather in the opposite way. The beginning of the welfare state was also the beginning of Marxism. Both had, in different ways, their background in the rise of the workers as an organized class and in the sharpened class conflicts after the depression of the mid-1870s, which finally sealed the fate of the traditions of 1848 — of plebeian radicalism as well as of steady *Nationalliberalismus*.

Class Challenge or Constitutional Deficit?

However, a class conflict perspective on the origins of welfare state development also has to confront another argument, which makes the constitution the central variable. The line of argument goes back at least to Gaston Rimlinger, is taken up by Peter Flora, and has received its highest elaboration so far in the important work of Jens Alber. The reasoning goes roughly like this. Schemes of social insurance were first introduced in predemocratic constitutional monarchies — Germany, Austria and Denmark — which as *such* were facing particular problems of legitimation vis-à-vis the rising labour movement. Social rights thus were installed as an *ersatz* for political rights. In contrast, parliamentary democracies — Britain, Belgium, France, the Netherlands and Switzerland — did not face a similar crisis of legitimation, and therefore proceeded more slowly in social development.[22]

As far as I can see, this is an incorrect way of viewing an important link between the working-class movement and the state. It is incorrect because it overlooks the fact that the so-called authoritarian regimes had to rally parliamentary majorities for their proposals. As well, the German *Reichstag* was elected by universal male suffrage, whereas the parliamentary "democracies" of Belgium, Britain and the Netherlands still had a census franchise. Furthermore, because of the duality between government and Parliament, Bismarck, Taaffe and Estrup had a weaker position vis-à-vis Parliament with regard to social legislation than had, say, Lloyd George. The former had no firm parliamentary basis, yet had to obtain a parliamentary majority for their social proposals.

Some understanding of labour history is called for here. The modern labour movement rose in a country that was developed but had experienced an abortive bourgeois revolution — in Germany — and spread from there along the lines of diffusion of German culture after the Prussian victory over the French in 1871. The new labour movement grew most rapidly where bourgeois politics were least developed — in Germany, Scandinavia and Austria.

In short, social policy was more Parliament-dependent in Germany, Austria and Denmark than in Belgium, Britain and France, but an industrial revolution without any developed bourgeois politics made for an earlier challenge by a united, distinctive working-class movement.

State Forms and Class Relations

One important reason for the intricate complexity of welfare state history is the fact that public social policy commitments can take a number of different forms, and questions of form have often aroused more controversy and conflict than the principle of public social responsibility per se (or the magnitude of the latter). This pattern of welfare state politics has existed from the very beginning of modern welfare state developments. Thus, for instance, while the first major state initiatives were clearly related to a working-class challenge perceived from above, the German, Austrian and Danish labour movements all opposed these initiatives by the state.[23]

Like that of parliamentary democracy, the historical development of the welfare state cannot be grasped as something emanating from a particular force or agent, be it industrialization, capital accumulation, the bourgeoisie, the working class or Social Democracy. Parliamentary democracy and the welfare state have both risen out of the welter of contradictions and conflicts of capitalist societies and states. The two most important direct determinants of welfare state forms seem to be institutional state traditions — law, state structures and state-society relations — and class perspectives. The timing of new applications and elaborations of institutional traditions and the extent of the assertion of a particular class perspective should be seen as being determined, for the most part, by the balance of socio-political forces and by the conjunctures of capital accumulation.

State Institutional Backgrounds

The reason that Germany pioneered the development of social insurance was not just that the Wilhelmine government was facing the challenge of the first modern labour movement. German welfare state commitment took the form of obligatory social insurance, supervised and regulated by the state, and involved representatives of employers and workers in its administration because this was an institution already existent in Germany. The model of social insurance derived from the preliberal guild regulations — more specifically, from the *Knappschaft* insurance system in the mines. This was carried over into the liberal capitalist era, in a modernized form, by the Prussion Mine Act of 1865.[24]

It was easy for the Austrian government to follow suit, not only because of the strong Prussian influence on Austrian political culture, but also because a similar, albeit more loosely regulated, institution was at hand in the Austrian mines: the *Bruderladen*. The Austrian Mine Act of 1854 had given this institution a modern legal form.[25] Denmark, the third avant garde country, possessed no mines and had a very different system of state-society relations. These domestic traditions prevailed over the strong German influences on the Danish Conservative government, and set Danish welfare state development going in a different direction from that of Germany and Austria, a direction characterized by an absence of obligatory social insurance and an absence of bipartite or tripartite forms of administration. Instead, Denmark started from vigorous and autonomous municipal institutions in a society of prosperous and well-organized farmers. The result was a municipally organized, but partly state-subsidized, pension system whereby old "deserving" poor were provided with municipal pensions without any punitive Poor Law consequences. Health insurance took the form of state and municipal subsidies to recognized local friendly societies.[26]

The British Old Age Pension Act of 1908 was probably the first major system of income maintenance upon which organized labour left a clear and important imprint (in the Act's provision of a general, non-contributory system financed by taxation). But its non-insurance character derived also from the absence of any domestic experience with public insurance — which made the idea of non-contribution acceptable also to some Conservative politicians — and from the seemingly too difficult administrative tasks of state insurance. In comparison with Scandinavia, the greater weakness and lesser financial autonomy of British municipal institutions favoured a centralized national system, although the representatives of local councils were to determine eligibility.[27] The immediate legal background to the British act was, as in Denmark, the Poor Law, and the perceived problem was seen in individual, not class, terms (i.e., in terms of the "deserving poor").

A very particular legal and institutional tradition has strongly influenced Dutch welfare state development. One aspect of it is a particular legalism expressed in the notion — which was operative till the end of the 1950s — that social policy cannot derive from expediency, but must follow from a *rechstgrond*, a superordinate, founding legal principle. In the dominant political circles (i.e., the confessional parties, remarkably often directed by professors of law) this legal foundation of social policy was the "just wage." From this followed the principles of social policy as insurance, of a coverage limited to wage workers and employees, and of financing through employers' and employees' contributions. Another important feature of the Dutch welfare state is the conception that social insurance should be administered by "those concerned" (the *belanghebbenden*), meaning bipartite or tripartite institutions. This idea has its roots in the decentralized Calvinist Church order, in the explicit corporatism of the social Encyclas and in the principle of autonomy for the religious community, common to both the Calvinist and the Catholic *zuilen* (pillars) of Dutch society.[28]

Systematic comparative research on welfare state institutions is still only in its initial stages. In a preliminary way only, we may try to summarize some of the most important institutional determinants of the first welfare state developments. We may formulate them provisionally through a set of dichotomizing questions:

1. Do preindustrial, publicly regulated insurance systems exist? In countries where they do, social policy developments from the late nineteenth century onwards tend to pioneer in, and to concentrate on, creating obligatory insurance schemes. Since such was the case with the older insurance institutions, these new obligatory schemes tend to have a corporatist form of organization. (This pattern is exemplified by Germany, Austria and, to a more limited extent, France.)[29]
2. Do local and provincial authorities have a wide competence and a significant fiscal autonomy or not? Where they have, modern

social politics begin to grow primarily on the basis of these authorities. (Scandinavia in general; Denmark in particular; and Switzerland[30] and Belgium in the case of unemployment insurance.)[31]

3. Do strong categorical institutions of private social security exist, catering for particular social categories? Where they do, the new public social policy tends to buttress these institutions with financial subsidies, legal recognition and legal protection. (This pattern is exemplified by Belgium, France and the Netherlands.)

In a country such as Britain, for which the answer would be no to all three questions, the institutional heritage would predispose the country to development of a welfare state system in which social insurance comes relatively late and is not regarded as *the* dominant institution of social policy, and one in which a relatively centralized system catering to individual citizens in need is developed. The available evidence seems to bear this out.

Our argument so far may be summed up in this way. The development towards a welfare state began on a broad scale in those countries that first experienced the challenge of a working-class party. The new social policies adopted were initiated from above and were largely shaped by distinctive national traditions of law, state structures and state-society relations prior to late nineteenth-century industrial capitalism. These traditions are in many ways still visible in their contemporary effects, and the adaptations of them before World War I in turn left a further institutional heritage to later generations.

However, the growth of the labour movement meant the emergence of another set of determinants of welfare state politics and policies: the demands and the perspectives of the classes of industrial capitalism. On the basis of existing institutions, the outcomes of industrial patterns of class conflict have shaped the welfare states of today.

The Working-Class Perspective

The histories of the welfare state have hitherto, on the whole, been written from above, with the historian's searchlight fixed on governments and civil servants and mainly with a view to looking into what and when they contributed to the development of what from today's perspective appears to be *the* main features of the welfare state: social insurance and other large-scale income-maintenance programs. The typical trajectory pictured in these histories is one from poor relief to income maintenance, as indicated by the title of the work of Jens Alber and the subtitle of that by Hugh Heclo, mentioned above.

Against the background of this conventional wisdom, the following questions need to be asked: What did the workers and the workers' movement think and do about the "workers' question"? What did they demand and what did they fight for? But such questions have a further implication. By answering it, we also begin to get a basis from which to assess how much the labour movement has contributed — directly, and not only as a threat to the existing social order — to the making of contemporary welfare states.

In another essay I have tried to develop a working-class perspective on social policy. Properly speaking, that is a task for large-scale, social-historical research. My own contribution is more limited, based first of all on an overview reading of nineteenth-century labour and social policy historiography (particularly of the major European countries), and, secondly, on a study of the programs and congress resolutions of the First, Second and Third Internationals, as well as of the major parties of the Second International. This latter source gives us the perspective of organized labour before it was shaped by national constraints in conjunctures involving parliamentary responsibility and delimited governmental margins of manoeuvre. The former, the secondary sources, provide at least a possible check on whether or not the early programmatic statements of labour parties were consistent with the demands and strivings of workers in struggle.[32]

From such research a set of characteristics of the working-class perspective on social policy may be formulated.

The Guiding Principle

Most immediately and most directly, what workers rose and organized to fight for were workers' rights to a livelihood and to a decent human life. A conception of workers' rights seems to be the guiding principle running through working-class perspectives on social policy — a principle opposed to insurance as well as to charity, an assertion overriding liberal arguments about the requirements of capital accumulation, dangers to competitiveness and the necessity of incentives. The labour perspective is first of all an assertion of the rights of working persons against any logic involving objects of charity, market commodities or thrifty savers.

One cannot deny that this working-class principle may at times overlap with the compassion of humanitarian middle-class reformers, an aristocratic sense of paternal obligation, a radical conception of citizens' rights or the enlightened self-interest of businessmen and statesmen concerned with the reproduction of the labour force, of the soldier force or of the existing social order. But there are also occasions and issues on which the working class tends to be left alone with its principles, and on which other concerns take on an overriding importance for other groups and classes. Unemployment and the treatment of the unemployed is such a crucial issue. Shall the unemployed have the same rights and conditions as the workers (whom it is profitable to employ) in public works employment or as benefits recipients? Should the prevention of unemployment be a task of social policy overriding all others? Questions like these form touchstones of class perspectives.

Task Priorities
The first working-class priority is undoubtedly protection of the class itself (*Arbeiterschutz* or workers' protection, as it is termed tellingly in German): safety at work, union rights and leisure from work.

The labour movement has always been male-dominated and, in spite of the explicit demands for the legal equality of women, this workers' protection orientation often includes a patriarchal, special protectionist attitude towards women (often assimilated with children) and women's work.[33] Class also has a gender aspect.

The second priority of the labour movement has been the *right to work*, the maintenance of employment under non-punitive conditions. Income maintenance and social insurance arranged by the state is *not* an original working-class demand. Insurance by means of associations of mutual aid developed early in working-class history, but state insurance comes from elsewhere. For instance, it does not figure in the Social Democratic Gotha Programme of 1875, in spite of the program's half-Lassallean, pro-state perspective.[34] The founding congress of the Austrian Social Democratic Workers' Party, in December–January 1888–1889, dismissed the Workers' Insurance organized by the state, and just adopted in Germany and Austria. It was rejected both because of its lack of significance to the social problems of the "worker who is capable of working" and because of its directly negative effects on "the partial transfer of the cost of poor relief from the municipalities to the working class and the restriction as much as possible, where feasible the shoving aside, of the independent support organizations of the workers." Instead the congress demanded, as long as the capitalist mode of production prevailed, "an honest worker protection legislation without loopholes and its energetic carrying out."[35]

When the labour movement comes to demand extension of social insurance, this is always seen in relation to incapacity to work, not in terms of breadwinner responsibilities and family size. Universal public education is an early demand, whereas public housing and housing hygiene appear somewhat later. Housing does not appear in the Erfurt Programme, for instance; it is brought to the Sixth Congress of the International in Amsterdam in 1904 by the British delegation.[36]

Administrative Control

The issue of who should administer social insurance and welfare state benefit schemes has been a central theme in the class conflicts regarding social policy and social institutions. From the French and German miners in the 1850s and 1860s, through the Second International, to the 1928 Comintern program for the time after the revolution, autonomous *self-management* has been a persistent demand of the workers' movement, with bipartite or tripartite forms as second and third best. There have been several objectives behind this concern: to establish and to guarantee entitlement to benefits independently of the employer's discretion and punishment; to ensure a human, non-bureaucratic consideration of claims and claimants; to prevent the use of the funds involved by the employers or by the state; to train administrative cadres of the working-class organization; and to boost the recruitment of members.

Coverage and Organizational Form

A *wide coverage and uniform organization* of social regulations and social institutions have been part of the strivings of labour from very early on. A regional organization encompassing all the mining companies was fought for by the French and the Saxon miners mentioned above. Later this was extended to demands for international or internationally congruent regulations of work and leisure and to uniform state organization of national insurance. Coverage had to be wide, embracing all wage workers and salaried employees, with particular attention paid to bringing agricultural, domestic and foreign workers into the schemes. Somewhat later, but at least by the first decade of this century, demands were raised for including low-income earners in general.

These are demands that ought to be expected from a rational working-class point of view as ones maximizing autonomy from particular employers and the unity of class and its potential allies. General schemes covering the whole population, however, can be only at most a second-best strategy, erosive of class unity and difficult to combine with working-class forms of administration. And demands for such schemes do not seem to be found in the early and the classical periods of the labour movement up to the Depression and the social democratic breakthroughs in Scandinavia and New Zealand. As an international conception, schemes of universal income maintenance seem to be an effect of the national anti-Fascist war effort, the context of the unexpectedly enthusiastic reception of the Beveridge Report of 1942.[37]

Demands for administrative control and the concern to facilitate organizational recruitment may sometimes make working-class organizations opt for less than full class coverage. This holds particularly for the case when specific class organizations have been the only ones to provide certain benefits. It would then be in the interest of the labour movement to restrict public insurance for such benefits to those who are or will become members. The field where this has occurred in Europe has been mainly unemployment insurance.[38]

Finance

The very origin of the labour movement was a protest against, among other things, the existing distribution of income and life chances. When issues of public insurance and public social services were raised, the labour movement always insisted on a *redistributive mode of finance* either through progressive taxation (or luxury taxation) or employers' contributions. This redistributive principle is, of course, different from and in conflict with the insurance principle, though between the two, different compromises may be struck.

One kind of compromise may come out of the possible conflict between redistributive, non-contributory financing and having a say in administration. The latter may be difficult or impossible to get without financial contribution. Before World War I, the French *Confédération général de travailleurs* (CGT) and the Guesdist wing of the Socialist Party waged a vehement resistance against workers' contributions to a public pensions insurance and against the bill as a whole, which became law in 1910. The law was a failure; the CGT had expressed the interests of the French workers on this issue. (The critique also referred to the capitalization scheme and the high age of retirement.) After the war, however, the CGT became a champion of social insurance with principled acceptance of workers' contributions as the legitimate basis for trade union control of the administration. (And the belated health and old age insurance act of 1930 was also accepted and supported in practice by the workers.)[39]

Part of the redistributive perspective is also an early demand for *public services* free of charge: education, health care and later a wide range of municipal services (not necessarily free of users' tariffs).[40]

Opposed Social Policy Perspectives

The corresponding bourgeois principles are most difficult to arrive at inductively because the bourgeoisie is much less publicly organized. However, from the bourgeoisie's socio-economic location we might derive something like this. The overriding principle should be the maintenance of favourable conditions for capital accumulation, which includes the securing of an adequately skilled, motivated and stable labour force. Administrative control of social security schemes should be in the hands of the employers or of private insurance companies, and above all not in the hands of the unions or the state. The organizational forms should therefore be allowed to vary, and coverage should be restricted to the employees of each enterprise, or possibly to each branch of an enterprise, to ensure uniform conditions of competition (possibly supplemented by residual programs for the marginalized poor and for the unemployed and the unemployable at a level clearly beneath the lowest wage rate). The method of finance should mainly be non-redistributive insurance and, as much as possible, the use of public services and facilities at market price should be charged.

How these class perspectives have been fought out in the course of twentieth-century welfare state politics is a story that cannot be told here. This mode of analysis has, however, been applied to the Swedish case, and its categories also fit very well with, for example, the issues and the alignment of forces in the controversies around social policies right after World War II in France, Germany and the Netherlands.[41]

In Britain, national enthusiasm for the Beveridge Report created a more complex political situation. On the other hand, the social policies of the postwar Labour government may be seen also as a tilting of the political balance of social forces towards the perspective expressed by the Labour Party Conference in May 1942, in a resolution ringing with classical working-class concerns:

> ... in the view of the Labour Party there should be: (a) One comprehensive system of social security; (b) Adequate cash payments to provide security whatever the contingency; (c) The provision of cash payments from national funds for all children through a scheme of Family Allowance; (d) The right of all forms of medical attention and treatment through a National Health Service.[42]

The controversy over superannuation involves a lineup along the class lines indicated above.[43]

In brief, the forms and principles of public social commitments have been politically controversial. These controversies have not been merely conjunctural, and have not only pitted individual politicians or civil servants and political parties and interest groups against each other. They have also developed along class lines, and the various specific issues are to a significant degree intelligible in terms of opposite class perspectives.[44] Classes are not decision-making bodies, which is a fundamental reason why policy making is inherently irreducible to class conflict and class power. Yet a class analysis provides an explanatory framework that can make the study of politics and policy into something more than a modernized *histoire événementielle* of strings of episodes acted out by individual policy makers (i.e., into an understanding of the historical dynamics and societal development).

The issues central to Bismarck and his age — those of state organization and of class relations — have, contrary to prevailing academic opinion, subsequently remained parts of welfare state history and politics. In the present crisis of the welfare state, they have become burning issues of social conflict. It is high time for historians and social scientists to try to understand and to unravel them.

Capital and Labour on Social Policy in 1981

Let us end this section by bringing forth the current class conflict over social policy and the future of the welfare state, that is, by asking if it is possible to discern, through the lenses of empirical scholarship, any distinctive class perspectives on the social policy issues of today.

The handiest, non-arbitrary way of doing this seems to be to look at the views expressed by the Business and Industry Advisory Committee to the Organization for Economic Co-operation and Development (OECD) and by the Trade Union Advisory Committee to the OECD. Both submitted their views on the topic to an OECD seminar, the proceedings of which have been published under the title, *The Welfare State in Crisis*.[45] Table 7.2 compares these views of 1981 with the class perspectives outlined above, the working-class part of which, it will be remembered, was inductively arrived at from a study of labour history prior to World War I.

The Welfare State in State History

In the reorientation of welfare state research and political understanding, which this paper tries to call for by pointing to some central issues of state organization, class relations and power, at least one more question has to be raised. It is important to raise it here, however briefly, not mainly because it is one unasked hitherto, but above all because the answer to it elucidates the socio-political struggles of today. The question is seemingly simple: When does a state become a welfare state?

To take the question seriously, however, implies that the welfare state has to be located in state history, the study of which has not run very deeply on this side of the age of Absolutism. And like that of liberal democracy, the history of the establishment of welfare states *qua* states has tended to dissolve in evolutionary mythologies. Often the two mythologies run together. Let us listen to one specimen, taken from one of the very best and one of the most history-conscious researchers on the welfare state.

This is his considered view of the historical rise of the welfare state:

> Democratic welfare states have moved through three general stages in the last 100 years, each with somewhat different ways of relating politics, the economy and social policy.[46]

The stages are "Experimentation" (1870s–1920s), "Consolidation" (1930s–1940s) and "Expansion" (1950s–1960s). A fourth stage is also distinguished, beginning in the 1970s and continuing to the present: "Reformulation."

There is something strange about this image of the "democratic welfare state" as a kind of ark floating through the decades of the

TABLE 7.2

Business and Trade Union Views on Social Policy in 1981 Compared with
Analytical Class Perspectives

Business View	Class Perspectives
1. "The decisive starting-point for any reflection on social policy-making in the '80s is the economic situation. ... Policy-makers desiring to guarantee higher social benefits must also create or improve the conditions for sufficient, non-inflationary economic growth." "Principle for a Revision of Social Policies"	*Guiding Principle:* Favourable conditions for capital accumulation
2. "The tendency of politicians in many OECD Countries to cover practically all risks as far as possible for all groups in society has to be stopped."	*Coverage and Organizational Form:* More restricted
3. "In particular, the individual's incentive to work efficiently must not be dampened by income levelling. The redistribution of the burden of financing social benefits is especially important in order to avoid misuse of the services offered ... and to prevent the trend of permanently growing expenditures."	*Finance:* Non-redistributive mode of finance (in relation to market-determined income) *Finance:* Insurance principles
4. "As far as insurance against basic risks ... is concerned, experience with income linked contributions of 50 per cent to be paid by both the employer and the worker and with the self-administration of the social institutions has been a good one. On the other hand, tax-finances and state-run social services have normally led to inefficiency and high costs."	*Administrative Control:* Against union and state control
5. "... avoid narrowing differences between the income of those working and the income of those who receive unemployment or pension benefits."	*Guiding Principle:* Incentives
6. "Employers ... should review the voluntary social benefits ... to see whether they correspond to a real need of the employees or whether they have become superfluous due to the expansion of the social benefits required by collective agreement."	No corresponding analytical perspective.

7. "Finally, not only the scope of social benefits but their costs and, in particular, the extent to which each individual must be contributing to these costs has to be made known to all parties involved. This includes evaluating whether the public or the private sector can do a better job providing goods and services and making the administrative expenditures necessary to the contribution of social benefits more transparent."

Finance: Non-redistribution

Coverage and Organizational Form: Against uniform public organization

Trade-Union Views

1. "Full Employment as the Major Aim" "Each human being has the fundamental right to a decent job. ... For the trade unions the real issue in the immediate future is to reorient economic policy so that it would stimulate such economic activity which would restore full employment."

The Guiding Principle: Workers' rights to livelihood; to a decent human life

2. "Alternatives Through Cooperation" "Free collective bargaining in lean years is difficult enough, and the governments should not aggravate the task of trade unions by attacking this valuable channel through which many crucial measures of social policy can also be negotiated."
"Priority should also be given to an analysis on the extent to which programmes fail to reach those who would be eligible: in this again, cooperation with the trade unions is necessary."

Administrative Control: Workers' self-management with bipartite or tripartite arrangements as second and third best

3. "Selective Growth and Basic Values" "Growth has never solved social problems alone. Even selective growth does not eliminate tension between social and economic aims. Social policies in the 1980s should create a framework for workers and their unions to exert an increasing influence in the decision-making process at all levels, including the enterprise level. ..."

Administrative Control: Workers' self-management; bipartite or tripartite arrangements

4. "Equality and Income Distribution" "Equality is one of the fundamental objectives of democratic societies, yet in this aspect, too,

Finance: Redistribution by progressive taxation

social policy and the economy have been pulling in opposite directions." "One of the major objectives of social policies in the 1980s should be to increase their impact on the taxation policies and to make this impact more concrete, so as to make taxation policies in all aspects be consistent with social policy objectives."	or employers' contributions
5. "A certain level of protection should be extended to each individual in society, for the society's own sake. ... Selective protection of disadvantaged groups is not an alternative to universal action, but it must come on top of it, to ensure equality."	*Coverage and Organizational Form:* Wide
6. "Educational policies are an essential part of this overall policy aiming at full employment, to guarantee retraining and the continuous upgrading of skills in the face of technological developments."	No corresponding analytical principle.
7. "The question of work-sharing or part-time work should not be confused with the basic trade union demand for the shortening of the working time. A consequent and general shortening of the working time. ... is socially desirable and feasible in the light of technological developments.	In part, no corresponding *analytical* principle. In part, *Task Priorities:* Worker protection; leisure from work
8. "Questions of policies to address the quality of work ought to occupy a central role in the deliberations of this Conference. The improvement of working conditions would alleviate a number of problems. ..."	*Task Priorities:* Worker protection, safety at work
9. "A certain degree of centralization in the government's social policy programmes is necessary in order to guarantee equality for the beneficiaries. A loss of uniformity in standards and contents of social benefits, and in their potential outcomes implied may well threaten the equalizing goals of social policy." "... TUAC [Trade Union Advisory Committee] opposes any increased Privatization of social services."	*Coverage and Organizational Form:* Uniform

Sources: Business Views: Business and Advisory Committee to the OECD, "A View from the Entrepreneur," in *The Welfare State in Crisis* (Paris 1981), 84–87; Trade Union Views: Trade Union Advisory Committee to the OECD, "A Frame of Reference for Priorities," in *The Welfare State in Crisis*, 87–93; Class Perspective: see the text of the previous section of this paper.

Of the sixteen different demands, here listed in the chronological order of the sources, fifteen (or fourteen-and-a-half) can be located along the dimensions of opposite class perspectives. Thus, current social policy controversies are clearly located within the classical nexus of capital-labour class conflict. As well, the declarations above can also tell us something about the balance of the class forces within the advanced capitalist countries, as it was perceived at the top level in 1980–1981.

Business has accepted a relatively extended social policy and that the unions have some say in the administration of it. The unions, for their part, do not demand workers' management of social institutions, but only a right to co-operate, and give a rather low priority to worker protection or conditions of work. Both sides are putting forward rather modest and rather defensive demands; the general situation emerging is one of mutual fears and uncertainty. Both sides testify to the increased importance of the state as a specific organization by criticizing "politicians," state organization and "governments," but not explicitly the other class (see business views no. 2 and 4; and trade union view no. 2). The class relations of advanced capitalism have to a very important extent become mediated by the state.

---

past century. When was that ark built? A century ago; no democracy, in the current sense of the word, existed anywhere in the world.

With regard to liberal democracy there is at least a set of criteria around which a certain consensus emerges relatively easily once the criteria have been made explicit. It is more difficult and more controversial to determine if a certain state should properly be called a welfare state.

The prevailing implied definition seems to be that a "welfare state" is any set of large-scale regulations and/or provisions undertaken by the state that entitles citizens to certain means of subsistence and some amount of care in case they cannot support themselves by their labour. This kind of definition is not very adequate for at least two reasons. Most generally, it pays no attention to other activities of the state, which makes it inappropriate for the characterization and understanding of different kinds of state. More specifically, because of the blind eye turned towards the rest of the state, the dominant implicit definition is inappropriate for any probings into the historical development of states, including welfare activities.

Therefore I would propose the following definition:

A welfare state is a state in which transfer payments to households

— other than the remuneration to holders of state positions and other than payments of interest to lenders of money to the state.

— and/or the caring and the education of other people than state employees constitute the quantitatively predominant everyday routine spending and activities of the state and its employees.

In less formalized prose, the proposed definition would read: *A welfare state is a state in which welfare activities dominate everyday state routine.*

Two remarks should be made on the definition. The emphasis on everyday routine is crucial because the arrival of welfare states has not meant that the other classical activities of the state have withered away: making or preparing for war, extraction of resources, punishing the breakers of the state's law and order, or the provision of infrastructure (transportation and communication). In case it should turn out that the name proposed for the kind of state defined runs too much counter to tenacious language habits, the conceptualization offered could go under another name, for instance, "a developed welfare state."

The Arrival of the (Developed) Welfare State

Elsewhere I have tried to give a first overview, in empirical and quantitative terms, of the historical development of Western European states, from the pre-bourgeois war machines to contemporary welfare states.[47] In this context, I will confine myself to showing two things: the limited ranged of two famous modern welfare efforts, and the largely unnoticed great change, which has taken place over the last twenty years.

Welfare activities comprise a wide range of endeavours, but for the purpose of comparisons between states over time and across frontiers, the composition of public expenditure and public employment will be both an adequate and manageable measure.

Two countries where an early change of the state into a welfare state might be expected would be Britain and Sweden. Britain is the country of the Beveridge Plan, of the post-World War II Labour government, of Bevan's National Health Service and the country where the expression "welfare state" was first struck. Sweden has been governed by a strong and vigorous social democracy since 1932, and has been, in its own words, reaping its "harvest" after World War II. Let us see what these states looked like around 1950. (See Table 7.3.)

What happened after World War II was more a growth than a structural change of the state. In Britain in 1931, and in Sweden in 1930, the proportions of social or welfare expenditures were 44 per cent and 39 per cent, respectively (as calculated from the same sources used in Table 7.3).[48] The proportion of welfare state employment in Britain was 21 per cent in 1931; in Sweden, it was 31 per cent.[49]

It was in the 1960s and 1970s that the social transformation of advanced capitalist states accelerated. Around 1970, the first welfare states appeared (in the sense of states) in which expenditures on welfare state activities — income maintenance, care, education, etc.,

---

TABLE 7.3

Expenditure on and Employment in Public Social Services in Britain in 1951 and Sweden in 1950 (Per cent of total public expenditure and of total public employment, respectively)

	Britain	Sweden
Social Expenditure[a]	38	43
Social Employment[b]	20	28

Notes:
[a] Social insurance, social assistance and other income maintenance programs (except agricultural subsidies), health and social care, public education, public housing and housing allowances.
[b] Employees in health care, education and social work.
Sources:
Social Expenditure, Britain: I. Gough, The Political Economy of the Welfare State (London 1979), 77; Social Expenditure, Sweden: calculations from E. Höök, Den offentliga sektorns expansion (Stockholm 1962). (A detailed account of the calculations made from Höök's material is given in my "When, How and Why Does a State Become a Welfare State?" paper presented to the ECPR Joint Workshops meeting in Freiburg, March 1983, 23.; Social Employment, Britain: R. Parry, "United Kingdom Public Employment: Patterns of Change 1951–1976" (Centre for the Study of Public Policy, University of Strathclyde, Glasgow, 1980), 42, 43, 46; Social Employment, Sweden: Göran Therborn, Klasstruckturen i Sverige 1930–80 (Lund 1981), 116 (calculations from census data).

---

became predominant. The three first (developed) welfare states were Belgium, Netherlands and Sweden.[50]

The pattern of state employment has changed rather drastically. By 1975 in Sweden, 47 per cent of public employees were occupied with teaching, caring, social assistance, feeding and cleaning work. In the United Kingdom in 1976, 40 per cent of all public employees were in education, the National Health Service or in central and local social security services.[51]

Thus, a change has taken place, completely overshadowing the immediate effects of World War II, Beveridge and the tide of Social Democracy and labourism. History eludes her court chroniclers. Large-scale social forces were at work throughout the advanced capitalist world. In the United States, for instance, school employees, for the first time since the U.S. turned into an imperial world power, became significantly more numerous than military and civilian defence personnel in 1970, at a time when the Vietnam War was still on.[52] In a country like Canada, however, the changes seem to have been moderate. The proportion of education and hospital employees out of all civilian public employees was 34 per cent in 1951, 38 per cent in 1961, 39 per cent in 1971 and (a bare) 39 per cent in 1974.[53] For the current situation on public expenditure patterns, a recent study by the OECD Secretariat may be used.[54] Table 7.4 shows that in the course of the 1970s, most advanced capitalist state have become welfare states.

Envoi

The current crisis of the welfare state is something that has broken out, not because of gerontological ailments, but right after a quiet but historically unique acceleration of welfare state developments throughout the Western world. The crisis is one of maturity and rigour, not of old age. The reasons for this recent growth, overshadowing all the *gestae* of the heroes of the conventional chroniclers, still need to be laid bare. People with a knowledge of and/or a commitment to the labour movement should take notice of the fact that the maturation of the welfare state in the 1960s and 1970s coincides with the second prolonged historical period of growth of the labour movement, as indicated in unionizations, labour party votes and increasing labour strength at the workplace.[56]

At the beginning of this paper we noticed that the first major developments of the welfare state took place in the first growth period

TABLE 7.4

Welfare State Expenditure[a] as a Percentage of Total Public Expenditure in 1981, and Total Outlays of Government as a Percentage of GDP in 1981

	Welfare State Expenditure	Total Expenditure
Canada	53	41
United States	59	35
Japan	57	34
Australia	61[b]	34
New Zealand	51	—
Austria	58	50
Belgium	74[b]	56
Denmark	53[c]	59
Finland	56[d]	39
France	61[e]	49
Germany	66	49
Greece	38[b]	36
Ireland	52	55[b]
Italy	64	51
Netherlands	61	62
Norway	56	48
Sweden	(52)[f]	65
Switzerland	48[g]	28[h]
United Kingdom	55	47

Notes: [a] "Estimates of total expenditure on education, health and social welfare. The estimates include final consumption expenditures by government, capital formation, subsidies, current transfers to households and capital transfers."
[b] 1980.
[c] 1978.
[d] 1974.
[e] 1979.
[f] Data incomparable with the others; expenditures on "social welfare services" includes "social security and welfare transfers only."
[g] 1975.
[h] Current disbursements only.
Sources: Calculations from OECD Secretariat, "Statistical and Technical Annex," mimeograph (Paris: OECD Secretariat, June 1983), Table A (welfare state expenditure); *OECD Economic Outlook* 33 (July 1983), Table R8.

According to this rather generous definition of welfare state expenditure, a welfare state emerged, after some European pioneers, in Canada from 1968, in the United States from 1971, in Japan from 1974 and in the U.K. from 1976. In terms of public employment, the current situation is still little explored.[55] In some vanguard countries, like Belgium and the Netherlands, it is complicated by the fact that a large part of welfare activities, while being publicly financed, is carried out by legally private institutions.

A look at two columns at the same time gives another interesting picture. If we exclude less developed Greece, it appears clearly that advanced capitalist states today differ much more in their size than in the relative importance of their welfare commitments. This implies that there are two kinds of forces at work here, one determining the size of the state, another the kind of everyday state activities — something that also came out of our earlier look at British and Swedish developments.

---

of the labour movement. The connection seems worth pursuing. Bismarck's hope and intention with his social insurance legislation was to bind the working class to the existing order. In his attempt, Bismarck suffered a complete failure. Imperial social policies did not prevent ever larger portions of the German working class from rallying under the banner of Social Democracy, which at that time stood for a socialist republic. (The integration of 1914 was an effect of nationalism.) Later on, far-left writers made Bismarck's hopes their fears. They too have been disconfirmed by historical developments. The growth of the welfare state in the 1960s and the 1970s was accompanied by an increased industrial militancy of the working class everywhere in the advanced capitalist world, and by new socialist projects in France, Britain and Sweden — to cite the most clear examples — alongside the advances of the Italian Communist Party. It is just because of the recent and rapid arrival of a welfare state, and because this arrival has not meant the final integration of the working class, that the current, ferocious onslaughts on the welfare states by the New Right, spearheaded by the governments of Thatcher and Reagan have to be understood as a socio-political *revanchisme*. The stakes in this battle are high and serious, but instead of whimpering at blows received, the labour left should be aware that it is being attacked in positions of strength.

Notes

1. Göran Therborn, "The Rule of Capital and the Rise of Democracy," *New Left Review* 103 (1977), 3–41.
2. D. Zöllner, "Landesbericht Deutschland," in *Ein Jahrhundert Sozialversicherung*, P. Köhler and H. Zacher (eds.) (Berlin 1981), 87.
3. The best monograph remains W. Vogel, *Bismarck's Arbeiter Vorsicherung* (Braunschweig 1951), 152ff. and passim. See also D. Zöllner, "Landesbericht Deutschland," 86ff.
4. Vogel, *Bismarck's Arbeiter Vorsicherung*, 158–159.

5. Peter Flora and Arnold Heidenheimer (eds.), *The Development of Welfare States in Europe and America* (London 1981), 8–9.

6. Ibid., 23.

7. Peter Flora, "Solutions or Source of Crisis? The Welfare State in Historical Perspective," in *The Emergence of the Welfare State in Britain and Germany*, W.J. Mommsen (ed.) (London 1981), 343–389.

8. H. Zacher (ed.), *Bedingungen für die Entustehung und Entwicklung von Sozialversicherung* (Berlin 1979); P. Köhler and H. Zacher (eds.), *Ein Jahrhundert Sozialversicherung* (Berlin 1981), esp. 15, 27ff.

9. H. Wilensky, *The Welfare State and Equality* (Berkeley 1975).

10. Francis Castles, *The Impact of Parties* (London 1982).

11. Staffan Marklund, *Klass, Stat, Socialpolitik* (Lund 1982).

12. Ian Gough, *The Political Economy of the Welfare State* (London 1979).

13. G. Esping-Andersen, and W. Korpi, "From Poor Relief to Institutional Welfare States: The Development of Scandinavian Social Policy," paper presented at the ECPR Joint Workshops in Freiburg, March 20–25, 1983.

14. Köhler and Zacher, *Ein Jahrhundert*, 18ff.; G. Rimlinger, *Welfare Policy and Industrialization in Europe, America, and Russia* (New York 1971), Chapter 3.

15. W. Vogel, *Bismarck's Arbeiter Vorsicherung*, 142ff.

16. Ibid., 25ff.

17. I. Horneman Moller, *Klassekamp og sociallovgivning 1850–1970* (Copenhagen 1981), 38–39.

18. P. Hennock, "The Origins of British National Insurance and the German Precedent 1891–1914," in *The Emergence of the Welfare State in Britain and Germany*, W.J. Mommsen (ed.) (London: 1981), 84ff.; H. Heclo, *Modern Social Politics in Britain and Sweden* (New Haven and London 1974), 170ff.

19 . M. Liebman, *Les socialistes belges 1885–1914* (Brussels 1979), 46ff; Kritak, *Wat Zoudt Gij Zonder 't Werkvolk Zijn?* (Leuven 1977), 38–39.

20. F. Tenstedt, *Sozialgeschichte der Sozialpolitik in Deutschland* (Göttingen 1981), 222.

21. G. Haupt, "Marx e marxismo," in *Storia del marxismo*, E. Hobsbawn et al. (eds.) (Torino 1978), 1:297ff., 350ff.; G. Haupt, *L'historien et le mouvement social* (Paris 1980).

22. Jen Albers, *Von Armenhaus zum Wohlfahrtsstaat* (Frankfurt and New York 1982), 132ff.

23. For Germany, See H. Wachenheim, *Die deutsche Arbeiterbewegung 1844–1914* (Cologne 1967), 233ff. Austrian social democracy condemned the social insurance proposals at its founding congress in Hainfeld. See *Beschlüsse des Parteitages des sozialdemokratischen Partei österreichs zu Painfeld ... ergänst am Parteitag zu Wein*, reprinted in *Kleine Bibliothek des Wissens und des Fortschritts* (Frankfurt circa 1982), 1:2401–2402; for Denmark, see O. Bertolt et al., *En bygning vi rejser* (Copenhagen circa 1950s), 1:220–221.

24. Vogel, *Bismarck's Arbeiter*, 20–21; D. Zöllner, "Landesbericht Deutschland," in Köhler and Zacker, *Ein Jahrhundert*, 82ff.

25. H. Hofmeister, "Landesbericht österreich," in Köhler and Zacher, *Ein Jahrhundert*, 49ff.

26. The Danish discussion on the social question in the last third of the nineteenth century may be followed in *Arbeidersporgsmalet og Landarbeiderorganisationen 1864 til 1900* (Copenhagen 1983); an overview of social policy decisions is given by I. Horneman Möller, *Klassenkamp og sociallovgivning 1850–1970* (Copenhagen 1981), Chapter 1; and by S. Kuhnle, *Velferdsstatens utvikling* (Oslo 1983), Chapter 8.

27. A good overview of the making of the British Old Age Pension Act is given by H. Heclo, *Modern Social Politics in Britain and Sweden*, 158ff. An interesting comparison with Germany is given by E.P. Hennock, "The Origins of British National Insurance and the German Precedent 1880–1914," in Mommsen, *Emergence of the Welfare State*, 84–106.

28. The best overview of Dutch social policy developments is given by G.M.C. Veldkamp (ed.), *Sociale Zekerheid* (Deventer 1978), vol. 1; an accessible introduction to the legal debate is provided by the collection *Tien jaren Raden van Arbeid* (Amsterdam 1929).

29. This pattern is exemplified by Germany, Austria and, to a more limited extent, France. See H. Hatzfeld, *Du paupérisme à la sécurité sociale* (Paris 1979), 111–249.

30. The Swiss refused the German system of social insurance and developed a decentralized one of their own. See Maurer, "Landesbericht Schweiz," in Köhler and Zacher (eds.), *Ein Jahrhundert*, 784ff.

31. See Veldkamp, *Sociale Zekerheid*, 198–199.

32. Göran Therborn, "The Working Class and the Welfare State," paper presented to the Fifth Nordic Congress of Research in the History of the Labour Movement, in Murikka, Finland, August 1983. (To be published in Congress proceedings.)

33. The Social Democratic women demanded no prohibition of nightwork for women, for instance. (Nor did they demand family or child allowance, but this was in agreement with the male perspective; see further below.) *Huitième Congrès Socialiste International* (Gand 1911), 492–495.

34. Of its six specific demands, one deals with education and five deal with worker protection in the German-Scandinavian sense. From Karl Marx, "Kritik des Gothaer Programms," in *Marx-Engels Werke*, 19: 30ff.

35. *Beschlüsse des Parteitages* 2401–2402.

36. *Programm der sozialdemokratischen Partei Deutschlands* (Berlin 1891).

37. The universalism of the Swedish old age pensions insurance of 1913 was incidental, and followed most directly from the pragmatic character of Swedish politics. The originally proposed, very wide coverage derived, however, from Swedish class relations — from the political strength of the peasantry and its link to the working class. From early on it was clear that pensions scheme should comprise those two classes together. See Therborn, "The Working Class and the Welfare State."

38. Thus, at the time of the introduction of unemployment insurance in Britain (by the Liberal Lloyd George government) the Parliamentary Committee of the TUC proposed that the insurance should be restricted to unionists. The government refused this, naturally enough for such a government. See J. Harris, *Unemployment and Politics* (Oxford 1972), 317–318. In Sweden, unemployment insurance is still wholly in the hands of the unions, as it is in Belgium to a predominant extent.

39. Hatzfeld, *Du pauperisme*, 229ff.

40. At the Paris Congress of the Second International, in 1900, the Belgians had a resolution passed on "municipal socialism" concerning the promotion of municipal services as "embryos of the collectivist society." *Cinquième Congrès Socialiste International* (Genève 1980), 112ff. The most important development of municipal socialism came after World War I, headed by the Socialists of Vienna.

41. See H.C. Galant, *Histoire politique de la sécurité sociale francaise 1945–1952* (Paris1955); H.G. Hockerts, *Sozialpolitische Entscheidungen im Nachkriegsdeutschland* (Stuttgart 1980); T. Berban and G. Janssen, "Vakbeweging en sociale zekerheid in Nederland na 1945," M.A. thesis, Institute for Political Science, Catholic University, Nijmegen, Netherlands, 1982.

42. *The Labour Party 41st Annual Conference Report 1942*, 132, here quoted from J. Hess, "The Social Policy of the Atlee Government," in Mommsen, *Emergence of the Welfare State*, 297.

43. See Heclo, *Modern Social Politics*, 253–283. Heclo himself does not see it that way, but a reader whose attention has been directed to the class perspectives outlined above will certainly recognize them in Heclo's narrative.

44. This is true also of non-European countries. For instance, opposite class alignments with regard to the organization of unemployment insurance in the 1930s or of health insurance after World War II emerge clearly, albeit in passing, from the studies of Canadian social reforms by Don Swartz and Alvin Finkel in *The Canadian State*, Leo Panitch (ed.) (Toronto 1977), 323, 329, 353.

45. Organization for Economic Co-operation and Development, *The Welfare State in Crisis* (Paris 1981).

46. H. Heclo, "Towards a New Welfare State?" and in Flora and Heidenheimer, *Development of Welfare States*, 384.

47. G. Therborn, "When, How and Why Does a State Become a Welfare State?" paper presented to the ECPR Joint Workshops Meeting in Freiburg, March 1983, part 2.

48. The Swedish figure does not include municipal housing expenditure.

49. M. Abramowitz and V. Eliasberg, *The Growth of Public Employment in Britain* (Princeton 1957), 101; Göran Therborn, *Klasstrukturen i Sverige 1930–1980* (Lund 1980), 116. The Swedish employment figures are based on detailed occupational breakdowns, which tend to give slightly higher figures than statistics based on departmental lump sums. Calculations on the basis of the latter-type of materials have yielded Swedish figures for 1930 and 1950 of 28 and 27 per cent, respectively.

50. Therborn, "When, How and Why," 30. The sources used there are International Labour Organization (ILO) figures on social security and OECD figures on education expenditure and total public expenditure (including capital formation).

51. The sources are the same as those of Table 7.3.

52. United States, Bureau of Census, *The Statistical History of the United States from Colonial Times to the Present* (New York 1976), 1102, 1104, 1141.

53. H. Armstrong, "The Labour Force and State Workers in Canada," in Panitch, *Canadian State*, 299, 300, 302 (tables 4–6).

54. Calculations on the basis of national statistics and of monographic studies or with the help of ILO social statistics have shown that the OECD Secretariat's estimates

of social expenditure in the 1960s are sometimes mysteriously inflated with no visible basis in public national statistics and little consonance with known later changes (Netherlands); or they include large-scale war-related schemes (Belgium, Germany, Italy), and schemes for public employees only (Austria, Germany). But with the development of more standardized national accounts, thanks to the efforts of the OECD Secretariat, and with the decreased importance of the particular effects of war damage and of particular privileges for public employees, the most recent OECD figures will be fairly adequate for our purposes here.

55. A rough overview is provided by the OECD publication, *Employment in the Public Sector* (Paris 1982).

56. See G. Therborn, "The Labour Movement in Advanced Capitalist Countries," paper presented to the Marx Centenary Conference of the Roundtable of Cavtat, Yugoslavia, October 1983. (To be published in the forthcoming *Socialism in the World*.)

Chapter Eight

The Conceptual Politics of Struggle: Wife Battering, the Women's Movement and the State

Gillian Walker

Introduction

This paper traces a crucial process whereby the efforts of feminist activists concerned with wife beating have been transformed and absorbed into existing institutional structures. The result of this process is that although we have achieved much and are still working, struggling and angry, the sites of our struggles are dispersed, disconnected and depoliticized. The process of absorption is not magical or mysterious, but it is not an easy one to uncover, partly because of its complexity and partly, as I will argue, because it involves ways of thinking and using language that obscure important aspects of what we need to understand. The dilemmas we face as feminists are embedded in the conceptual practices that we must adopt when we take up our struggle in relation to the state. As we work to understand the relationship between women, the women's movement and state practices, it becomes increasingly evident that one-dimensional views of the state as a monolith, with either benign or hostile intentions towards women, are not adequate. The analysis developed in my study reveals a layered web of negotiated discursive relations in which ideological constructs play a coordinating role. In the face of pressures for social change, these provide a basis for developing government policies and the particular funding, reporting and accounting procedures of different state institutions.

My work deals with a facet of the interaction between the state and the women's movement, and must be seen within the framework of the organization of social relations linking the local, everyday activities and practices of people with the general and abstracted procedures of ruling and administering an advanced capitalist society. In particular, this study examines part of a political process of control that shapes and develops "issues" and lodges them in the administrative procedures through which Canadian society is ordered, organized and ruled. Particularly, it explores how concepts as ways of thinking, naming and knowing coordinate and make possible the process of institutional articulation and absorption. This approach allows the development of a framework that delineates the process in several stages, which loosely correspond both to the temporal sequence of events and to the ideological aspects of how the struggle for control and action were played out.

The struggle can be characterized for analytic purposes as having three stages. The first involved the efforts of the women's movement to make the situation of women being beaten by their menfolk visible and actionable. At this stage, the women's movement struggled to define a "women's issue" in feminist terms in the face of professional attempts to remove the issue from the political "movement" context and organization and substitute a conception of the problem that revolved around the notion of "troubled families." The second stage saw the resulting struggle within the women's movement as the work of doing something about "the issue" was translated to and generalized within the relations of the state. Feminists strove to formulate an account of the problem, providing both an analysis of its roots and a basis for action in relation to increasing state involvement. In the third stage movement activists, service providers and others in various professional fields succeeded in getting particular sections of the ruling apparatus to respond to the needs of battered women. It marked a transformation and reorganization of the relations of the women's movement to the issue and to the agencies and institutions of the state. This study is part of a fourth stage in which dissatisfaction with outcomes provoked a number of theoretical and strategic re-examinations of this enterprise.[1] The temporal nature of these stages can be counterposed with a conceptual mapping of the process in question. This aspect of the process provides the focus for what follows.

The Language of Ruling

In the early years of recognizing and organizing around the plight of women beaten and brutalized by husbands and intimates, women did not have a term to define their situation. The process of making the experience of oppression in our own homes visible to ourselves and then getting it accepted as a matter of public concern involved defining it as a problem in our terms. The language available to us to do this kind of work presents us with a contradiction; it is the "oppressor's language," controlled by those who have the power to define its content and meaning.[2] We must use it, however, to express our concerns.

In detailing the conceptual processes underlying these developments, the use of language presents me with a problem. It is important to distinguish language used descriptively in relation to activities and experiences from the conceptual forms produced by ideological practices that identify the relations of ruling. I am in no way denying the fact that men treat women in a variety of oppressive ways, some of which are brutal and coercive, in order to enforce their demands and desires. What I am addressing here is something different; I am mapping a discursive process, embedded in the work of intellectuals, professionals and administrators, through which certain activities are selected and named as categories, intended to identify particular problems and particular solutions. To mark and clarify this distinction, I have used the device of placing certain terms in quotation marks when I address the technical nature of their ideological functioning as ruling concepts. Concepts, when they operate in this technical way, are not simply descriptive linguistic conventions; they organize the social construction of knowledge: ways of thinking about, defining and giving abstract and generalized meaning to our particular experience. Knowledge, thus produced, provides for particular courses of action. Understood in this way, concepts can be seen to do more than name a phenomenon. They are part of a social relation (used here to signify an ongoing, concerted course of action involving more than one person) that brings into being and organizes particular phenomena in specific ways, and provides for a response to what has been thus identified.

In detailing this conceptual process I want to look first at the way particular aspects of women's experience — wife beating, battering and abuse — have been isolated and described so as to become accepted as discrete phenomena and taken up as "women's issues." Then I shall explore the struggle over terms and definitions — "male violence," "domestic violence" and "family violence" — which took place both within the women's movement and in relation to institutional structures and professional practices. Finally I show that the common ground provided by the concept of "violence" has allowed for combined strategies among activists and professionals, which led to the acceptance of wife battering as primarily a problem of assault under the Criminal Code. While this has important short-term implications for the protection of individual women and the possibility of public sanctioning of men's violent behaviour, I argue that it is part of the process of absorption, a process that we need to understand if we are to develop strategies to avoid fragmentation and absorption in the future. While some of the data for this account and analysis are provided by documents or drawn from academic discourse, I also discuss some specific events in which I took part.

In Vancouver in the early 1970s I worked with a United Way task force aimed at providing information and education, coordinating services and pressuring government and agencies to recognize and respond to "the issue" of family violence. Here, as elsewhere, women's movement groups often found themselves in opposition to the approaches put forward by professionals from institutions and agencies. As "the issue" was made more visible through the work being done at the local level all over the country, feminists with connections to the federal government sought to make an impact at that level by organizing, in 1980, a National Consultation of women's groups working in the area of wife battering. This consultation and later events such as federal and provincial (Ontario) public hearings before standing committees of both legislative bodies, which took place in 1981 and 1982, and the reports that resulted from both hearings contributed key data to the analysis.

The Battered Wife

When women first spoke out about being hit and beaten by husbands or common-law partners, the terms "battered wife" and "wife abuse" were not available as ways to think about the experience. As women strove to make the situation public in various local sites in which organization was taking place, these terms were extrapolated from the existing discourse on child abuse, already "discovered" and designated as a "syndrome" by medical practitioners in the 1960s.[3] "Battered babies" had already made media headlines, especially in Britain. The use of the word "battering" in this connection was an adaptation from legal terminology, "assault and battery" being a categorization of the degree of severity of an assault under the British Criminal Code. Though the terms may have arisen in the professional discourse in Europe and the United States, they were elaborated in the media and their use in reference to wife beating was in common parlance by the early 1970s. Women identify themselves as battered wives in some of the letters that Erin Pizzey published in her groundbreaking 1974 book. She herself uses "battering" occasionally as an adjective to describe continued and severe beatings and refers to battered wives only once, qualified by quotation marks, which imply some skepticism as to its professional implications:

> As far as I can see the reason why "battered wives" are getting a hearing is that for the first time a middle-class woman has said, "It's happening to me." That makes it respectable and all the more shocking. Now — just as "battered babies" were once called "manslaughter" — wife beating has become the "battered wife syndrome." But it is not enough to call it a new name and then carry on as before.[4]

My memory of my own involvement with Vancouver Transition House and other related projects in those days is that we initially used the terms "wife beating," "battering" and "abuse" in a loose and relatively interchangeable way. Any concern we may have had at the time about the implications of the terms related to whether using the term "wife" would act either to prevent women who were not legally married to their abusers from seeing themselves as welcome at the house or to allow professional agencies to refuse them welfare and other services.

Del Martin's book, *Battered Wives*, published in 1976, contains an introduction by Diane Russel, an activist and academic doing research in the area of rape. Russel gives battering an actual definition as a more severe and extreme form of the phenomenon of wife beating, which she links with rape as a similar means of coercion and control of women. Martin took up the term "wife battering" in the same way as we did in Vancouver, as problematic only in relation to the marital status of the victim; she opted to continue using the word "wife" because it conveyed the intimate nature of the relationship involved.[5] For Martin, "battering" was a specific descriptive term. Her book was a significant factor in the development of a discourse promoting the adoption of the term "battered wife," which could counter neutralizing and degendering alternatives such as "spouse abuse" and "interspousal violent episodes." These were the terms employed by professionals responding to the issue, who tended to link it with child abuse under the rubric of family or domestic violence.

Family Violence and Our Discontents

Activists in other places shared similar experiences as those of us working with the United Way in Vancouver. We found that linking wife battering and child abuse focused the issue in such a way that women's experience came to be subsumed by the professional emphasis on child abuse and services to men who battered their wives. We discovered that we had to be vigilant, vigorous and persistent to counteract the way that the framework of "family violence" obscured the actual actions of men and the suffering of women, so that who did what to whom disappeared in an objectified professional language.

The designation of violence as occurring in the family or in the domestic realm also maintained it as a private matter concerned with the interpersonal relations of individuals. This framework arose out of and fed back into the work of professional agencies and institutions whose mandate was to maintain the organization and existing power relations of the family. In response, the political objective on which many of us focused our work was to force the professionals to recognize wife battering and abuse as an issue in its own right and indeed as representing the overwhelming preponderance of instances of "family violence." This also involved us in a critique of "the family." The feminist analysis of the family as an institution embodying the political oppression of women at its most personal was not accepted readily by the professionals with whom we struggled. Their professional mandate of maintaining the traditional family form inclined them towards interventions designed to fix up the family and help "it" deal with "its" violence.[6] We fought for the maintenance of the women's movement's control of its definition of the issue against attempts by professionals to remove the issue from its context in a political movement.

For some feminists, however, the use of the terms "family" and "domestic" violence served as conscious change strategy. In her 1981 update to the second edition of *Battered Wives*, for example, Martin notes that in the early stages the term "domestic violence" was used because it was necessary to cloak "the realities" in "diplomatic language ... to get people to listen, or to keep from alienating those whose help we needed."[7] The coordinator of the Vancouver United Way task force reacted with anger to the suggestion that "family violence" as a term worked against women's interests. She insisted that, on the contrary, it allowed her to "slip women in" in circumstances where wife battering itself would have been "too contentious an issue."[8]

Male Violence Against Women

This division over the uses of terms like "family" and "domestic" violence was not the only one among feminists working on the issue. At the National Consultation organized by the Canadian Advisory Council on the Status of Women in March 1980, the Council attempted to find a common position in relation to professional concerns for the proper management of the problem and the conflicting accounts of the roots of the issue put forward by activists.[9] While we had no difficulty in agreeing that men's violence towards women must be addressed in the short term in any strategy for change, some of us concentrated on the structural features of women's dependence in relation to the family and the workforce, emphasizing the trap that this creates for women, particularly women with children. Others saw the organization of the family as only a manifestation of the overriding issue of ultimate control of women by force or the threat of force in a patriarchal system. For them, male dominance and male violence thus became the primary target for action.

The proceedings published by the Council after the consultation show how our work was drawn together to emphasize this latter position. By taking up the theme of one presentation (that battering is something we all share), which extended the definition of wife battering to include almost every form of women's experience of oppression, especially rape, incest and sexual harassment, the document packaged the various positions into one that could be adopted to stand for all: "We women" stand opposed to "male violence," which must be countered; we women must maintain control of the issue. This was an attempt to link definitions that operate at a bureaucratic and professional level, such as family and domestic violence, to those with a political mobilizing intent such as wife battering, violence against women and male violence. Slogans such as "Wife battering is Everywoman's issue" brought us together as women and dissolved differences in location between professionals, service providers, activists and women who were beaten, all of whom became women vulnerable to male violence.[10] The term "wife battering" was taken up in a way that linked movement organization and impetus to bureaucratic and professional forms.

Assault under the Law

What was actually accomplished at this stage of the process was that, through focusing on violence itself, the male violence framework could be married to that of family violence. This gave women who occupied a range of positions a way to organize their work in opposition to violence as behaviour that should be brought under the rule of law. The issue of wife battering was reformulated in terms of the laws on assault, which ostensibly protect everyone from violent attack by other members of society. The struggle concentrated on extending the application of the law to those women whose status as wives or intimates had hitherto left them unprotected within the private realm of the family, traditionally beyond legal intervention in any situation short of murder. In the process, the analysis of women's oppression in the broader structures of society became secondary to the strategy of invoking women's rights as individuals under the law. The emphasis on individual rights in the criminal justice system specifically obscured the different experiences and location in the social structure of Black, minority, Native, immigrant and White working-class women and men. Class differences between the men who batter could only be accounted for in ideological terms, set up by a framework that designates family violence as crossing all cultures and classes.

The coalescence of this strategy and its consequences for lodging wife battering within particular institutional sites of the state's "social problem apparatus" provide the focus of my analysis of the events that took place before the federal Parliament's Standing Committee on Health, Welfare and Social Affairs and the Ontario Legislature's Standing Committee on Social Development.[11] Representatives of a range of women's groups, social service organizations, government departments and their researchers appeared before both committees. In the transcripts of the hearings and in the reports produced by each committee, it was possible to trace the development of a framework that allowed committee members to define the problem in ways that linked specific aspects to particular institutions and agencies within the government. Some of the conceptual underpinnings of that framework are detailed here.[12]

Conceptual Practices

I have described the struggle over definition and control of the issue sequentially to illustrate that the process is one that has taken place over time and within activities and events, not as merely an abstract or linguistic concern. It could equally be presented systematically like this:

Male Violence

Wife Battering

Family Violence

Violence = Assault

As a concept, "family violence" organizes both a phenomenon and a course of action. How it is constructed, however, is in some ways invisible. It appears as the natural conjunction of two recognizable features of our society: "the family" and "violence." This conjunction is not a straightforward naming of related entities; it developed out of the work of professionals, researchers, theorists and information disseminators as a discourse with distinctive properties. The conjunction of "family" and "violence" treats as naturalistic and conflates two concepts already developed for our understanding by sociological procedures or as administrative products. These procedures construct as social facts the "ordinary forms in which the features of our society become observable to us as its features — mental illness, neighbours, crime, riots leisure, work satisfaction, etc."[13] The processes by which these features are constructed is the making of ideology. Ideology understood in this way is a method of thinking and working that ruptures our ideas from the practical, everyday world of lived experience in which they arise, and enters them into theories within a discourse that represents the relevancies of those who order and rule. The practical actions, activities and locations that make up social relations are stripped away and dropped out of the conceptual form and replaced by connectives, which account for experiences in terms of theory and discourse.

Feminists have struggled against the concept of "family violence." But I suggest that there is a prior conceptual stage with regard to wife battering as a category, which has seldom been addressed in our definitional debates. Although Pizzey acknowledged some ambivalence towards the naming of women who were beaten as "battered wives," it was Dorothy Smith who challenged the category itself.[14] As she pointed out, taking a particular aspect of women's experience of oppression out of context, and putting it through a process of abstraction that constructs a category — the "battered wife" — is also an ideological process, producing the conceptual forms through which professional intervention operates. Such a process is, she suggests, one of the ways that women's protest is absorbed into institutional structures:

> The issue of men's violence against women in the family setting is being transformed into a professional psychiatric or counselling problem. The "battered wife" concept is substituted for the political analysis of violence by men against women. There are conferences, a literature, the elaboration of a professional practice (often focusing more on men than on women).[15]

The significance of Smith's challenge was not fully appreciated at the time. The struggles to combat subsuming "wife battering" under the rubric of "family violence" obscured some of the implications of the term itself. Wife beating or battering might have some claim to the status of mere description, but "the battered wife" is clearly a social construction. Its ideological properties as a category ruptured from the social relations of women's lives allows "the battered wife" to be treated as an instance of "family violence," or as part of a theoretical framework that separates features of people's lives into pieces that can be managed and administered.

A subsequent development added a dimension not evident in 1979 when Smith first issued her warning. The political analysis of violence by men against women was elaborated into a framework that became a major organizing focus for feminists in the early 1980s. In this process "the battered wife" was treated as an instance of the victimization of women by male violence. I would argue that this is also an ideological feature of a discourse equally ruptured from the social relations in which women's lives are embedded. The initial mobilizing efforts of the women's movement centred on oppression as part of the broad social structures of the division of labour in the workplace and in the family. This was displaced by theories that emphasize men's violent domination of women as the overreaching determinant of women's oppression throughout history. This shift in focus denotes a major rift in the contemporary women's movement.[16] Theories of male domination provided the basis for the conceptual coordination of the issue of wife beating as "violence," defined as assault under the law. With this definition, the work of the women's movement could be aligned with that of the criminal justice system.

The Concept of "Violence"

Feminists on many fronts drew attention to the ideological construction of "the family" as both normative and problematic for women.[17] "Violence," on the other hand, has been used extensively by feminists as if it were a purely descriptive term for behaviours or activities in which physical force is used to inflict injury, either randomly or to gain some specific end such as control. In the case of male violence against women, its definition has been extended to include verbal threats and abuse, economic deprivation, sexual coercion or deprivation and the creation of a general climate of fear, which limits the full participation of women in society. Yet "violence" as a term also holds properties beyond the descriptive. Here I will simply sketch in some of the dimensions and implications of its current usage.

When a concept such as "violence" is constructed by the process of "making ideology," it is detached from its grounding in the social relations in which events and activities take place, and put through an abstract reorganization that conforms to the relevances of a particular or a number of discourses.[18] In this process, it takes on a reified form as a single coherent phenomenon or force to which causal efficacy, as well as explanatory powers, can be ascribed. There is a shift in the concept; it ceases to describe what someone does — hitting, punching, kicking, stabbing or shooting someone else. The presence of people doing things disappears and is replaced by a term expressing the action in a general form, but without the actor. "Violence breaks out" in families, in the streets, on the picket line; outbreaks of "violence" "occur." "Violence" can then be treated as a causal factor and motivator in a range of discourses that intersect and articulate several disciplines. Within the broad discourses of the social sciences, "violence" appears as integral in the psychosocial and sociobiological discourses concerning aggression, dominance, instinctual behaviour and sex roles. In sociology and criminology, it operates as a feature of the discourses of law and order and victimology. In legal discourse, "violence" is of particular significance in relation to the rule of law. "Violence" knits together these discourses and is given both a clinical and a criminal organization, each of which is salient to the analysis I am making here.

Already made available by the ideological practices of mainstream social scientists, building upon "the primary administrative work which constitutes murders, suicides, etc.,"[19] "violence" has taken its place as the unquestioned focus of two relatively new discourses: the professional discourse of "family violence" and a feminist discourse of "male violence." It provides a link both between these discourses and with the socio-legal discourse on "violence" in relation to the state.

"Violence" and the State

The sanctioned use of force in contemporary society is monopolized by the state as a feature of the practices of ruling. The state has developed myriad bureaucratic procedures to license and control its use by the police, the military and other functionaries such as coast guards, prison guards and mental hospital attendants. It is in relation to the state's claim to the legitimate use of force in certain circumstances that "violence" as a concept can be seen to designate uncontrolled, unregulated and illegitimate use of force. "Violence" within this framework has been worked up ideologically from a term in common usage, describing a wide range of activities used to enforce will, inflict injury or express discontent, into a technical category for the designation of non-sanctioned acts beyond the bounds of law. This is part of a historical process in which the use of physical force to gain power and maintain order and control has been superseded by ideological procedures that regulate society through bureaucratic and professional operations.[20]

Brutal physical practices such as hanging, flogging, maiming and torture are no longer officially accepted in democratic societies as regularized features of the rule of law. Corporal punishment in schools is increasingly prohibited and, in countries such as Sweden, it is illegal to smack one's own children. This represents both a change in methods of law enforcement and a shift in the designation of the realm to which the rule of law applies. The internal governance of family matters was regarded until relatively recently as the domain of the male head of the household. The patriarchal organization of earlier family forms resulted from a hierarchical social structure whereby the chain of authority of the state was extended to the "pater familias." He was responsible for ensuring the law-abiding behaviour of the family members, servants, apprentices and employees within his household by such measures as he saw fit including physical correction. This responsibility, however, was not isolated from community, kin and state intervention. It is only in later forms of capitalist organization that the family takes on the restricted and relatively "private" nuclear grouping now taken as normative.

The juxtaposition within the professional discourse of the concepts "family" and "violence" has only taken place over the past decade and a half. At the same time, child abuse has also been subject to the processes of medicalization and legalization.[21] Feminist campaigns for child protection and the relief of women bound to brutal husbands in the last century and the early years of this century were not couched in terms of "family violence." They dealt with issues in terms of the husband's legal right of chastisement and his authority over his wife and children as property.[22] As late as 1969, wife beating had not yet been fully included in what prominent sociologist James Q. Wilson designated as "domestic violence":

> There are two kinds of domestic violence for which we would like to estimate future rates and thus two kinds of problems which make such estimates very difficult, if not impossible. The first kind is individual violence — murders, suicides, assaults, child-beatings — and the second is collective violence — riots, civil insurrections, internal wars and the like.[23]

Conceptualizing "violence" as a single coherent phenomenon spanning a range from individual pathology to large-scale social pathology opens the way for designating protest, dissent or resistance to the dominant class as riots, insurrections, terrorism or mob rule. That such definitions are operating unseen when "family violence" is considered can be seen in both the definitions of "domestic violence" offered by Wilson.

This conflated framework of individual and collective behaviour permits the kind of theory used by Dutton et al. They pull together a number of seemingly contradictory possibilities, theoretically reconciled into a causal hypothesis that suggests a form of personalized, "deindividuated" "violence" engaged in by men as individuals towards their mates. "Deindividuated violence" is a psychosocial construct that refers to theories of mass, uncontrolled, uninhibited and pleasurable rage expressed in vandalism, mob rampages and riots. "Violence" as a conceptual organizer enables the actions of people (here acknowledged as men) to be treated as if the acts are governed by a force independent of the will of the actors. Women are thought to remain with "violent" men because they, in turn, develop inappropriate but intense "trauma bonding" as a result of the erratic nature of their partner's behaviour. (This theory is based on studies of the hostage, or "Stockholm" syndrome.) Stress and "interpersonal aspects of the battering relationship" act as triggers of male rage.[24] A feature of the theory of individual yet "deindividuated" violence is that men, once past the rage threshold, have no control over and no memory of their actions, and thus presumably no responsibility for them; women, in turn, are helplessly unable to escape because of their own trauma. Theories such as these, often produced by state-funded research, provide the constructs necessary to direct the nature of state intervention into areas defined as social problems. "Violence" comes to be understood as a feature of social life, one that must be both deplored and managed, a pressing social problem in all its manifestations.

The Dilemma of "Violence"

The feminist discourse of "male violence" did make visible the gender and power relations involved in "family" or "domestic" "violence." It helped advance the struggle for definitional control and action, and made the professional discourse accommodate women's experience. It has, however, produced a number of anomalies that mitigate its ultimate usefulness as a strategic base. At the simplest level it presents an explanation that suggests that every instance of the abuse and control of women is either an inevitable outcome of pathological models of masculinity produced by society through socialization, or the result of innate, inherent and sociobiological characteristics that doom all men to dominate each other and all women by aggression and force.

These positions offer the option of a massive and immediate resocialization of the entire society or the setting up of a separatist society divided on gender lines. Neither position accounts for the anomalous situation of men who do not beat, rape, harass and abuse women, in spite of growing up in so-called "cradles of violence," or those who did not experience or witness physical abuse and do perpetuate it. Liddle points out that, despite the importance of the insights supplied by feminist theorists concerning both the pervasiveness and impact of violence against women, one-dimensional models of male agency and simplistic conceptions of male "interests" as the motivations for violence fail to adequately address the situation.[25] Nor do they give us any way to understand why some women abuse children or other dependants. These positions also open the way for clinical and legal initiatives that tie the most radical aspects of feminist mobilization into a conservative law and order framework for social control. In this process, men's actions towards their wives become instances of assault. The actors are again subsumed under the legal terms of perpetrator and victim and both gender and relational aspects are dissolved. This obscures any political understanding of society as structured through fundamental inequalities that render it disastrously out of tune with human need.

Dissecting the Dilemma

The process I have examined can now be assembled schematically in a more complex and elaborate fashion:

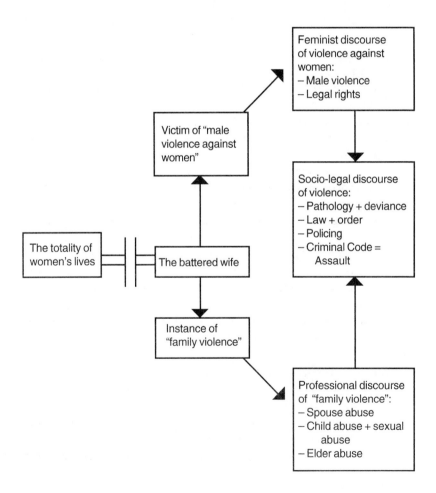

The dilemma of "violence" as a conceptual practice points to the larger dilemma for the women's movement, which has been detailed in this paper. In order to act in ways that would alter the oppressive conditions that women experience in differing ways in the totality of their lives, experiences designated as belonging to the private realm had to be made public. The terms available in the public discourses, however, were more than a mere language of description. They were part of the conceptual coinage of ruling relations in contemporary society. When we took up such terms as the "battered wife" or "violence," we played a part in constructing the phenomenon and the terms in which it was to be made comprehensible. The language of abstraction is part of the making of ideology, which transforms our understanding of our daily experience, and implicates us in our own regulation by shaping our concerns into "issues" organized on the grounds and within the relevancies and imperatives of the institutions and practices of ruling. Through this process the woman becomes the victim of "violence," constituted as an abstraction by procedures that rupture the experience being named from the general context of her life. The category thus constituted can then be assembled, with others, as an issue or social problem from which professional intervention extracts the political focus by providing social service or legal solutions.

The dilemma faced by feminists is contained in the practices through which ruling is accomplished. Naming the experience is a double-edged sword. It coordinates our mobilization and identifies our difficulties to ourselves and each other. Many women have spoken of the power that being able to identify themselves as "battered wives" gave them. It was a first step for some in recognizing that the experience was widely shared and that taking action was a legitimate response. At the same time, it directed such action into particular channels: seeking "help" in the form of social services or legal redress. Neither of these mobilize women unless they are put in a feminist context, nor do they address the totality of women's lives.

Concepts as Ruling Practices

"Violence" can no longer be regarded as a straightforward term describing a pre-existing phenomenon. It is established by ideological practices as one of the concepts forming discourses that are the knowledge base for the exercise of power in contemporary society; it is a ruling concept, a ruling practice. As feminists we have taken the term into our own language to counter the ideology of "family violence" and to attempt to reattribute the activities it names to the men who commit the acts of cruelty and coercion that it purports to describe. In the process, however, "violence" comes to be accepted as an independent force directing the activities of all men for all time.

This process, I suggest, has involved us in some strange alliances. Within the women's movement the position of "we women," battered or oppressed in other ways, mobilizing to change the actual conditions of our lives and the structures that enforce them, has been fragmented by strategies that align us with different aspects of the state's practices. Our organization becomes its organization. We take up "violence" within the family and use the linkages with the legal discourse to support the equation of certain forms of "violence" with assault. This allows feminists with differing political commitments to ally themselves with professionals and within a civil rights framework in seeking legal sanctions and protection for women under the law.

We become actors in a process that reflects shifts and tensions in the jurisdictional boundaries of state practices in relation to individual rights and family forms. As the organization of the family unit around the assumption of a single male wage deteriorates, men's authority in the family is challenged. At the same time, the individual rights model of participation and democracy permeates the ideology of the state. The relatively recently won right of women to be considered as persons makes arguments against their right as individuals to freedom from assault harder to defend. "Family violence" seems to present a way of deflecting part of the focus from the criminal justice model and maintaining the power of intervention in the hands of those professionals more directly concerned with maintaining or implementing the family as represented in the ideology of the state. "Violence" as assault allows for either the treatment of men to "cure" them of their violence or the removal of men who "abuse their authority in the family," and the subsequent supporting of a new family form made up of women and children dependent upon the state. The clinical dimension of the concept of "violence" links together the two lines of development, "family violence" and "male violence," to give them a particular character. A framework for action is set up. The process of developing this framework gathers up local and particular threads, homogenizes and coordinates them, and then allows for the reapplication of the definition or diagnosis at the local level via appropriate divisions of the social problem apparatus. The particular dimensions of situations — those that relate to gender, class location, racial or ethnic factors, the abuse of alcohol or any other way in which we might understand what is going on in a broader social context — are written out. At the same time, women's struggles against the many forms of coercion and abuse that arise in the context of oppression and inequality are subsumed within theories of a sick society in which individuals need treatment. The power relations inherent in the structure of "the family" are, at best, modified.

What is being modified, I would argue, is not men's authority in the family but their abuse of that authority. "Family violence" deflects the focus from the legal system towards health, welfare and social services institutions, but "male violence," reformulated in professional discourses in terms such as "spouse assault," paves the way for the entry of legal discourse. Patriarchal family relations are thus reduced to actions that support or defy the law and the hidden "law and order" frame that "violence" references.[26] Allying ourselves with aspects of the ruling apparatus, and particularly the state, by accepting the "male violence/family violence" conceptual frame risks substituting what Brown has called public patriarchy for private patriarchy.[27] It is ironic that the appropriation of "male violence" provides for short-term solutions that invoke the rule of law since feminists have often characterized the legal system as one that maintains male domination. Control of the issue is delivered over to those in the social problem apparatus who are charged with maintaining "the family" and who are encouraged to enforce further legal sanctions against individuals within the family unit.

Wife Battering and the Women's Movement Reviewed

I have identified a three-stage process of generalization and appropriation in which issues that seemingly come out of "nowhere" are articulated to structures where there is a possibility of getting something done to address them. The paper is not an attempt to write a history of wife battering. Rather, it describes some of the conceptual practices of the woman's movement as it struggled to make public this particular aspect of women's experience. My work stands beside that of other commentators in a fourth stage of reflection and assessment, which seeks to account for some of the outcomes of the struggle so far. Writing in the early 1980s, both Tierney and Morgan conclude that as far as the experience in the United States was concerned, the women's movement had lost any form of control over the disposition of the issue.[28] Susan Schechter's analytically perceptive and comprehensive review of the U.S. shelter movement, published in 1982, ended on a more optimistic note, which called for feminists to continue to struggle against wife battering itself and against bureaucratic attempts to depoliticize it. Schechter, however, may have been overly optimistic. According to a recent report on the difficulties faced by the movement, in many states it is impossible to find government funding or services for battered women except through drug and alcohol treatment programs.[29]

Recent work in Canada has also explored the impact of government policies and practices on the women's movement's actions with regard to wife battering.[30] Much of this work confronts the limitations of reform as an effective social response. G. Geller documents examples of judicial indifference, prejudice and hostility that trivialize and undermine the strategy of laying assault charges by imposing inadequate or meaningless sentences on men convicted of rape, incest and wife beating.[31] In the same vein N.Z. Hinton argues that failure to address the role of patriarchy and the structural features of oppression by treating wife battering as a matter of individual rights leaves the justice system free to manage violence in ways that bolster and reassert the status quo.[32] She pressed for a more effective justice system and resistance to any attempt to individualize and reprivatize the issue. Loseke and Cahill, on the other hand, suggest that the work of the women's movement has created a new class of experts who focus on battered women and a new population of deviants, i.e., women who refuse to leave relationships in which they are abused. Ignoring the history of struggle over the form in which women's suffering could be made visible and the many different positions taken by feminists and professionals in that struggle, these authors recommend the reprivatization of personal relationships and respect for the right of adult women to choose their own fate. Though they fail to address power relations and structural oppression, Loseke and Cahill provide useful data that call into question the specificity of battered women's actions and experiences, showing that some of the features of the "battered women syndrome" are present in most marriages and not necessarily contingent on a "violent" relationship.[33]

Using the experience of the Transition House movement in the Maritime provinces as an example, Andrea Currie suggests that the feminist analysis of wife battering as assault has been responsible for some of the dissatisfaction expressed by working-class, Aboriginal, ethnic and racial minority groups who feel excluded from services. Her persuasive discussion of what she describes as "one of the worst expressions of men's abusive power over women" leads her to the conclusion that only direct and adequate responses from the state in the form of fully funded and far-ranging services can meet the immediate needs of individual women and their children.[34] Political action to change the circumstances that make women the targets of violence, she suggests, should be the responsibility of a broadly based social movement in which battered women from all class and racial backgrounds would work alongside feminist activists. Currie acknowledges the fact that it was the work of the women's movement in founding transition houses that first brought wife battering to public awareness. If, however, shelters and other services continue to be run by professionals whose approach to the problem is guided by concepts such as "family violence," it is not clear, as Currie suggests, how women will be exposed to the political analysis required for membership in a broader battered women's movement. The experience of the Vancouver Transition House also indicates that full government funding is not necessarily a secure option. The only one in the country at the time to be entirely funded by the provincial government, the Vancouver Transition House was a victim of the 1983 Social Credit policy of cutbacks and restraint. Despite a vigorous struggle, which included a sit-in and occupation by staff, activists and residents, the house was eventually closed. A Salvation Army Women's Shelter receives provincial funding as a transition house and there is a small shelter for women run independently of all government funding, but Vancouver is without a transition house as such to this day.

A number of questions raised in these studies support my argument that part of the problem with the outcome of the struggle so far stems from the ways in which we have come to conceptualize the experiences involved. I have been concerned with the ways in which our thinking came to be organized so that the state, through its social problem apparatus, could be induced, shamed or pressured to respond. Wife battering was first linked with "family violence" to provide an articulation to existing family policies and service agencies. The struggle to include wife assault introduced the possibility that sanctions already existing in the Criminal Code could be invoked. In the process of coordinating the work of government agencies and institutions, however, aspects of the mobilization of a movement for political change got lost. The work done with battered women has become, in many cases, the site for professional and voluntary service provision. This has taken the place of consciousness-raising within the context of a fully mobilized women's movement, which might allow the issue to be linked with others in the wider struggle against women's oppression. Working in women's shelters has become part of a career process in which women develop experience and expertise as social service workers or use their existing skills to provide services. This is not in itself negative or culpable, but it is assimilative. It is in this way that women's movement representatives come to be professionalized as experts speaking for and about battered women.

The contradiction embodied in this process of professionalization lies in the fact that its very success eliminates the possibility of a more radical critique. This is not a new problem or one confined to the "battered women's movement" or the "shelter movement," or what is more commonly known in Canada as the "transitional house movement." The professionalization and institutionalization of social movements have a long history. Social work, education (particularly adult education), labour and popular health movements and the initiatives of the previous wave of feminist organizing have all been subject to these processes. The extent to which this has class implications is revealed by the way in which the conceptually coordinated organization of state responses to wife battering creates divisions between volunteer and paid staff who work in shelters, and transforms the women using transition houses into welfare problems. Indeed, an informant suggested to me that shelters have become the new "poorhouses," with all the attendant poverty and stigma that the term implies. The implications of criminalization and its clinical correlates as a protective and "preventative" strategy for different segments of the population are eliminated from view, let alone discussion. Women who are beaten become a welfare problem; their batterers become a problem for the criminal justice system. Differences in the power relations of women and men are dissolved into individual difficulties and reformulated as a social problem affecting a mass of individuals — a new population to be managed. At the same time, class relations and operation of racism are also dissolved. Thus, linking "male violence" and "family violence" by defining wife battering as assault shifts the attention of activists and governments alike to the global and undifferentiated problem of "violence" and "its" management and away from structural features of oppression.

Conclusion

Several commentators draw attention to the limitations of feminist use of "violence" as an untheorized and unproblematic concept, though the arguments they present are in a somewhat different context from mine.[35] I want to emphasize that this analysis is not intended as a moral judgment of the success or failure of strategies employed by the women's movement. It is a matter of seeing how social relations are socially constructed. In investigating this process I attempted not to proceed ideologically by starting with concepts to be defined and discovered, but to discover instead their organization as part of a social relation. In this context concepts are technical work processes that organize both phenomena and courses of action; thus their construction is integral to social relations. Categories and concepts of ideologies *substitute* the ideological expression of a textually mediated discourse for actual relations, that is, actual practices, work processes and organization of practical knowledge of actual individuals. Thus an examination of the actual relations, practices and processes, and the discursive forms substituted for them, reveals the ideological features of social organization.

"Issue politics," formulated in relation to state practices, have provided for the creation of isolated organizations. Ideological constructs such as "the battered wife" lifted the experience of women who are beaten and abused out of the general experiences of women and made wife battering available as an issue to be absorbed into the social problem apparatus. The task of relocating it in the broader structures of the reproduction of relations of domination and control, which are the relations of ruling, confronts the women's movement with the necessity of renewing efforts to address the relations of knowledge and power and how we are incorporated into them.

This study attempts to move our efforts forward by uncovering for our understanding one feature of how our work comes to be organized against us by the process in which we engage. I agree with Currie that the battle, though complex, is not over. How to organize to change the oppressive conditions of women's lives without being appropriated through our interactions with the ruling apparatus and participation in the relations of ruling is the dilemma that confronts the women's movement as it moves into the nineties.

Notes

Parts of this paper are taken from my Ph.D. thesis, "Conceptual Practices and the Political Process: Family Violence as Ideology" (University of Toronto, 1988), to be published by the University of Toronto Press in Fall 1990 under the title *Family Violence and the Women's Movement: The Conceptual Politics of Struggle*, and appear here with the permission of the publisher. My thanks go to Roberta Hamilton, Arlene McLaren, Barbara Neis and Jane Ursel for their helpful comments on an earlier draft, and to Iris Taylor for her work in revising and adapting the manuscript.

1. See, for example, P. Morgan, "From Battered Wife to Program Client: The State's Shaping of Social Problems," *Kapitaliste* 9 (1981); S. Schechter, *Women and Male Violence: The Visions and Struggles of the Battered Women's Movement* (Boston: South End Press, 1982); K. Tierney, "The Battered Woman Movement and the Creation of the Wife Beating Problem," *Social Problems* 29/3 (1982). For more recent appraisals in a specifically Canadian context, see N.Z. Hinton, "One in Ten: the Struggles and Disempowerment of the Battered Women's Movement," *Canadian Journal of Family Law* 7 (1989); Andrea Currie, "A Roof Is Not Enough: Feminism, Transition Houses and the Battle Against Abuse," *New Maritimes* (September/October 1989).

2. D.E. Smith, "Using the Oppressor's Language," *Resources for Feminist Research. Special Issue on Feminist Theory* (Spring 1979).

3. See E.H. Newberger and R. Bourne, "The Medicalization and Legalization of Child Abuse," in A.Skolnick and J.H. Skolnick (eds.), *Family in Transition*, 5th ed. (Boston: Little, Brown & Co., 1986), 440–455, for a critical appraisal of the medicalization of child abuse.

4. E. Pizzey, *Scream Quietly or the Neighbours Will Hear* (London: Penguin Books, 1974), 46.

5. D. Martin, *Battered Wives* (San Francisco: New Glide Publications, 1976), ix.

6. This battle has by no means been won. See, for example, R.L. Neely and G. Robinson-Simpson, "The Truth About Domestic Violence: A Falsely Framed Issue," *Social Work* (Nov./Dec. 1987), a paper that reviews major "family violence" studies to "prove" that women are *more* violent than men. Ignoring the many critiques of the data produced by these studies, the authors specifically refute every feminist tenet and all attempts to modify the "family violence" framework, developing an argument that is anti-feminist and punitively anti-women.

7. D. Martin, *Battered Wives*, 2nd ed. (San Francisco: Volcano Press Inc., 1981), 279.

8. Flora MacCloud, personal communication with author, 1981.

9. For an expanded account of the consultation, see G. Walker, *Family Violence and the Women's Movement: The Conceptual Politics of Struggle* (Toronto: University of Toronto Press, forthcoming 1990), Chapter 3.

10. L. MacLeod, *Wife Battering Is Every Woman's Issue: A Summary Report of the CACSW Consultation on Wife Battering* (Ottawa: Canadian Advisory Council on the Status of Women, 1980).

11. Morgan, "From Battered Wife to Program Client," 18, describes the mental health, welfare and the criminal justice systems as part of an apparatus designed to combat designated "social problems."

12. See Canada, House of Commons, Standing Committee on Health, Welfare and Social Affairs, *Minutes of Proceedings — Hansard* (Nos. 24–29, 1982); and

Sociology for Women," paper presented to the Political Economy of Gender Relations in Education Conference, University of Toronto, 1981; A. Griffith, "Ideology, Education and Single Parent Families: The Normative Ordering of Families Through Schooling," Ph.D. thesis, University of Toronto, 1984; M. Barrett and M. McIntosh, *The Anti-Social Family* (London: Verso Editions, 1982); B. Thorne and M. Yalom (eds.), *Rethinking the Family: Some Feminist Questions* (New York: Longman Inc., 1982); Segal, *Is the Future Female* and many others.

18. Smith, "The Ideological Practice of Sociology."

19. Ibid., 53.

20. D.E. Smith, "Women and Violence," lecture given at Faculty of Social Work, University of Toronto, Fall 1986; and D.E. Smith, "Feminist Reflections on Political Economy," *Studies in Political Economy* 30 (Autumn 1989), 42.

21. Newberger and Bourne, "The Medicalization and Legalization of Child Abuse."

22. L. Gordon, *Heroes of Their Own Lives; The Politics and History of Family Violence, Boston 1880–1960* (New York: Viking Press, 1988); E. Pleck, "Feminist Response to 'Crimes Against Women,' 1868–1896," *Signs* 8/3 (1983), 451–470; E. Pleck, *Domestic Tyranny; The Making of American Social Policy Against Family Violence from Colonial Times to the Present* (New York: Oxford University Press, 1987); C. Bauer and L. Ritt, "'A Husband Is a Beating Animal,' Frances Power Cobbe Confronts the Wife Abuse Problem in Victorian England," *International Journal on Women's Studies* 6/2 (1983), 88–118; C. Bauer and L. Ritt "Wife Abuse, Late Victorian English Feminists, and the Legacy of Frances Power Cobbe," *International Journal of Women's Studies* 6/3 (1983), 195–207.

23. J.Q. Wilson, "Violence," in D. Bell (ed.), *Toward the Year 2000* (Boston: Beacon Press, 1969), 53, cited in Smith, "the Ideological Practices of Sociology."

24. D. Dutton and S.L. Painter, with D. Patterson and C. Taylor, "Male Domestic Violence and Its Effects on the Victim," Report to the Health Promotions Directorate, Health and Welfare Canada,1980; S.L Painter and D. Dutton, "Patterns of Emotional Bonding in Battered Women: Traumatic Bonding," *International Journal of Women's Studies* 8/4 (1985).

25. A.M. Liddle, "Feminist Contributions to an Understanding of Violence Against Women — Three Steps Forward, Two Steps Back," *Canadian Review of Sociology and Anthropology* 26/5 (1989).

26. I am grateful to Ian Taylor for making this point in comments on an earlier paper, and for drawing my attention to the news release from the Department of Justice, Ottawa, December 21, 1983.

27. C. Brown, "Mothers, Fathers and Children: From Private to Public Patriarchy," in L. Sargent (ed.), *Women and Revolution: A Discussion of the Unhappy Marriage of Marxism and Feminism* (Montreal: Black Rose Books, 1981), 239–267.

28. Tierney, "The Battered Women's Movement"; Morgan, "From Battered Wife."

29. Schechter, *Women and Male Violence*; Adele Mueller, personal communication with author, 1989.

30. See, for example, M. Beaudry, *Battered Women*, L. Houston and M. Heap (trans.) (Montreal: Black Rose Books, 1985); L. MacLeod, *Battered But Not Beaten* (Ottawa: Canadian Advisory Council on the Status of Women, 1987); J. Barnsley,

Feminist Action, Institutional Reaction: Responses to Wife Assault (Vancouver: Women's Research Centre, 1985).

31. G. Geller, A Feminist Case Against Patriarchal 'Justice' for Women Victims of Abuse," paper presented at the Canadian Sociology and Anthropology Association Sessions, Learned Societies Meetings, Quebec City, 1989.

32. Hinton, "One in Ten," 334.

33. I. Loseke and K. Cahill, "The Social Construction of Deviance: Experts on Battered Women," *Social Problems* 31/3 (1984).

34. Currie, "A Roof Is Not Enough," 17.

35. See Liddle, "Feminist Contributions to an Understanding of Violence Against Women"; M. Poster's review of Pleck's *Domestic Tyranny* in *Signs* 14/1 (1988), 216–219.

Chapter Nine

Depoliticizing Insurgency: The Politics of the Family in Alberta

Lois Harder

In 1990 the Alberta government, under the premiership of Don Getty, launched a broad initiative to raise the profile of "the family" in Alberta's public policy and social life. In the moment, Getty's family fervour appeared to be the reaction of a troubled and politically well-placed father to the very public disclosure of his son's cocaine habit. Yet the vigour with which the family initiative was pursued, the ideological context to which the Alberta state was shifting and the economic situation that was encouraging the restructuring of the provincial welfare state suggest that Alberta's family initiative had a rationale that was considerably more coherent than such an idiosyncratic explanation would allow.

With the province now under the administration of Ralph Klein, attention to "the family" has become less explicit. Although the statutory mid-winter holiday known as Family Day persists, the Getty-inspired Premier's Council in Support of Alberta Families was disbanded in 1995. Nonetheless, the neo-liberal ideology that underscores Klein's cuts to health care, education and social assistance assumes that Alberta's families, but particularly Alberta women, will fill the void left by provincial retrenchment.

This article explores the political and strategic implications of the Alberta state's reclamation of "the family" for feminist organizing in the province. Drawing on the work of Iris Young and Nancy Fraser, I argue that the provincial state has attempted to contain Alberta feminists' demands for equality through a rhetorical campaign celebrating the traditional nuclear family and, with the installation of the neo-liberal state, a policy program that relies on the unpaid work of women in the home for its success. The effects of neo-liberalism on the process of feminist claims-making should serve as a cautionary tale for social activists in other jurisdictions in which the neo-liberal state threatens to delegitimize the practice of democratic politics.

The insights of Iris Young and Nancy Fraser address three key questions that frame the paper's argument regarding the use of "the family" by the Alberta state as a tool to delegitimize the struggles and achievements of Alberta feminists. The first question is concerned with the historical context, which precipitated the province's efforts to depoliticize[1] Alberta feminists by reclaiming "the family." The second question asks how discourse has been used in the service of depoliticizing feminist claims-makers. Finally, the third question queries the shift in the strategy of depoliticization from the explicit use of family values discourse in the dying days of the Alberta welfare state to deficit-reduction discourse and program cuts in the emergence of the new neo-liberal state form. The first section of the paper will outline these questions in the context of the insights contained in Young's *Justice and the Politics of Difference* and Fraser's "Struggle Over Needs: Outline of a Socialist-Feminist Critical Theory of Late-Capitalist Political Culture," while the remainder of the paper will apply these insights in the Alberta context.

Distributive Justice and Neo-liberalism

For the purposes of examining the use of the family by the Alberta state as a tool to depoliticize feminist claims-makers, Young's work, *Justice and the Politics of Difference*, provides three important insights. First, the book provides a careful analysis of the metamorphosis of justice in the context of the contestatory environment of claims-making. Second, Young places the dynamic character of claims-making in a framework of insurgency and containment. She argues that the potential for social groups to make their mark on political processes and policies emerges when the state fails to maintain a balance between ensuring the conditions for the accumulation of capital and protecting the collective well-being of citizens. In response to this unsettling of the regime of claims-making, the state and supportive social groups attempt to reclaim the old structures of claims-making and contain insurgent groups within the established process. This framework is particularly useful for understanding feminist struggles with the Alberta state in the period following the crash of the world price of oil. With decreasing revenues available to meet the needs of citizens and a growing public perception of government mismanagement, an opportunity emerged for expanding the category of legitimate social actors on the provincial political scene. Finally, Young points to the uses of neo-liberal economic discourse as a tool of containment and depoliticization.

Young argues many policy makers and liberal democratic theorists understand social justice as limited to "the morally proper distribution of benefits and burdens among society's members."[2] Her difficulties with such an understanding surround the conceptual limits of distribution itself. Young posits that attention to distribution has tended to focus on the allocation of resources rather than on the political, economic and social systems in which that allocation takes place. Further, when considering the distribution of non-material resources, such as decision making power, security of the person or the division of labour, the distributive paradigm represents them as static, as unaffected by the social processes through which they operate and are made comprehensible.[3] In essence, the distributive paradigm of justice is insufficiently aware of the political realm in which it operates and which, by general acceptance of such a paradigm, it helps to form.

Young situates her critique of distributive justice within discussions of a number of state practices and governing principles, central among which is interest group pluralism. Working from a liberal conception of the state as a neutral arbiter among a variety of competing demands, proponents of the distributive paradigm argue that all groups have an equal chance of having their demands met by the state. The determination of how resources should be distributed among these groups relates solely to the skill with which competing interest groups can make their claims. This is a conceptualization of arbitration among competing interests, or conflict resolution, that is roughly analogous to the market in that "various interests compete with one another for people's loyalties, and those that amass the most members and money have the market advantage in lobbying for legislation, regulations, and the distribution of tax dollars."[4]

Understanding the distribution of state resources on the basis of a market model is inadequate, in Young's view, for several reasons. First, such an understanding is unaware of its own normative framework and consequently is blind to the moral basis on which choices between demands are made. Young argues that "in its process of conflict resolution, interest-group pluralism makes no distinction between the assertion of selfish interests and normative claims to justice or right."[5] A successful outcome for an interest group is the result of amassing support for one's position. While justice may be a part of gathering that support, it functions as a discursive and rhetorical tool rather than as the guiding principle on which determinations of state provision are made. Effectively, normative claims for justice are collapsed into the selfish desires of an interest group, resulting in the delegitimation of both the group and its demands.[6]

While I concur with Young's critique of the liberal version of claims-making, her analysis ends too soon. If one situates her observation regarding the lack of normative awareness in the exercise of distributive justice in a political context, one is forced to consider why adherence to the liberal model is so compelling for politicians and policy makers as well as for liberal theorists. Young argues that normative standards of justice are indeed at work in the process of deciding among competing claims, but that the expression of these standards is obscured by an adherence to procedural fairness — the arbitration among competing demands on the basis of the most successful statement of claim. There are considerable political advantages in taking up the mantle of procedural fairness in the face of competing claims to justice. First, it masks the state's own interest in the outcome. The state can simply represent itself as the impartial judge and hence is not compelled to provide its own thick interpretation of justice. Second, liberal justice as procedural fairness avoids the nasty political problem of articulating a clear position on what justice is. Because the state is the most identifiable site from which justice is meted out, its interpretation of justice forms the standard for society. Other interpretations of justice whose normative frameworks are more explicitly articulated become positions between which the state must arbitrate, rather than viable alternatives that the state itself might adopt. By assuming the role of arbitrator and guarantor of fairness, the state's agents can avoid questions concerning the basis on which certain groups are included or excluded from the political process.

There are two risks involved in the effort to cloak the state's normative framework in the veil of procedural fairness in the distribution of justice. First, it requires that the state actually maintains a modicum of fairness. Neutrality is a difficult disguise to maintain when groups with strong claims are regularly excluded in the distribution of resources. Hence, to the extent that the appearance of state neutrality is desired, a variety of groups whose positions may pose a challenge to the state's actual normative framework may have to be included among the contenders for state resources. Second, the risk of revealing the normative framework through which state policy is operating is a constant danger, especially for politicians whose electoral success or failure often depends upon their positions on questions of morality and the identifiable expression of that morality in public policy. In fact, I would assert that the negotiation of the tension between the façade of normative neutrality and the explicit expression of a public morality has been a key feature of post-oil boom politics in Alberta.

While the attempt to maintain the ruse of procedural fairness in the face of competing claims was fairly successful under the welfare state, the shift to a neo-liberal state form created a crisis in the established rules of interest group politics. Young reads this crisis as the failure of the capitalist state to walk the line between ensuring adequate conditions for the accumulation of capital and maximizing collective welfare.[7] In Young's view, this failure represents a potential moment of insurgency, the possibility for a marked growth in politicization. Thus, it follows that, in the face of the state's inability or unwillingness to meet the needs of its citizens, we should be witnessing vigorous social claims-making and challenges to the practice of interest group pluralism. Interestingly, however, while there is evidence of such an invigoration in the period immediately following the crash of oil prices, it is less clear that insurgency has continued under the clear retreat from ensuring collective welfare instituted by the Klein administration.

Young suggests that the failure to realize a radical politicization of the social realm at present is the product of a shift in economic thinking from Keynesianism to the monetarist discourse of neo-liberalism. The content of most social movement demands has been focused either on meeting previously unaddressed needs or on revising existing methods of service delivery. These kinds of demands, however, become increasingly futile when service provision itself is called into question, as is the case in current economic thinking focused on deficit reduction. When groups must defend the limited benefits they have received from the welfare state rather than criticizing the way in which those benefits have been bestowed, they become, in Young's view, increasingly susceptible to reabsorption within the competitive, pluralist framework.[8] What Young fails to appreciate is that the transformation of state form has redefined the process of containment. The neo-liberal state does not contain insurgent demands by attempting to corral them into the old game of distributing resources on the basis of procedural fairness and a market model of competition among interest groups. Instead, the neo-liberal model delegitimizes virtually all claims-makers whose objectives are not directly linked to the accumulation of capital.

Young's observation that the character of monetarism has placed unique limits on the possibility of insurgency is an important qualification to her discussion of the distributive paradigm of justice. Yet, interestingly, she is largely unwilling to acknowledge its long-term importance. Instead, Young focuses on the possibility of democratizing the state and social life by challenging the distributive paradigm of justice in favour of a notion of justice centred on empowerment. This suggests an unwillingness to take the new form of containment established by the neo-liberal state very seriously. However, the ways in which this shift in state form has affected the discourse of claims-making is likely to be considerably more transformative than Young's theory allows. The work of Nancy Fraser provides some suggestions as to why Young's theory, while accurate in its critique of interest group pluralism as a mechanism of distributive justice, is strained when confronting the current political climate.

Fraser's Politics of Needs Interpretation

Nancy Fraser's work on the struggle over needs and needs interpretation addresses issues similar to those outlined in Young's work. Fraser, however, offers a richer theorization of the dynamics of claims-making and containment by defining a series of needs discourses that may come into play as demands are made and addressed. It is the theorization of the creation and interaction of these discourses, and the sensitivity to historical specificities that such a focus implies, that is most useful in helping to overcome the limitations of Young's analysis in making sense of the current political moment in Alberta politics. In addition, Fraser is more sensitive than Young to the political realm as a site in which groups not only contend with the state but also form alliances with and oppositions to each other.

For Fraser, as for Young, the primary function of the welfare state is to identify and address a variety of needs in social and economic life. Fraser identifies this function as the politics of needs interpretation. The distinctly political aspect of interpreting needs is found in the contestation of competing networks of "in-order-to" relations.[9] That is, the manner in which one answers the question, what must be done in order for a certain outcome to be realized, is an inherently political process. For example, feminist groups in Alberta, such as Options for Women and the Alberta Status of Women Action Committee, have argued since the late 1970s that, in order to address the problem of women's unequal access to employment, the provincial government should pass employment equity legislation, and provide training programs with child care and transportation subsidies for participants. The Conservative government, by contrast, has argued that the formal declaration of women's equality and career counselling would provide adequate means to meet the challenge of equality in the workplace.

For the most part, contestation over needs interpretation occurs when needs can no longer be contained within existing discursive parameters. In Fraser's theory, the contradictions in the state's role of facilitating capital accumulation and maximizing the collective welfare may form the context for social change, but so might the course of various social struggles or particular local events. The needs that are articulated in these moments of potential social change are "markers of major social-structural shifts in the boundaries separating what are classified as 'political,' 'economic,' and 'domestic' or 'personal' spheres of life."[10] Fraser calls these "runaway needs" and suggests three categories of needs discourses that inhabit the unsettled social realm they occupy: oppositional, reprivatization and expert.

Oppositional discourses arise when needs are politicized "from below." Groups attempt to put issues on the political agenda that are considered private and/or "natural," and hence not open to public scrutiny, debate or regulation. Formerly non-politized groups argue that relations of power inform and infuse the issues with which they are concerned and, thus, that these are legitimate political issues. This persuasive effort poses a challenge to hegemonic notions of the political and previously existing patterns of needs interpretation.[11] The contestation that surrounds this process can contribute to the formation of a group identity as people organize around a particular cause and carve out an identity that is somehow representative of that cause.

Reprivatization discourses emerge as a response to oppositional discourses and are an attempt to maintain emergent claims in their private and depoliticized form. The motivation behind this conservative reaction is the desire to prevent the recognition and fulfillment of new needs by the state. In the process, however, reprivatization discourses articulate interpretations of social life that previously had simply been assumed. Hence, people espousing reprivatization discourses can, contrary to their objective, actually contribute to the politicization of oppositional needs by making the hegemonic position explicit and consequently more open to contestation. As Fraser notes, this articulation of the old is also a modification, since in resisting the new, oppositional discourse, reprivatization discourse defines itself both in terms of the hegemonic view of the social but also in reference to the new discourse.[12] Finally, expert discourses arise once the proponents of oppositional discourses have successfully politicized their claims. These needs discourses are the means through which runaway needs are transformed into the objects of state intervention.[13]

The effects of expert discourses are to depoliticize the process of needs interpretation by sterilizing it. The use of juridical, scientific, specialist language in creating the conditions in which oppositional needs can be administered abstracts from the context in those needs arose and reduces the groups who promoted the runaway needs to individual claimants. They become passive recipients, while those who administer do so behind the guise of institutional objectivity.[14] Hence, while the expression of the initial politicization may succeed in convincing the state to address runaway needs, the cost of that success is a discounting of those needs. The systematic conditions that gave rise to them are reduced to the problems of specific individuals to be addressed on a case by case basis. By addressing the need and individualizing the solution, expert discourse diffuses the possibility of continued collective identification and response to a particular concern. The reinterpretation of needs through expert discourse thus amounts to depoliticization, though not through a return to the private or natural.

Feminism and the Family

Under conditions of a change from the welfare to the neo-liberal state form, reprivatization discourse, deployed by social groups, as well as the Conservative government and the Alberta state, has provided the primary means for addressing the "runaway needs" articulated by Alberta feminists.[15] Furthermore, the "traditional" family has served as the locus of this particular manifestation of reprivatization discourse. Indeed, the deployment of the "traditional" nuclear family as a means of reprivatizating the oppositional discourse of "women's issues" represents the consummate strategy for containing the demands of Alberta feminists.

The usefulness of the "traditional family" for depoliticizing feminist demands stems from two significant cultural phenomena. The first is the desire to invoke some control and familiarity in a historical moment marked by insecurity and unpredictability. The globalization of capital, the decline of the Keynesian welfare state and the resulting precariousness of employment create anxiety. For conservatives, this anxiety is often expressed in terms of moral crisis — a perception of increased violence, untamed sexuality and disrespect for authority. The family is invoked in this moment as a stalwart against the disquiet of the postmodern condition.[16]

The second phenomenon relates to the discursive construction of "women's issues" as articulated by the feminist movement. Dubbed "Wollstonecraft's Dilemma" by Carole Pateman, and more commonly known as the equality versus difference debate, feminist theorists and activists have struggled over the question of whether to articulate their needs in such a way as to obtain treatment equal to that of men, or whether to make claims on the basis of their difference from men, both in terms of the capacity to bear children and in their socially assigned responsibility for caregiving.[17]

The problem with adopting the equality strategy is that equality has a tendency to be equated with sameness. When women are treated "the same" as men, the specificity of women's various experiences within the gendered organization of social life and the particular expectations for women that this social organization implies cannot be addressed. The oft-used illustration of this problem is the inclusion of maternity leave under "disability" compensation in the framework of an employee benefits package. The equality strategy also risks homogenizing all women and all men, so that class and racial inequalities among women and between women and men are obscured. In light of the challenge posed by women from a variety of racial, ethnic and class backgrounds to the White, middle-class mainstream of the feminist movement, the equality strategy has largely been abandoned in recent claims-making efforts.

Demanding that needs be interpreted on the basis of difference, however, poses its own set of difficulties for feminist struggles. In the context of this discussion, the primary risk of the difference strategy is the institutionalization of the existing gendered division of labour and women's subordinate position within that structure. When feminist claims-making is structured around addressing women's needs for child care, elder care, respite care, protection against the objectification of pornography and freedom from domestic violence, we enter the debate from a position of subordination. These issues are "women's issues" because women are responsible for activities that are undervalued and to which political power does not accrue. Of course, feminist campaigns in these areas are focused on revaluing "women's work" and sharing the burden of care among all members of the household. But as long as the gendered subtext is maintained, so too is the possibility of conservative retrenchment expressed through reprivatization discourse.

"The family" represents a peculiarly vexed institution for feminist analysis. On the one hand, the family has been a central location of women's oppression while, on the other hand, participation in family life has been and continues to be extremely meaningful and rewarding. Michelle Barrett and Mary McIntosh contextualize the self-fulfilling attributes of the family as the limited reward for participating in an otherwise highly atomized society. While their arguments focuses on the extremely anti-social nature of the reification of the family, which prevents the strengthening of community, they also recognize that existing historical conditions make participation in the family an overwhelmingly rational choice for women.[18] In a less radical theoretical intervention, Mimi Abramovitz, too, qualifies her critical position on the family, arguing that

> ... the critique of the family ethic is not meant to devalue the experience of sharing one's life with a partner or that of bearing, raising, and loving children. Rather it suggests that institutionally enforced rules of family organization do not necessarily enhance family life and they frequently disadvantage women.[19]

The combination of the continuing importance of the family to the organization of social life and individual identity and the pursuit of feminist claims-making strategies based on women's "difference" has produced an oppositional discourse around the family that is particularly amenable to reframing by groups who would cling to conservative notions of family form and function. It is this vulnerability to the reprivatization discourse of family values and the manifestations of this discourse in public policy that has posed the most significant challenge for feminist claims for justice vis-à-vis the Alberta state in the last ten years.

The explicit use of family values discourse by the Getty government and the unarticulated necessity of a two-parent family for the realization of the Klein government's deficit-reduction strategy provide a significant instantiation of Young's critique of distributive justice, her theory of insurgency and containment, her observations surrounding the effects of neo-liberal ideology on claims-making and Fraser's theory of needs interpretation. In an effort to situate their insights in the context of feminist claims-making in Alberta, I will now turn to an examination of the provincial state's use of "the family" as a reprivatization discourse and as a means of depoliticizing Alberta's organized feminist groups. This examination will involve a consideration of the political climate that attenuated the Getty government's embrace of family values, the discursive expression of these values in the legislature and in the official documents of the Premier's Council in Support of Alberta Families, and a discussion of the Klein government's approach to the family and the depoliticization of feminist organizations.

The Getty Government and the Family: "There's No Place Like Home"

When Don Getty succeeded Peter Lougheed as the premier of Alberta in 1985, the province was in the midst of coping with the collapse of world oil prices and a reorientation of the political realm. This reorientation was the product of a number of political scandals that expressed the problems of adjustment to decreasing wealth, the election of the federal Conservatives to the House of Commons on a platform of pro-western initiatives (thereby undermining the Lougheed strategy of defusing internal political conflict by insisting on a united front to fight the federal government) and a declining ability to buy off dissent through state largesse. When decreasing government revenues eventually resulted in attempts to reduce spending on education, health and welfare, Albertans were no longer prepared to support the government's definition of the public interest.[20]

Growing discontent among Albertans manifested itself in the election returns of 1986 and 1989 and in the growth of social movements. Both of these elections augmented the ranks of the provincial opposition and increased the number of women in the legislature, among whom were some vocal critics of the gendered subtext of many government policies. As for the Conservative Party, its recognition of impending electoral misfortune inspired a move to court "new" electoral players, including women. As a result, mainstream feminist demands began to gain some political legitimacy thereby creating an opportunity for the articulation of a feminist oppositional discourse within provincial politics.

For feminists, the Alberta state's acknowledgement of their enhanced power was reflected in: the reconstruction of the Alberta Women's Bureau as the Women's Secretariat with a larger, more competent staff, expanded mandate and increased budget; the appointment of an interdepartmental committee and a Cabinet committee on women's issues; and, two years later in 1986, the establishment of the Alberta Advisory Council on Women's Issues (AACWI).[21] These initiatives marked a significant departure from the government's insistence that the equality of women had been formally recognized in the Individual Rights Protection Act and that any further initiatives to ensure equality would constitute special treatment and, hence, discrimination. It was no longer possible to contain feminist demands by ignoring them. Instead, an attempt would be made to contain them by institutional means.

The province's feminist groups, however, were not deceived. Their long experience of running up against the locked doors of Alberta legislators had made them suspicious of the government's initiatives and, as it turned out, their suspicions were well-founded. The first incarnation of AACWI was chaired by Margaret Leahy, a political climber who was so out of touch with provincial women's groups as to suggest that she wanted a "very strong male" from the private sector, who turned out to be Peter Pocklington, to be considered as a Council member.[22] While Pocklington did not, in fact, get the job, the Council was nonetheless stacked with Tory supporters. Even with the Council populated by the party faithful, however, AACWI's recommendations to government were systematically ignored. The Women's Secretariat, though employing well-intentioned feminists, had limited success in persuading government departments to consider the implications of their policies for women or to consult with the Secretariat on proposed legislation. Predictably, the Secretariat was also sorely understaffed. In light of these developments and as a result of the internal politics of grassroots feminist organizations, by the late 1980s the province's feminists had largely refocused their energies on constitutional reform and free trade or had retreated from claims-making and intensified their involvement in community service.

An additional restraint on the capacity of Alberta feminists to reap the limited rewards of state sanction was the concurrent attainment of political legitimacy by the anti-feminist group, the Alberta Federation of Women United for Families (AFWUF). The emergence of AFWUF is illustrative of Young's critique of the normative weakness inherent in a distributive notion of justice. AFWUF was formed in direct response to the pro-choice position of the province's largest feminist organization, the Alberta Status of Women Action Committee (ASWAC). Formed in 1981 after its founder was expelled from ASWAC for claiming that she would "destroy the organization if it's the last thing I do," AFWUF promptly embarked on a campaign to secure government funding.[23] AFWUF argued that if the provincial government was providing funding ($5,000 as a conference grant) to a pro-choice, anti-family, feminist organization, then AFWUF, with its Christian morality, surely deserved treatment at least equal to that of ASWAC.

In response to rumours of AFWUF's impending funding request, the first impulse of the Minister Responsible for Women's Issues in this pre-oil bust context was to consider withdrawing funding for all women's groups, feminist, anti-feminist or otherwise.[24] The cooler heads of bureaucrats prevailed, however, and a funding policy was proposed that would ensure all groups an equal opportunity to apply for available monies.[25] Thus, rather than consider which of the groups had a more just claim, the state chose to avoid difficult normative questions by establishing a fair process and distributing justice with the help of its chequebook.

Six years later, when feminists had secured a place within the apparatus of the state, AFWUF's initiatives to eliminate state support for feminist groups continued, as did state's adherence to a model of distributive justice. In 1987, ASWAC again found itself the target of an attempt to have its funding withdrawn. Upon hearing revelations from "pro-family" women regarding their experiences at ASWAC's annual conference, Ken Rostad, Solicitor General, wrote to the Minister Responsible for Women's Issues, (Elaine McCoy, who was fairly sympathetic to feminist demands) expressing his displeasure. He reported that, while his initial perception was that his constituents were overreacting, he had received reports from "level headed people" that ASWAC

> ... was expressing their promotion of occults, ending their session with a form of witchcraft chant as well as promoting the formation and enhancement of lesbian groups in Edmonton. ... The ASWAC group was thought to be destructive to the women's movement, to the family and an insult to the feminine gender.[26]

In response to these reports, Rostad wrote that he was distressed that the government would fund such a group and requested information on the amount of funding provided and McCoy's "latest intelligence" on ASWAC.[27] McCoy's response to Rostad was that while "ASWAC has generated considerable controversy as a result of topics which the group had addressed, ... I believe the group as a whole and the majority of its members have added, in a constructive way, to the debate on many issues facing women today."[28] In response to a similar concern expressed by one of Rostad's constituents, McCoy wrote "I am certain that the government is aware that a number of the groups it funds have views that vary significantly from those of the government and many women. Diversity of opinion is important in a democratic society."[29]

Faced with containment through co-optation and an inability to diffuse the archaic notions of gender professed by AFWUF because of the unwillingness of the state to engage in a substantive discussion of justice, Alberta feminist groups were understandably disheartened with the politics of claims-making. Yet co-optation and the politics of interest group pluralism were relatively common and predictable tools for the containment of claims-makers, feminist or otherwise. The espousal of family values, by contrast, was an entirely new innovation.

While the province's organized feminist groups had weakened the intensity of their claims-making on the provincial state in the late 1980s, feminist demands continued to confront the government during this period. A number of NDP and Liberal members of the legislature ensured that the government regularly faced questions relating to the continuing inequality of the province's women, and the Minister Responsible for Women's Issues was herself supportive of many feminist objectives. AFWUF continued its lobbying efforts on behalf of the traditional family and in opposition to policies that would enhance an understanding of women as individuals rather than as wives and mothers. As Fraser suggests, this attempt to reprivatize feminist oppositional discourse only served to maintain feminist demands on the political agenda. Finally, by 1989, the government's thinly veiled contempt for the AACWI had knocked the Council's members from their neutral stance into a much more activist and pro-feminist position. The appointment of a new chair to the council, though a former campaign manager for one of the Cabinet ministers, also served to invigorate the Council's role as a gadfly for women.

It is difficult to know precisely what combination of events sparked the provincial government's embrace of family values discourse. Certainly the Premier's personal difficulties cannot be discounted, nor can the growing influence of AFWUF within the Conservative caucus. The 1980s also saw some troubling statistics reflecting the social ill health of the province, including the country's highest rate of teenage pregnancy and divorce.[30] It would not be surprising if certain bureaucrats and MLAs linked these social ills to another statistic — that Alberta's women have the highest labour force participation rate in Canada.[31] In any event, beginning with the throne speech in 1986, but intensifying with the Lieutenant-Governor's Conference on the Family and the establishment of the Premier's Council in Support of Alberta Families in 1990, the discourse of family values came to be a feature of the province's political debate.

Public statements by Conservative caucus members indicate the general character of the government's use of the family in response to the advances of women in attaining a level of personal autonomy. In response to the Mulroney government's child care initiative, Getty stated in the legislature:

> Our initiative is to strengthen the family, to provide reasons why the family is stronger, why mothers will stay in the house with the family. ... I get frustrated when most of the initiatives seem to be taking children out of the home or moving parents out of the home.[32]

John Oldring, the Minister of Family and Social Services, addressed the annual meeting of AFWUF in November 1989. In the question period, he stated that a homosexual relationship does not constitute a family, that he was involved in a pro-life group in his constituency and that he did not support universal day care.[33]

Stockwell Day, an MLA and the first chair of the Premier's Council in Support of Alberta Families and the current Minister of Labour in the Klein government, noted in an interview preceding the release of a Council report that the Council's statistics

> ... showed conclusively that children whose parents are divorced are more likely to have emotional and psychological problems that lead to drug abuse, crime and suicide than the children of couples who do not get divorced. "These statistics are the reality of what may happen to your kids should you choose divorce."[34]

With regard to the issue of family violence, Premier Getty observed that the problem had not been solved by state spending. Instead, perversely, he argued that the issue should be addressed by a return to the foundation of the family itself.[35]

In addition to the limited appreciation of the reality of women's lives that such statements reveal, they also indicate a rethinking of the state's role in social service provision and the consideration of the family unit as a low-cost alternative. Rather than acknowledging a social obligation to ensure the welfare of citizens in the context of a widespread recession, the province turned instead to an emphasis on family support. By emphasizing the family as the solution to problems of poverty, substance abuse and violence, the government heralded a low-cost response to social ills that also had considerable moral force. With Ralph Klein's assumption of the premiership, this reclamation of the family in the interest of offsetting the costs of social service provision has become considerably more explicit.

This "Ozzie and Harriet" conception of the family was also manifested in the Premier's Council in Support of Alberta Families and the conference, hosted by the Lieutenant-Governor, that served as its inspiration. The knowledge and analysis of families that feminist groups had acquired over their years of activism were not initially welcome in this officially sanctioned forum, nor was much opportunity provided for open discussion. An ASWAC newsletter reporting on the event noted that only three of the twenty scheduled hours of the conference were devoted to discussion. It also notes that a number of organizations whose work focuses on reproductive rights and the status of women and children in poverty were initially excluded from the event.[36]

The Getty administration's most profound initiative in the rhetorical campaign to reclaim the traditional family, however, was the establishment of the Premier's Council. Chaired by a member of the Conservative caucus, with members appointed by the Cabinet and supported by a constituency of social groups that were much less suspicious of the provincial government and the Alberta state than the feminist groups to whom AACWI was to cater, the Premier's council was, from the outset, much better suited to the task of reprivatizing the "runaway needs" politicized by feminist groups than AACWI proved to be. Some examples from the Council's public consultations and publications should serve to demonstrate the particular character of its reprivatization discourse.

The Council asserted that its mandate was the product of a broadly representative (both geographically and ideologically) consultative process in which 3,000 Albertans were given the opportunity to express their concerns about families. While it might have been possible to critique "the family" within that consultative process, the documents produced from the consultation offer no acknowledgement of such a critique. Indeed, the Council declares that it "is guided in its mandate by the belief that the family has always been and remains the best environment in which the skills and values vital to a strong, democratic environment are acquired,"[37] and that "the family is the single greatest influence on our lives, shaping who we are, how we feel about ourselves and how we approach the challenges of life."[38] The list of participants suggests that more critical insights into the family and the character of citizenship might well have been put forward, but these insights were apparently deemed insufficiently representative to merit attention in the consultation summary or in the Council's subsequent publications.

The Premier's Council documents provide a number of examples of the dynamic between oppositional and reprivatization discourses outlined by Fraser. In the context of family form, feminist groups in the province had long challenged the nuclear family model implicit in many of the province's social policies. Criticism of the application of the "spouse-in-the-house" rule to women on social assistance (i.e., presuming that the presence of a man in the household requires his financial contribution to the care of the woman and her children), of the government's refusal to include protection on the grounds of sexual orientation in the province's human rights legislation and of the widows' pension plan, which provided assistance to women between the ages of fifty-five and sixty-four whose spouses had died but not to women who had divorced or never married, suggest efforts on the part of feminist groups to install an appreciation in state policy for the range of relationships through which people organize their intimate lives. Interestingly, the Premier's Council begins virtually all of its documents with the claim that the government needs to recognize the diversity of Alberta families. On the face of it, such a claim suggests that the definition of the family employed by the Council must be quite broad, although, interestingly, the closest the documents come is to claim that the definition of the family most frequently cited in their public consultations was "two or more persons related by birth, marriage, or adoption."[39]

The documents do recognize that other, broader definitions exist, but there are many indications that "the best" family is the heterosexual, two-parent, nuclear model in which "traditional" gender roles are the norm.

These indications range from the absence of any reference to same-sex couples to the claim that "a strong partnership between spouses is ... important in modeling and teaching caring and loving behaviour to family members."[40] Another indication of the pre-eminence of the nuclear family model is provided in an appendix listing the issues identified through the consultative process. Here we learn that the roles and responsibilities of family members can be categorized as nurturer, provider and contributor. Issues relating to the nurturer role include acknowledgement of the value of parenting and providing greater support, recognition and respect for stay-at-home mothers. In order to enhance the capacity of the provider role, the report identifies the need to increase the ability of a single income to meet basic family needs. As for contributors — that is, women employed in paid labour — the Council observes

> ... while many households require two earners, ... some families become two income households by choice rather than necessity. Some argue that this has chipped away at the family foundation by reducing family time and by placing an emphasis on accumulating possessions and material wealth to achieve happiness or success.[41]

By beginning their discussion of family roles from the perspective of appreciating family diversity, the Premier's Council takes up the oppositional discourse of provincial feminist groups surrounding the multiplicity of arrangements for one's intimate life. However, the Council then turns this observation back into the nuclear family model — now couched in the gender-neutral terms of nurturer, provider and contributor. Similarly, while acknowledging that many families require two incomes to sustain them, the goal of families maintained by a single income earner is very much alive. This acknowledgement, however reluctant, also demonstrates Fraser's point regarding the tendency of reprivatization discourse to further politicize the oppositional claim by making the unarticulated assumptions of reprivatization discourse more explicit. In this case, the assumption is that the ideal family model is that of a two-parent family with a single (male) income earner. Given that, by the late 1980s, sixty-five to eighty hours of work per week were required to sustain a family as opposed to forty-five hours per week in the 1970s, the suggestion that women work simply to provide the family with luxury items is certainly worth contesting.[42]

Of course, the Premier's Council was neither an institution with much power nor could the Council itself exercise any influence on the way people lived their lives. Its primary purpose seemed to be to provide the Getty government with some empirical support for the government's rhetorical position. The Klein government, by contrast, has embraced the family in terms that may be less rhetorically explicit, but have considerably more meaning for the organization of people's lives and women's lives in particular.

Neo-liberalism and the Family: "Now You See It, Now You Don't"

The debt and deficit reduction policies of the Klein government provide an excellent forum for observing the effects of neo-liberalism on the politics of claims-making, particularly as it applies to notions of the traditional family and feminist activism. As Dacks, Green and Trimble have recently pointed out,

> ... the policies of the Klein government both assume and foster the notion that a woman's full-time focus should be the family. With this model in mind, the government can discount the burdens it places on the working women and single mothers when it reduces social programs and cuts public sector employment in ways that disproportionately harm women.[43]

While the nuclear family model is strongly implied in Klein's policies, as will be discussed below, the Klein government has moved with stealth to remove outward signs of the necessity of the family for neo-liberal policies and to displace the struggle between feminist and "pro-family" claims-makers from the public forum of the state. Extrapolating from Fraser, one can read this disengagement as a recognition of the tendency of reprivatization discourse to, contrary to its intent, actually further politicize the issues raised in oppositional discourse. The government's decision to disband the Premier's Council in Support of Alberta Families in the summer of 1995 suggests a desire to overcome this dilemma. The chair of the council, Lyle Olberg, in discussing the decision to dismantle the Council, provided the following rationale:

> We sat down with our board and we said: "You know, it's time that the state got out of the family. We've given it a good start in the International Year of the Family, but it's time that we got out. It's time to turn the baton over to families to allow them to control their own destiny."[44]

Similarly, the AACWI is also scheduled for disbanding in 1996 as per the legislation under which it was established. While the Women's Council has been asked to conduct public meetings with the province's women's groups in order to establish the appropriate vehicle through which their interests might be conveyed to government, the government's lengthy history of ignoring the Council's recommendations and the responsible Minister's own comments that "times have changed, women's groups have multiplied and grown in strength, and they can and want to speak for themselves to government without a publicly funded intermediary," suggest that the Klein government is attempting to put some distance between itself and feminist claims-makers.[45]

These efforts to depoliticize the debate between the competing conceptions of justice put forward by feminist groups and the "pro-family" lobby are indicative of a larger tendency inherent in the neo-liberal state to avoid all issues that may incite competing claims regarding the substance of the collective good.[46] This objective stems from a particular analysis of the crisis of "ungovernability" of the welfare state: the formation and politicization of various social groups and the challenges posed by these groups to the organization of the state and its role in the economy are at the root of this crisis. In order to re-establish some level of governability, then, the neo-liberal state attempts to remake itself for the purposes of ensuring the efficacious functioning of the free market and to devolve from its role in compensating for the inequities that exist among citizens. Since proponents of the neo-liberal state are ill-disposed towards political conflict and debate, they argue that ridding the state of its redistributive functions and, hence, the need to articulate some inevitably contestatory notion of "the good" will allow for the imposition of a more lasting consensus around an apparently apolitical and minimalist notion of the state.[47] If the state is no longer the site at which claims for democracy, equality and justice are to be made, it need no longer address the difficult moral questions with which politics is so intimately concerned.

There is an obvious logical flaw in the assertion that the pursuit of state policies designed to facilitate the market is an endeavour that frees the state from normative concerns. The decision to intensify the state's role in facilitating the accumulation of capital is itself normative, and the policies that emerge from this endeavour are similarly laden with normative assumptions. Indeed, the argument that reducing the deficit must take precedence over all other social concerns is a clear articulation of the substance of the good. The presumption of the nuclear family form and the availability of women's unpaid labour to compensate for the caring work that has been abandoned through cuts to government services and employment are significant examples of the normative assumptions implicit in the neo-liberal state.

Cuts to health care and education have relied on the volunteer labour, primarily performed by women because of their flexible position in the labour force, in order to succeed. Hospital stays have been reduced, but the overall recovery time for many procedures remains the same. Hence, many patients are sent home requiring twenty-four hour care.[48] The presumption here is that not only will someone be available to care for the patient, but that the caregiver will actually have the skills with which to perform the required tasks. Nursing is, after all, a highly skilled profession and to presume that a family member can do the job is both irresponsible and demeaning to the (female-dominated) profession of nursing. Equally irresponsible are the Premier's suggestion that educational program reductions can be addressed through the volunteer labour of parents and his decision to effect a 50 per cent reduction in kindergarten funding.[49] These cuts have cost teachers their jobs and have compromised the capacity of many other women to participate in the labour market as a result of their increased responsibilities for the education of their children.

The Klein government's normative assumptions surrounding the nuclear family can also be detected in its treatment of single mothers on social assistance. While the government's efforts to implement a workfare scheme have suggested that single women with children are presumed to be workers rather than mothers, the absence of adequate child care facilities, the low-wage jobs in which many of these women are employed and the province's insistence on maintaining the minimum wage at $5.00 per hour, the second lowest in Canada,[50] suggest that the only way for these women to attain a reasonable standard of living is to attach themselves to an employed man or return to their parental home.

The off-loading of state provision onto the private realm presumes that the family, but especially women, will take on responsibilities previously undertaken by the state. Drastic reductions to nursing care, decreasing resources for child care and education and a growing emphasis on family support for elder care all impose new burdens on women's domestic labour. The assumption on the part of politicians and policy makers is that women's labour is infinitely elastic.[51] However, as Linda McDowell argues, the social speed-up that flows from increasing demands on both women's productive and reproductive work is not infinitely extendible.[52]

With the embarrassment of riches that have flowed into the coffers of the Alberta treasury as a result of a recent increase in natural gas prices, the Klein government's deficit elimination target has been achieved. Given the dire terms in which the province's finances were cast during the 1993 election, the insistence that considerable suffering would have to be endured, and the hardship that many Albertans have withstood, the too-hasty achievement of budget surpluses is likely to reignite the energies of many claims-makers whose demands were sidelined in the drive for deficit elimination. It remains to be seen whether efforts to depoliticize feminist claims through the traditional family rhetoric of the Getty government and the policies of Klein's neo-liberal state will have a lasting effect on women's struggles for equality and justice.

Notes

I would like to thank Caroline Andrew, Pat Armstrong, Pat Connelly and Linda Trimble for their comments on an earlier draft of this paper. I would also like to thank the Social Sciences and Humanities Research Council for its financial support.

1. The term "depoliticize" refers to the process of removing issues and their advocates from the public realm of the political. While the issues remain salient in the broadest sense of the political as relations of power, and groups that advance these issues remain organized, the process of depoliticization attempts to remove the issues in question from the public agenda and from the realm of policy making.

2. Iris Marion Young, *Justice and the Politics of Difference* (Princeton: Princeton University Press, 1990), 15.

3. Ibid., 16.

4. Ibid., 74.

5. Ibid., 72.

6. Ibid.

7. Ibid., 81.

8. Ibid., 90.

9. Nancy Fraser, "Struggle Over Needs: Outline of a Socialist-Feminist Critical Theory of Late Capitalist Political Culture," in Linda Gordon (ed.), *Women, the State, and Welfare* (Madison: University of Wisconsin Press, 1990), 201.

10. Ibid., 209.

11. Ibid.

12. Ibid., 210.

13. Ibid., 211.

14. Ibid., 212.

15. Expert discourse, at least as it is defined by Fraser, has played a less significant role in recent struggles over needs interpretation due to the perception of fiscal crisis and the decision to address this crisis through spending reductions. A weakened capacity for spending thus limits the possibility of establishing public programs to address the needs advanced by social groups and thus the opportunity to reframe these needs in the language of policy experts.

16. Lise Gotell, "Policing Desire: Obscenity Law, Pornography Politics, and Feminism in Canada," in Janine Brodie (ed.), *Women and Canadian Public Policy* (Toronto: Harcourt and Brace, 1996), 292, 300.

17. See Carole Pateman, "The Patriarchal Welfare State," in Linda McDowell and Rosemary Pringle (eds.), *Defining Women: Social Institutions and Gender Divisions* (London: Polity Press, 1992), 223–245; Anne Phillips, *Democracy and Difference* (University Park, PA: University of Pennsylvania Press, 1993); Joan Scott, "Deconstructing Equality-Versus-Difference: Or, the Uses of Poststructuralist Theory for Feminism," in Marianne Hirsch and Evelyn Fox Keller (eds.), *Conflicts in Feminism* (New York: Routledge, 1990), 134–148.

18. Michelle Barrett and Mary McIntosh, *The Anti-Social Family*, 2nd ed. (London: Verso, 1991).

19. Mimi Abramovitz, *Regulating the Lives of Women: Social Welfare Policy from Colonial Times to the Present* (Boston: South End Press, 1989), 9.

20. Linda Trimble, "The Politics of Gender in Modern Alberta," in Allan Tupper and Roger Gibbons (eds.), *Government and Politics in Alberta* (Edmonton: University of Alberta Press, 1992), 233.

21. The job of the Secretariat was to act as an internal watchdog on government policy and legislation, advise the Minister Responsible for the Status of Women and provide a link to the community. See Government of Alberta, News Release, February 28, 1984. The interdepartmental committee on women's issues was composed of senior bureaucrats from key departments. Minutes of the committee's meetings and memos between the Director of the Women's Secretariat and the Minister Responsible for Women's Issues indicate that the interdepartmental committee held monthly meetings for one year and then continued on an ad hoc basis for another six months, while the Cabinet committee on women's issues only met twice.

22. *Edmonton Journal* (May 16, 1986).

23. ASWAC to Mary LeMessurier, Minister of Culture, January 5, 1982, Women's Secretariat Documents, Provincial Archives of Alberta, Edmonton.

24. Les Young, Minister of Labour and Minister Responsible for Women's Issues, to Al Kennedy, Associate Director, Planning and Research, Alberta Labour, March 1, 1982, Women's Secretariat Documents, Provincial Archives of Alberta, Edmonton.

25. Al Kennedy to Les Young, March 25, 1982, Women's Secretariat Documents, Provincial Archives of Alberta, Edmonton.

26. Ken Rostad to Elaine McCoy, November 18, 1987, Women's Secretariat Documents, Provincial Archives of Alberta, Edmonton.

27. Ibid.

28. Elaine McCoy to Ken Rostad, December 17, 1987, Women's Secretariat Documents, Provincial Archives of Alberta, Edmonton.

29. Elaine McCoy to Patricia Good, December 16, 1987, Women's Secretariat Documents, Provincial Archives of Alberta, Edmonton.

30. Howard Palmer and Tamara Palmer*, Alberta: A New History* (Edmonton: Hurtig Publishers, 1990), 106.

31. Statistics Canada, Labour Force Annual Averages, cited in Pat Armstrong and Hugh Armstrong, *The Double Ghetto: Canadian Women and Their Segregated Work*, 3rd ed. (Toronto: McClelland and Stewart, 1994), 49.

32. *Calgary Herald* (June 12, 1988).

33. *Alberta Report* (November 13, 1989).

34. *Financial Post Daily* (June 13/15, 1992).

35. Alberta Legislative Assembly, *Debates* (June 29, 1992).

36. *Alberta Status of Women Action Committee Newsletter* (May 1990).

37. Premier's Council in Support of Alberta Families, *Directions for the Future* (Edmonton: Government of Alberta, 1992), 3.

38. Premier's Council in Support of Alberta Families, *Family Policy Grid* (Edmonton: Government of Alberta, 1992), 6.

39. Premier's Council in Support of Alberta Families, *Albertans Speak Out About Families* (Edmonton: Government of Alberta, 1992), 6.

40. Premier's Council in Support of Alberta Families, *Perspectives on Family Well-Being* (Edmonton: Government of Alberta, 1993), 2.

41. Premier's Council, *Albertans Speak Out About Families*, 10.

42. Judy Fudge, "Fragmentation and Feminization: The Challenge of Equity for Labour Relations Policy," in Janine Brodie (ed.), *Women and Canadian Public Policy* (Toronto: Harcourt Brace, 1996), 67.

43. Gurston Dacks, Joyce Green and Linda Trimble, "Road Kill: Women in Alberta's Drive Toward Deficit Elimination," in Trevor Harrison and Gordon Laxer (eds.), *The Trojan Horse: Alberta and the Future of Canada* (Montreal: Black Rose Books, 1995), 282.

44. Alberta Legislative Assembly, *Debates* (March 1, 1995), 293.

45. Ibid., (March 27, 1995), 839.

46. See Anna Yeatman, *Postmodern Revisionings of the Political* (New York: Routledge, 1994).

47. See Robert Devigne, *Recasting Conservatism: Oakeshott, Strauss and the Response to Postmodernism* (New Haven: Yale University Press, 1994), esp. chapters 3 and 4.

48. Dacks, Green and Trimble, "Road Kill," 277.

49. Laurie Adkin, "Life in Kleinland: Democratic Resistance to Folksy Fascism," *Canadian Dimension* 25 (April–May 1995), 35.

50. Dacks, Green and Trimble, "Road Kill," 282.

51. Isabella Bakker, "Engendering Macro-economic Policy Reform in the Era of Global Restructuring and Adjustment," in *idem* (ed.), *The Strategic Silence: Gender and Economic Policy* (London: Zed Books, 1994), 8.

52. Linda McDowell, "Gender Divisions in a Post-Fordist Era: New Contradictions or the Same Old Story?" in Linda McDowell and Rosemary Pringle (eds.), *Defining Women: Social Institutions and Gender Divisions* (Cambridge: Polity Press, 1992), 192.

Conclusion

The Pasts (and Futures) of Feminist Political Economy in Canada: Reviving the Debate

Leah F. Vosko

In the last three decades, Canadian scholars have played a central role in shaping the field of feminist political economy. We have contributed to challenging the gender-blindness of political economy scholarship and advancing debates in feminist theory. Globalization, accelerating commodification and welfare state retrenchment, however, pose a number of challenges and opportunities to scholars in the field. These challenges require feminist political economists to engage more effectively in debates in applied contemporary feminist theory, particularly debates between feminist critical and poststructural theorists, and to deepen analyses of reprivatization, feminization and other consequences of neo-liberal restructuring.

With a view to examining where feminist political economy has been and where it is headed, this chapter reviews the Canadian feminist political economy literature and locates it in a broader context. Focusing centrally on scholarship in the journal *Studies in Political Economy* and other leading contributions, it argues that Canadian scholarship in feminist political economy has proceeded through four overlapping phases since the early 1970s, cultivating a vibrant community of scholars and an extensive body of gender-sensitive political economy research. Yet critical engagement between Canadian feminist political economists and feminist theorists has waned in recent years, resulting in several missed opportunities for intervention in central debates in contemporary feminist theory. This development is regrettable since a prime strength of early Canadian feminist political economy scholarship was its contributions to various branches of feminist theory. However, recent debates among a group of principally U.S. feminist theorists — debates generating significant scholarly attention — offer an opening for scholars to reinvigorate feminist political economy since a growing number of theorists are referring to issues and debates critical to the field.

One set of debates calling for greater intervention from feminist political economists surrounds Nancy Fraser's "recognition-redistribution dilemma" or the dichotomous positioning of the "politics of recognition" and the "politics of redistribution." Within this dichotomy "recognition politics" are cast essentially as struggles for cultural or symbolic change and/or group recognition, while "redistributive politics" are cast largely as struggles related to socioeconomic injustices (i.e., class struggles narrowly conceived).[2] Some critics of this characterization, such as Judith Butler and Iris Marion Young, argue that feminist thinkers are increasingly trapped in a false opposition that mystifies the overlapping political struggles of marginalized groups and that Fraser's ideal typology is limited in theory and in practice. In criticizing those taking the recognition-redistribution dilemma as given, these theorists have looked to early debates in feminist political economy — debates in which Canadian scholars played leading roles — but with insufficient depth. Combined with recent work on intersectional theorizing and racialization critical to advancing scholarship in the field, however, feminist work on the gender-blindness of political economy and debates over causality and levels of analysis offer insights to those attempting to transcend or displace this dichotomy.

To develop this argument and raise questions critical to the continued development of feminist political economy in Canada, the ensuing discussion unfolds in three parts. Part One traces what I label the four overlapping phases characterizing the Canadian feminist political economy scholarship in the last three decades, highlighting both the prime contributions and the range of theoretical and practical issues raised in each phase. It devotes considerable attention to several prominent themes in *Studies in Political Economy* reflected in the articles and commentaries in this volume, specifically, production and reproduction (Armstrong and Armstrong), the state (Andrew) and manufacturing (Clement).[3] Part Two examines a pivotal debate in contemporary feminist theory between the "politics of recognition" and the "politics of redistribution," which has commanded considerable attention in a range of feminist circles in North America, Europe and Australia since the mid-1990s. Finally, the concluding section links the overview of the four phases of feminist political economy scholarship in Canada and the sketch of the recognition/ redistribution debate. It explores how we might strengthen feminist *political economy*[4] in Canada, on the one hand, and how *feminist* political economy could contribute to deepening debates between feminist critical and poststructural theorists on the other hand.

Phases of Feminist Political Economy in Canada

Since the mid-1970s, feminist scholarship in political economy has moved through four overlapping phases. The first identifiable phase focused on raising the issue of "gender-blindness" in political economy. Second stage debates explored questions related to "levels of analysis," examining how to explain sexual inequality under capitalism and where to locate "women's work" (paid and unpaid) in the mode of production. Building on the abstract theorizing of the second stage and the tentative resolution to the "levels of analysis" debate, applied works in feminist political economy dominated the third stage of discussion. The trajectory of feminist political economy scholarship then took two complementary turns. In the fourth stage, which prevails to the present, scholars began to explore more deeply the interrelationships between gender, race and ethnicity in shaping women's relationship to capitalism — this strain in the literature is frequently labelled feminist intersectional theorizing. At the same time, a growing body of scholarship on the welfare state and the law, shaped largely by feminist political economists influenced by intersectional theorizing, emerged.

Before describing these four phases of feminist political economy scholarship in Canada, four caveats are in order. First, in delineating these phases, I am schematizing (and thus simplifying) what I recognize is a wide and diverse body of scholarship that overlaps chronologically and in subject matter. While any effort at categorization is inevitably artificial, I take this route since mapping scholarly interventions is illuminating in charting new directions for the field, the central task of this intervention.

Second, in my sketch, I use the label feminist political economy in an inclusive manner. In the ensuing discussion, therefore, I make reference to the work of scholars whom I locate in the feminist political economy tradition but who may view their work differently. I take this inclusive approach since my aim is to upset narrow economistic notions of *political economy* and identify challenges for *feminist* political economy and since, in my view, feminist political economy is a diverse terrain.

Third, in this survey, I cover considerable ground. As a result, although I draw examples from a range of disciplinary angles, my review is necessarily partial; I have selected a limited number of examples from a wide body of scholarship in feminist political economy to advance my arguments. Furthermore, my interpretations of debates in feminist political economy may not correspond with the understandings of those involved in them. A central objective of this chapter, however, is to initiate a dialogue between those feminist political economists intimately involved in field-defining debates and scholars whose writing may be peripheral to these debates but whose scholarship nevertheless builds on this tradition.

Fourth, and finally, while many debates in contemporary feminist theory call for intervention from feminist political economists, I deliberately take a debate occurring largely in the journals *New Left Review* and *Social Text* as a case study for two reasons. First, I aim to intervene in debates among feminist critical and poststructural theorists since they have had a chilling effect in certain domains of feminist scholarship including, to some degree, in feminist political economy where few scholars have challenged formally and/or directly leading U.S. feminist theorists in particular. Second, I aim to use these debates to recover the under-recognized contributions of feminist political economists loosely associated with the broader scholarly tradition known as the "New Canadian Political Economy" since they offer an opening for reinvigorating the field.

Phase 1: Raising the Issue of Gender-Blindness

Paralleling developments in Britain, Australia and Western Europe as a whole, the earliest set of interventions inaugurating the field of feminist political economy in Canada focused on the gender-blindness characterizing classic works in the field. When Canadian scholars — such as Pat Armstrong and Hugh Armstrong, Marjorie Cohen, Pat Connelly, Meg Luxton, Angela Miles and Martha MacDonald — began to raise the issue of the gender-blindness apparent in political economy analysis, they drew on the contributions of scholars such as Maggie Benston, Heidi Hartmann, Mary MacIntosh and Juliet Mitchell, who had formally recognized some of the conceptual problems inherent in the writings of Marx and Engels. The focus of this scholarship, however, was not to rehash these issues. Rather, as Armstrong and Armstrong noted in the early 1980s, citing Sheila Rowbotham, "Karl Marx and Friedrich Engels were still just a couple of bourgeois men." Thus, the aim should be to move beyond taking them to task for their errors and omissions to use the political economy method to *gender* class analysis and to make class more integral to gender analysis.[5]

Scholarship building on such objectives followed two complementary trajectories. The first trajectory included writings describing and examining women's situation under capitalism, focusing on the various manifestations of sex/gender divisions of labour. Works belonging to this trajectory focused on wage inequality, the sex/gender division of labour in households and labour market segmentation by sex. Meg Luxton's study, *More Than a Labour of Love*, is a case in point, as is her subsequent article, "Two Hands for the Clock," which illustrated that despite women's increased labour force participation, the sexual division of labour in the domestic sphere in Flin Flon, Manitoba (the site of her initial study) remained virtually unchanged.[6] In the second trajectory, the aim was to locate the roots of women's disadvantaged position as waged and wageless workers, largely through theoretically grounded case studies; the writings of Armstrong and Armstrong, Connelly and Miles as well as several works by Luxton fit into this category. In each of these cases, much of the debate focused on domestic labour and the central question underpinning discussions was: Is there a third department in the mode of production that encompasses daily and intergenerational reproduction? This set of feminist work attempted to highlight the narrow economism of the malestream political economy scholarship by revealing the necessary and integral relationship between production for surplus and social reproduction and by illustrating why these departments of production should be located and studied at corresponding levels of abstraction.

Both strands of debate paralleled discussions in journals outside Canada, like the *New Left Review*, where the work of Jane Lewis, Wally Seccombe (one of the earliest writers to speak of a third department of production) and Iris Young figured prominently, and in Bonnie Fox's edited volume, *Hidden in the Household*.[7] In this period, differences over the significance of women's domestic labour under capitalism (i.e., the "domestic labour debate") also reinforced divisions between those positing a dual system of patriarchy and capitalism and those arguing for unified systems approach. The two groups differed over the relative importance of the ideological and material causes of women's disadvantaged position.

Phase 2: "Levels of Analysis" Debates

What began as a discussion over the problem of gender-blindness in political economy analysis and led to a central focus on the domestic sphere (and, hence, theoretical discussion surrounding daily and intergenerational reproduction) transformed into a full-fledged debate over levels of analysis in the mid-1980s. By this time, the lines in the feminist political economy scholarly community were being drawn between those convinced that ideology was the driving force behind women's position under capitalism, influenced significantly by the work of Michelle Barrett[8] as well as scholars like Mary McIntosh and Christine Delphy, and those intent on rooting women's situation primarily in material relations. While a third grouping of scholars seeking a balance between these two positions (and owing a debt to Joan Acker)[9] arose gradually, the result of this split between identifying causality in ideological or material relations was that feminist political economists began distancing themselves from discussions locating causes per se. The scholarship thus began to drift towards determining the appropriate level (or levels) of analysis at which to specify women's disadvantaged position in the economy, broadly defined.

Initially, this debate took place at a high level of abstraction. Again, two strands of analysis dominated. On the one hand, the goal for scholars — like Armstrong and Armstrong, Seccombe, Luxton and others joining the debate like Roberta Hamilton — was to understand the sexual division of labour at all levels of analysis, but especially at the level of the mode of production. As Armstrong and Armstrong noted, for these scholars, "the issue [was] not 'women's questions' or the 'question of women' but the efficacy of an analytical framework which fails to recognize or explain how and why sex differences pervade every aspect of human activity."[10] In contrast, led by Barrett and other scholars preoccupied with the role of ideology, another group of writers created a split interpretation that located the "class question" at the level of the mode of production and the "gender question" at the level of the social formation. As a result, the debate began to polarize even further than it had at the end of Phase 1.

Early on in this debate, Pat Connelly intervened in an attempt to move beyond the increasingly entrenched set of competing arguments.

In her article "On Marxism and Feminism," which began with a review of the contributions of the domestic labour debate, she responded to earlier work by Angela Miles from one angle, and Armstrong and Armstrong from another, and drew on work by Barrett, representing yet another angle, to break down the ideology/materialism divide. At this time, Connelly characterized this debate as one between radical feminists and socialist feminists that operated as follows: she argued that radical feminists focus too narrowly on gender relations as the ultimate source of women's oppression, without considering the specific historical and economic context of these relations, while socialist feminists overemphasize "how gender relations which preceded capitalism have been affected historically by capitalist relations of production — by class domination and class struggle."[11] For Connelly, socialist feminists were merely "adding women" and radical feminists were merely "adding class" to their respective theoretical paradigms when the truly important challenge was to "develop a coherent and integrated perspective with which to analyze the oppression of women in capitalist society."[12] In her view, both Armstrong and Armstrong and Barrett were certainly trying to address this challenge. However, Armstrong and Armstrong were concerned with responding to the challenge at all levels of analysis since they located the sexual division of labour at the highest level of abstraction while Barrett aimed to shift the focus towards the *gender* division of labour, locating class divisions at the level of the mode of production and gender divisions as "historically constituted integral part[s] of, but not a necessary condition for, the capitalist mode of production."[13]

Although Connelly was sympathetic to scholars viewing the sexual division of labour as operating at the highest level of abstraction, she argued that it is impossible to understand all aspects of women's oppression using the categories of malestream political economy. She also contended that it is unclear whether the sex/gender division of labour actually predates capitalism. As a result, Connelly advocated that analyses of women's oppression proceed at the level of the social formation. She suggested that focusing scholarship at this concrete level was the most promising way out of the impasse between those giving primacy to material factors, like Armstrong and Armstrong, versus those preoccupied with ideological forces, like Barrett. Connelly argued further that probing women's situation at the level of the social formation would enable scholars to reject functionalism in favour of examining the role of women's domestic and waged labour in specific historical contexts, abandon the view that "biology is destiny," take greater account of geographical variation in women's condition and place more weight on ideological forces without rejecting materialist analyses.

The pragmatic strategy that Connelly advanced marked a critical turning point in feminist political economy scholarship in Canada, one that led many scholars to set aside their unresolved differences over critical levels of analysis questions. However, it is also important to note that the shift away from discussions of causality in feminist political economy scholarship coincided with and, to some extent, reflected the emerging critique of political economy as a singular body of social and political thought. Connelly's intervention nevertheless typified the nature of interventions in the field in the mid- to late 1980s when scholars began to apply various theories with this type of integrative goal in mind rather than pursue debates over levels of analysis.

Phase 3: Theoretically Grounded Applied Case Studies

Many case studies grew out of the levels of analysis debate in the Canadian feminist political economy literature. Chief among them were Martha MacDonald's critique of the discipline of economics building on debates in *Studies in Political Economy*, Marjorie Cohen's work on the problem of "economic man" and Marilyn Porter's application of these insights to maritime political economy. At the same time, works like *Feminism and Political Economy* (1987), edited by Luxton and Maroney, Ester Reiter's book *Making Fast Food* (1991) and Linda Briskin's work on socialist feminist praxis exploring the tension between adopting strategies aimed at mainstreaming feminist concerns and opting for disengagement moved scholarship beyond the levels of analysis debate.[14] Still, the widely cited work that definitively reflected the turn towards applied case studies was Jane Jenson's article "Gender and Reproduction or Babies and the State."[15] Emerging after the controversy over levels of analysis, Jenson's article had a formidable impact in charting the direction of feminist political economy scholarship. Specifically, it contributed to ensuring that the research agenda among Canadian feminist political economists focused on analyses aimed at elaborating women's situation at the level of the social formation.

In her examination of early British and French state policies regarding maternity, Jenson's most provocative assertion, which clearly grew out of debates over levels of analysis debate, was:

[T]here must be a clear distinction among levels of analysis so that, while abstractly designating the fact of the state's contribution to the reproduction of the mode of production, the description of *how* that role is organized is found in analyses of political struggle in concrete social formations.[16]

The impact of Jenson's adoption of this position was far-reaching in that it led her to introduce the concept "universe of political discourse," which enabled her to draw the following conclusion contra Armstrong and Armstrong as well as Barrett. According to Jenson, based on her detailed study of the historical roots of maternity policies in France in Britain, "a system of gendered power can be acknowledged and resisted without immediately requiring that it be articulated at the highest level of abstraction to the capitalist mode of production."[17] Jenson's intervention cemented the movement to bring the levels of analysis debate to a halt. However, at the same time, the reference that she made to the "inevitably gendered character of childbirth" also provided an opening for reviving this debate. Indeed, this assumption, which Jenson raised as an aside, moved her important applied study, which operates at the level of the social formation, to a higher level of abstraction, although her brief reference was never taken in this direction.

Feminist political economy's turn towards applied case studies was not universal in the late 1980s, however. Indeed, from the mid- to late 1980s, there was considerable debate over questions related to the significance of "experience" and how to define the apparatus surrounding the "relations of ruling" dominant in late capitalist societies. For example, in this period, Dorothy Smith wrote rather abstractly about the importance of shifting standpoints to where women's "experience" in the "everyday world" becomes visible and is no longer objectified. In her article "Feminist Reflections on Political Economy," Smith's goal was to acknowledge and articulate multiple sites of experience beyond the site of production and criticize contemporary political economists for what she termed as "accepting relations of ruling." Her contribution had a significant influence on feminist political economy. Yet, despite the nature of this early article, Smith's theoretical starting point, which crystallized in her subsequent analyses, eschewed debate over levels of analysis as well as theorizing at the highest level of abstraction. Hence, her work reinforced the move towards applied case studies.

Phase 4: Intersections of Race, Class and Gender

The most important outcome of what began as a movement away from debates over causes and levels of analysis, and prompted an emphasis on theoretically grounded case studies, was the emergence of two complementary strains in the feminist political economy scholarship in Canada in the late 1980s and early 1990s. In Phase 4, which prevails to date, scholarship probing intersecting systems of domination and scholarship grounding work on intersectionality in explorations of women, the law and the welfare state both began to lead, and indeed transform, the field.

Work on racism and racialization was central to introducing an analysis of intersectionality in this fourth phase of scholarship, and the examples are numerous. Ruth Frager's article on "Class and Ethnic Barriers to Feminist Perspective in Toronto's Jewish Labour Movement" is a key example of a work initiating feminist intersectional theorizing in Canada. In this article, through her exploration of gender and class relations in the Jewish labour movement, Frager argued that certain historical conditions might encourage the dominance of ethnicity and class over gender as a basis for action.[18] At the same time, however, she illustrated that strategies that do not take women-specific concerns into account often have contradictory results for women. Sedef Arat-Koc's work, including her contribution to *Through the Kitchen Window* (1990), her article "In the Privacy of Our Home" and her contribution to *Not One in the Family* (1997), also rests squarely in this grouping. Her scholarship on paid domestic work identifies and calls attention to the inequalities between largely White, Canadian-born, middle- and upper-class women and foreign domestic workers.[19] It reveals the private sphere as a site of racialized sex/gender divisions of labour. Notably, in the three works named above, Arat-Koc placed emphasis on social reproduction, building on scholarship from the first phase of feminist political economy in Canada. Yet, at the same time, she tied this dimension of production to the racialized character of the international division of labour, deepening analyses of the public/private split under capitalism.

The growth of intersectional theorizing, reflected in leading case studies by Arat-Koc and Frager, continued into the 1990s. In the mid-1990s, its significance was underscored by a special issue of *Studies in Political Economy* on "Intersections of Gender, Race and Class" (1996), edited by Gillian Creese and Daiva Stasiulus. Taking inspiration from the work of Chandra Mohanty, Ann Russo and Lourdes

Torres,[20] among others, this special issue was devoted to examining the multiple and contradictory intersections of gender, race and class and to developing a fuller consideration of the power relationships flowing from them. One of its central aims was to unsettle certain established strands of feminist political economy in a manner similar to the way feminists writing at the inception of the journal challenged the gender-blindness of malestream political economy. Creese and Stasiulus noted accordingly:

> Feminist political economy, like its non-feminist counterparts, inherited a theoretical legacy that privileges economic relations over cultural and ideological relations, while failing to acknowledge the degree to which the former shaped the latter ... [one that] tended to treat white, European groups as socially normative, rather than merely dominant.[21]

They went on to suggest further that "race, ethnicity and related axes of exclusion and subordination are often named, but seldom form an integral part of feminist and non-feminist political economy," a claim of a similar order to that raised by feminist political economists over a decade earlier.[22] More specifically, in her contribution to the same special issue of *Studies in Political Economy* entitled "Post-Modern Race and Gender Essentialism or a Post-Mortem of Scholarship," Radha Jhappan examined the pitfalls of race and gender essentialism, arguing for a "contextualized essentialism."[23] Tania Das Gupta, another contributor and author of *Racism and Paid Work*, linked the everyday harassment of Black women nurses to systemic racism in hospital management in Toronto.[24] Finally, Gillian Creese and Laurie Peterson provided a comparison of the media depiction of Chinese Canadians in the 1920s and 1980s, and Wenona Giles and Valerie Preston pointed to the importance of ethnic cultural differences in shaping female homeworkers' evaluation of their work.[25]

Along with a range of other works theorizing intersectionality, including works by Caroline Andrew, Himani Bannerji, Daiva Stasiulus and Abigail Bakan,[26] contributions to this special issue of *Studies in Political Economy* placed considerations of the interconnectedness of race, class and gender at the centre of analysis. They cultivated a feminist political economy attentive to racialization and racism more generally. Scholarship on intersectionality originating in the late 1980s thus widened applied research, raising new questions for feminist political economy and strengthening the claim that struggles based on race and ethnicity are political economic struggles. While it operated on a parallel track, in the 1980s and 1990s, intersectional theorizing by feminist political economists also addressed similar themes and issues to those raised in debates in feminist theory.[27]

Feminist intersectional theorizing remains central to the feminist political economy literature to date, with recent work focusing on theoretically grounded case studies exploring, in particular, racialized sex/gender divisions of labour in paid and unpaid work and in trade union structure. However, in the present period, there is growing emphasis, complementing this type of theorizing, on probing developments at the level of the state and changes in the legal arena in the field.[28] Work on women and the welfare state, sex/gender and social policy and women and the law, therefore, represents the other dominant strain in this fourth phase.

Recent scholarship on welfare state restructuring by Isabella Bakker, Janine Brodie, Marjorie Cohen and Patricia Evans figures prominently in this subgrouping. Bakker's edited volume, *Rethinking Restructuring* (1996), unpacks the "gendered paradox" of restructuring in Canada, which she argues is marked by the simultaneous erosion and intensification of gender. Bakker and several contributors to her volume suggest that, at present, "gender appears to be less important in understanding the global political economy and, at the same time, more of a determining factor in its transformation."[29] For example, contributions exploring developments in the labour market by Pat Armstrong, Barbara Cameron, Martha MacDonald and Pat Connelly and Jane Jenson demonstrate that the current restructuring means that more women are joining the labour force. Yet, at the same time, changes in labour market regulation are prompting the feminization of employment or the erosion of employment norms.[30]

Janine Brodie's work in the mid-1990s in *Politics on the Margins* and *Politics on the Boundaries*, as well as her contributions to Bakker's collection and the journal *Citizenship Studies*, tackles the question of gender and restructuring through the lens of citizenship.[31] Much of her work documents the shift in the gender order, a term coined by R.W. Connell, from the Keynesian period to the present. In unpacking the new citizenship order of the neo-liberal state, Brodie highlights five central gendered dimensions: privatization, commodification, familialization (i.e., the reconstitution of the domestic hetero-patriarchal family as the foundation of society), decentralization and criminalization. Brodie's conclusion about the nature of change echoes a central finding of Marjorie Cohen's work on globalization and free trade — namely, that changes in the global economy and their manifestations domestically undermine equality and democracy and particularly the democratic traditions of the Canadian women's movement.[32] Other contributions to this latest phase in the scholarship, particularly those examining citizenship through an intersectional lens and bridging the two dominant strains, such as work by Yasmeen Abu-Laban, and those seeking to expand comparative welfare state analysis to take greater account of race/ethnicity, such as work by Fiona Williams, substantiate these conclusions.[33]

Reinforcing this direction in the scholarship, feminist scholars in the field of law take up similar questions to those focusing on the citizenship and the neo-liberal state, although, even more than their counterparts in other fields, their analyses operate largely at a meso-level. Contributors to Susan Boyd's *Challenging the Public/Private Divide* (1997) and Elizabeth Comack's *Locating the Law: Race/Class/Gender* (1999), for example, explore the themes of reprivatization, the feminization of employment and changing state forms as do contributors to *Feminization, Privatization and the Law*, the forthcoming volume co-edited by Judy Fudge and Brenda Cossman.[34] Taking privatization as a lens to explore a tectonic shift in public policy, however, Fudge and Cossman's introduction explicitly recognizes the importance of theorizing the relationship between discourse and political economy, taking up a pivotal challenge to contemporary feminist political economy. The volume also begins to address this challenge by combining an analysis of law as a discourse central to privatization with an exploration of assumptions about the supposed elasticity of social reproduction. In this way, Fudge and Cossman take seriously Brodie's claim that "the restructuring imperative [and its by-product privatization] has been accompanied by a subtle but palpable shift in the organizing terms of the social sciences and, *in particular, of political economy*" (emphasis added).[35]

The magnitude and scope of contributions to the Canadian feminist political economy literature in Phase 4 — not to mention the three phases reviewed previously — should not be underestimated. However, the strains dominating the contemporary literature (and the mode of debate that they generate) have failed largely to alter the movement away from debates and discussions about levels of analysis. With the exception of recent works engaging feminist political economy and the law and a few articles exploring welfare state restructuring, which may affect a change in course, attempts to synthesize recent case studies with unresolved debates and questions in feminist political economy are limited, reflecting a continued focus on theorizing at the level of the social formation.[36] Given recent developments in various strains of contemporary feminist theory, however, there is a pressing need for feminist political economists to revisit early debates with greater sensitivity to the intersections of race, class, sexuality and gender. The final segment of this article explores this dual challenge by delving into a contemporary debate.

The "Recognition-Redistribution Dilemma": A Central Debate in Contemporary Feminist Theory Meets Feminist Political Economy

In exploring the need for renewed interaction between feminist political economists and feminist theorists, a set of concurrent developments that began in the mid-1990s comes to the fore. In this period, feminist political economists in Canada and elsewhere remained focused on elaborating women's position under capitalism, albeit with increasing attention to interlocking systems of domination. Yet, at the same time, several leading U.S. feminist theorists returned to concepts and ideas originating in feminist political economy with surprisingly limited acknowledgement of their contested meanings or their roots. These corresponding trends are paradoxical since prominent debates among feminist theorists, especially between feminist critical and poststructural theorists, are making concerns pivotal to feminist political economy once again central to core debates in feminist theory — they are reviving debates over gender-blindness, causality and levels of analysis.

The debate surrounding "recognition-redistribution dilemma" or "the politics of recognition" versus "the politics of redistribution," initiated by Nancy Fraser and pursued actively by Judith Butler, Iris Marion Young and Ann Phillips among others, belongs to this grouping. It is an important debate to consider since Fraser and her interlocutors refer to early debates in feminist political economy, where the gender-blindness of political economy analysis was scrutinized and where the position of women, and eventually other marginalized groups, in the mode production was hotly debated. I view the debate over the "recognition-redistribution dilemma" as exemplifying the need for greater engagement between feminist political economists and feminist theorists since its contributions are constrained by a weak understanding of pivotal debates in feminist political economy since the 1970s — on the part of virtually every central participant — even though the political-theoretical debate over justice claims rests upon a foundation of feminist political economy.

The Parameters of the Debate

As interpreted by Nancy Fraser, the central divide among North American feminist theorists today is between those who support the "politics of recognition" and those advancing a "politics of redistribution" as a means of reconciling gender inequality. The current impasse, she argues, is framed by two analytically distinct understandings of justice: the first understanding is cultural or symbolic and therefore related to social patterns of representation, and the second understanding is socio-economic and therefore rooted in the political economic structure of society. According to Fraser, from the early 1980s to the mid-1990s, feminist theorizing in this geographic context proceeded along two divergent paths. One current, which gradually evolved into the *politics of recognition*, was first marked by the emergence of a "politics of identity" that characterized the struggles of various marginalized groups as principally struggles for recognition, and subsequently by a turn towards difference. Scholars following this trajectory criticized liberal feminism for its tendency to overgeneralize about "women's" oppression and a strand of socialist feminism for its adoption of universalistic (and often economistic) categories rooted in Marxist orthodoxy.[37] Another current, which evolved into the *politics of redistribution*, kept redistributive concerns at the centre of analysis, although this current refused to assign class (defined narrowly in relation to production for the market) a more central role in relations of domination than gendered and racialized relations.[38] For approximately fifteen years, these two currents proceeded along different tracks, but in the mid-1990s Fraser suggests that they diverged further. A number of scholars belonging to the first grouping shifted their lens of analysis to embrace more fully the insights of psychoanalysis, often emphasizing symbolic change. Simultaneously, a number of scholars belonging to the second current moved more towards applied studies of interlocking forms of oppression, in many instances advocating redistributive strategies.

Nancy Fraser urges feminist scholars to address the growing split between these currents in her article "From Redistribution to Recognition? Dilemmas of Justice in a 'Post-Socialist' Age" (1995). In this contribution, as well as in her subsequent book, *Justice Interruptus* (1997), and her recent article "Rethinking Recognition" (2000), Fraser raises the following questions: "how should we view the eclipse of the socialist imaginary centered on terms such as 'interest', 'exploitation' and 'redistribution'? What should we make of the rise of a new political imaginary centered on notions of 'identity,' 'difference,''cultural domination' and 'recognition'?"[39] By posing these questions, she addresses the rise of identity politics and the contradictions that it generates, suggesting that identity politics, along with an economistic class politics, exacerbate her recognition-redistribution dilemma. To overcome this dilemma, Fraser proposes that feminist scholars adopt a transformative critical theory of recognition grounded in socialist (i.e., redistributive) principles, on the one hand, and deconstruction, on the other. To establish the conditions under which "a politics of recognition could support the politics of redistribution," she constructs an axis of struggle (based on a Weberian typology)[40] designed to operate at a high level of abstraction, where cultural and socio-economic struggles are intricately intertwined. Yet she chooses to retain an analytical distinction between redistribution and recognition struggles for "heuristic purposes."[41]

While Fraser maintains that "economic injustice and cultural injustice are usually interimbricated so as to reinforce one another dialectically,"[42] she is criticized harshly for reinforcing this distinction. For example, Fraser uses struggles over sexual orientation as a prototypical example of recognition struggles. She notes accordingly:

> Sexuality in this conception is a mode of social differentiation whose roots do not lie in the political economy because homosexuals are distributed through the entire class structure of capitalist society, occupy no distinctive position in the division of labour, and do not constitute an exploited class. Rather, their mode of collectivity is that of a despised sexuality, rooted in the cultural-valuational structure of society. *From this perspective, the injustice that they suffer is quintessentially a matter of recognition.* Gays and lesbians suffer from heterosexism: the authoritative construction of norms that privilege heterosexuality. ... The remedy for the injustice, consequently, is recognition, not redistribution.[43]

Fraser speaks of "exploited classes," which may include one gender (women) and various racialized groups, on the one hand, and "despised sexualities," on the other hand, but whose members are unified by economic injustice. She also speaks of "bivalent collectivities" (e.g., lesbians, women of colour, disabled women), arguing that redistribution is key to eradicating gender inequalities, but that recognition is most central to remedying inequalities based on sexual orientation, thereby suggesting that gender and race are concepts of a different order than, for example, sexual orientation and disability. This distinction leads her to advocate the destabilization of group identities (i.e., deconstruction) and, at the same time, to call for socialism in the economy. These parallel prescriptions lie at the root of her transformative agenda.

A number of feminist scholars object to Fraser's dichotomous framework. Iris Marion Young, for example, characterizes her theory as reminiscent of dual systems analyses that treat capitalism and patriarchy as separate systems of oppression confronted by women. She thus advocates pluralizing categories rather than a return to "marxist-feminist orthodoxy."[44] From a different perspective, Anne Phillips agrees with Fraser on the danger of displacing redistributive claims in favour of the politics of identity. Yet she takes seriously Young's concerns about the potential return to orthodoxy if Fraser's transformative agenda is embraced. For Phillips, the "recognition-redistribution dilemma," as posed by Fraser, raises two issues: "whether it is theoretically and/or politically appropriate to make this distinction between redistribution and recognition; and whether Fraser's analysis ends up reinstating economic injustice [narrowly defined] as her central concern."[45]

Judith Butler, however, provides the most detailed and widely discussed response to Fraser based on their history of productive exchange. Her response to Fraser — and their debate over social justice more generally — is most interesting from our perspective since it depends upon the assumed prior resolution of conceptual and theoretical issues in feminist political economy. In her article, "Merely Cultural" (1998), where she first critiques Fraser's recognition-redistribution dilemma, Butler is especially critical of Fraser's characterization of "gender" and "race" as belonging to the redistributive side of her continuum and "sexuality" to the recognition side. She argues *against* Fraser's ideal typology and, at the same time, *for* characterizing sexuality as critical to political economy, as critical as gender and race, a surprising move for Butler, who normally locates her work in the feminist poststructuralist rather than the political economy tradition. To respond to Fraser, Butler cites Paul Gilroy and Stuart Hall, who argue that "race may be one modality in which class is lived" and "in this way, race and class are rendered distinct analytically only to realize that the analysis of the one cannot proceed without the analysis of the other."[46] Critical to this project, however, Butler returns to central debates in feminist political economy in the late 1970s and early 1980s in extending the logic of this type of claim to sexuality, debates at the heart of the Canadian literature, as well as broader debates where psychoanalytic insights figured prominently.

Drawing on the contributions of socialist feminist scholars who bridged political economy and psychoanalysis in these decades, Butler asks, "why would a movement concerned to criticize and transform the ways in which sexuality is socially regulated not be understood as central to the functioning of political economy?"[47] In response to this question, she argues that Marx and Engels insisted that the mode of production concept included forms of social association; in her view, Marx "makes clear ... that a mode of production is always combined with a mode of cooperation" and Engels identifies social reproduction as central to the mode of production.[48] Furthermore, Butler argues that psychoanalysis's contribution is to show how the very production of gender has to be understood as a part of the production of human beings themselves, according to norms that reproduce the heterosexual normative family. She credits Gayle Rubin for developing an analogous argument.

Unlike Phillips, who characterizes the contributions of feminist political economy as "short-lived,"[49] Butler also acknowledges the significance of the feminist political economy scholarship in the late 1970s and early 1980s, which established the sphere of sexual reproduction as part of the material conditions of life and therefore central to political economy analysis. Contra Fraser, Butler's conclusion is that struggles to transform the social field of sexuality are critical to political economy "because they cannot be understood without an expansion of the 'economic sphere' itself to include both the production of goods as well as the social reproduction of persons."[50] She views the social regulation of sexuality as integral to the process of production and thus part of political economy. This analysis of sexuality, in part, leads Butler to firmly reject Fraser's effective dichotomization of redistributive and recognition struggles.

Butler's counterargument raises a range of issues that are worthy of discussion and debate, but her references to the contributions of feminist political economists in the late 1970s and early 1980s (as well as references made by Fraser and others participating in the debate) are especially noteworthy. Still, Fraser primarily responds to Butler on different grounds, choosing to clarify her method and to argue that, for her, "the recognition-redistribution dilemma" is merely an analytical distinction, maintaining her Weberian ideal-type approach. For example, in "Rethinking Recognition," her most recent intervention in this debate, Fraser goes to great lengths to clarify what she means by recognition and asserts that "cultural forms of social ordering" and "economic forms ordering ... are interimbricated"[51] but maintains her typology.[52] Fraser also defends forcefully her placement of sexuality on the recognition side of her continuum. In her article "Heterosexism, Misrecognition and Capitalism: A Response to Judith Butler," Fraser replies to Butler's claims about the relationship between sexuality and the political-economic structure by questioning how "the heteronormative regulation of sexuality is part of the economic structure by definition, *despite the fact that it structures neither the social division of labour nor the mode of exploitation of labour-power in capitalist society.*"[53]

Critical to this discussion, in defending her characterization of sexuality, Fraser fails to discuss (or even acknowledge) the privatized character of the heterosexual nuclear family under capitalism, let alone the escalating reprivatization of women's work in late capitalism. Rather, she contends that in the present period the rise of "personal life" — Eli Zaretsky's term — makes sexuality disconnected from production and reproduction, asserting that:

> [I]n the late capitalist society of the twentieth century ... the links between sexuality and surplus-value accumulation have been still further attenuated by the rise of ... "personal life": a space of intimate relations, including sexuality, friendship, and love, *that can no longer be identified with the family that is lived as disconnected from the imperatives of production and reproduction* [emphasis added].[54]

She suggests further that "if sexual struggles, therefore, are economic, they are not economic in the same sense as are struggles over the rate of exploitation."[55] In advancing these linked claims,

Fraser relies on an inaccurate representation of central insights and debates in feminist political economy of the 1970s and 1980s. For example, her claim that the central socialist feminist insight in this period was that "the family" is part of the mode of production misrepresents critical debates. As the foregoing review of the Canadian literature demonstrates, notions of "the family" and "production" (i.e., production for subsistence, surplus and social reproduction) were highly contested among feminist political economists in the time period to which Fraser refers, especially in the initial three phases of the scholarship. Moreover, with one broad sweep, Fraser discounts an entire strand of the feminist political economy literature, led by scholars in the United Kingdom, arguing that the culture of romantic love and, hence, marriage and "the family" is a crucial mechanism in the process of women's subordination.

My project here is not to evaluate the merits and shortcomings of each specific argument — neither Fraser's initial formulation nor the responses of Young, Phillips or Butler or Fraser's counter-responses to her interlocutors. Instead, the aim is to reveal the critical absences and flaws in this debate, especially concerning issues related to the position of women, racialized groups and "despised sexualities," etc., under capitalism. Furthermore, I want to suggest that the silences in the debate provide an important opening to revisit the feminist political economy scholarship of the 1970s and 1980s and continuing work on social reproduction aiming to understand sex/gender relations at all levels of abstraction. What is critical about the recognition-redistribution debate is that Fraser, Young, Phillips and Butler make references (both implicit and explicit) to early insights and debates in feminist political economy, specifically to the long-standing feminist insight that social reproduction is critical to production and related debates about "the family" and "production" under capitalism. But neither Fraser nor her interlocutors engage in a detailed discussion of the nature of social reproduction (i.e., its gendered and racialized character and dominant norms and assumptions about the heterosexual nuclear family) and how it should be understood at all levels of analysis. They thus make little acknowledgement of discussions and, most critically, the unresolved debates that prefigured the contemporary recognition-redistribution debate. The basis of their disagreements nevertheless belongs partly to the terrain of feminist political economy since it rests in how feminist political economists have understood, debated and, at some level, left unresolved the relationship between sex, sexuality, gender and race and "production," a neglected history of scholarship requiring reconsideration.

Beyond the Recognition-Redistribution Dilemma: Towards a Renewed Understanding of Feminist Political Economy

How might the feminist political economy scholarship advance prevailing debates over the "politics of recognition" and the "politics of redistribution" as well as other central challenges currently confronting feminist theorists? How could feminist political economists move this debate in contemporary feminist theory in a direction that promotes a return to theorizing at all levels of analysis, while avoiding the narrow economism still pervasive in much of the political economy literature? In light of feminist theorists' recent calls to early feminist political economy, how might greater interaction between feminist political economists and feminist theorists expand and reinvigorate debates in feminist political economy?

From a feminist political economy perspective, the critical feature of recent debates over Fraser's recognition-redistribution dilemma among Butler, Fraser, Phillips and Young is that this enduring disagreement around social justice rests upon a prior understanding of the processes of social reproduction. The arguments of each scholar in some way invoke a supply-side insight central to feminist political economy. This insight is that what is distinct about capitalism is that it depends on the production of workers outside the "productive" or "surplus" system — that social reproduction is central to the political economy, whether it is achieved through a sex/gender division of labour based on women's unpaid domestic labour and rooted in the heterosexual nuclear family form or, as is true for immigrants, an international division of labour reliant primarily on resources (including women's unpaid domestic labour) from a sending country.[56] Hence, many struggles for gender equality as well as many struggles against racism and heterosexism, are, by definition, struggles for redistribution. For example, Fraser and Butler both conceptualize class broadly enough to view redistribution as critical to redressing inequalities among women and racialized groups as well as, for Butler, among "despised sexualities." Again, following Gilroy and Hall, even Butler emphasizes that race is one way in which class is lived and she adds that sexuality is another. Still, evident in this conception of class are its deep-rooted narrow association with production for surplus and its much weaker association with social reproduction. Fraser and Butler, as well as Young, Phillips and others, thus understand that redistribution is a necessary remedy for advancing the struggles of women and racialized groups. But all four scholars effectively (although not self-consciously) call on feminist theorists to take social reproduction more seriously without sufficient elaboration of the contested and ever-expanding meaning of this dimension of production and other concepts, such as "the family," linked to it.

Many claims made by both Fraser and Butler rest on early insights in feminist political economy — several evolving from discussions led by Canadian scholars — about the significance of social reproduction. Still, their common acknowledgement of its importance comes from differing (even divergent) views of the relationship between accumulation and family formation. One view emphasizes the role of ideological and discursive processes; Butler, in this case, follows socialist feminists influenced by psychoanalysis like Gayle Rubin and, more recently, Michelle Barrett. Another view highlights the centrality of material processes like child-bearing; Fraser, in this case, ultimately follows the tradition of feminists influenced by historical materialists, although her kinship with historical materialism is weak. At the root of the disagreement between Fraser, Butler and other parties in this debate, therefore, are differences over causality and levels of analysis that pervaded the first and second phases of feminist political economy in Canada and beyond. Yet key differences over causality have yet to be revisited by feminist political economists. Nor has recent work on racialization, sexuality and intersectionality more generally been linked sufficiently to these debates.

There is a pressing need, therefore, for feminist scholars working in the field of political economy to draw on the wide range of applied research and new directions in theorizing pursued in the last few decades and revisit questions related to social reproduction at all levels of abstraction. Feminist political economists in Canada are in a strong position to pursue this agenda given our influence on political economy analysis and given our many contributions to the expansion of feminist theory evident in the four overlapping phases of the scholarship since the 1970s.

Notes

1. The author gratefully acknowledges the Canada Research Chair Programme of the Canadian Federal Government and the Social Sciences and Humanities Research Council Standard Grant Programme for their generous financial support. This chapter has benefited from comments from Greg Albo, Caroline Andrew, Pat Armstrong, Hugh Armstrong, Kate Bezanson, Linda Briskin, Wallace Clement, Judy Fudge, Gerald Kernerman, Rianne Mahon and Joan Sangster.
2. Nancy Fraser, *Justice Interruptus: Critical Reflections on the "Post-Socialist Condition* (New York: Routledge, 1997), 15.
3. To be clear, my aim is not to undertake a comprehensive review of the literature in Part One.
4. This objective entails preventing political economy from returning to a narrow economism that treats gender and race relations as an adjunct to class relations rather than as integral to them at all levels of abstraction.
5. Pat Armstrong and Hugh Armstrong, "Beyond a Sexless Class: Towards Marxist Feminism," *Studies in Political Economy* 10 (1983).
6. Meg Luxton, *More Than a Labour of Love* (Toronto: The Women's Press, 1980); Meg Luxton, "Two Hands on the Clock," *Studies in Political Economy* 12 (1983), 27–44.
7. Bonnie Fox (ed.), *Hidden in the Household* (Toronto: Women's Press, 1980).
8. Michelle Barrett's work was highly influential among this grouping of scholars. See Michelle Barrett, *Women's Oppression Today: The Marxist-Feminist Encounter* (London: Verso Press, 1987). However, in the Canadian context, the collection *The Politics of Diversity* also paid a pivotal role in elevating discussions about ideology. See Roberta Hamilton and Michelle Barrett (eds.) *The Politics of Diversity: Feminism, Marxism and Nationalism* (Montreal: Book Center Inc., 1986).
9. Scholars belonging to this grouping owe a debt to Joan Acker since her contributions in this period cultivated an understanding of how relations of distribution shape gendered class relations.

    According to Acker, political economists (including feminists) tend to prioritize relations of production over relations of distribution and this limits the scope of a gender-integrated analysis of class. Since relations of distribution encourage women's dependence on men — through capitalist wage-relations, the ideology of the family wage and the creation of the state as "absent father" in households without a male wage — Acker argues that they vitally affect women's location within the class structure and hence shape the third department of production. See especially Joan Acker, "Gender, Class and Relations of Distribution," *Signs: Journal of Women Culture and Society* 13/3 (1988), 473–495.
10. Armstrong and Armstrong, "Beyond a Sexless Class," 7.
11. M. Patricia Connelly, "On Marxism and Feminism," *Studies in Political Economy* 12 (1983), 155.
12. Ibid., 153–161.
13. Ibid., 156.
14. Linda Briskin, "Socialist Feminism: From the Standpoint of Practice," *Studies in Political Economy* 30 (1989), 87–114; Meg Luxton and Heather Jon Maroney,

Feminism and Political Economy: Women's Work, Women's Struggles (Toronto: University of Toronto Press, 1987); Martha MacDonald, "Economics: The Dismal Science," *Studies in Political Economy* 15 (1984), 151–183; Marilyn Porter, "Peripheral Women: Towards a Feminist Analysis of the Atlantic Region," *Studies in Political Economy* 23 (1987), 41–71; Ester Reiter, *Making Fast Food: From the Frying Pan into the Fire* (Montreal: McGill-Queen's University Press, 1991).

15. Jane Jenson, "Gender and Reproduction or Babies and the State," *Studies in Political Economy* 20 (1986), 9–46.

16. Ibid., 14.

17. Ibid., 24.

18. Ruth A. Frager, "Class and Ethnic Barriers to Feminist Perspectives in Toronto's Jewish Labour Movement, 1919–1939," *Studies in Political Economy* 30 (1989), 143–166.

19. Sedef Arat-Koc, "In the Privacy of Our Home: Foreign Domestic Workers as a Solution to the Crisis of the Domestic Sphere in Canada," in Pat Armstrong and Patricia Connelly (eds.), *Feminism in Action* (Ottawa: Carleton University Press, 1987).

20. See, for example, Chandra Mohanty, Ann Russo and Lourdes Torres (eds.), *Third World Women and the Politics of Feminism* (Bloomington: Indiana University Press, 1991).

21. Gillian Creese and Daiva Stasiulus, *Studies in Political Economy* Special Issue "Intersections of Gender, Race and Class" 51 (1996), 6.

22. Ibid.

23. Rhada Jhappan, "Post-Modern Race and Gender Essentialism or a Post-Mortem of Scholarship," *Studies in Political Economy* 51 (1996), 15–64.

24. Tania Das Gupta, "Anti-Black Racism in Nursing in Ontario," *Studies in Political Economy* 51 (1996), 97–116.

25. Gillian Creese and Laurie Peterson, "Making the News, Racialized in Chinese Canadians," *Studies in Political Economy* 51 (1996), 117–146; Wenona Giles and Valerie Preston, "The Domestification of Women's Work: A Comparison of Chinese and Portuguese Immigrant Women Homeworkers," *Studies in Political Economy* 51 (1996), 147–182.

26. See Caroline Andrew, "Ethnicities, Citizenship and Feminisms: Theorizing the Political Practices of Intersectionality," in Jean Laponce and William Safran (eds.), *Ethnicity and Citizenship: The Canadian Case* (London: Frank Cass, 1996), 64–81; Abigail Bakan and Daiva Stasiulus, *Not One in the Family* (Toronto: University of Toronto Press, 1998); Himani Bannerji, "But Who Speaks for Us? Experience and Agency in Conventional Feminist Paradigms," in Himani Bannerji et al. (eds.), *Unsettling Relations: The University as a Site of Feminist Struggles* (Toronto: Women's Press, 1991), 67–81; Daiva Stasiulus, "The Political Economy of Race, Ethnicity and Migration," in Wallace Clement (ed.), *Understanding Canada: Building on the New Canadian Political Economy* (Montreal and Kingston: McGill-Queen's University Press, 1997), 141–171; Daiva Stasiulus, "Feminist Intersectional Theorizing," in Peter S. Li (ed.), *Race and Ethnic Relations in Canada*, 2nd ed. (Toronto: Oxford University Press, 1999), 347–398.

27. Still, with a few notable exceptions, Canadian feminist political economists advancing this strain have yet to extend sufficiently intersectional theorizing to struggles related to sexuality, a significant weakness. See, for example, Becki L. Ross, "Bumping and Grinding on the Line: Making Nudity Pay," *Labour/Le Travail* 46 (Fall 2000), 221–250.

28. See, for example, Lois Harder, "Depoliticizing Insurgency: The Politics of the Family in Alberta," *Studies in Political Economy* 50 (1996), 37–64; Meg Luxton and Leah F. Vosko, "Where Women's Efforts Count: The 1996 Census Campaign and 'Family Politics' in Canada," *Studies in Political Economy* 56 (1998), 43–82; Katherine Scott, "The Dilemmas of Liberal Citizenship: Women and Social Assistance Reform in the 1990s," *Studies in Political Economy* 50 (1996), 1–36; Katherine Teghtsoonian, "Gendering Policy Analysis in the Government of British Columbia: Strategies, Possibilities and Constraints," *Studies in Political Economy* 61 (2000), 105–127.

29. Isabella Bakker (ed.), *Rethinking Restructuring: Gender and Change in Canada* (Toronto: University of Toronto Press, 1996), 7.

30. A case in point is Barbara Cameron's study of gender and training policy, which highlights the uneven and contradictory effects of the federal government's equity policy in the Canadian Job Strategy (CJS). In her examination of training, Cameron illustrates how the CJS gave women greater access to federal training programs, on the one hand, but concentrated them in low-skilled jobs, on the other. Barbara Cameron, "From Equal Opportunity to Symbolic Equality: Three Decades of Federal Training Policy for Women," in Isabella Bakker (ed.), *Rethinking Restructuring: Gender and Change in Canada* (Toronto: University of Toronto Press, 1996), 55–81.

31. Janine Brodie, "Meso-Discourses, State Forms and the Gendering of Liberal-Democratic Citizenship," *Citizenship Studies* 1, 2 (1997), 223–242; Janine Brodie, *Politics on the Margins: Restructuring and the Canadian Women's Movement* (Halifax: Fernwood, 1995); Janine Brodie, *Politics on the Boundaries: Restructuring and the Canadian Women's Movement* (Toronto: Robarts Centre for Canadian Studies, 1994); Janine Brodie, "Restructuring and the New Citizenship," in Isabella Bakker (ed.), *Rethinking Restructuring: Gender and Change in Canada* (Toronto: University of Toronto Press, 1996), 126–141.

32. Marjorie Cohen, "New International Trade Agreements: Their Reactionary Role in Creating Markets and Retarding Social Welfare," in Isabella Bakker (ed.), *Rethinking Restructuring: Gender and Change in Canada* (Toronto: University of Toronto Press, 1996), 187–202.

33. Yasmeen Abu-Laban, "Keeping 'em Out: Gender, Race, and Class Biases in Canadian Immigration Policy," in Sherrill Grace, Veronica Strong-Boag, Joan Anderson and Avigail Eisenberg, *Painting the Maple* (Vancouver: UBC Press, 1998), 69–84; Fiona Williams, "Race/Ethnicity, Gender and Class in Welfare States: A Framework for Comparative Analysis," *Social Politics* (Summer 1995), 127–159; Fiona Williams, "Reflections on the Intersections of Social Relations in the New Political Economy," *Studies in Political Economy* 55 (Spring 1998), 173–190.

34. See Susan B. Boyd (ed.), *Challenging the Public/Private Divide: Feminism, Law and Public Policy* (Toronto: University of Toronto Press, 1997); Elizabeth Comack (ed.), *Locating the Law: Race/Class/Gender* (Halifax: Fernwood, 1999); Judy Fudge and Brenda Cossman, "Introduction: Feminist Privatization and the Law," in Brenda Cossman and Judy Fudge (eds.), *Privatization, Law, and the Challenge to Feminism* (Toronto: University of Toronto Press, 2002).

35. Brodie, "Meso-Discourses," 224.

36. I include much of my own scholarship in this category. See Meg Luxton and Leah F. Vosko, "Where Women's Efforts Count: The 1996 Census Campaign and 'Family Politics' in Canada," *Studies in Political Economy* 56 (1998), 43–82; Leah F. Vosko, "*Irregular* Workers, *New* Involuntary Social Exiles: Women and UI Reform," in Jane Pulkingham and Gordon Ternowetsky (eds.), *Remaking Canadian Social Policy: Social Security in the Late 1990s* (Toronto: Fernwood Press, 1996), 265; Leah F. Vosko, "Recreating Dependency: Women and UI Reform," in Daniel Drache and Andrew Ranikin (eds.), *Warm Heart, Cold Country* (Toronto: Caledon Press, 1995), 213.

37. The work of Iris Marion Young epitomizes the nature of early scholarship following this trajectory. See, for example, *Justice and the Politics of Difference* (Princeton: Princeton University Press, 1990). However, by the late 1980s, a sizable group of feminist scholars branched off and began to engage in discourse analysis. See, for example, Judith Butler, *Gender Trouble* (New York: Routledge, 1990).

38. Works by Chandra Mohanty in the United States and Abigail Bakan, Daiva Stasiulus and Roxana Ng in Canada fall into this broad category. See Chandra Mohanty, Ann Russo and Lourdes Torres (eds.), *Third World Women and the Politics of Feminism* (Bloomington: Indiana University Press, 1991); Abigail Bakan and Daiva Stasiulus (eds.), *Not One of the Family* (Toronto: University of Toronto Press, 1997).

39. Nancy Fraser, "From Redistribution to Recognition? Dilemmas of Justice in a 'Post-Socialist' Age," *New Left Review* 22 (1995), 68–93.

40. Fraser has been criticized for her Weberian approach, especially by socialist feminists, yet she defends it to the present by clarifying how she understands class and its relationship to recognition. For example, in her most recent intervention in this debate, entitled "Rethinking Recognition," Fraser defends her Weberian typology as a route towards a transformative deconstructive critical theory of recognition and argues further that Weberian and Marxian concepts and approaches are not necessarily incompatible. Regarding the notion of class, she notes that:

> This Weberian conception of class as an *economic* category suits my interest in distribution as a normative dimension of justice better than the Marxian conception of class as a *social* category. Nevertheless, I do not mean to reject the Marxian idea of the "capitalist mode of production" as a social totality. On the contrary, I find that idea useful as an overarching frame within which we can situate Weberian understandings of both status and class. Thus, I reject the standard view of Marx and Weber as antithetical and irreconcilable thinkers.

Nancy Fraser, "Rethinking Recognition," *New Left Review* 3 (2000), 117.

41. Fraser, "From Redistribution to Recognition?" 69.

42. Ibid., 72.

43. Nancy Fraser, *Justice Interruptus* (Princeton: Princeton University Press, 1998), 18–19, emphasis added.

44. Iris Marion Young, "Unruly Categories: A Critique of Nancy Fraser's Dual System Theory," *New Left Review* 22 (1997), 147.

In response, Fraser depicts Young as creating a range of categories of struggle and misreading and conflating her three levels of analysis — the philosophical, the social-theoretical and the political. She also labels Young's critique as a "brief for the politics of affirmative recognition" (see Nancy Fraser, "A Rejoinder to Iris Young," *New Left Review* 223 (1997), 127, 129). Ironically, however, other feminist scholars like Rosemary Hennessy criticize Fraser for failing to address sufficiently the connections between relations of production and identity and, therefore, ultimately advocating a pluralistic vision in which class is conceived as largely a cultural category.

45. Anne Phillips, "From Inequality to Difference: A Severe Case of Displacement?" *New Left Review* 224 (1997), 143–153.

46. Judith Butler, "Merely Cultural," *New Left Review* 227 (1998), 33–44.

47. Ibid., 39.

48. Ibid.

49. In describing the evolution of feminist critiques of orthodox understandings of class, Phillips notes that:

> Much feminist work in the 1970s, for example, continued to work within a framework derived from Marx, building on his insights even while addressing his blind spots about women's oppression. Class was not so much "displaced as retheorized in its racialized and gendered complexity, while those who adopted a "dual systems" approach to sexual and class oppression typically developed their theories of patriarchal relations on a model derived from the analysis of class. *Such initiatives proved rather short-lived, however, and rapidly developed into a deeper questioning of the primacy attached to political economy per se. It was not just the domination of class that had to be questioned. It was also the underlying hierarchy of causation that had distinguished an economic base from a political and cultural superstructure, or defined "real" interests through location in economic relations* [emphasis added].

My review of the second and third stages of the feminist political economy scholarship in Canada, where debates over causation raged in 1980s, reveals that Phillips's depiction of the shift among feminist scholars towards *questioning* political economy to be only partial. Rather than "questioning the primacy of *political economy*" in this period, many feminist scholars chose to continue to theorize political economy broadly and to continue to reject its malestream variants.

50. Butler, "Merely Cultural," 41.

51. Fraser, "Rethinking Recognition," 119.

52. Notably, in this article, Fraser acknowledges the danger, raised by her critics, that a narrow pursuit of the "politics of recognition" may generate two problems — the

problems of reification and the problem of displacement. Yet her response to this danger is that "everything depends on how recognition is approached" (Fraser 2000, 109). Fraser thus suggests that progressive groups rethink the politics of recognition such that it is integrated with struggles for redistribution. She argues further that the ideal route towards integration involves bringing a Weberian notion of class as an economic category (i.e., status) and a Marxian notion of class as a social relation together.

Fraser's view is that "vulgar Marxism once allowed the politics of redistribution to displace the politics of recognition" and "vulgar culturalism is no more adequate for understanding contemporary society than vulgar economism was" (Fraser 2000, 111). Thus, while she adds complexity to her dichotomous characterization by suggesting that misrecognition is partly about "status subordination," Fraser is ultimately unwilling to breakdown the recognition-redistribution dilemma, let alone move beyond it by drawing on the insights of feminist political economy.

53. Nancy Fraser, "Heterosexism, Misrecognition and Capitalism: A Response to Judith Butler," *New Left Review* 228 (1998), 145.

54. Ibid., 145.

55. Ibid., 146.

56. For a rigorous discussion developing this supply-side insight based on the British case, see Antonella Picchio, *Social Reproduction: The Political Economy of the Labour Market* (Cambridge, UK: Cambridge University Press, 1992).

References

Abel, E.K. 1991. *Who Cares for the Elderly? Pubic Policy and the Experiences of Adult Daughters*. Philadelphia: Temple University Press.

Abramovitz, Mimi. 1989. *Regulating the Lives of Women: Social Welfare Policy from Colonial Times to the Present*. Boston: South End Press.

Abramowitz, M. and V. Eliasberg. 1957. *The Growth of Public Employment in Britain*. Princeton.

Abu-Laban, Yasmeen. 1998. "Keeping 'em Out: Gender, Race, and Class Biases in Canadian Immigration Policy." In *Painting the Maple*, edited by Sherrill Grace, Veronica Strong-Boag, Joan Anderson and Avigail Eisenberg. Vancouver: UBC Press.

Acker, Joan. 1988. "Gender, Class and Relations of Distribution." *Signs: Journal of Women Culture and Society* 13(3).

Adam, E. 1991. *To Be a Nurse*, 2nd ed. New York: W.B. Saunders.

Adkin, Laurie. 1995. "Life in Kleinland: Democratic Resistance to Folksy Fascism." *Canadian Dimension* 25 (April–May).

Albers, Jen. 1982. *Von Armenhaus zum Wohlfahrtsstaat*. Frankfurt and New York.

Alberta Legislative Assembly. 1992. *Debates* (June 29).

_____. 1995a. *Debates* (March 1).

_____. 1995b. *Debates* (March 27).

Allen, Sheila and Carol Wolkowitz. 1986. "Homeworking and the Control of Women's Work: in Feminist Review." In *Waged Work: A Reader*, edited by Sheila Allen and Carol Wolkowitz. London: Virago Press.

Amott, Teresa. 1993. *Caught in the Crisis: Women and the U.S. Economy Today*. New York: Basic Books.

Amott, Teresa and Julie Matthaei. 1991. *Race, Gender, and Work*. Montreal: Black Rose Books.

333

Andrew, Caroline. 1996. "Ethnicities, Citizenship and Feminisms: Theorizing the Political Practices of Intersectionality." In *Ethnicity and Citizenship: The Canadian Case*, edited by Jean Laponce and William Safran. London: Frank Cass.

Applebaum, A. 1987. "Technology and the Redesign of Work in the Insurance Industry." In *Women, Work and Technology*, edited by B.D. Wright, M.F. Ferree, G. Mellow, L. Lewis, M.D. Samper, R. Asher and K. Claspell. Ann Arbor: University of Michigan Press.

Arat-Koc, Sedef. 1987. "In the Privacy of Our Home: Foreign Domestic Workers As a Solution to the Crisis of the Domestic Sphere in Canada." In *Feminism in Action*, edited by Pat Armstrong and Patricia Connelly. Ottawa: Carleton University Press.

_____. 1990. "Importing Housewives: Non-Citizen Domestic Workers and the Crisis of the Domestic Sphere in Canada." In *Through the Kitchen Window: The Politics of Home and Family*, edited by M. Luxton, H. Rosenberg and S. Arat-Koc. Toronto: Garamond Press.

Arbeidersporgsmalet og Landarbeiderorganisationen 1864 til 1900. 1983. Copenhagen.

Armstrong, Pat. 1988. "Where Have All the Nurses Gone?" *Healthsharing* (Summer).

_____. 1994. "Closer to Home: More Work for Women." In *Take Care: Warning Signals for Canada's Health Care System*, edited by P. Armstrong, J. Choiniere, G. Feldberg and J. White. Toronto: Garamond.

_____. 1996. "The Feminization of the Labour Force: Harmonizing Down in a Global Economy." In *Rethinking Restructuring: Gender and Change in Canada*, edited by I. Bakker. Toronto: University of Toronto Press.

Armstrong, Pat and Hugh Armstrong. 1983. "Beyond a Sexless Class: Towards Marxist Feminism." *Studies in Political Economy* 10.

_____. 1994. *The Double Ghetto: Canadian Women and Their Segregated Work*, 3rd ed. Toronto: McClelland and Stewart.

Aronson, J. 1990. "Old Women's Experiences of Needing Care: Choice or Compulsion?" *Canadian Journal on Aging* 9.

_____. 1992a. "Are We Really Listening? Beyond the Official Discourse on Needs of Old People." *Canadian Social Work Review* 9.

_____. 1992b. "Women's Sense of Responsibility for the Care of Old People: 'But Who Else Is Going to Do It?'" *Gender & Society* 6.

_____. 1993. "Giving Consumers a Say in Policy Development: Influencing Policy or Just Being Heard?" *Canadian Public Policy* XIX.

Aronson, J. and S. Neysmith. 1996. "'You're Not Just in There to Do the Work': Depersonalizing Policies and the Exploitation of Home Care Workers' Labour." *Gender & Society* 10.

ASWAC to Mary LeMessurier. January 5, 1982. Women's Secretariat Documents, Provincial Archives of Alberta, Edmonton.

Atkinson, J. 1988. "Recent Changes in the International Labour Market Structure in the UK." In *Technology and Work*, edited by W. Buitelaar. Aldershot: Avebury.

Badgely, R. 1975. "Health Workers Strike," *International Journal of Health Services* 5(1).

Baehre, Rainer. 1980. "Victorian Psychiatry and Canadian Motherhood." *Canadian Women's Studies* 2(1).

Baines, C.T., P.M. Evans and S.M. Neysmith. 1991. *Women's Caring: Feminist Perspectives on Social Welfare*. Toronto: McClelland and Stewart.

Bakan, Abigail and Daiva Stasiulus (eds.). 1997. *Not One of the Family*. Toronto: University of Toronto Press.

Bakker, Isabella. 1994. "Engendering Macro-economic Policy Reform in the Era of Global Restructuring and Adjustment." In *The Strategic Silence: Gender and Economic Policy*, edited by Isabella Bakker. London: Zed Books.

_____. 1996. *Rethinking Restructuring: Gender and Change in Canada*. Toronto: University of Toronto Press.

Baldock, J. and C. Ungerson. 1993. "Consumer Perceptions of an Emerging Mixed Economy of Care." In *Balancing Pluralism: New Welfare Mixes in Care for the Elderly*, edited by A. Evers and I. Svetlik. Aldershot: Avebury.

Bannerji, Himani. 1991. "But Who Speaks for Us? Experience and Agency in Conventional Feminist Paradigms." In *Unsettling Relations: The University As a Site of Feminist Struggles*, edited by Himani Bannerji et al. Toronto: Women's Press.

Baran, A. and S. Teegarden. 1987. "Women's Labor in the Office of the Future: A Case Study of the Insurance Industry." In *Women, Households and the Economy*, edited by L. Beneria and C. Stimpson. New Brunswick, NJ: Rutgers University Press.

Barnsley, J. 1985. *Feminist Action, Institutional Reaction: Responses to Wife Assault*. Vancouver: Women's Research Centre.

Barrett, Michelle. 1987. *Women's Oppression Today: The Marxist-Feminist Encounter*. London: Verso Press.

Barrett, Michelle and Mary McIntosh. 1982. *The Anti-Social Family*. London: Verso Editions.

_____. 1991. *The Anti-Social Family*, 2nd ed. London: Verso.

Bauer, C. and L. Ritt. 1983. "'A Husband Is a Beating Animal': Frances Power Cobbe Confronts the Wife Abuse Problem in Victorian England." *International Journal on Women's Studies* 6(2).

_____. 1983b. "Wife Abuse, Late Victorian English Feminists, and the Legacy of Frances Power Cobbe." *International Journal of Women's Studies* 6(3).

Beaudry, M. 1985. *Battered Women*, translated by L. Houston and M. Heap. Montreal: Black Rose Books.

Beschlüsse des Parteitages des sozialdemokratischen Partei österreichs zu Painfeld ... ergänst am Parteitag zu Wein. 1982. Reprinted in *Kleine Bibliothek des Wissens und des Fortschritts*. Frankfurt.

Beechey, V. 1987. "Conceptualizing Part-Time Work." In *Unequal Work*, edited by V. Beechey. London: Verso.

Benston, Margaret. 1971. "The Political Economy of Women's Liberation." In *Voices from Women's Liberation*, edited by Leslie Tanner. New York: New American Library.

Berban, T. and G. Janssen. 1982. "Vakbeweging en sociale zekerheid in Nederland na 1945." M.A. thesis, Institute for Political Science, Catholic University, Nijmegen, Netherlands.

Bergthold, L.A., C.L. Estes and A. Villanueva. 1990. "Public Light and Private Dark: The Privatization of Home Health Services for the Elderly in the United States." *Home Health Care Services Quarterly* 11.

Bertolt, O. et al. n.d. *En bygning vi rejser.* Copenhagen.

Betcherman, G., K. McMullen, N. Leckie and C. Caron. 1994. *The Canadian Workplace in Transition.* Kingston: Queen's University, Industrial Relations Centre.

Boehm, J. 1988. "Letter." *Edmonton Journal* (February 13):B1.

Borowy, Jan. 1996. "Super Fitness, Super Scam." *Our Times* 15(2).

Borowy, Jan and Fanny Yuen. 1993. *The International Ladies Garment Workers' Union 1993 Homeworkers' Study: An Investigation into Wages and Working Conditions of Chinese-Speaking Homeworkers in Metropolitan Toronto.* Toronto: ILGWU.

Bottomley, Gill. 1991. "Representing the 'Second Generation': Subjects, Objects and Ways of Knowing." In *Intersexions: Gender, Class, Culture and Ethnicity,* edited by G. Bottomley, M. de Lepervanche and J. Martin (eds.). Sydney: Allen and Unwin.

_____. 1995. "Living Across Difference: Connecting Gender, Ethnicity, Class and Ageing in Australia." Paper presented to the Workshops on the Political Economy of Marriage and the Family, York University. November.

Bottomley, Gill and Marie de Lepervanche (eds.). 1984. *Ethnicity, Class and Gender in Australia.* Sydney: Allen and Unwin.

Bowers, B. 1990. "Family Perceptions of Care in a Nursing Home." In *Circles of Care: Work and Identity in Women's Lives,* edited by E. Abel and M. Nelson. New York: SUNY Press.

Boyd, Monica. 1990. "Immigrant Women: Language, Socioeconomic Inequalities and Policy Issues." In *Ethnic Demography, Canadian Immigrant, Racial and Cultural Variations,* edited by S.S. Halli, F. Trovato and L. Dreidger. Ottawa: Carleton University Press.

_____. 1992. "Gender, Visible Minority and Immigrant Earnings Inequality: Reassessing an Employment Equity Premise." In *Deconstructing a Nation: Immigration, Multiculturalism and Racism in the '90s in Canada,* edited by V. Satzewich. Toronto: Fernwood Press.

Boyd, Susan B. (ed.). 1997. *Challenging the Public/Private Divide: Feminism, Law and Public Policy.* Toronto: University of Toronto Press.

Braverman, Harry. 1974. *Labor and Monopoly Capital.* New York: Monthly Review Press.

Briskin, Linda. 1989. "Socialist Feminism: From the Standpoint of Practice." *Studies in Political Economy* 30.

Brodie, Janine. 1994. *Politics on the Boundaries: Restructuring and the Canadian Women's Movement.* Toronto: Robarts Centre for Canadian Studies.

_____. 1995. *Politics on the Margins: Restructuring and the Canadian Women's Movement.* Halifax: Fernwood.

_____. 1996. "Restructuring and the New Citizenship." In *Rethinking Restructuring: Gender and Change in Canada,* edited by Isabella Bakker. Toronto: University of Toronto Press.

_____. 1997. "Meso-Discourses, State Forms and the Gendering of Liberal-Democratic Citizenship." *Citizenship Studies* 1(2).

Brown, C.A. 1975. "Women Workers in the Health Service Industry." *International Journal of Health Services* 5(1).

Brown, C. 1981. "Mothers, Fathers and Children: From Private to Public Patriarchy." In *Women and Revolution: A Discussion of the Unhappy Marriage of Marxism and Feminism*, edited by L. Sargent. Montreal: Black Rose Books.

Brown, H. and H. Smith. 1993. "Women Caring for People: The Mismatch Between Rhetoric and Women's Reality?" *Policy and Politics* 21.

Buckley, Suzann. 1979. "Ladies or Midwives? Efforts to Reduce Infant and Maternal Mortality." In *A Not Unreasonable Claim*, edited by Linda Kealey. Toronto: Women's Press.

Bulmer, M. 1987. *The Social Basis of Community Care*. London: Allen and Unwin.

Burgess, Jacquelin. 1990. "The Production and Consumption of Environmental Meanings in the Mass Media: A Research Agenda for the 1990s." *Transactions of the Institute of British Geographers* 15(2).

Burawoy, Michael. 1979. *Manufacturing Consent*. Chicago: University of Chicago Press.

_____. 1985. *The Politics of Production*. London: Verso.

Burstyn, Varda. "Masculine Dominance and the State." 1986. In *Women, Class, Family and the State*, edited by Varda Burstyn and Dorothy E. Smith. Toronto: Garamond Press.

Butler, Judith. 1990. *Gender Trouble*. New York: Routledge.

_____. 1998. "Merely Cultural." *New Left Review* 227.

Cameron, Barbara. 1996. "From Equal Opportunity to Symbolic Equality: Three Decades of Federal Training Policy for Women." In *Rethinking Restructuring: Gender and Change in Canada*, edited by Isabella Bakker. Toronto: University of Toronto Press.

Cameron, Barbara and Teresa Mak. 1991. "Chinese Speaking Homeworkers in Toronto: Summary of Results of a Survey Conducted by the ILGWU." Toronto: ILGWU.

Campbell, M. 1987. "The Structure of Stress in Nurses' Work." In *Health and Canadian Society: Sociological Perspectives*, edited by D. Coburn. Markham: Fitzhenry and Whiteside.

_____. 1988. "Management As 'Ruling': A Class Phenomenon in Nursing." *Studies in Political Economy* 27 (Autumn).

Canada, House of Commons, Standing Committee on Health, Welfare and Social Affairs. 1982a. *Minutes of Proceedings — Hansard*. Nos. 24–29.

_____. 1982b. *Report on Violence in the Family: Wife Battering*. Ottawa.

Canada, Treasury Board. 1992. *Telework Policy*.

Carpenter, M. 1994. *Normality Is Hard Work: Trade Unions and the Politics of Community Care*. London: Lawrence and Wishart.

Carter, V. 1987. "Office Technology and Relations of Control in Clerical Work Organizations." In *Women, Work and Technology*, edited by B.D. Wright et al. Ann Arbor: University of Michigan Press.

Cashman and Others v. Central Regional Health Authority. Employment Court Wellington Registry, WEC3/96, W119/95.

Castells, Manuel and A. Portes. 1989. "World Underneath: The Origins, Dynamics and Effects of the Informal Economy." In *The Informal Economy: Studies in Advanced* and Less Developed Countries, edited by A. Portes, M. Castells and L.A. Benton. Baltimore and London: Johns Hopkins University Press.

Castles, Francis. 1982. The Impact of Parties. London.

Chappell, N.L., L.A. Strain and A.A. Blandford. 1986. Aging and Health Care: A Social Perspective. Toronto: Holt, Rinehart and Winston.

Chichin, E.R. and M.H. Kantor. 1992. "The Home Care Industry: Strategies for Survival in an Era of Dwindling Resources." Journal of Aging and Social Policy 4.

Chouinard, Vera and Ruth Fincher. 1987. "State Formation in Capitalist Societies: A Conjunctural Approach." Antipode 19(3).

Chouinard Vera and Pamela Moss. 1992. "Gender and Class Formation in Waged Domestic Labour Processes and the State." Paper presented to a special session on "The Politics of the Local State: Production, Consumption and Labour Process in Britain and North America,"Annual Conference of the Association of American Geographers, San Diego, California. April.

Christensen, Kathleen. 1988a. Testimony before the Employment and Housing Subcommittee, Committee on Government Operations, U.S. House of Representatives, Washington, D.C.

_____. 1988b. The New Era of Home-Based Work. Boulder: Westview Press.

_____. 1992. Presentation to "A Conference on Homeworking: From the Double Day to the Endless Day," Regis College, Toronto, November 13–15.

Christopherson, Susan. 1989. "Flexibility in the U.S. Service Economy and the Emerging Spatial Division of Labour." Transactions Institute of British Geographers 14.

Clement, Wallace and John Myles. 1994. Relations of Ruling: Class and Gender in Postindustrial Societies. Montreal: McGill-Queen's University Press.

Cockburn, Cynthia. 1983. Brothers. London: Pluto.

_____. 1985. Machinery of Dominance. Boston: Northwestern University Press.

Cohen, Marjorie Griffin. 1985. "The MacDonald Report and Its Implications for Women." Toronto: National Action Committee on the Status of Women.

_____. 1987. Free Trade and the Future of Women's Work: Manufacturing and Service Industries. Toronto: Garamond Press.

_____. 1994. "The Implications of Economic Restructuring for Women: The Canadian Situation." In The Strategic Silence: Gender and Economic Policy, edited by Isabella Bakker. London: Zed Books.

_____. 1996. "New International Trade Agreements: Their Reactionary Role in Creating Markets and Retarding Social Welfare." In Rethinking Restructuring: Gender and Change in Canada, edited by Isabella Bakker. Toronto: University of Toronto Press.

Cohen, Sheila. 1987. "A Labour Process to Nowhere?" New Left Review 165.

Comack, Elizabeth (ed.). 1999. Locating the Law: Race/Class/Gender. Halifax: Fernwood.

Conference Handbook Committee (CHC). 1992. From the Double Day to the Endless Day. Proceedings from the Conference on Homeworking, Ottawa: Canadian Centre for Policy Alternatives.

Connelly, Patricia. 1978. Last Hired, First Fired. Toronto: Women's Educational Press.

_____. 1982. "Women's Work and Family Wage in Canada." In Women and the World of Work, edited by Anne Hoiberg. New York: Plenum Press.

_____. 1983. "On Marxism and Feminism." *Studies in Political Economy* 12.

Connelly, Patricia and Martha MacDonald. 1993. "Women's Work: Domestic and Wage Labour in a Nova Scotia Community." *Studies in Political Economy* 10 (Winter).

Cooper, D.J. and D. Neu. 1995. "The Politics of Debt and Deficit in Alberta." In *The Trojan Horse: Alberta and the Future of Canada*, edited by G. Laxer and T. Harrison. Montreal: Black Rose.

Corrigan, P., H. Ramsey and D. Saver. 1978. *Socialist Construction and Marxist Theory*. London: Macmillan.

Coulson, Margaret , Bianka Magas and Hilary Wainwright. 1975. "The Housewife and Her Labour under Capitalism — A Critique." *New Left Review* 89.

Cox, Kevin and Andrew Mair. 1988. "Locality and Community in the Politics of Local Economic Development." *Annals of the Association of American Geographers* 78.

Creese, Gillian and Laurie Peterson. 1996. "Making the News, Racialized in Chinese Canadians." *Studies in Political Economy* 51.

Creese, Gillian and Daiva Stasiulus. 1996. "Intersections of Gender, Race and Class." *Studies in Political Economy* 51 (Special Issue).

Crompton, R. and G. Jones. 1984. *White-Collar Proletariat*. London: MacMillan Press.

Crompton, Rosemary and Kay Sanderson. 1990. *Gendered Jobs and Social Change*. London: Unwin Hyman.

Crown, W., M. McAdam and E. Sadowsky. 1992. *Caring* (April).

Cunnison, S. 1986. "Gender, Consent and Exploitation Among Sheltered Housing Wardens." In *The Changing Experience of Employment: Restructuring and Recession*, edited by K. Purcell, S. Wood, A. Waton and S. Allen. London: MacMillan.

Currie, Andrea. 1989. "A Roof Is Not Enough: Feminism, Transition Houses and the Battle Against Abuse." *New Maritimes* (September/October).

Daatland, S. 1990. "What Are Families For? On Family Solidarity and Preference for Help." *Ageing and Society* 10.

_____. 1994. "Recent Trends and Future Prospects for the Elderly in Scandinavia." *Journal of Aging and Social Policy* 6.

Dacks, Gurston, Joyce Green and Linda Trimble. 1995. "Road Kill: Women in Alberta's Drive Toward Deficit Elimination." In *The Trojan Horse: Alberta and the Future of Canada*, edited by Trevor Harrison and Gordon Laxer. Montreal: Black Rose Books.

Dalla Costa, Mariarosa and Selma James. 1972. *The Power of Women and the Subversion of the Community*. Bristol: Falling Wall Press.

Daniels, A. Kaplan. 1987. "Invisible Work." *Social Problems* 34.

Das Gupta, Tania. 1996. "Anti-Black Racism in Nursing in Ontario." *Studies in Political Economy* 51.

Davies, Margaret Llewelyn. [1915] 1978. *Maternity: Letters from Working Women*. Essex: Tiptree.

Davis, Angela. 1981. *Women, Race and Class*. New York: Women's Press.

Deber, R.B. and A.P. Williams. 1995. "Policy, Payment and Participation: Long Term Care Reform in Ontario." *Canadian Journal on Aging* 14.

de la Cuesta, C. 1993. "Fringe Work: Peripheral Work in Health Visiting." *Sociology of Health and Illness* 15.

Delaney, Janice, Mary Jane Lupton and Emily Toth. 1977. *The Curse*. New York: Dutton.

Delphy, Christine. 1972. "L'ennemi principal." In *Libération des femmes année zero*. Partisans: Paris.

_____. 1981. "Women in Stratification Studies." In *Doing Feminist Research*, edited by Helen Roberts. London: Routledge & Kegan Paul.

Devault, M.L. 1991. *Feeding the Family: The Social Organization of Caring As Gendered Work*. Chicago: University of Chicago Press.

Devigne, Robert. 1994. *Recasting Conservatism: Oakeshott, Strauss and the Response to Postmodernism*. New Haven: Yale University Press.

de Wolff, Alice. 1992. *Review of the Situation of Women in Canada*. Toronto: National Action Committee on the Status of Women.

_____. 1995. "Job Loss and Entry-Level Information Workers: Training and Adjustment Strategies for Clerical Workers in Metro Toronto." Toronto: Report of the Metro Toronto Clerical Workers Labour Adjustment Committee.

Dey, I. 1989. "Flexible Parts and Ridged Fulls: The Limited Revolution in Work-time Patterns." *Work, Employment and Society* 3(4) (December).

Diamond, T. 1992. *Making Gray Gold: Narratives of Nursing Home Care*. Chicago: University of Chicago Press.

Dohse, D., J. Ulrich and T. Malsch. 1985. "From 'Fordism' to 'Toyotism'? The Social Organization of the Labor Process in the Japanese Automobile Industry." *Politics and Society* 14(2).

Donovan, R. 1989. "'We Care for the Most Important People in Your Life': Home Care Workers in New York City." *Women's Studies Quarterly* 1.

Donovan, R., P.A. Kurzman and C. Rotman. 1993. "Improving the Lives of Home Care Workers." *Social Work* 38.

Doray, Bernard. 1988. *From Taylorism to Fordism: A Rational Madness*. London: Free Association Books.

Duffy, A. and N. Pupo. 1992. *Part-Time Paradox: Connecting Gender, Work and Family*. Toronto: McClelland & Stewart.

Duncan, James S. and John A. Agnew (eds.). 1989. *The Power of Place*. Boston: Unwin Hyman.

Duncan M.T. and D.L. Morgan. 1994. "Sharing the Caring: Family Caregivers' Views of Their Relationships with Nursing Home Staff." *Gerontologist* 34.

Dutton, D., S.L. Painter et al. 1980. "Male Domestic Violence and Its Effects on the Victim." Report to the Health Promotions Directorate, Health and Welfare Canada.

Dyck, Isabel. 1989. "Integrating Home and Wage Workplace: Women's Daily Lives in a Canadian Suburb." *The Canadian Geographer* 33.

Economic Council of Canada. 1986. *Aging with Limited Resources*. Ottawa: Ministry of Supply and Services.

Edwards, R. 1979. *Contested Terrain: The Transformation of the Workplace in the Twentieth Century*. London: Heinemann.

Ehrenreich, B. and J. Ehrenreich. 1973. "Hospital Workers: A Case Study of the New Working Class." *Monthly Review* 24(8).

Ehrenreich, Barbara and Deirdre English. 1973. *Complaints and Disorders*. Old Westbury, NY: Feminist Press.

Engels, Frederick. 1968, 1983. *The Origin of the Family, Private Property and the State*. Moscow: Progress Pub.

———. 1970. "Letter to J. Bloch in Konigsberg." In *Selected Works in Three Volumes*, Vol. 3, by K. Marx and F. Engels. Moscow: Progress Publishers.

Esping-Andersen, G. and W. Korpi. 1983. "From Poor Relief to Institutional Welfare States: The Development of Scandinavian Social Policy." Paper presented to the ECPR Joint Workshops, Freiburg, Germany. March 20–25.

Estable, Alma. 1986. *Immigrant Women in Canada: Current Issues*. Ottawa: Canadian Advisory Council on the Status of Women.

Eustis, N.N., R.A. Kane and L.R. Fischer. 1993. "Home Care Quality and the Home Care Worker: Beyond Quality Assurance As Usual." *Gerontologist* 33.

Evers, A. 1993. "The Welfare Mix Approach: Understanding the Pluralism of Welfare Systems." In *Balancing Pluralism: New Welfare Mixes in Care for the Elderly*, edited by A. Evers and I. Svetlik. Aldershot: Avebury.

Eyles, John. 1985. *Senses of Place*. Warrington: Silverbrook Press.

———. 1987. "Housing Advertisements As Signs: Locality Creation and Meaning-Systems." *Geografiska Annaler* 69B(2).

Feldberg, R. and E.N. Glenn. 1987. "Technology and the Transformation of Clerical Work." In *Technology and the Transformation of White-Collar Work*, edited by R. Kraut. Hillsdate, NJ: Lawrence Erlbaum Associates.

Ferguson, Ann. 1989. *Blood at the Root*. London: Pandora.

Ferman, Louis A., Stuart Henry and Michele M. Hoyman. 1987. "Issues and Prospects for the Study of Informal Economies: Concepts, Research Strategies, and Policy." *Annals of the American Academy of Political and Social Science* 493.

Finch J. and D. Groves. 1983. *A Labour of Love: Women, Work and Caring*. London: Routledge and Kegan Paul.

Fincher, Ruth, Ian Campbell and Michael Webber. 1993. "Multiculturalism, Settlement and Migrants' Income and Employment Strategies." In *Multiculturalism, Difference and Postmodernism*, edited by G. Clark, D. Forbes and R. Francis. Melbourne: Longman Cheshire.

Findlay, Sue. 1993. "Reinventing the 'Community': A First Step in the Process of Democratization." *Studies in Political Economy* 42 (Autumn).

Firestone, Shulamith. 1970. *The Dialectic of Sex*. New York.

Flora, Peter. 1981. "Solutions or Source of Crisis? The Welfare State in Historical Perspective." In *The Emergence of the Welfare State in Britain and Germany*, edited by W.J. Mommsen. London.

Flora, Peter and Arnold Heidenheimer (eds.). 1981. *The Development of Welfare States in Europe and America*. London.

Fox, Bonnie (ed.). 1980. Hidden in the Household: Women's Domestic Labour Under Capitalism. *Toronto: Women's Press.*

———. 1980. "Women's Double Work Day: Twentieth-Century Changes in the Reproduction of Daily Life." In *Hidden in the Household: Women's Domestic Labour under Capitalism*, edited by Bonnie Fox. Toronto: Women's Press.

Fox, Bonnie and Pamela Sugiman. 1999. "Flexible Work, Flexible Workers: the Restructuring of Clerical Work in a Large Telecommunications Company." *Studies in Political Economy* 60 (Fall).

Fraad, Harriet, Stephen Resnick and Richard Wolff. 1989. "For Every Knight in Shining Armor, There's a Castle Waiting to Be Cleaned: A Marxist-Feminist Analysis of the Household." *Rethinking Marxism* 2(4).

Frager, Ruth A. 1989. "Class and Ethnic Barriers to Feminist Perspectives in Toronto's Jewish Labour Movement, 1919–1939." *Studies in Political Economy* 30.

Frankenburg, Ruth. 1993. *White Women, Race Matters: The Social Construction of Whiteness.* London: Routledge.

Fraser, Nancy. 1989. *Unruly Practices: Power, Discourse and Gender in Contemporary Social Theory.* Minneapolis: University of Minnesota Press.

_____. 1990. "Struggle Over Needs: Outline of a Socialist-Feminist Critical Theory of Late Capitalist Political Culture." In *Women, the State, and Welfare*, edited by Linda Gordon. Madison: University of Wisconsin Press.

_____. 1995. "From Redistribution to Recognition? Dilemmas of Justice in a 'Post-Socialist' Age." *New Left Review* 22.

_____. 1997a. "A Rejoinder to Iris Young." *New Left Review* 223.

_____. 1997b. *Justice Interruptus: Critical Reflections on the "Post-Socialist" Condition."* New York: Routledge.

_____. 1998. "Heterosexism, Misrecognition and Capitalism: A Response to Judith Butler." *New Left Review* 228.

_____. 2000. "Rethinking Recognition." *New Left Review* 3.

Friedman, A. 1977. *Industry and Labour.* London: Macmillan.

"From Localised Social Structures to Localities As Agents." 1991. *Environment and Planning D: Society and Space* 23.

"Frustration Caused Strike." 1988. *Edmonton Journal* (February 11):A7.

Fudge, Judy. 1996. "Fragmentation and Feminization: The Challenge of Equity for Labour Relations Policy." In *Women and Canadian Public Policy*, edited by Janine Brodie. Toronto: Harcourt Brace.

Fudge, Judy and Brenda Cossman. 2002. "Introduction: Feminist Privatization and the Law." In *Privatization, Law, and the Challenge to Feminism*, edited by Brenda Cossman and Judy Fudge. Toronto: University of Toronto Press.

Fuller, L. and V. Smith. 1991. "Consumers' Reports: Management by Customers in a Changing Economy." *Work Employment, and Society* 5(1).

Gabbacia, Donna (ed.). 1992. *Seeking Common Ground: Multidisciplinary Studies of Immigrant Women in the United States.* Westport: Praeger.

Gagnon, M. 1990. "Reflections on the Public Sector Contract Negotiations." *Studies in Political Economy* 31 (Spring).

Galant, H.C. 1955. *Histoire politique de la sécurité sociale francaise 1945–1952.* Paris.

Galt, Virginia. 1992. "Oh Give Me a Home..." *The Globe and Mail* (September 19).

Gamarniko, Eva et al. 1983. *Class, Gender and Work.* London: Heinemann.

Gardiner, Jean. 1975. "Women's Domestic Labour." *New Left Review* 89.

_____. 1976. "Political Economy of Domestic Labour in Capitalist Society." In *Dependence and Exploitation in Work and Marriage*, edited by Diana Leonard Barker and Sheila Allen. London: Longman.

_____. 1977. "Women in the Labour Process and Class Structure." In *Class and Class Structure*, edited by Alan Hunt. London: Lawrence and Wishart.

Garson, A. 1988. *The Electronic Sweatshop*. New York: Simon & Schuster.

Geller, G. 1989. "A Feminist Case Against Patriarchal 'Justice' for Women Victims of Abuse." Paper presented at the Canadian Sociology and Anthropology Association Sessions, Learned Societies Meetings, Quebec City.

Gibson, D. and J. Allen. 1993. "Parasitism and Phallocentrism in Social Problems of the Aged." *Policy Sciences* 26.

Giles, Wenona. 1993. "Clean Jobs, Dirty Jobs: Ethnicity, Social Reproduction and Gendered Identity." *Culture* 13(2).

_____. n.d. *The Gender Relations of a Labour Migration: Two Generations of Portuguese Women in Toronto* (working title; forthcoming).

Giles, Wenona and Sedef Arat-Koc. 1994. *Maid in the Market: Women's Paid Domestic Labour*. Halifax: Fernwood Publishing.

Giles, Wenona and Valerie Preston. 1996. "The Domestication of Women's Work: A Comparison of Chinese and Portuguese Immigrant Women Homeworkers." *Studies in Political Economy* 51 (Fall).

Glaser, N.Y. 1990. "The Home As Workshop: Women As Amateur Nurses and Medical Care Providers." *Gender & Society* 4.

_____. 1993. *Women's Paid and Unpaid Labour: The Work Transfer in Health Care and Retailing*. Philadelphia: Temple University Press.

Glucksmann, Miriam. 1990. *Women Assemble*. New York: Routledge.

Goldfarb Corporation. 1988. *The Nursing Crisis*. Toronto: Ontario Nurses' Association.

Gordon, Linda. 1979. "The Struggle for Reproductive Freedom: Three Stages of Feminism." In *Capitalist Patriarchy and the Case for Feminist Socialism*, edited by Zillah Eisenstein. New York: Monthly Review Press.

_____. 1988. *Heroes of Their Own Lives: The Politics and History of Family Violence, Boston 1880–1960*. New York: Viking Press.

Gorelick, Sherry. 1989. "The Changer and the Changed: Methodological Reflections on Studying Jewish Feminists." In *Gender/Body/Knowledge*, edited by Alison M. Jagger and Susan R. Bordo. New Brunswick: Rutgers University Press.

Gotell, Lise. 1996. "Policing Desire: Obscenity Law, Pornography Politics, and Feminism in Canada." In *Women and Canadian Public Policy*, edited by Janine Brodie. Toronto: Harcourt and Brace.

Gottfried, H. and L. Graham. 1993. "Constructing Difference: The Making of Gendered Subcultures in a Japanese Automobile Plant." *Sociology* 27(4).

Gough, Ian. 1979. *The Political Economy of the Welfare State*. London.

Government of Alberta. 1984. News Release. February 28.

Government of Ontario. 1994. *An Act Respecting Long-Term Care*.

Graham, H. 1993. "Social Divisions of Caring." *Women's Studies International Forum* 16.

Graham, Julie. 1990. "Theory and Essentialism in Marxist Geography." *Antipode* 22(1).

Gramsci, Antonio. 1971. In *Selections from the Prison Notebooks*, edited by Q. Hoare and G. Nowell-Smith. New York: Lawrence and Wishart.

Grant, D. 1985. "Bed-Blockers Blamed for Emergency Ward Crunch." *The Globe and Mail* (February 18).

Gregory, Derek. 1978. *Ideology, Science, and Human Geography*. London: Hutchinson.

Griffith, A. 1984. "Ideology, Education and Single Parent Families: The Normative Ordering of Families Through Schooling." Ph.D. thesis, University of Toronto.

Grosner, Lucia. 1995. "A Canadian Profile: Toronto's Portuguese and Brazilian Communities." Toronto: Portuguese Interagency Network.

Growe, S. 1991. *Who Cares?* Toronto: McClelland and Stewart.

Guettel, Charnie. 1974. *Marxism and Feminism.* Toronto: Women's Press.

Gurr, T.R. 1970. *Why Men Rebel.* Princeton: Princeton University Press.

Hacker, S. 1979. "Sex Stratification, Technology and Organizational Change: A Longitudinal Case Study of AT&T." *Social Problems* 26.

Hadley, K. 1994. "Working Lean and Mean: A Gendered Experience of Restructuring in an Electronics Manufacturing Plant." Unpublished Ph.D. thesis, Ontario Institute for Studies in Education.

Hakim, C. 1987. "Trends in the Flexible Workforce." *Employment Gazette* (November).

Hamilton, Roberta. 1978. *The Liberation of Women.* London: Allen & Unwin.

Hamilton, Roberta and Michèle Barrett (eds.). 1986. *The Politics of Diversity: Feminism, Marxism and Nationalism.* Montreal: Book Center Inc.

Hanson, Susan and Geraldine Pratt. 1990. "Geographic Perspectives on the Occupational Segregation of Women." *National Geographic Research* 6.

_____. 1992. "Dynamic Dependencies: A Geographic Investigation of Local Labor Markets." *Economic Geography* 68.

Harder, Lois. 1996. "Depoliticizing Insurgency: The Politics of the Family in Alberta." *Studies in Political Economy* 50.

Harman, H., R. Kraut and L. Tilly (eds.). 1987. *Computer Chips and Paper Clips*, Vol. 1. Washington, DC: Panel on Technology and Women's Employment, Commission on Behavioral and Social Sciences and Education. National Research Council, National Academy Press.

Harrington, M. 1992. "What Exactly Is Wrong with the Liberal State As an Agent of Change?" In *Gendered States: Feminist (Re)visions of International Relations Theory*, edited by V. Spike Peterson. Boulder and London: Lynne Reinner Publishers.

Harris, J. 1972. *Unemployment and Politics.* Oxford.

Harrison, Bennett. 1994. *Lean and Mean: The Changing Landscape of Corporate Power in the Age of Flexibility.* New York: Basic Books.

Harrison, John. 1973. "The Political Economy of Housework." *Bulletin of the Conference of Social Economists* (Winter).

Hartmann, Heidi. 1981. "The Unhappy Marriage of Marxism and Feminism: Towards a More Progressive Union." In *Women and Revolution*, edited by Lydia Sargent. Montreal: Black Rose Books.

Harvey, David. 1989. *The Condition of Postmodernity.* Oxford: Oxford University Press.

Hatzfeld, H. 1979. *Du paupérisme à la sécurité sociale.* Paris.

Haupt, G. 1978. "Marx e marxismo." In *Storia del marxismo*, edited by E. Hobsbawn et al. Torino.

_____. 1980. *L'historien et le mouvement social.* Paris.

Heclo, H. 1974. *Modern Social Politics in Britain and Sweden.* New Haven and London.

Hennock, P. 1981. "The Origins of British National Insurance and the German Precedent 1891–1914." In *The Emergence of the Welfare State in Britain and Germany*, edited by W.J. Mommsen. London.

Henry, David. 1973. *Social Justice and the City*. Baltimore: The Johns Hopkins University Press.

_____. 1985. *The Urban Experience*. Baltimore: The Johns Hopkins University Press.

Hinton, N.Z. 1989. "One in Ten: the Struggles and Disempowerment of the Battered Women's Movement." *Canadian Journal of Family Law* 7.

Hockerts, H.G. 1980. *Sozialpolitische Entscheidungen im Nachkriegsdeutschland*. Stuttgart.

Holter, H. (ed.). 1984. *Patriarchy in a Welfare Society*. Oslo: Universitisforlaget.

Hoyman, Michele. 1987. "Female Participation in the Informal Economy: A Neglected Issue." *The Annals of the American Academy of Political and Social Science* 493.

Huitième Congrès Socialiste International. 1911. Gand.

Huws, U. 1984. *The New Homeworkers, New Technology and the Changing Location of White Collar Work*. London: Low Pay Unit.

Inglis, C., A. Birch and G. Sherington. 1994. "An Overview of Australian and Canadian Migration Patterns and Policies." In *Immigration and Refugee Policy: Australia and Canada Compared*, Vol. 1, edited by H. Adelman, A. Borowski, M. Burstein and L. Foster. Carlton: Melbourne University Press.

International Ladies Garment Workers' Union (ILGWU). 1991. *Homeworkers: Fair Wages and Working Conditions for Homeworkers: A Brief to the Government of Ontario*.

James, N. 1992. "Care = Organization + Physical Labour + Emotional Labour." *Sociology of Health and Illness* 14.

Januario, Ilda. 1993. "Some Statistical Data on the Portuguese-Canadian Population." Mimeo. Toronto: Portuguese-Canadian Educators' Association.

Jenny, J. 1982. *Issues Affecting Nurses' Hospital Employment in the 80s*. Toronto: Canadian Hospital Association.

Jenson, Jane. 1986. "Gender and Reproduction or Babies and the State." Studies in Political Economy 20.

_____. 1989. "The Talents of Women, the Skills of Men: Flexible Specialization and Women." In *The Transformation of Work?*, edited by S. Wood. London: Hutchinson.

_____. 1992. "Gender and Reproduction, or Babies and the State." In *Feminism in Action: Studies in Political Economy*, edited by M. Patricia Connolly and Pat Armstrong. Toronto: Canadian Scholars' Press.

Jhappan, Rhada. 1996. "Post-Modern Race and Gender Essentialism or a Post-Mortem of Scholarship." *Studies in Political Economy* 51.

Johnson, Theresa. 1992. "Work at Home: New Draft Policy: But What Does It All Mean?" *Alliance* (Public Service Alliance of Canada) (Spring).

Jones, E. 1996. "The Privatization of Home Care in Manitoba." *Canadian Review of Social Policy* 37.

Jones, P. 1987. "Labour Market Flexibility." *Labour and Society* 12(1) (January).

Kane, R. and A. Caplan. 1993. *Ethical Conflicts in the Management of Home Care: The Case Manager's Dilemma*. New York: Springer Publishing.

Katznelson, Ira. 1981. *City Trenches*. Chicago: University of Chicago Press.

Kaye, L.W. 1986. "Worker Views of the Intensity of Affective Expression During the Delivery of Home Care Services for the Elderly." *Home Health Care Services* 7.

Kelsey, J. 1995. *The New Zealand Experiment: A World Model for Structural Adjustment?* Auckland: Auckland University Press.

Kennedy, Al to Les Young. March 25, 1982. Memo. Women's Secretariat Documents, Provincial Archives of Alberta, Edmonton.

Knopp, Lawrence and Mickey Lauria. 1987. "Gender Relations As a Patriarchal Form of Social Relations." *Antipode* 19(1).

Knopp, Lawrence and Richard S. Kujawa. 1993. "Ideology and Urban Landscapes: Conceptions of the Market in Portland, Maine." *Antipode* 25(3).

Köhler, P. and H. Zacher (eds.). 1981. *Ein Jahrhundert Sozialversicherung*. Berlin.

Kritak. 1977. *Wat Zoudt Gij Zonder 't Werkvolk Zijn?* Leuven.

Kroc, Sedef. 1989. "In the Privacy of Their Own Home: Foreign Domestic Workers As Solution to Crisis of the Domestic Sphere." *Studies in Political Economy* 28 (Spring).

Kuhnle, S. 1983. *Velferdsstatens utvikling*. Oslo.

Labelle, M., G. Turcotte, M. Kempeneers and D. Meintel. 1987. *Histories d'Immigrées, Itinéraires d'Ouvrières Columbiennes, Greques, Haïtennes et Portugaises de Montréal*. Montréal: Boréal.

Lamphere, Louis. 1987. *From Working Daughters to Working Mothers: Immigrant Women in a New England Industrial Community*. Ithaca: Cornell University Press.

_____. 1992. *Structuring Diversity: Ethnographic Perspectives on the New Immigration*. Chicago and London: University of Chicago Press.

Lane, B. "New Technology and Clerical Work." In *Employment in Britain*, edited by D. Gallie. Oxford: Basil Blackwell.

Leach, Belinda. 1992. "Ideas About Work and Family: Outwork in Contemporary Ontario." Ph.D. dissertation, Department of Anthropology, University of Toronto.

_____. 1993. "'Flexible' Work, Precarious Future: Some Lessons from the Canadian Clothing Industry." *Canadian Review of Sociology and Anthropology* 30(1).

Lee, B. 1988. "ICU a Real Pressure Cooker." *Hamilton Spectator* (April 25):B1.

Leeson, Joyce and Judith Gray. 1978. *Women and Medicine*. London: Tavistock Publications.

Leidner, Robin. 1991. "Selling Hamburgers, Selling Insurance: Gender, Work and Identity." *Gender and Society* 5.

_____. 1993. *Fast Food, Fast Talk, Service Work and the Routinization of Everyday Life*. Berkeley: University of California Press.

Letourneau, Claire. 1990. "Telecommuting and Electronic Homework in Canada." Ottawa: Womens Bureau, Labour Canada.

Li, Peter S. 1988. *The Chinese in Canada*. Toronto: Oxford University Press.

Lichtman, Richard. 1975. "Marx's Theory of Ideology." *Socialist Revolution* 23.

Liddle, A.M. 1989. "Feminist Contributions to an Understanding of Violence Against Women — Three Steps Forward, Two Steps Back." *Canadian Review of Sociology and Anthropology* 26(5).

Liebman, M. 1979. *Les socialistes belges 1885–1914*. Brussels.

Lipsig-Mummé, Carla. 1983. "The Renaissance of Homeworking in Developed Economies." *Industrial Relations* 38.

_____. 1987. "Organizing Women in the Clothing Trades: Homework in the 1983 Garment Strike." *Studies in Political Economy* 22 (Spring).

Little, Margaret. 1995. "The Blurring of Boundaries: Private and Public Welfare for Single Mothers in Ontario." *Studies in Political Economy* 47 (Summer).

Liu, Xiaofeng. 1995. "New Mainland Chinese Immigrants: A Case Study in Metro Toronto." Ph.D. dissertation, Department of Geography, York University.

Lorraine, Tamsin. 1990. *Gender Identity and the Production of Meaning.* Boulder: Westview.

Loseke, I. and K. Cahill. 1984. "The Social Construction of Deviance: Experts on Battered Women." *Social Problems* 31(3).

Lukàcs, Georg. 1971. *History and Class Consciousness.* London: Merlin Press.

_____. 1980. *Labour.* London: Merlin Press.

Luxton, Meg. 1980. *More Than a Labour of Love: Three Generations of Women's Work in the Home.* Toronto: Women's Press.

_____. 1983. "Two Hands for the Clock: Changing Patterns in the Gendered Division of Labour." *Studies in Political Economy* 12 (Fall).

Luxton, Meg and Leah F. Vosko. 1998. "Where Women's Efforts Count: The 1996 Census Campaign and 'Family Politics' in Canada." *Studies in Political Economy* 56.

MacDonald, Martha. 1984. "Economics: The Dismal Science." *Studies in Political Economy* 15.

_____. 1991a. "Post-Fordism and the Flexibility Debate." *Studies in Political Economy* 36.

_____. 1991b. "The Flex Spec Debates." *Studies in Political Economy* 36 (Autumn).

Machung, A. 1984. "Word Processing: Forward for Business, Backward for Women." In *My Troubles Are Going to Have Trouble with Me*, edited by K. Sacks and D. Remy. New Brunswick, NJ: Rutgers University Press.

Mackenzie, Suzanne. 1986. "Women's Responses to Economic Restructuring: Changing Gender, Changing Space." In *The Politics of Diversity: Feminism, Marxism and Nationalism*, edited by Roberta Hamilton and Michèle Barrett. Montreal: The Book Center.

_____. 1988. "Building Women, Building Cities: Toward Gender Sensitive Theory in the Environmental Disciplines." In *Life Spaces: Gender, Household, Employment*, edited by C. Andrew and B.M. Milroy. Vancouver: UBC Press.

MacLeod, L. 1980. *Wife Battering Is Every Woman's Issue: A Summary Report of the CACSW Consultation on Wife Battering.* Ottawa: Canadian Advisory Council on the Status of Women.

_____. 1987. *Battered But Not Beaten.* Ottawa: Canadian Advisory Council on the Status of Women.

Manga, P. 1993. "Health Economics and the Current Health Care Cost Crisis." *Health and Canadian Society* 1.

Marklund, Staffan. 1982. *Klass, Stat, Socialpolitik.* Lund.

Maroney, Heather Jon. 1992. "'Who Has the Baby?' Nationalism, Pronatalism, and the Construction of a 'Demographic Crisis' in Quebec 1960–1988." *Studies in Political Economy* 39 (Autumn).

Maroney, Heather Jon and Meg Luxton. 1987. *Feminism and Political Economy: Women's Work, Women's Struggles*. Toronto: University of Toronto Press.

———. 1987. "From Feminism and Political Economy to Feminist Political Economy." In *Feminism and Political Economy: Women's Work, Women's Struggles*, edited by Heather Jon Maroney and Meg Luxton. Toronto: Methuen.

———. 1997. "Gender at Work: Canadian Feminist Political Economy since 1988." In *Understanding Canada: Building on the New Canadian Political Economy*, edited by Wallace Clement. Montreal: McGill-Queen's University Press.

Martin, D. 1976. *Battered Wives*. San Francisco: New Glide Publications.

———. 1981. *Battered Wives*, 2nd ed. San Francisco: Volcano Press Inc.

Marx, Karl and Friedrich Engels. 1988. *The German Ideology*. New York: International Publishers.

Massey, Doreen. 1984. *Spatial Divisions of Labour*. London: Macmillan.

Mathera, D. 1985. "Nurses Pay: How Part-timers Are Doing." *R.N.* (December).

Matthews, A. Martin. 1992. *Homemakers' Services to the Elderly: Provider Characteristics and Client Benefit, 1989–1992*. Guelph: Gerontology Research Centre.

McArthur, J. 1988. "Pay Is Not the Problem." *Toronto Star* (February 16).

McCoy, Elaine to Patricia Good. December 16, 1987. Women's Secretariat Documents, Provincial Archives of Alberta, Edmonton.

McCoy, Elaine to Ken Rostad. December 17, 1987. Memo. Women's Secretariat Documents, Provincial Archives of Alberta, Edmonton.

McDowell, Linda. 1986. "Beyond Patriarchy: A Class Based Explanation of Women's Subordination." *Antipode* 18(3).

———. 1991. "Life Without Father and Ford: The New Gender Order of Post-Fordism." *Transactions of the Institute of British Geographers* 16(4).

———. 1992. "Gender Divisions in a Post-Fordist Era: New Contradictions or the Same Old Story?" In *Defining Women: Social Institutions and Gender Divisions*, edited by Linda McDowell and Rosemary Pringle. Cambridge: Polity Press.

McLaren, Angus. 1977. "Women's Work and the Regulation of Family Size: The Question of Abortion in the Nineteenth Century." *History Workshop* 4.

———. 1978. "Birth Control and Abortion in Canada, 1870–1920." *Canadian Historical Review* 59(3) (September).

McQuaig, Linda. 1995. *Shooting the Hippo*. Toronto: Viking.

Meltz, N. 1988. *The Nursing Shortage*. Toronto: Registered Nurses' Association of Ontario.

Menzies, Heather. 1982. *Women and the Chip*. Montreal: the Institute for Research on Public Policy.

———. 1996. *Whose Brave New World?* Toronto: Between the Lines Press.

———. 1997. "Telework, Shadow Work: The Privatization of Work in the New Digital Economy." *Studies in Political Economy* 53 (Summer).

Milkman, R. 1985. *Women, Work and Protest*. New York: Routledge and Kegan Paul.

Milkman, R. and C. Pullman. 1991. "Technological Change in an Auto Assembly Plant: The Impact on Workers, Tasks, and Skills." *Work and Occupations* 18(2).

Milliband, Ralph. 1977. *Marxism and Politics*. Oxford: Oxford University Press.

Mills, C. Wright. 1962. *The Marxists*. New York: Dell Publishing.

Mitchell, Juliet. 1972. "Marxism and Women's Revolution." *Social Praxis* 1(1).

Mitter, S. 1986. "Industrial Restructuring and Manufacturing Homework: Immigrant Women in the Clothing Industry." *Capital and Class* 27.

Mohanty, Chandra, Ann Russo and Lourdes Torres (eds.). 1991. *Third World Women and the Politics of Feminism*. Bloomington: Indiana University Press.

Moller, I. Horneman. 1981. *Klassekamp og sociallovgivning 1850–1970*. Copenhagen.

Molyneux, Maxine. 1979. "Beyond the Domestic Labour Debate." *New Left Review* 116.

Moore, B. 1978. *Injustice: The Social Basis of Obedience and Revolt*. London: Macmillan.

Morgan, Glenn and David Knights. 1991. "Gendering Jobs: Corporate Strategy, Managerial Control and the Dynamics of Job Segregation." *Work, Employment and Society* 5.

Morgan, P. 1981. "From Battered Wife to Program Client: The State's Shaping of Social Problems." *Kapitaliste* 9.

Morton, Peggy. 1972. "Women's Work Is Never Done." In *Women Unite!*, edited by Canadian Women's Educational Press. Toronto: Canadian Women's Educational Press.

Moss, P. 1995. "The 'Gap' As Part of the Politics of Research Design." *Antipode* 27(1) (January).

Murdie, Robert. 1994. "Economic Restructuring and Social Polarization in Toronto: Impacts on an Immigrant Population." Mimeo. North York, ON: Department of Geography, York University.

National Advisory Council on Aging. 1995. *The NACA Position on Community Services in Health Care for Seniors: Progress and Challenges*. Ottawa: Ministry of Supply and Services.

Neal, Rusty and Virginia Neale. 1987. "'As Long As You Know How to Do Housework': Portuguese Canadian Women and the Office Cleaning Industry in Toronto." *Canadian Women's Studies Journal* 16(1).

Neely, R.L. and G. Robinson-Simpson. 1987. "The Truth About Domestic Violence: A Falsely Framed Issue." *Social Work* (November/December).

Newberger, E.H. and R. Bourne. 1986. "The Medicalization and Legalization of Child Abuse." In *Family in Transition*, 5th ed., edited by A. Skolnick and J.H. Skolnick. Boston: Little, Brown & Co.

Neysmith, S.M. 1981. "Parental Care: Another Female Family Function?" *Canadian Journal of Social Work Education* 7.

_____. 1995. "Power in Relationships of Trust: A Feminist Analysis of Elder Abuse." In *Abuse and Neglect of Older Canadians: Strategies for Change*, edited by M. McLean. Toronto: Thompson Educational Publishing.

_____. 1997. "Toward a Woman Friendly Long-Term Care Policy." In *Women and the Canadian Welfare State: Challenges and Change*, edited by P. Evans and G. Wekerle. Toronto: University of Toronto Press.

Neysmith, S.M. and J. Aronson. 1995. "Negotiating Issues of Culture and Race Within the Home." Paper presented to the conference of the Canadian Association on Gerontology, Vancouver.

_____. 1996. "Home Care Workers Discuss Their Work: The Skills Required to Use Your 'Common Sense.'" *Journal of Aging Studies* 10.

Ng, Roxana. 1992. "Managing Female Immigration: A Case of Institutional Sexism and Racism." *Canadian Women's Studies Journal* 12(3).

_____. 1993a. "Sexism, Racism and Canadian Nationalism." In *Feminism and the Politics of Difference*, edited by Snega Gunew and Anna Yeatman. Halifax: Fernwood.

_____. 1993b. "Sexism, Racism and Canadian Nationalism." In *Returning the Gaze: Essays on Racism, Feminism and Politics*, edited by Himani Bannerji. Toronto: Sister Vision Press.

Ng, Roxana and Alma Estable. 1987. "Immigrant Women in the Labour Force: An Overview of Present Knowledge and Research Gaps." *Resources for Feminist Research* 16(1).

Nicholson, Linda (ed.). 1987. *Feminism/Postmodernism*. New York: Routledge.

Noble, Joey. 1979. "'Class-ifying' the Poor: Toronto Charities, 1850–1880." *Studies in Political Economy* 2 (Autumn).

Norcliffe, Glen, Michael Goldrick and Leon Muszynski. 1986. "Cyclical Factors, Technological Change, Capital Mobility, and Deindustrialization in Metropolitan Toronto." *Urban Geography* 7.

Nye, Andrea. 1988. *Feminist Theory and the Philosophies of Man*. New York: Routledge.

Oakley, Ann. 1981. *Subject Women*. New York: Pantheon Books.

OECD. 1981. *The Welfare State in Crisis*. Paris.

_____. 1982. *Employment in the Public Sector*. Paris.

Oldfield, Margaret. 1991. "The Electronic Cottage — Boon or Bane for Mothers." In *Proceedings of the Conference on Women, Work and Computerization*, edited by A.M. Letito and I. Ericsson. Helsinki.

Ontario Advisory Council on the Status of Women. 1989. *Recommendations for Changes to the Employment Standards Act*. Toronto.

Ontario Ministry of Community and Social Services. 1991. *Redirection of Long-Term Care and Support Services in Ontario*. Toronto: Queen's Printer for Ontario.

Ontario Ministry of Health, Ministry of Community and Social Services and Ministry of Citizenship. 1993. *Partnerships in Long-Term Care: A New Way to Plan, Manage and Deliver Services and Community Support*. Toronto: Queen's Printer for Ontario.

Ontario Nurses' Association. 1988. *An Industry in Crisis* (April). Toronto: Ontario Nurses' Association.

Orser, Barbara and Mary Foster. 1992. *Home Enterprise, Canadians and Home-Based Work*. Ottawa: The National Home-Based Business Project Committee.

Owens, R.J. 1995. "The Peripheral Worker: Women and the Legal Regulation of Outwork." In *Public and Private: Feminist Legal Debates*, edited by M. Thornton. Melbourne: OUP.

Painter, S.L. and D. Dutton. 1985. "Patterns of Emotional Bonding in Battered Women: Traumatic Bonding." *International Journal of Women's Studies* 8(4).

Palmer, Howard and Tamara Palmer. 1990. *Alberta: A New History*. Edmonton: Hurtig Publishers.

Palmer, Phyllis. 1989. *Domesticity and Dirt*. Philadelphia: Temple University Press.

Panitch, Leo. 1977. *The Canadian State: Political Economy and Political Power*. Toronto: University of Toronto Press.

Parker, M. and J. Slaughter. 1989. *Choosing Sides: Unions and the Team Concept*. Boston: South End Press.

Parr, Joy. 1990. *The Gender of Breadwinners*. Toronto: University of Toronto Press.

Pateman, Carole. 1992. "The Patriarchal Welfare State." In *Defining Women: Social Institutions and Gender Divisions*, edited by Linda McDowell and Rosemary Pringle. London: Polity Press.

Peet, Richard (ed.). 1987. *International Capitalism and Industrial Restructuring*. London: Allen and Unwin.

Personal Narratives Group. 1989. *Interpreting Women's Lives*. Bloomington: Indiana University Press.

Phillips, Anne. 1987. *Divided Loyalties*. London: Virago.

_____. 1993. *Democracy and Difference*. University Park, PA: University of Pennsylvania Press.

_____. 1997. "From Inequality to Difference: A Severe Case of Displacement?" *New Left Review* 224.

Phillips, R. 1995. *A Second Look at the Clients in the Community Programs for People with Cognitive Impairments in Metro Toronto (January 1–March 31, 1994)*. Toronto: Toronto Long Term Care Office, Ontario Ministry of Health.

Phizacklea, Anne and Mary Wolkowitz. 1995. *Homeworking Women: Gender, Racism and Class at Work*. London: Sage Publications.

Picchio, Antonella. 1992. *Social Reproduction: The Political Economy of the Labour Market*. Cambridge, UK: Cambridge University Press.

Pignon, D. and J. Querzola. 1978. "Dictatorship and Democracy in Production." In *The Division of Labour*, edited by Andre Gorz. Sussex, England: Harvester Press.

Piore, M.J. 1986. "Perspectives on Labour Market Flexibility." *Industrial Relations* 25(2).

Pizzey, E. 1974. *Scream Quietly or the Neighbours Will Hear*. London: Penguin Books.

Pleck, E. 1983."Feminist Response to 'Crimes Against Women,' 1868–1896." *Signs* 8(3).

_____. 1987. *Domestic Tyranny: The Making of American Social Policy Against Family Violence from Colonial Times to the Present*. New York: Oxford University Press.

Pollert, A. 1988. "Dismantling Flexibility." *Capital and Class* 34 (May).

Porter, Marilyn. 1987. "Peripheral Women: Towards a Feminist Analysis of the Atlantic Region." *Studies in Political Economy* 23.

Poster, M. 1988. "Review of Pleck's *Domestic Tyranny*." *Signs* 14(1)

Poulantzas, Nicos. 1975. *Classes in Contemporary Capitalism*. London: New Left Review.

Premier's Council in Support of Alberta Families. 1992a. *Albertans Speak Out About Families*. Edmonton: Government of Alberta.

_____. 1992b. *Directions for the Future*. Edmonton: Government of Alberta.

_____. 1992c. *Family Policy Grid*. Edmonton: Government of Alberta.

_____. 1993. *Perspectives on Family Well-Being*. Edmonton: Government of Alberta.

Preston, Valerie and Wenona Giles. 1991. "Ethnicity, Gender and Labour Markets in Canada: A Case Study of Immigrant Women in Toronto." Paper presented to Canadian Sociology and Anthropology Association Meetings, Kingston, Ontario.

Proctor, S., M. Rowlinson, L. McArdle, J. Hassard and P. Forrester. 1994. "Flexibility, Politics and Strategy: In Defense of the Model of the Flexible Firm." *Work, Employment and Society* 8(2).

Programm der sozialdemokratischen Partei Deutschlands. 1891. Berlin.

Province of Ontario, Legislature, Standing Committee on Social Development. 1982a. *Minutes — Hansard.* Nos. 4, 10, 11, 12 (May).

_____. 1982b. *Minutes — Hansard.* Nos. 19, 20, 21, 23, 26, 27, 28, 29, 30 (July).

_____. 1982c. *First Report on Family Violence: Wife Battering.* Toronto.

Przeworski, Adam. 1985. *Capitalism and Social Democracy.* New York: Cambridge University Press.

Purcell, K. 1979. "Militancy and Acquiescence Amongst Women Workers." In *Fit Work for Women,* edited by S. Burman. London: Croom Helm.

Qureshi, H. 1990. "Boundaries Between Formal and Informal Caregiving Work." In *Gender and Caring Work: Work and Welfare in Britain and Scandinavia,* edited by C. Ungerson. London: Harvester Wheatsheaf.

Qureshi, H. and A. Walker. 1989. *The Caring Relationship: Elderly People and Their Families.* London: MacMillan.

Ramsay, Harvie, Anna Pollert and Helen Rainbird. 1992. "A Decade of Transformation? Labour Market Flexibility and Work Organization in the United Kingdom." *New Directions in Work Organization: The Industrial Relations Response.*

Reinhart, J., C. Huxley and D. Robertson. 1997. *Just Another Car Factory? Lean Production and Its Discontents.* Ithaca, NY: ILR Press.

Reiter, Ester. 1991. *Making Fast Food: From the Frying Pan into the Fire.* Montreal: McGill-Queen's University Press.

Rimlinger, G. 1971. *Welfare Policy and Industrialization in Europe, America, and Russia.* New York.

Ross, Becki L. 2000. "Bumping and Grinding on the Line: Making Nudity Pay." *Labour/ Le Travail* 46 (Fall).

Rostad, Ken to Elaine McCoy. November 18, 1987. Memo. Women's Secretariat Documents, Provincial Archives of Alberta, Edmonton.

Rich, Adrienne. 1977. *Of Woman Born.* London: Norton.

Rinehart, J. 1987. *The Tyranny of Work,* 2nd ed. Toronto: HBJ.

Robertson, B., J. Rinehart, C. Huxley and the CAW Research Group on CAMMI. 1992. "Team Concept and Kaizen: Japanese Production Management in a Unionized Canadian Auto Plant." *Studies in Political Economy* 39.

Rollins, Judith. 1985. *Between Women.* Philadelphia: Temple University Press.

Romero, Mary. 1992. *Maid in the U.S.A.* New York: Routledge.

Rowbotham, Sheila. 1974. *Women, Resistance and Revolution.* New York: Pantheon Books.

_____. 1977. *A New World for Women: Stella Browne — Socialist Feminist.* London: Pluto Press.

Rubin, Gayle. 1975. "The Traffic of Women: Notes on the 'Political Economy' of Sex." In *Toward an Anthropology of Women,* edited by Rayna Rapp Reiter. New York: Monthly Review Press.

Russell, B. n.d. "The Subtle Labour Process and the Great Skill Debate: Evidence from a Potash Mine-Mill Operation." *Canadian Journal of Sociology* 20(3).

Sabel, Charles. 1982. *Work and Politics*. Cambridge: Cambridge University Press.

Salaman, G. 1986. *Working*. London: Tavistock Pub.

Saraceno, C. 1987. "Division of Family Labour and Gender Identity." In *Women and the State*, edited by A. Showstack Sassoon. London: Unwin Hyman.

Sassen, Saskia. 1990. *The Global City*. Princeton: Princeton University Press.

_____. 1991. "The Informal Economy." In *Dual City, Restructuring New York*, edited by J.H. Mollenkopf and M. Castells. New York: Russell Sage Foundation.

Sayer, Andrew. 1984. *Method in Social Science: A Realist Approach*. London: Hutchinson.

Scott, Joan. 1990. "Deconstructing Equality-Versus-Difference: Or, the Uses of Poststructuralist Theory for Feminism." In *Conflicts in Feminism*, edited by Marianne Hirsch and Evelyn Fox Keller. New York: Routledge.

Scott, Katherine. 1996. "The Dilemmas of Liberal Citizenship: Women and Social Assistance Reform in the 1990s." *Studies in Political Economy* 50.

Seccombe, Wally. 1974. "The Housewife and Her Labour Under Capitalism." *New Left Review* 83.

_____. 1975. "Domestic Labour — A Reply to Critics." *New Left Review* 94.

_____. 1980. "Domestic Labour and the Working-Class Household." In *Hidden in the Household: Women's Domestic Labour under Capitalism*, edited by Bonnie Fox. Toronto: Women's Press.

_____. 1980. "The Expanded Reproduction Cycle of Labour Power in Twentieth-Century Capitalism." In *Hidden in the Household: Women's Domestic Labour under Capitalism*, edited by Bonnie Fox. Toronto: Women's Press.

Schechter, S. 1982. *Women and Male Violence: The Visions and Struggles of the Battered Women's Movement*. Boston: South End Press.

Schmid, H. and Y. Hasenfeld. 1993. "Organizational Dilemmas in the Provision of Home Care Services." *Social Service Review* 67.

Segal, L. 1987. *Is the Future Female? Troubled Thoughts on Contemporary Feminism* London: Virago Press.

Seward, S. and K. McDade. 1988. *Immigrant Women in Canada: A Policy Perspective*. Ottawa: Canadian Advisory Council on the Status of Women.

Shaiken, H., S. Herzenberg and S. Kuhn. 1986. "The Work Process Under More Flexible Production." *Industrial Relations* 25(2).

Siim, B. 1988. "Toward a Feminist Rethinking of the Welfare State." In *The Political Interests of Gender: Developing Theory and Research with a Feminist Face*, edited by K. Jones and A. Jonasdottor. London: Sage.

Sinclair, A. 1992. "The Tyranny of a Team Ideology." *Organization Studies* 13(4).

Singh, Navsharan. 1999. "Of GIFTS, GAMETRICS, Victim Women and Surplus Peoples: Reproductive Technologies and the Representation of 'Third World' Women." In *Feminism, Political Economy and the State: Contested Terrain*, edited by Pat Armstrong and M. Patricia Connolly. Toronto: Canadian Scholars' Press.

Sky, L. 1995. *Lean and Mean Health Care: The Creation of the Generic Worker and the Deregulation of Health Care*. Don Mills: Ontario Federation of Labour.

Smith, D.E. 1973. "Women, the Family and Corporate Capitalism." In *Women in Canada*, edited by Marylee Stephenson. Toronto: New Press.

_____. 1974. "The Ideological Practice of Sociology." *Catalyst* 8.

_____. 1977. *Feminism and Marxism: A Place to Begin, a Way to Go.* Vancouver: New Star Books.

_____. 1979a. "Using the Oppressor's Language." *Resources for Feminist Research. Special Issue on Feminist Theory* (Spring).

_____. 1979b. "Where There Is Oppression There Is Resistance." *Branching Out* 6.

_____. 1979c. "Women and the Politics of Professionalism." Unpublished manuscript. Department of Sociology in Education, OISE.

_____. 1981. "Institutional Ethnography: A Method of Sociology for Women." Paper presented to the Political Economy of Gender Relations in Education Conference, University of Toronto.

_____. 1986. "Women and Violence." Lecture at Faculty of Social Work, University of Toronto, Toronto. Fall.

_____. 1989. "Feminist Reflections on Political Economy." *Studies in Political Economy* 30 (Autumn).

Smith, Heather. 1988. Interview, "Morningside," CBC Radio. October 11.

Smith, Paul. 1978. "Domestic Labour and Marx's Theory of Value." In *Feminism and Materialism*, edited by Annette Kuhn and Anne Marie Wolpe. London: Routledge.

Smith, V. 1994. "Braverman's Legacy: The Labour Process Tradition at 20." *Work and Occupations* 21(4).

Soja, Edward W. 1989. *Postmodern Geographies.* London: Verso.

Spelman, Elizabeth V. 1988. *Inessential Woman.* Boston: Beacon Press.

Stanford, J. 1996. "Discipline, Insecurity and Productivity: The Economics Behind Labour Market 'Flexibility.'" In *Remaking Canadian Social Policy*, edited by J. Pulkingham and G. Ternowetsky. Halifax: Fernwood Press.

Stasiulus, Daiva. 1997. "The Political Economy of Race, Ethnicity and Migration." In *Understanding Canada: Building on the New Canadian Political Economy*, edited by Wallace Clement. Montreal and Kingston: McGill-Queen's University Press.

_____. 2000. "Feminist Intersectional Theorizing." In *Race and Ethnic Relations in Canada*, 2nd ed., edited by Peter S. Li. Toronto: Oxford University Press.

Statistics Canada. 1975. *Canada Year Book 1975.* Ottawa.

Stone, Leroy O. and Claude Marceau. *Canadian Population Trends and Public Policy Through the 1980s.* Montreal: McGill-Queen's University Press.

Strain, L. and B. Payne. 1992. "Social Networks and Patterns of Social Interaction Among Ever-Single and Separated/Divorced Elderly Canadians." *Canadian Journal on Aging* 11.

Stricklin, M.Y. 1993. "Home Care Consumers Speak Out on Quality." *Home Healthcare Nurse* 11.

Sutherland, Neil. 1976. *Children in English-Canadian Society.* Toronto: University of Toronto Press.

Swartz, Don and Alvin Finkel. 1977. In *The Canadian State*, edited by Leo Panitch. Toronto.

Szebehely, M. 1995. *Vardagens Organisering: Om vardbitraden och gamla i hemtjansten* [The Organization of Everyday Life: On Home Helpers and Elderly People in Sweden]. Lund: Arkiv Forlag.

Teghtsoonian, Katherine. 2000. "Gendering Policy Analysis in the Government of British Columbia: Strategies, Possibilities and Constraints." *Studies in Political Economy* 61.

Teixeira, Jose Carlos and Gilles Lavigne. 1992. *The Portuguese in Canada: A Bibliography*. Toronto: Institute for Social Research, York University.

Tenstedt, F. 1981. *Sozialgeschichte der Sozialpolitik in Deutschland*. Göttingen.

Tentler, L. 1979. *Wage-Earning Women: Industrial Work and Family Life in the United States, 1900–1914*. New York: Oxford Press.

Therborn, Göran. 1977. "The Rule of Capital and the Rise of Democracy." *New Left Review* 103.

_____. 1980. *Klasstrukturen i Sverige 1930–1980*. Lund.

_____. 1983a. "When, How and Why Does a State Become a Welfare State?" Paper presented to the ECPR Joint Workshops Meeting, Freiburg, March 1983.

_____. 1983b. "The Labour Movement in Advanced Capitalist Countries." Paper presented to the Marx Centenary Conference of the Roundtable of Cavtat, Yugoslavia, October 1983.

_____. 1983c. "The Working Class and the Welfare State." Paper presented to the Fifth Nordic Congress of Research in the History of the Labour Movement, Murikka, Finland, August 1983.

Thompson, E.P. 1963/1980. *The Making of the English Working Class*. New York: Penguin.

Thompson, P. 1983. *The Nature of Work*. London: Macmillan.

Thorne, A. and M. Yalom (eds.). 1982. *Rethinking the Family: Some Feminist Questions*. New York: Longman Inc.

Tierney, K. 1982. "The Battered Woman Movement and the Creation of the Wife Beating Problem." *Social Problems* 29(3).

Tilly, Louise A. and Joan W. Scott. 1978. *Women, Work and Family*. New York: Holt, Rinehart, and Winston.

Tivers, Jaqueline. 1995. *Women Attached: The Daily Lives of Women with Young Children*. London: Croom Helm.

Toomaney, J. 1990. "The Reality of Workplace Flexibility." *Capital and Class* 40.

Toughill, K. 1995. "Health Care Cuts Killing Seniors, Group Says." *Toronto Star* (April 20).

Townson, M. 1995. *Women's Financial Futures: Mid-Life Prospects for a Secure Retirement*. Ottawa: Canadian Advisory Council on the Status of Women.

Trimble, Linda. 1992. "The Politics of Gender in Modern Alberta." In *Government and Politics in Alberta*, edited by Allan Tupper and Roger Gibbons. Edmonton: University of Alberta Press.

Ungerson, C. 1987. *Policy Is Personal: Sex, Gender and Informal Care*. London: Tavistock.

United States, Bureau of Census. 1976. *The Statistical History of the United States from Colonial Times to the Present*. New York.

Urban Dimensions Group. 1989. *Growth of the Contingent Workforce in Ontario: Structural Trends, Statistical Dimensions and Policy Implications*. Toronto: Ontario Women's Directorate.

Veldkamp, G.M.C. (ed.). 1978. *Sociale Zekerheid*, Vol. 1. Deventer.

Vogel, W. 1951. *Bismarck's Arbeiter Vorsicherung*. Braunschweig.

Vosko, Leah F. 1995. "Recreating Dependency: Women and UI Reform." In *Warm Heart, Cold Country*, edited by Daniel Drache and Andrew Ranikin. Toronto: Caledon Press.

_____. 1996. "Irregular Workers, New Involuntary Social Exiles: Women and UI Reform." In *Remaking Canadian Social Policy: Social Security in the Late 1990s*, edited by Jane Pulkingham and Gordon Ternowetsky. Toronto: Fernwood Press.

_____. 2000. *Temporary Work: The Gendered Rise of a Precarious Employment Relationship*. Toronto: University of Toronto Press.

Wachenheim, H. 1967. *Die deutsche Arbeiterbewegung 1844–1914*. Cologne.

Walby, S. 1989. "Flexibility and the Changing Sexual Division of Labour." In *The Transformation of Work?*, edited by S. Wood. London: Hutchinson.

Walker, A. 1995. "The Future of Long-Term Care in Canada: A British Perspective." *Canadian Journal on Aging* 14.

Walker, G. 1990. *Family Violence and the Women's Movement: The Conceptual Politics of Struggle*. Toronto: University of Toronto Press.

Walker, Richard. 1985. "Is There a Service Economy? The Changing Capitalist Division of Labour." *Science and Society* 49(1).

Warburton, R. and W. Carroll. "Class and Gender in Nursing." In *Health and Canadian Society: Sociological Perspectives*, edited by D. Coburn. Markham: Fitzhenry and Whiteside.

Ward, K. 1990. *Women Workers and Global Restructuring*. Ithaca: L.R. Press.

Wardell, P. 1990. "Labour and Labour Process." In *Labour Process Theory*, edited by D. Knights and H. Willmott. London: Macmillan.

Warren, L. 1990. "'We're Home Helps Because We Care': The Experiences of Home Helps Caring for Elderly People." In *New Directions in the Sociology of Health*, edited by P. Abbott and G. Payne. London: Falmer Press.

Webber, Michael, Ian Campbell and Ruth Fincher. 1990. "Ethnicity, Gender, and Industrial Restructuring in Australia, 1971–1986." *Journal of Intercultural Studies* 11.

Weintraub, L.S. 1995. *No Place Like Home: A Discussion Paper About Living and Working in Ontario's Long Term Care Facilities*. Don Mills: Ontario Federation of Labour.

Weir, Lorna and Jasmin Habib. 1999. "A Critical Feminist Analysis of the *Final Report* of the Royal Commission on New Reproductive Technologies." In *Feminism, Political Economy and the State: Contested Terrain*, edited by Pat Armstrong and M. Patricia Connolly. Toronto: Canadian Scholars' Press.

Wells, D. 1993. "Are Strong Unions Compatible with the new Model of Human Resource Management?" *Relations Industrielles* 48(1).

Wertz, Richard W. and Dorothy C. Wertz. 1979. *Lying-In: A History of Childbirth in America*. New York: Free Press.

White, J.P. 1988. "Women, Labour Process and Public Sector Militancy." Address to the 8th Annual Conference on Labour Process, University of Manchester Institute of Science and Technology, Manchester.

_____. 1990. *Hospital Strike: Women, Unions and Conflict in the Public Sector*. Toronto: Thompson Educational Pub.

_____. 1993. "Changing Labour Processes and the Nursing Crisis in Canadian Hospitals." *Studies in Political Economy* 40.

Wilensky, H. 1975. *The Welfare State and Equality*. Berkeley.

Williams, Fiona. 1995. "Race/Ethnicity, Gender and Class in Welfare States: A Framework for Comparative Analysis." *Social Politics* (Summer).

_____. 1998. "Reflections on the Intersections of Social Relations in the New Political Economy." *Studies in Political Economy* 55 (Spring).

Willmott, H. 1990. "Subjectivity and the Dialectic of Praxis: Opening Up the Core of Labour Process Analysis." In *Labour Process Theory*, edited by D. Knights and H. Willmott. London: Macmillan.

Wilson, David. 1989. "Local State Dynamics and Gentrification in Indianapolis, Indiana." *Urban Geography* 10.

Wilson, J.Q. 1969. "Violence." In *Toward the Year 2000*, edited by D. Bell. Boston: Beacon Press.

Women and Work Research and Education Society (WWRES) and International Ladies Garment Workers' Union (ILGWU). 1993. "Industrial Homework and Employment Standards: A Community Approach to 'Visibility' and Understanding." Brief prepared for Improved Employment Legislation to the Ministry of Women's Equality, Vancouver, British Columbia.

Women's Book Committee, Chinese Canadian National Council. 1992. *Jin Guo: Voices of Chinese Canadian Women*. Toronto: Women's Press.

Wood, S. (ed.). 1982. *The Degradation of Work*. London: Hutchinson Press.

Wright, E.O. 1976. "Class Boundaries in Advanced Capitalist Societies." *New Left Review* 98.

_____. 1978. *Class Crisis and the State*. London: New Left Books.

_____. 1985. *Classes*. London: Verso.

_____. 1989. *The Debate on Classes*. London: Verso.

Yeatman, Anna. 1994. *Postmodern Revisionings of the Political*. New York: Routledge.

Young, Iris Marion. 1981. "Beyond the Unhappy Marriage: A Critique of the Dual Systems Theory." In *Women and Revolution*, edited by Lydia Sargent. Montreal: Black Rose Books.

_____. 1990. *Justice and the Politics of Difference*. Princeton: Princeton University Press.

_____. 1997. "Unruly Categories: A Critique of Nancy Fraser's Dual System Theory." *New Left Review* 22. (1997)

Young, Les to Al Kennedy. Memo. March 1, 1982. Women's Secretariat Documents, Provincial Archives of Alberta, Edmonton.

Yuval-Davis, Nira. 1994. "Identity Politics and Women's Ethnicity." In *Identity, Politics and Women: Cultural Reassertions and Feminisms in International Perspective*, edited by Valentine Moghadam. Boulder: Westview Press.

Zacher, H. (ed.). 1979. *Bedingungen für die Entustehung und Entwicklung von Sozialversicherung*. Berlin.

Zöllner, D. 1981. "Landesbericht Deutschland." In *Ein Jahrhundert Sozialversicherung*, edited by P. Köhler and H. Zacher. Berlin.

Zuboff, S. 1988. *In the Age of the Smart Machine: The Future of Work and Power*. New York: Basic Books.

About the Contributors

Caroline Andrew is Dean of Social Sciences at the University of Ottawa.

Jane Aronson is Professor of Social Work at McMaster University.

Pat Armstrong holds a Chair in Health Services Research at York University.

Hugh Armstrong is Professor of Social Work and Political Economy at Carleton University.

Wallace Clement holds a Chancellor's Professorship at Carleton University.

Bonnie Fox is Associate Professor of Sociology at the University of Toronto.

Wenona Giles is Chair of Social Sciences in the Atkinson Faculty of Liberal and Professional Studies, York University.

Lois Harder is Assistant Professor of Political Science at the University of Alberta.

Pamela Moss is Professor of Human and Social Development at the University of Victoria.

Sheila M. Neysmith is Professor of Social Work at the University of Toronto.

Valerie Preston is Associate Professor of Geography at York University.

Pamela Sugiman is Associate Professor of Sociology at McMaster University.

Göran Therborn is Professor of Sociology and Director of the Swedish Collegium for Advanced Study in the Social Sciences, in Uppsala.

Leah F. Vosko holds a Canada Research Chair in Feminist Political Economy at York University.

Gillian Walker is Professor of Social Work at Carleton University.

Jerry White is Professor of Sociology at the University of Western Ontario.

Publisher's Acknowledgements

Chapter One, "Beyond Sexless Class and Classless Sex: Towards Feminist Marxism," by Pat Armstrong and Hugh Armstrong, was originally published in *Studies in Political Economy* 10, Winter 1993.

Chapter Two, "Spatially Differentiated Conceptions of Gender in the Workplace," by Pamela Moss, was originally published in *Studies in Political Economy* 43, Spring 1994.

Chapter Three, "The Retreat of the State and Long-Term Care Provision: Implications for Frail Elderly People, Unpaid Family Carers and Paid Home Care Workers," by Jane Aronson and Sheila M. Neysmith, was originally published in *Studies in Political Economy* 53, Summer 1997.

Chapter Four, "Changing Labour Process and the Nursing Crisis in Canadian Hospitals," by Jerry White, was originally published in *Studies in Political Economy* 40, Spring 1993.

Chapter Five, "The Domestication of Women's Work: A Comparison of Chinese and Portuguese Immigrant Women Homeworkers," by Wenona Giles and Valerie Preston, was originally published in *Studies in Political Economy* 51, Autumn 1996.

Chapter Six, "Flexible Work, Flexible Workers: The Restructuring of Clerical Work in a Large Telecommunications Company," by Bonnie Fox and Pamela Sugiman, was originally published in *Studies in Political Economy* 60, Autumn 1999.

Chapter Seven, "Classes and States: Welfare State Developments, 1881–1981," by Göran Therborn, was originally published in *Studies in Political Economy* 14, Summer 1984.

Chapter Eight, "The Conceptual Politics of Struggle: Wife Battering, the Women's Movement and the State," by Gillian Walker, was originally published in *Studies in Political Economy* 33, Autumn 1990.

Chapter Nine, "Depoliticizing Insurgency: The Politics of the Family in Alberta," by Lois Harder, was originally published in *Studies in Political Economy* 50, Summer 1996.

The Conclusion, "The Pasts (and Futures) of Feminist Political Economy in Canada: Reviving the Debate," by Leah F. Vosko, was originally published in *Studies in Political Economy* 68, Summer 2002.

All reprinted with permission of the authors.